Social Criticism & Nineteenth-
Century American Fictions

Social Criticism & Nineteenth-Century American Fictions

ROBERT SHULMAN

University of Missouri Press
Columbia, 1987

Copyright © 1987 by
The Curators of the University of Missouri
University of Missouri Press, Columbia, Missouri 65211
Printed and bound in the United States of America
All rights reserved

Library of Congress Cataloging-in-Publication Data

Shulman, Robert, 1930–

   Social criticism and nineteenth-century American fictions.
   Includes index.
   1. American literature—19th century—History and
criticism. 2. Social change in literature. 3. Capitalism and
literature. I. Title.
PS217.S58S5   1987   810'.9'355   87–5933
ISBN 0–8262–0648–4 (alk. paper)

∞™ This paper meets the minimum requirements of the American National
Standard for Permanence of Paper for Printed Library Materials, Z39.48, 1984.

For Sandy, David, and Natasha

PREFACE

In *Social Criticism and Nineteenth-Century American Fictions*, I examine the ways American authors responded to the changing market society that increasingly dominated nineteenth-century American life. Because writers, like the rest of us, are not simply passive receivers of forces beyond their control or comprehension, they accept, resist, criticize, and sometimes imagine alternatives to the practices and values that have deeply affected them. Writers are inevitably involved in the crosscurrents of the hegemonic process. My own understanding of this process is indebted to Antonio Gramsci and Raymond Williams.[1] To explain how dominant classes maintain their control, Gramsci shifted attention away from the police, the recourse to force, and focused on the way dominant classes achieve a sense of legitimacy. For Gramsci, through their influence on educational and religious institutions and the media, ruling groups preempt the high ground of universal morality and truth. They penetrate the consciousness of those in subordinate classes, who give them their willing if often uneasy support. But however deep and widespread, dominance is never absolute; counter-hegemonic forces always exist to challenge those in power.

I use Gramsci's ideas about the hegemonic process to help me examine writers and their creations as part of an ongoing political-historical process that includes the emergence of new classes, the shifting power relations between dominant and subordinate classes, and the pervasive results of the way people actually do their everyday work. In probing the consciousness of creators and their characters, I have tried to see them in relation to the conflicts of their society and history rather than abstracting them from the emerging market society. I draw on particular

1. Antonio Gramsci, *Selections from the Prison Notebooks*, ed. Quentin Hoare and Geoffrey Smith (New York: International Publishers, 1971) is the primary source in English for contemporary thinking about hegemony. Raymond Williams develops his version of Gramsci in *Marxism and Literature* (New York: Oxford, 1977), pp. 108–14. See also Joseph Femia, *Gramsci's Political Thought: Hegemony, Consciousness, and the Revolutionary Process* (Oxford University Press, 1981), pp. 23–60; Martin Clark, *Antonio Gramsci and the Revolution that Failed* (New Haven: Yale University Press, 1977), pp. 46–73, 210–26; and Perry Anderson, "The Antinomies of Antonio Gramsci," *New Left Review* 100 (1976/1977): 5–78.

historical and critical studies as the occasion demands. Repeatedly, though, I use the insights into freedom and alienation C. B. Macpherson develops in *The Political Theory of Possessive Individualism: Hobbes to Locke*.[2] In taking us to the philosophical origins of the English and American market society, Macpherson helped me account for the divided selves and social fragmentation I was encountering in my work on nineteenth-century American literature. Macpherson's phrases "possessive individualism" and "possessive market society" also allow me an occasional alternative to "capitalism," a fact of American experience as pervasive as the word is rhetorically provocative.

Marx and Lukacs on the basic processes of commodification or reification provide a related way of understanding the divisive pressures of American capitalism.[3] By the middle of the nineteenth century, industrial capitalism, particularly in Europe, was producing things on a heretofore unimaginable scale. The sheer magnitude of productive forces, the division of labor, and the scale of production and distribution made it difficult for those involved in the process to see any connection between their human labor and its results. Even more pervasively than in the earlier phases of capitalism, the connection is mystified, as Marx puts it in his famous chapter on "The Fetishism of Commodities." "A commodity is therefore a mysterious thing," he writes, "simply because in it the social character of men's labour appears to them as an objective character stamped upon the product of that labour; because the relation of the producers to the sum total of their own labour is presented to them as a social relation, existing not between themselves, but between the products of their labor. . . . To them, their own social action takes the form of the action of objects, which rule the producers instead of being ruled by them."[4] For Lukacs in "Reification and the Consciousness of the Proletariat," "the essence of commodity structure . . . is that a relation between people takes on the character of a thing and thus acquires a 'phantom objectivity,' an autonomy that seems so strictly rational and all-embracing as to conceal every trace of its fundamental nature: the

2. C. B. Macpherson, *The Political Theory of Possessive Individualism: Hobbes to Locke* (New York: Oxford, 1962).

3. Carolyn Porter makes suggestive use of insights about commodification or reification in her groundbreaking study of American literature and society, *Seeing and Being: The Plight of the Participant Observer in Emerson, James, Adams, and Faulkner* (Middletown, Conn.: Wesleyan University Press, 1981). See also Bertell Ollman, *Alienation: Marx's Conception of Man in Capitalist Society*, 2d ed. (Cambridge University Press, 1976), and Joachim Isreal, *Alienation from Marx to Modern Sociology* (Boston: Allyn and Bacon, 1971).

4. *Capital: A Critique of Political Economy*, trans. Samuel Moore and Edward Aveling, ed. Frederick Engels, 3 vols. (New York: International Publishers, 1967), 1:72, 75.

relation between people."[5] Speaking of "two of Marxism's fundamental critiques of the pathology of capitalism—those of alienation and of reification," Alvin W. Gouldner perceptively comments that the criticism "is an indictment of a society in which men make their own history without knowing it is they who are making it, and without having control over the history they make."[6]

Compounding the problem, as goods enter into the complex exchange system of capitalism, instead of being used to satisfy immediate needs they become a means of exchange; they become commodities in a system of commodity exchange. In this system the use-value of objects becomes separated from their exchange-value.[7] Particularly important, the self becomes commodified, becomes fragmented, and people are free to sell their alienated labor as a commodity for what it will command. This fragmentation of self and society was endemic in nineteenth-century America, with consequences that pervade our literature. The pervasive impact of reification or commodification, however, makes it difficult for some readers to see and accept. Because it emerges from an intellectual tradition not always familiar to Americans, moreover, the concept can seem foreign and arbitrary. My experience, though, is that the theory usefully clarifies divisions within American selves and society. I would simply ask skeptical readers to suspend judgment until they have gone through five or six chapters.

Another of my major sources is Tocqueville's *Democracy in America*. In important ways, Tocqueville's insights into the dynamics of American restlessness and loneliness independently confirm Marx and Lukacs. In my study of nineteenth-century American literature I examine the still unresolved conflict between America as a democracy and America as a market society. In another sense I explore what we might call the political psychology of American capitalism as it emerges in the works of our major nineteenth-century writers. By political psychology I mean the market society's impact on the depths of consciousness of those who inevitably absorb and resist the prevailing power relations, values, and practices.

In my own critical practice I focus intensively on particular works. I have not tried to homogenize them, to impose a preconceived conclusion and, *voilà*, to discover that our writers all say pretty much the same thing. They do not. Strains, contradictions, degrees of difference are

5. George Lukacs, *History and Class Consciousness: Studies in Marxist Dialectics* (Cambridge: MIT Press, 1971), p. 83.

6. *Against Fragmentation: The Origins of Marxism and the Sociology of Intellectuals* (New York: Oxford University Press, 1985), pp. 230–31.

7. Lukacs, *History and Class Consciousness*, pp. 84, 89.

crucial within works and between writers. Successive chapters do not
develop a deductive argument or a nineteenth-century narrative. They
do take us under the surface and bring into the open the urgency,
energy, and variety of response of a range of significant writers. The
recurring concern with divided selves, for example, indicates that the
alienating power of the market society, not the particular author, is at
issue.

I concentrate on mainstream writers not because I am indifferent to
the need to rethink the established canon but because I want to assume
and not have to demonstrate the value of the works I consider.[8] For
those of us who teach American literature, these works occupy the
center of our curriculum. As they emerge in the hundreds of books and
articles devoted to them year after year, they are for the most part
politically sanitized. I hope my book will sharpen the issues, provide
incentive and models for those dissatisfied with the prevailing criticism,
and reinforce the promising recent work of critics like Carolyn Porter,
Michael Rogin, Michael Gilmore, Alan Trachtenberg, and Michael Spindler.[9]

American universities are hierarchical and compartmentalized. Theory, as brilliant and abstruse as possible, commands the highest prestige.
On the lowest rung of the prestige ladder is the classroom. In literature
departments graduate students do theory in seminars and the old new
criticism in the classes they teach. Throughout the university disciplines
are separated. My book emerged from the give-and-take of my own
teaching. Without simplifying or talking down I try to speak to the
needs of the classroom and across disciplinary lines to those with common interests in and out of the university.

R. P. S.
May 1987

---

8. For practical modifications of the established canon, see *Restructuring American Literature: Courses, Syllabi, Issues*, ed. Paul Lauter (Old Westbury, N.Y.: The Feminist Press,
1983).

9. Carolyn Porter, *Seeing and Being*; Michael Paul Rogin, *Subversive Genealogy: The Politics
and Art of Herman Melville* (New York: Knopf, 1983); Michael T. Gilmore, *American Romanticism and the Marketplace* (University of Chicago Press, 1985); Alan Trachtenberg, *The Incorporation of America: Culture and Society in the Gilded Age* (New York: Hill and Wang, 1982);
and Michael Spindler, *American Literature and Social Change: William Dean Howells to Arthur
Miller* (London: Macmillan, 1983).

ACKNOWLEDGMENTS

I am grateful to the friends and colleagues who have commented on my work and who over the years have given indispensable moral and intellectual support. Robert Hudspeth has provided an ideal audience; he and Richard Baldwin were with me from the earliest stages. More recently Evan Watkins has given me lucid commentary and a deepened understanding of cultural politics. The example of William Charvat, Roy Harvey Pearce, Walter Sutton, and David Owen has always been important. In ways they may not be aware of I have benefited from the responses of John Griffith, Ken Requa, David Nye, Ross Posnock, Catherine Ingraham, Allen Hibbert, Don Kartiganer, Mark Patterson, Martha Banta, Larry Frank, Everett Carter, and Viola Sachs. As editors of *One Hundred Years of "Huckleberry Finn,"* J. Donald Crowley and Robert Sattelmeyer raised questions and made suggestions that greatly improved Chapter 2. Louis Budd and an anonymous reader for the University of Missouri Press both made perceptive comments that helped me strengthen the book. I was fortunate to receive their mix of intelligent understanding and specific suggestions for improvement.

While I was working on the book, the English Department at the University of Washington encouraged me to try out my ideas in a series of special topics courses, honors seminars, and graduate classes. The students in these classes made the entire project come alive. A sabbatical leave from the University of Washington allowed me to do much of the writing. In the final stages, Jerry Barnett of the University of Washington Humanities Computer Center did his best to help me master the word processor. I am indebted to him for his assistance in getting the manuscript in shape.

Parts of the book have appeared as essays: a version of Chapter 2 in *One Hundred Years of "Huckleberry Finn": The Boy, His Book, and American Culture*, ed. Robert Sattelmeyer and J. Donald Crowley (Columbia: University of Missouri Press, 1985), pp. 325–40; a portion of Chapter 11 in *Lamar Journal of the Humanities* 8 (1982): 18–25; a portion of Chapter 9 in *Studies in English Literature* 14 (1984): 79–88; and part of Chapter 13 in *Perspectives on Contemporary Literature* 11 (1985): 10–19. I presented part of Chapter 1 at the Claremont Nineteenth-Century Interdisciplinary

Conference on "Representing the Real," April 1986; a version of Chapter 10 at the American Studies section of the Western Social Science Association meeting in 1981; a portion of Chapter 13 at the Twentieth-Century Literature Conference on "The Politics of Literature" in Louisville in 1984; and part of Chapter 14 at the fiction workshop of the Rome, 1984, meeting of the European Association for American Studies.

CONTENTS

Community & Fragmentation in America

INTRODUCTION TO COMMUNITY AND FRAGMENTATION IN AMERICA

Most Americans see a conflict between the individual and society. The "and" comes through as "versus." Most of us feel that we need to protect the private, inner self from the pressures of group or social life. The danger is that in protecting ourselves from the power of society, in pursuing private as opposed to public goals, we may end in that dungeon of the heart Tocqueville saw as defining the American individualist. Most of us find it difficult to imagine an individuality coming into the fullness of its possibilities in the midst of a community, instead of at odds with it.[1] Instead of the fusing of the personal and the public to the advantage of both, during the nineteenth and twentieth centuries Americans experienced the energies of a corporate and bureaucratically powerful capitalism that has produced immense wealth, inequality, and fragmentation. In America the States may be United but selves and society are more or less acutely divided. Along with all the benefits of American capitalism, the underlying imperatives to expand, to maximize profits, and to commodify relations—to make consumer and commodity exchange relations the model for human relations—these powerful tendencies have fragmented American society, whose divisions often reappear as internal splits within individuals.[2]

Melville's "Bartleby, the Scrivener" (1853) has an uncanny prophetic quality because Melville penetrates to the Wall Street center of American life. In a style that resists easy resolutions, he enters deeply into the lawyer-narrator's representative American consciousness, which is as divided as the Wall Street office that has shaped his inner life. Melville also illuminates the situation of those who do the dreary, routine office work of an emerging capitalism. For Melville the circumstances of their

1. Ellen Wood, *Mind and Politics* (Berkeley: University of California Press, 1972), examines the philosophical traditions relevant to this central conflict.

2. For a revealing theoretical analysis, see Nancy Hartsock, *Money, Sex, and Power: Toward a Feminist Historical Materialism* (Boston: Northeastern University Press, 1985), esp. pp. 95–114. On the fragmenting of ideology under the pressure of large-scale corporate dominance in the twentieth century, see David E. Nye, *Image Worlds: Corporate Identities at General Electric* (Cambridge: MIT Press, 1985), esp. pp. 130–34.

lives separate them from each other, cut them off from the natural world, and wall them off from communion with a divinity that has become inaccessibly remote.

Thirty years later in *Adventures of Huckleberry Finn*, Twain probes the world of the "diseased," a sickness that divides Huck and relates him to basic conflicts within the America of the Gilded Age. Huck's alienation shows the persistence of those divisive pressures Melville had earlier explored in an urban milieu far removed from the raft and the river. Jim's status as a black slave—as a commodity, a black, and a human being—locates the novel at the heart of our still unresolved conflicts about race and about property versus human values. Twain centers his novel around conflicts between contrasting families, culminating in the opposition between the Duke and the Dauphin and Huck and Jim. In the process, Twain illuminates the need for community and its precariousness in the fragmenting, acquisitive world of the diseased.

Charles Chesnutt, for his part, gives us insights into the conjure world, a world that draws cohesive energy from sources outside the dominant American society. Chesnutt was writing as technology and corporate power were fragmenting modern America along class, sex, and racial lines. In opposing the official ideology, Chesnutt helps us see the value of a residual communal culture that inspires resistance even as it is increasingly threatened by the dominant society. Responsive as he is to voice and language, in *The Conjure Woman* Chesnutt creates both a black narrator of the conjure stories and a white narrator of the frame tales. The contrasts—and our own tendency to accept uncritically the genteel white voice—give *The Conjure Woman* a subversive power that reveals both the fragmenting pressures of the dominant society and Chesnutt's strategies of resistance.

Like Twain and Chesnutt at the height of their power, Melville at the end of his career in *Billy Budd* uses the past as a way to illuminate the present. In *Billy Budd* he writes "an inside narrative" that takes us deep into the inner workings of the emerging bureaucratic America. As Melville was writing his final masterpiece, Americans were developing professionalism and bureaucracy to unify a nation Robert Wiebe characterizes as in "search for order."[3] Under the chronic threat of war, these centralizing tendencies have intensified during the twentieth century. As in *Billy Budd* bureaucracy, professionalism and the centralized state under the pressure of revolutionary threat are key American alternatives to genuine community. Through Vere, Melville probes the consciousness and ideology of one of the new men, one of the patricians who

---

3. Robert Wiebe, *Search for Order, 1877–1920* (New York: Hill and Wang, 1967).

from the 1880s on controlled power in the emerging American bureaucracies. Melville shows the way ideology legitimizes power in a
system of dominance and subordination; that is, he explores the dynamics of the hegemonic process within one of its dominant-class members
and within a representative institution of the new order. In his image of
Vere, "rigid as a musket," and in his treatment of Billy Budd, Melville
also dramatizes the price we can pay for order.

Before considering Melville's final achievement, though, we must
turn in detail to "Bartleby, the Scrivener."

one

DIVIDED SOCIETY, DIVIDED SELVES
"Bartleby, the Scrivener" and the Market Society

More deeply than any of his predecessors, in "Bartleby, the Scrivener: A Story of Wall Street" (1853), Melville explores the interior of the emerging new world of power, hierarchy, and deadly, routine office work. He goes to the symbolic center of the urban market society that was increasingly to dominate nineteenth and twentieth-century American life. Melville shows that this society fragments people internally and separates them from each other. At a time when America was still predominantly rural and was still seen as basically egalitarian, Melville seizes on contrasting and emerging realities. As a pioneer explorer of the urban work place, Melville was a century ahead of his countrymen. Instead of the continent, Melville explores the geography of an office world whose structure embodies widely shared dominant-class views about authority, power, and class relations. These views precede and are the precondition of the routine office work that was to become a familiar part of the American urban landscape. The lawyer-narrator's assumptions about what is reasonable, about who should command and who should obey, about how work is to be done and divided—these assumptions go deep into the consciousness of all the inhabitants of his Wall Street world. These views and the structures of power they legitimize are basic to the hegemony of American capitalism.

From seventeenth-century England on, capitalism creates and is premised on the political psychology of the divided self. "If a single criterion of the possessive market society is wanted," C. B. Macpherson stresses, "it is that man's labour is a commodity, i.e., that a man's energy and skill are his own, yet are regarded not as integral parts of his personality, but as possessions, the use and disposal of which he is free to hand over to others for a price. It is to emphasize this characteristic of the fully market society that I have called it the *possessive* market society. Possessive market *society* also implies that where labour has become a market commodity, market relations so shape or permeate all social

6

relations that it may properly be called a market society, not merely a market economy."[1] But as "Bartleby" shows, when people divide themselves and sell their labor as a commodity they nonetheless continue to regard their labor as integral to their personalities. In "Bartleby, the Scrivener" the result is the warped personalities and divided selves who inhabit an office divided by its screen and its class and power barriers. The factory is the classic capitalistic workplace, and artisan or factory labor is the center of our most powerful nineteenth-century analyses of capitalism, Marx's *Capital* and Engels' *The Condition of the Working Class in England.* Melville shifts the focus to a Wall Street law office. He goes to the center of American capitalism and exposes the dynamics of the hegemonic process in an office world whose enigmas continue to challenge us.

No wonder most readers at one time or another become impatient with Bartleby or become acutely, unsympathetically critical of him. The hegemony Bartleby rejects has for most of us penetrated our own consciousness so deeply that it has come to seem the very embodiment of the real, of the human and the possible.[2] In rejecting the "common sense" and "common usage" of the office, Bartleby opens himself to the rejection that attacks on the basis of our lives understandably inspire. We may long for alternatives to the common sense of our ordinary lives, but we are also deeply affected by the prevailing hegemony. Melville arranges the story so that we are pulled in opposing directions, so that Bartleby inspires conflicting responses, appeals to conflicting needs and perceptions, as does the lawyer. Instead of constructing a work with a clearly defined protagonist and antagonist, Melville sees both the lawyer and Bartleby in a mixed light. They reflect on each other. Our sympathies shift. We no sooner begin to side with Bartleby against the lawyer than Melville contrives it so that the lawyer appears as humane or reasonable. In the unstable equilibrium of "Bartleby," there is no firm, fixed resting point. As is even more evident in *The Confidence-Man,* there is no stable point of view to help us decide on the matters that count.

Early in the development of American capitalism, Melville has seized on its implications and carried them to their logical (or illogical) conclusions. In "Bartleby" the corrosive mobility of the market society, its dynamics of change, the priorities of capitalism and its impact on older religious and secular values all combine to undercut a stable, normative

1. C. B. Macpherson, *The Political Theory of Possessive Individualism: Hobbes to Locke* (New York: Oxford, 1962), p. 48.

2. I am echoing Raymond Williams's definition of hegemony in his lucid account in *Marxism and Literature* (New York: Oxford, 1977), pp. 108–14.

point of view that can be trusted regardless. Instead, we are moving toward the open, unstable world of *The Confidence-Man*. In "Bartleby," too, at bottom everything is open to interpretation. We no sooner feel safe about our view of the lawyer or Bartleby than our position is undermined. Soon the principle of trust itself will be undermined. As Benjamin Franklin knew, trust was even more basic than the contracts that held the early market society together.

The market society and most of its exemplary personalities seem rocklike and assured in their drive and insensitivity. In "Bartleby," the other *Piazza Tales*, and *The Confidence-Man*, Melville was one of the first to expose the underlying instability and uncertainty. Philosophically and aesthetically a stable point of view is undermined. Psychologically, a fixed, stable personality is called into question. The double relation between the lawyer and Bartleby subverts official ideas of the stable, unified self. In a more extreme way the merging of identities in *The Confidence-Man*, the fluid guises of the confidence man, the merging of speakers as Frank Goodman argues with the Cosmopolitan all challenge the commonsense views of identity. Our shifting responses to Bartleby and the lawyer are intensified as we try to decide how to respond to the confidence man and his—are they victims? exploiters? what? Melville thus shows that capitalism undermines, makes unstable and unreliable, the simple, separate self, the bastion of self-interest and the very cornerstone of capitalism itself. In particular, the divisive tendencies of capitalism not only divide people from each other but also divide the self internally.

In "Bartleby," the lawyer and our shifting responses to him are the focus for these revelations. With the willing if not eager consent of his employees, the lawyer-narrator controls the office, just as he controls the narrative. At some point most readers rebel against the lawyer's control, against his version of the story, just as the employees react against his control in their own ways. The lawyer enjoys the profits, frustrations, and self-esteem of his position as a professional who does "a snug business among rich men's bonds, and mortgages, and title deeds."[3] His identity, his sense of who he is and why he counts, is inseparable from his business as a servicer of the rich. He identifies with those who own property and control wealth. Four years after John Jacob Astor died, leaving the largest fortune in the history of America, the lawyer stresses his connection with this symbol of "bullion" and power

---

3. Herman Melville, "Bartleby, the Scrivener: A Story of Wall Street" in *The Great Short Works of Herman Melville*, ed. Warner Berthoff (New York: Harper & Row, 1969), p. 40. Subsequent references will be abbreviated BTS and cited by page number in the text.

(BTS, p. 40). The lawyer's pervasive religious references, however, show that his identity, his way of seeing and valuing himself and others, is also inseparable from a Christianity that in part supports and in part conflicts with his business. No wonder the lawyer becomes increasingly troubled, irritated, and divided. Using the lawyer as his narrator, Melville is able to show how the world looks and feels from the point of view of someone who represents the dominant-class hegemony of America's emerging capitalism. Through the lawyer's voice and conflicting values, Melville is thus able to expose the recognizably human contradictions and limitations in a representative American consciousness.

The lawyer, with his constant stress on the "respectable" and the "gentlemanly," is a gentry version of the dominant class.[4] He is not ruthless and domineering in the style of Ahab, but he is nonetheless accustomed to controlling others and he expects obedience. He is not rich on the scale of John Jacob Astor, but he identifies with those who control great wealth and power, and on his more moderate scale he functions as their representative. As a gentry professional he expects deference, but his touchiness about ambition and insolence suggests that he also feels vulnerable to the social changes of the antebellum Jacksonian market society that gave him a comfortable but not inevitably secure position. The lawyer is not a monster or an abstract symbol of the evil tendencies of an acquisitive society. He is human, pulled in opposing directions, sometimes sympathetic to the misfortune he is partly responsible for, sometimes prudentially insensitive and unintentionally self-serving. He shows the dilemmas of the moderate, professionalized gentry caught in the crosscurrents of capitalistic and Christian demands.

In his moderate, gentlemanly way, he arranges the office for his convenience and for the efficient conduct of his business. The office he sets up is a model of the possessive market society. Because the lawyer's consciousness is deeply affected by the prevailing hegemony, he simply takes for granted the desirability and rightness of the divisions and hierarchy he implements. Most readers have had the disconcerting experience of accepting the lawyer's views about the structure of the office, a reminder of the extent to which he is our representative, too, speaking for our own inevitable involvement in the practices and structures Melville forces us to question. The process of critical exposure is subtle and deep and worth examining in close detail. "I should have stated before," Melville has the lawyer write, "that ground-glass folding-doors divided my premises into two parts, one of which was occupied

4. For insight into the American gentry, see Stow Persons, *The Decline of American Gentility* (New York: Columbia University Press, 1973).

by my scriveners, the other by myself" (BTS, p. 46). They are on one side, the lawyer is on the other. As employees, they are in one class, and the lawyer as employer is in another. As befitting the illusion of classlessness in America, the dividers are not solid stone. The ground-glass lets in light but separates people as effectively as the walls of a prison. The employees are not free to open the doors. In Melville's version, the power to open the doors is reserved to the employer. The structure of the office in the context of the story is not encouraging for those who believe that in America the doors of opportunity are open. Ginger-Nut, whose father has placed him in the office in the hopes of advancement, is likely to be as disappointed as the other clerks. Or perhaps he will thrive and intensify their sense of failure. The two parts of the office are in any case not equal. In a supposedly egalitarian society, the lawyer not only places his employees where they are, but presumably also has more space, a physical sign of his greater self-worth and value.

The lawyer is perfectly comfortable with his position of control. "According to my humor, I threw open these doors, or closed them. I resolved to assign Bartleby a corner by the folding-doors, but on my side of them, so as to have this quiet man within easy call, in case any trifling thing was to be done." Bartleby may be less pleased than the lawyer at being placed according to the lawyer's whim. The lawyer provides Bartleby a workplace walled in like a prison. Bartleby has "no view at all." He has no prospect and no prospects. He is also cut off from the other clerks and is separated from his employer, physically by a screen and more deeply by class and power differences and contrasts in basic orientation.

The details are haunting and expressionist. Beyond the enclosing walls, light filters down "from far above, between two lofty buildings, as from a very small opening in a dome" (BTS, p. 46). The divisions and confines of the new urban market society have metaphysical consequences. The light of heaven is now remote and inaccessible. The lawyer uses a green screen to divide Bartleby from him, to keep him within easy call but out of human sight. The screen is green but this divider, like the scene itself, lacks pastoral vitality. As the lawyer has said earlier in a sentence of marvelously unintentional irony, "The view might have been considered rather tame than otherwise, deficient in what landscape painters call 'life'" (BTS, p. 41). By experiencing nature in a picturesque landscape or through the intermediary of a picturesque landscape painting, mid-nineteenth-century Americans could commune with God and renew themselves from the pressures of the increasingly urban, industrial, commercial world that made unspoiled nature valuable as it became increasingly more threatened and more inaccessible. As with the value of real estate, nature increased in psychological and metaphysical value as it became scarcer.

Melville examines as related two tendencies we conventionally separate. For Melville the urbanizing, mechanizing tendencies of American life are inseparable from the Wall Street market society that provides the capital, incentives, and ideological justifications for the alienated labor of the office. Melville goes beyond a liberal or Jeffersonian critique of the impact of urbanization and mechanization by locating the entire process at the Wall Street center of American capitalism. The insights of "Bartleby" are the prelude to Melville's subsequent exploration of America in his fiction of the 1850s, including the dehumanizing and desexualizing factory labor of "The Tartarus of Maids."

As a social critic Melville is also impressive because he dramatizes the connection between metaphysics and social and economic arrangements, between the state of belief and the way people earn their living in the workplace. The walls are simultaneously metaphysical, psychological, and Wall Street walls. In the changing urban market society of Wall Street, walls divide people inside; outside other walls rise to block the view in the fullest sense imaginable. The "grimy back yards and bricks" and the walls pressing close to the window (BTS, p. 46) further define the Wall Street world as separated from a life-giving nature and the light of heaven. The entire hegemony of the urban market society is implicated. Consciously the lawyer believes that Christianity and capitalism are compatible. In "Bartleby," Melville applies pressure along a central fault line of his society. He exposes a basic contradiction between religious transcendence and urban capitalism, a contradiction many people sensed but refused to follow through on.

Thoreau was one of those who recognized and acted on his awareness of this basic conflict. During his interlude from pencil manufacturing and book production and sales, Thoreau at Walden tries an experiment in unalienated living close to the land and the water. He comes to know beans by cultivating a bean field. He builds his own house, the symbol of building his own life, and if the materials come from the railroad shack, the sun purifies the boards and Thoreau's own self-motivated labor builds the structure. As another part of his unalienated life, Thoreau at Walden can look deep into the pond, into the eye of God, and can see no separation between air and water, earth and heaven. His entire way of life makes this perception possible. As the opening chapter on "Economy" makes explicit, it is a way of life deliberately posed as an alternative to the conventional market economy. Walden Pond, Thoreau puns, is a walled-in pond but is not a prison.[5] Thoreau's freedom, however, involves important limits. Like Bartleby, Thoreau is single and celibate. Bacon realized that "he who marries gives a hostage to fortune"—or to the market society. Thoreau's simplification of life includes rejecting the complexity of family and sexual life. Thoreau achieves his freedom and individuality in a recognizably American way, alone and away from, not as a member of, a family or community within which his individuality comes to its fulfillment. Beyond the family, Thoreau, who wants to live deliberately, deliberately chooses not to work with others to change the society he acutely criticizes.

For all their similarities, including a strong tendency toward a desexualized privatization, Bartleby's situation is nonetheless in key ways the exact opposite of Thoreau's. Bartleby is an urban office worker whose employer arranges his environment and tells him when to work and what to work on. Behind his screen, separated from his employer and the other clerks, Bartleby does routine work and, not incidentally, has "dead-wall reveries." He wants to see, but his entire way of life as an employee doing alienated labor has affected his eyesight and makes it impossible for him to achieve the transcendence he seems to crave. Like Thoreau, Melville values the ability to live an unalienated life at odds with the market society. But Melville also recognizes that a desexualized privatization is fatal and that, in the modern world of alienated labor, transcendental insights are unavailable.

For his part, when the lawyer places Bartleby behind the screen he regards the arrangement as making Bartleby's situation even more "satisfactory" than before (BTS, p. 46). His use of value words is eye-opening. He isolates Bartleby but keeps him within easy call. "And thus in a manner," the lawyer concludes, "privacy and society were conjoined" (BTS, p. 46). In an individualistic society "privacy" and "society" are key words. Respect for personal rights, for the sanctity of private property and the control of one's person are connected with "privacy." Private affairs, private profit, the sanctity of the deepest recesses of the personality and the rewards of private enterprise are all connected with "privacy." In the theory of possessive individualism, property rights and personal rights are thus closely aligned. The private is in this sense at odds with the public or communal. In "Bartleby, the Scrivener," Melville exposes the unstable equilibrium of the possessive market-society equation. Melville shows property rights and power turned against the recesses of the personality and violating the innermost privacy of the self.

5. My colleague, Mark Patterson, called this pun to my attention.

The control of the person can be violated, not affirmed by the unequal distribution of power and property. Melville shows that the power of property ownership can lead to a deadly privatization.

"Society" in the sense of "companionship or company," "friendly association," "the condition of living in companionship with others or in a community rather than in isolation" (*Oxford Universal Dictionary*) is at odds with the privatizing tendency of possessive individualism. Melville has the lawyer play on a widely shared feeling that "society" and "privacy" are at odds and that their conflicting demands need to be reconciled. Melville also has the lawyer's complacent sophistry expose the alienation and the denial of community or companionship in the "satisfactory arrangement" he has contrived for his representative workplace.

As Raymond Williams shows, in Gramsci's view dominant classes establish their hegemony by universalizing their values, by preempting the territory of morality and universal values, and by gaining the legitimacy that follows when they and the subordinate classes accept the dominant-class views of what is satisfactory and just. In his description of the law office, Melville uses the lawyer to expose this process. Melville is exceptionally alert to the connections between consciousness, the nature of work, and questions of class power. From the lawyer's point of view, the nature of his work makes the workplace he arranges preeminently satisfactory. We also learn about the clerks from the lawyer's point of view. The discrepancy between the lawyer's dominant-class evaluations and other possibilities illuminates the divisive impact of the emerging market society on the consciousness of those who are free to sell their labor and to work in an office at the center of American capitalism.

Answering to the divided structure of the office and the routine, alienated labor they do, the clerks are divided internally. Turkey works well in the morning. He accommodates to his situation in a classic way: he drinks. In the afternoon his energy is deranged and violently out of control (BTS, p. 42). Nippers works effectively for half the day, too—in the afternoon. But in the morning he is nervous, irritable, and painfully unable to find the right position for his desk. The clerks are divided down the middle of their lives. To make something like a whole person, they would have to be combined. Their situation in the market society fragments their humanity, deranges their human energy, and divides their consciousness.

They are also divided from each other. It reflects both the narrator's consciousness, the nature of his concerns and values, and the realities of the workplace that the clerks are shown to cooperate in reading proof and in the other details of their employment but that they are not shown together in any deeper sense. Significantly, they do come together in their common attack on Bartleby, who has disrupted the precarious balance of the office. As in the lower depths of Redburn's London, Melville shows that those at the bottom attack each other. In his version the clerks are too depleted, too deeply affected by their involvement in the processes of dominant-class hegemony, to form a genuine community opposed to the practices that generate their hatred and their misery. As American office workers, they do not have the kind of working-class consciousness E. P. Thompson examines in *The Rise of the English Working Class* or that Herbert Gutman examines among American manual workers in *Work, Culture, and Society*.[6] Or is it that the lawyer as a gentry professional sees only what he is capable of seeing? In any case, the clerks' way of assimilating the conditions of their work leads to self-division, a warping of energy, and the consequent, ever-present threat of violence. Under the controlled surface of the office and its inhabitants, the suppression of their humanity produces a seething, angry violence. To the extent that the clerks accept the dominant-class view of themselves, they intensify the potential for violence by turning this internalized power against their own humanity. The violence expresses itself in momentary outbursts against Bartleby, in the grinding of teeth, in the barely suppressed possibility of violent explosion. Except for Bartleby's passive resistance, however, the potential for rebellion is contained. It poses a psychological but not, in the ordinary sense, a political threat.

The lawyer, for his part, explains Nippers's behavior as the result "of two evil powers—ambition and indigestion. The ambition was evinced by a certain impatience of the duties of a mere copyist, an unwarrantable usurpation of strictly professional affairs, such as the original drawing up of legal documents" (BTS, p. 43). We see that Nippers is desperately trying to sustain his humanity by doing something creative instead of the endless round of copying.[7] For the lawyer, however, this "usurpation," this declaration of independence, is a threat to the division of labor, prestige, and power that reserves independent, human activity to

6. *The Rise of the English Working Class* (New York: Vintage, 1963), and *Work, Culture, and Society in Industrializing America* (New York: Knopf, 1976).
7. The lawyer's hegemonic appeal and his control of the narrative condition the reader's response. The extent emerges in the fact that even sophisticated critics like Andrew Weeks and John Carlos Rowe accept the lawyer's evaluation of Nipper's "ambition." Andrew Weeks, *The Paradox of the Employee: Variants on a Social Theme in Modern Literature* (Berne: Peter Lang, 1980), p. 29, and John Carlos Rowe, *Through the Custom-House: Nineteenth-Century American Fiction and Modern Theory* (Baltimore: Johns Hopkins University Press, 1982), p. 128.

owners and to professionals. In the deepest sense the lawyer is comically inaccurate in using "ambition" to explain Nippers's behavior. But in another sense Melville has the lawyer correctly understand that "ambition," "the drive to succeed" (*Oxford Universal Dictionary*), would alter the power relations central to his own position in the market society. The lower classes were to be ambitious, to work hard, and to rise in the world, but they were also to be kept in their places. The lawyer as a gentry professional in the flux of Jacksonian capitalism is unusually sensitive to this issue.

As a gentry professional he values Nippers because he dressed respectably and thus "reflected credit upon my chambers" (BTS, p. 44). Turkey, though, "with so small an income could not afford to support such a lustrous face and a lustrous coat at one and the same time" (BTS, p. 44). Instead of paying Turkey more, the lawyer offers him one of his own discarded overcoats, "a highly respectable-looking coat" that can cover Turkey's smelly clothes because it buttons from top to bottom. Because he cannot afford to see the real causes of Turkey's divided self, the lawyer thinks his self-interested charity will cure Turkey's "rashness and obstreperousness of afternoons" (BTS, p. 44). Like other dominant-class Americans, he also cannot understand why the recipient of his discarded clothing resents the favor. "It made him insolent. He was a man whom prosperity harmed" (BTS, p. 44). The explanation is worthy of Mark Twain or perhaps of Ronald Reagan.

Although Turkey and Nippers accept the prevailing dominant-class hegemony, they do so in a troubled, disturbed way. Their bodies and their spirits protest through drink or through the grinding of teeth, but Turkey and Nippers nonetheless work within the structure of the market society. As their divided selves reveal, they have interiorized the dominant-class hegemony. They literally work within the structure of the office. More deeply, they have taken that structure inside their consciousness. Their protests are caused by their situation and represent a kind of counter-hegemony or at least the energy from which a revolution might emerge. Melville, however, is not at all encouraging about its prospects.

Unlike the other clerks, Bartleby refuses to play the market-society game. His confrontations with the lawyer repeatedly establish that Bartleby comes to reject the theoretical foundations of capitalism. The willingness to alienate the self and to sell one's labor on the market is basic to capitalism. Bartleby prefers not to. He comes to reject the "common sense" and "common usage" that govern his society, its division of labor, its division of the self, its definitions of life and of right and wrong. "'What earthly right have you to stay here?' the lawyer asks. 'Do

you pay any rent? Do you pay any taxes? Or is this property yours?'"
(BTS, p. 63). The Declaration of Independence tells Bartleby that he has
an "unalienable right" to "life, liberty, and the pursuit of happiness."
For Locke it was "life, liberty, and estate [property]." Americans tend to
equate the pursuit of happiness with the pursuit of property. Through
the lawyer and Bartleby, Melville focuses on the central conflict between
the unalienable right to life, property, and happiness, a conflict Jefferson's language successfully obscures.

In addition to Bartleby's unalienable right to life by virtue of his being
a human being, the lawyer also raises other issues in conflict with the
capitalistic emphasis on property, taxes, and "earthly rights." The lawyer sees Bartleby as a spiritual person who would then have spiritual or
heavenly rights. In the lawyer's eyes, Bartleby's walled-in corner of the
office is his "hermitage," the habitation of "one who has retired to a
solitary place for a life of religious seclusion" (Oxford Universal Dictionary). The almost schizoid incongruity of a divided Wall Street office
presented as a "hermitage" contributes to the subversive comedy of the
story. The lawyer cannot bring into conscious awareness the conflict
between his view of Bartleby as a religious figure, finally as a Christ-like
sacrificial figure, and his feelings about the property rights and common
usage of the market society. The lawyer's consciousness is as divided as
his clerks'. The bleak comedy of "Bartleby, the Scrivener" emerges from
this socially rooted doubleness.

Bartleby's civil disobedience, his "passive resistance" (BTS, p. 50), is a
rebellion against the dominant assumptions of capitalism. As the lawyer
helps us see, Bartleby's rebellion is rooted in the Enlightenment commitment to the unalienable right to life and in the Christian desire for a
transcendent relation with God beyond the confining walls of the market society and of the earth itself. In the context of the emerging capitalism of Jacksonian America, these versions of both the Enlightenment
and the Christian are what Raymond Williams calls residual elements,
cultural forces that are no longer dominant but are nonetheless available
as resources within selves and society.[8] The division within the lawyer's
consciousness shows the same elements in conflict, not as external
powers but as internal forces.

The other clerks give a grudging but willing consent to the "reasonable" procedures of the office. Bartleby withholds his consent. He rejects
the dominant-class hegemony and appropriately moves from the prison
of the office to the prison of the Tombs, the place where society sends
offenders against its basic rules. A society divided between religious and

8. *Marxism and Literature*, pp. 121–28.

capitalistic tendencies, however, has a serious choice to make. Melville contrives it so that the lawyer must define himself through his choices between the conflicting sides of his personality. First, however, he tries to persuade Bartleby. "Those are your own copies we are about to examine. It is labor saving to you, because one examination will answer for your four papers. It is common usage" (BTS, p. 48). Bartleby refuses. Does he reject the view that the copies are his? Perhaps he believes they are the lawyer's. Although it may be "labor saving" to Bartleby, it is even more labor-saving to the lawyer. Bartleby refuses to give his willing consent. He rejects the "reasonable demand" that he participate in the unequal distribution of ownership and to save labor at the owner's command, sanctioned as "reason," "common sense," and "common usage" (BTS, p. 49). These words, which are still compelling, embody a dominant-class view of the market society. They are central to the hegemony Bartleby rejects.

When Bartleby first appears, he at least accepts the necessity of offering his labor for sale on the market. Like others in his position, he is free to starve if he chooses to withhold his property in himself. Except for his clothing and a small savings of money, Bartleby's only property is his property in his labor. Melville shows that for people like Bartleby, Turkey, and Nippers, the prospects are grim. Their problem goes beyond the low wages, which can to an extent be improved, and beyond the mechanical work, which cannot. In the land of opportunity, the Eden of the new world, they suffer the added burden of seeing others thrive, of believing they themselves should get ahead, and yet of experiencing daily the routine of an office whose doors are opened and closed by the owner. In this sense they are failures in the land of success. They suffer the psychological wounds, the "hidden injuries of class" that Richard Sennett analyzes.[9]

No wonder Bartleby is pallid. Bartleby is a propertyless person in a land where self-worth is a function of property ownership and the freedom it confers. To the extent that he accepts the market-society evaluations of self-worth, his sense of self is understandably pallid, is understandably depleted. If he yearns for transcendence, as the lawyer suggests, his "dead-wall reveries" constitute another failure rooted in and intensifying his market-society situation. If the lawyer is correct, God has disappeared for Bartleby. That disappearance and its effects on Bartleby are rooted in the developments of an emerging urban market society, embodied in the physical structure, procedures, and hierarchy of the Wall Street office.

9. *The Hidden Injuries of Class* (New York: Vintage, 1970).

In rejecting the market society, Bartleby affirms himself as independently as he can of dominant-class standards. He draws on and affirms sources of inner strength at odds with the prevailing power. He acts, or more often refrains from acting, but on his own choice, not on his employer's. He goes about his own, not his employer's, business. He does not compensate through drink. First the lawyer places Bartleby, as other employers have presumably done before. Bartleby then reverses the process. As if affirming and transcending his "failure," Bartleby reverses the market society power-prestige system. For him the doors of opportunity are closed. He then deliberately keeps the door closed. He decides when the lawyer will enter. In the land of mobility, he chooses to stay where he is. He refuses to move. He rejects the entire system of command, ownership, rationality, prestige, and mobility. He says at the end, "I know where I am" (BTS, p. 71). His self-knowledge is inseparable from his place in society and in the universe.

Unlike Thoreau, who knows beans from cultivating a bean field, Bartleby is unable to work creatively, to have his knowledge emerge continuously from the processes of his labor. The work he has done gives him his bitter knowledge but does not allow him to continue developing. In his rebellion, Bartleby inevitably shows the effects of the alienated labor and alienated life he is reacting against. He accepts and intensifies the divisions and isolation of his routine work and the organization of the workplace. He is cut off from others. He is similarly cut off from transcendence. Melville shows that human life cannot continue under the combined pressure of separation from meaningful work, human community, and divinity.

Bartleby's rebellion is individual and isolated like the market society it emerges from and protests against. This rebellion subtly begins to affect the consciousness of the other workers and even the lawyer. They, too, begin to have preferences and to prefer not to. But, despite this promising beginning, Bartleby is unable to change the structure of the market-society world he lives in. The impact on consciousness is not sustained because a reciprocal relation is needed between a transformed work system and transformed consciousness in order to make the changes last. The lawyer, however, simply moves to a new office, presumably similar to the old one. Bartleby, cut off from human community, gazes rebelliously at the dead walls and dies in the Tombs. In the absence of community, his lonely, individual rebellion reaches a dead end. Bartleby's rebellion is fatally marked by the privatizing tendencies of the dominant-class American hegemony it opposes.

The lawyer represents a gentry version of possessive individualism. Bartleby shows the impact of this system but in the lawyer's eyes Bartleby also emerges as a representative of American religious absolutism, of Protestant individualism carried to an uncompromising extreme. As has often been noted, the lawyer and Bartleby are doubles.[10] For the lawyer, Bartleby represents the contemplative, spiritual side of his own nature, the side he has largely suppressed but which nonetheless attracts him, which he invites to rebel, which he tries to placate and to co-opt, which he engages with a baffling persistence whose energy comes from deep within. This double relation is rooted in the processes of the market society as workplace and as world view. Just as the office is divided, just as labor is divided, just as Turkey and Nippers are divided, so is the lawyer's consciousness divided.

The lawyer's Bartleby appropriately has no energy or desire for human connection. He has only his devotions, his "dead-wall reveries," his unsatisfied yearning for communion with the absolute. On this view, we have another kind of division of labor. For the lawyer, contemplative spirituality is cut off from all other processes of ordinary human life. Instead of being the central element of an organically functioning societal life that includes work, family, and politics, as it had been for John Winthrop, contemplative religion is in this version a specialized function separated from and at odds with the world of work, family, and politics.[11] The lawyer as a gentry professional is susceptible to the claims of fellow-feeling (BTS, p. 42), but he has almost no human connections with his employees and he is so indifferent to relations outside the office that he does not say whether or not he has a family. He creates or responds to precisely the sort of contemplative person who answers to his own situation as a gentry version of the market society. Instead of someone who is flexible, humane, and moderate, the lawyer is attracted to and feels the need for the polar opposite. He is an absolutist who complements but nonetheless bears the stamp of the lawyer's own hegemony. His Bartleby is thus if not weak at least lacking in energy and is even less concerned with his fellow human beings than the lawyer. The lawyer's Bartleby has eyes only for the dead wall he

10. See Mordecai Marcus, "Melville's Bartleby as Psychological Double," *College English* 23 (February 1962): 369-76; Kingsley Widmer, *The Ways of Nihilism: Herman Melville's Short Novels* (Los Angeles: The California State Colleges, 1970), pp. 107, 109, 119; and Rowe, *Through the Custom-House*, pp. 123-33. Biographical critics, beginning with Mumford, also saw Bartleby and Melville as doubles, which is not at all the same thing.

11. I do not want to idealize Winthrop and his followers. They represent the unstable equilibrium of the first generation Puritan synthesis, a combination of traditionalist late medieval organicism and modern capitalistic tendencies. But at best Winthrop spoke for a cohesion his own efforts helped to destroy. For a suggestive analysis of the dynamics of Puritan theology, see Christopher Hill, "Protestantism and the Rise of Capitalism," in David S. Landes, ed., *The Rise of Capitalism* (New York: Macmillan, 1966), pp. 41–52.

cannot penetrate. He embodies the situation of intense religion under the pressure of the emerging urban market society the lawyer represents. This religion can no longer animate a full human life or even concern itself with human beings. To preserve his integrity and humanity, the lawyer's Bartleby becomes increasingly dehumanized. The act of choice through which we affirm our humanity becomes for the lawyer's Bartleby an increasingly devitalizing process leading to the Tombs. He shows the dead end of an absolutist Protestant individualism under the pressures of the Jacksonian market society.[12]

Within the lawyer's consciousness the moderate mix of capitalistic and Christian beliefs is unequal: the claims of professional peer opinion and the lawyer's own deep involvement in possessive individualism finally prevail. The lawyer's consciousness is unequally divided not only between Christian and capitalistic tendencies but also between the old, intense Calvinistic Christianity of "Edwards on the Will" (BTS, p. 64) and the new, humane Christianity of sentiment and pity. Responsive to the conflict between Christianity and capitalism, the lawyer separates the conflicting sides of his personality and the conflicting sides of his religion. He projects his religious needs outside, onto Bartleby. What then emerges is an absolutist version of Christianity that shows the deep effects of the lawyer's dominant-class hegemony Bartleby's Christianity in part opposes, in part supports. What attracts the lawyer is an absolutism, an extreme spiritual commitment for which he feels the need. But under the circumstances of his market-society life, the lawyer's absolutist is a far cry from Jonathan Edwards.

Through the lawyer and Bartleby, the declining energy Melville attributes to Christianity shows his view of the situation of religion under the market-society pressures of Wall Street. Just as Turkey's energy is deranged, just as his self is divided, so the lawyer is fragmented such that his need for religious absolutism results in his attraction to Bartleby, an absolutist reified and deranged in his socially and economically generated isolation. Because of his divided consciousness the lawyer vacillates. As a Christian of both the old and the new persuasions he knows how he should treat Bartleby. He celebrates "the divine injunction: 'A new commandment give I unto you, that ye love one another'" (BTS, p. 64). But from this commitment to love as a unifying and saving principle, the lawyer immediately moves to a view of charity as a "prudent

12. Bartleby is also connected with Eastern religion. In the history of American Protestantism, intellectuals have a long-standing relation with forms of Oriental religion. H. Bruce Franklin examines Bartleby as a version of the Oriental ascetic, the Hindu Saniassi, in *The Wake of the Gods: Melville's Mythology* (Palo Alto: Stanford University Press, 1963), pp. 135–36. See also Rowe, *Through the Custom-House*, pp. 119–27.

principle," and he is soon enmeshed in a market-society argument for "self-interest" as the motive for charity. The comedy emerges from and reveals the confusions of the well-intentioned Christian gentry whose involvement in the market society finally undercuts his Christianity. Viewed in another way, Melville shows how difficult it is to maintain a genuine Christian commitment to love in a Wall Street society that systematically divides people and seeks to maximize self-interested profit.

As a descendent of the Calvinists, the lawyer reads "Edwards on the Will" (BTS, p. 64) and decides that caring for Bartleby is "the predestinated purpose of my life," "predestinated from eternity . . . for some mysterious purpose of an all-wise Providence" (BTS, p. 65). But in the next breath he again resolves to get rid of the now useless and embarrassing scrivener. He cannot sustain his old-fashioned Christian commitments under the pressure of the disapproval of his professional colleagues and of the market-society side of his own personality. The lawyer is especially disturbed because Bartleby "denies his authority" (BTS, p. 67), challenges his control, which is to say, challenges his class dominance as a gentry employer.

The drama of self-definition, social definition, and moral and religious choice reaches an intense climax. The lawyer is told directly, "You are responsible for the man you left there." He explicitly denies responsibility, although the phrase "in mercy's name" resonates with the values he sacrifices (BTS, p. 67). In one sense, in denying his responsibility to Bartleby, the lawyer commits a prolonged act of apostasy against the man he sees as a Christ-like sufferer and against his own Christian profession of love, mercy, and belief in the "predestinated purpose of his life." In another sense the lawyer denies a part of himself, rejects the risks and possibilities of change, of acting on his commitment to love. Bartleby's death is a death for the lawyer as well. Bartleby as a separate self may or may not be incurable. But the lawyer can affirm or deny the power of love within himself, a power Bartleby speaks to and challenges. In the Tombs the lawyer buries the spiritually sensitive, potentially renewing side of his own personality. Love as a cohesive, renewing power is the alternative to the fragmenting, self-interested impulses of possessive individualism. The lawyer senses that love and capitalism may be incompatible, that to love Bartleby unconditionally, to take him home unconditionally, to embrace Bartleby instead of offering him money is clearly a risky course. Following it the lawyer may or may not be able to function on Wall Street. As it turns out, through his choices the lawyer repeatedly affirms his market-society self at the expense of his Christian and humanistic impulses. At the end he is totally imprisoned in the market society. Bartleby achieves a perverse freedom through his choices that lead him to death and the prison and the prison of death. Bartleby is blind but he sees. The lawyer has eyesight but he is blind. Unlike Bartleby, he does not know where he is. He is in prison without knowing it. He has learned nothing. He has gained no insight into himself or into his society, and he has gained no understanding of Bartleby's rebellion. He has denied his own capacity to love. What remains is only the sentimentality that emerges in his final words of pity and self-pity, "Ah Bartleby! Ah Humanity!" (BTS, p. 74).

As he has throughout, the lawyer retains enough of his gentry decency and concern to voice the sentiment. The criticism of the lawyer as a moderate representative of the market society turns partly on the contradiction between his humane tendencies and his inability to actualize them. In response to market-society demands he has denied his responsibility to Bartleby, he has denied Bartleby's and his own humanity. But without realizing the full implications of his words or actions he continues to speak for humanity. Is Melville pointing to a corrosive incompatibility between the values of humanity and the market society, an incompatibility intensified by the lawyer's moderation and benign unawareness? For his own survival the lawyer needs to see himself as humane, as America and Americans do, despite systematic actions that destroy the values he professes. As a moderate he goes only so far in the direction of his humane principles. This behavior is prudent but also fatal to the qualities of love and humanity the lawyer needs to maintain in order to see himself as worthwhile. As an integral part of his dominant-class hegemony, the lawyer needs to see himself as a humane Christian. Melville subversively exposes this part of the hegemonic process.

As a gentry representative of the dominant class, the lawyer also protects himself by perceiving in a way that minimizes the seriousness and the nature of Bartleby's rebellion. He refuses to acknowledge that Bartleby has made a conscious, principled choice. "Poor fellow! thought I, he means no mischief" (BTS, p. 50). It is as necessary and as reassuring for the lawyer to believe Bartleby "don't mean anything" (BTS, p. 64) as it is for him to believe Bartleby's "eccentricities" are "involuntary" (BTS, p. 50). The "insolence" (BTS, p. 50) the lawyer refuses to attribute to his "gentlemanly" employee says more about the lawyer's concerns than about Bartleby's. When Bartleby speaks in his own voice, not from the lawyer's point of view, he says that he knows where he is. He deliberately refuses to work, to do alienated labor at his employer's command. He prefers not to move when the lawyer offers to take him home, a generous gesture vitiated by the condition "till we can conclude upon some convenient arrangement" (BTS, p. 69). The "satisfactory arrangement" of the office indicates whose convenience will be served. The lawyer tries to get Bartleby back to work, to get him to accept the market-society system. He does so in the name of "friendly" (BTS, p. 57) feelings like those that motivate his gift of the overcoat. He mixes the claims of friendship and business, as he does love, charity, and prudential self-interest. Bartleby prefers not to. What is at issue is the way the need for humane flexibility is manipulated, not hypocritically but as an expression of a set of deep, hegemonic assumptions. Perhaps Bartleby sees that the lawyer's mix always favors the claims of the market society, that the lawyer uses apparently disinterested and universal values to give legitimacy to his dominant-class control.

Bartleby rebels against the lawyer's entire system of power and legitimizing values. The lawyer maintains his own sense of superiority and control by downplaying the extent and causes of Bartleby's rebellion. As a representative of the dominant class, the lawyer's sense of self-esteem motivates him to perceive (or misperceive) so as to ignore the corrosive implications of Bartleby's reality. It is the reality of a member of a subordinate class in the process of rejecting the dominance of the market society.

At his best the lawyer appreciates the depths of Bartleby's loneliness. He sees Bartleby cast off like a wreck in the midst of the emptiness of Wall Street. It does not detract from the lawyer's perception if we see it as an intensification of his own isolation, modulated in his case by his prosperity and position. On Melville's view, everyone in the market society of Wall Street is isolated.

In one of the most challenging episodes in the story, the lawyer concludes that Bartleby's misery is hopeless, incurable. Because the lawyer's consciousness is divided between conflicting tendencies, Melville has his narrator go to the center of the conflict among Calvinistic Protestantism, its liberal successors, and the market society. His decision not to aid Bartleby, the lawyer argues, does not reflect Calvinistic, market-society man's "inherent selfishness." From the point of view not of a Calvinist but of his liberal, gentry successor, the lawyer asserts that Bartleby inspires pity, but when "at last it is perceived that such pity cannot lead to effectual succor, common sense bids the soul be rid of it." "What I saw that morning," the lawyer tellingly concludes, "persuaded me that the scrivener was the victim of innate and incurable disorder. I might give alms to his body; but his body did not pain him; it was his soul that suffered, and his soul I could not reach" (BTS, p. 56). The conclusion, not surprisingly, as the lawyer states, "Disqualified me for the time from church-going" (BTS, p. 56). The mix of values and value words is staggering. Without any sense of disparity the lawyer puts "common sense," the cornerstone of the market society, to work getting rid of "the soul," as if it were a spiritual duty to deny the Christian imperative to love unconditionally. The lawyer can speak as he does in a way that still compels attention because in contrast to the old Protestantism he articulates the American secular belief that every problem has a solution and that unsolvable problems do not have moral status—or rather, that we have a moral sanction to ignore unsolvable problems. In mixing theological and secular categories, moreover, the lawyer converts the old Calvinistic idea of innate depravity into the new secular vocabulary of medical disease, without, however, totally giving up the idea of "soul."

The lawyer's analysis, we should note, overlooks the extent to which Bartleby's physical and spiritual misery is rooted in the market society the lawyer represents. Even in his view that Bartleby is incurable, however, the lawyer does not consider what an unconditional attempt to aid Bartleby would do for the lawyer himself. It might renew him or unfit him for his work, it might radicalize him or spiritualize him or both. But it would not unfit him for church-going and it would not leave him complacently imprisoned at the end. The gentry lawyer is an effective spokesman for a market society that needs to recognize compassion to justify itself and that needs to keep compassion in its place to sustain its own underlying dynamics.

Internalized within the lawyer, this conflict illuminates the dynamics of authority, power, and control. The lawyer wants to control Bartleby. Well after Bartleby has announced that he prefers not to work, that he prefers not to be "a little reasonable" (BTS, p. 58), the lawyer "would inadvertently summon Bartleby, in a short, rapid tone" (BTS, p. 53). "I burned to be rebelled against again" (BTS, p. 52), the lawyer says. He needs to assert his power as a person and as an employer—the two categories are inseparable in his consciousness—but he also needs Bartleby's rebellion, which appeals to the spiritually suppressed side of his own nature. When he visits the deserted office on Sunday, however, Bartleby is in control. The conventional power relations are reversed. Instead of Bartleby's rebelling, the lawyer himself then experiences "sundry twinges of impotent rebellion against the mild effrontery of this unaccountable scrivener" (BTS, p. 54). As a gentry employer the lawyer has a special need to control his hired help, to have them defer to him. His inability to control Bartleby affects his sexuality, his sense of his masculinity. He feels impotent, "unmanned when he tranquilly permits his hired clerk to dictate to him, and order him away from his own premises" (BTS, p. 54). The dynamics of market-society control and rebellion affect the innermost recesses of the self, a person's sexuality,

which for the lawyer is closely aligned with a not always secure dominant-class position he needs continually to affirm.

More generally, the market society as an alienating system affects
both the lawyer and Bartleby's sexuality. The lawyer has alienated his
own contemplative, spiritual tendencies and embodied them in Bartleby. The lawyer's Bartleby is similarly alienated from his own sexuality. He is pallid; he has no appetite or appetites. Instead of animating
his spirituality, this separation from erotic sources reinforces Bartleby's
alienation from God, his dead-end, dead-wall reveries. The lawyer is as
asexual as Bartleby. In the lawyer and Bartleby the market society and
ascetic Protestantism combine and reinforce the sexually alienating tendencies of each system. Bartleby nonetheless poses the challenge of
love. For the lawyer it is spiritual or Christian love. In the context of the
office and the market society it represents, this separation of sexuality
and spirituality is itself significant. Melville contrives it so that the lawyer is challenged to love Bartleby, to touch him, to take him home in the
fullest sense. Ordinarily in the course of the lawyer's narrative we do
not notice that he has alienated or sublimated his sexuality, because in
the context of his market society and coming from his representative
consciousness we take the absence of sexuality for granted. We do not
expect and do not ordinarily notice the absence of a genuinely human,
overt sexuality, which we feel would be out of place in the lawyer's
world. But what if the lawyer had taken Bartleby home without conditions? Imagine the lawyer at home with Bartleby as Ishmael and Queequeg are at home with each other. The saving relation between Ishmael
and Queequeg is subversively at odds with conventional sexual, racial,
religious, and finally market-society values. The absence of such a relation between the lawyer and Bartleby and the systematic exclusion of
overt sexuality in their characterization are similarly perceptive and subversive.

Melville published "Bartleby" and several of his succeeding short-
story masterpieces in *Putnam's*. In the lawyer's market-society world,
which includes Bartleby, sexuality has been driven away or driven underground. For Melville, the middle-class Victorian decorum of magazines like *Putnam's* reinforces this tendency and calls forth the strategies
of indirection "Bartleby, the Scrivener" carries to new extremes in
Melville's writing career. "Bartleby" is a profound study of the workings
of the market society not because Melville is somehow abstracted from
these processes but because they have penetrated his consciousness: he
knows them from the inside because they are inside him. As a producer
for the literary marketplace, Melville was deeply involved in the processes of cultural hegemony. The results pervade the style and the sub-

versive insights of "Bartleby." In "Bartleby" Melville draws on, caricatures, and transforms his own experience as a title hunter, as a writer or
scrivener, as a notorious borrower from Shakespeare, Montaigne,
Browne, and Rabelais—a copyist indeed.[13] As a creative writer Melville
was presumably doing work the direct opposite of the routine, alienated
labor of the law office. But under the pressure of his own involvement in
the literary marketplace where "dollars damn me," Melville experienced
alienation at the center of his creative life. He jokes that he is a mechanical device: "I shall at last be worn out and perish, like an old nutmeg-
grater, grated to pieces by the constant attrition of the wood, that is, the
nutmeg." The reason, though, is not a joke: "What I feel most moved to
write, that is banned,—it will not pay. Yet, altogether, write the *other*
way I cannot. So the product is a final hash, and all my books are
botches."[14] In "Bartleby" Melville draws on his experience as a creative
writer in the marketplace and transforms it into an extraordinary probing of the urban market society. He simultaneously exposes, resists, and
shows the impact of the dominant society, which is to say that he takes
us deep into the processes of cultural hegemony.[15]

   To further illuminate Melville's involvement in the hegemonic process, it is worth stressing that in "Bartleby" he draws on and transforms
his entire family situation. He is unusually sensitive to the predicament
of his gentry, lawyer narrator partly because of his own family. His
Gansevoort and Melville grandparents were Revolutionary War heroes.
The Gansevoorts were wealthy landowners, his father was a prosperous

   13. Richard Chase established the connection between Bartleby and Melville as a writer
in *Herman Melville: A Critical Study* (New York: Macmillan, 1949), pp. 143–49. In his influential rejoinder, "Melville's Parable of the Walls," *Sewanee Review* 61 (October 1953): 602–27,
Leo Marx makes Bartleby a writer and systematically ignores the extent to which Melville
transforms and caricatures his own experience.
   14. *The Letters of Herman Melville*, ed. Merrill R. Davis and William Gilman (New Haven:
Yale University Press, 1960), p. 128.
   In his pioneering essays on Melville as a professional writer, William Charvat, *The
Profession of Authorship in America, 1800–1870* (Columbus: Ohio State University Press,
1968), established Melville's career-long "conflict with his readers," a conflict that became
more serious as Melville developed (p. 204). Although Melville made a comparatively
good living for a serious writer—an average of $1,600 a year for the period 1846–1851 (p.
193)—books like *Mardi* and *Moby-Dick* did not pay. A book needed to sell about 5,000
copies to be a commercial success. Only 2,915 copies of *Moby-Dick* were printed (p. 241). At
the same time writers like Susan Warner, author of *Wide, Wide World* (New York: Putnam,
1852), were selling in the 100,000 copy range. Melville had good reason to be disappointed
not only in the sales of *Moby-Dick* but also in the mixed critical response (pp. 241-42).
   15. For a stimulating view of "Bartleby" and the marketplace, but not of the dynamics of
cultural hegemony, see Michael Gilmore, *American Romanticism and the Marketplace* (University of Chicago Press, 1985), pp. 132–45.

importer. In the flux of Jacksonian America, however, his father went bankrupt trying to import French luxury goods against the grain of current taste and commercial practices.[16] Allan Melville died a bankrupt after a period of insanity. At twelve Melville was suddenly thrust into a hard world. He experienced deeply and at first hand the instability of the market society. His ambivalence toward the authority figures of official society emerges in his treatment of the lawyer. A similar ambivalence characterizes his view of his lawyer brothers, Gansevoort and Allan, and even more his complex feelings about his father-in-law and father surrogate, Chief Justice Lemuel Shaw, the distinguished head of the Massachusetts Supreme Court.[17]

Melville did not write "Bartleby, the Scrivener: A Story of Wall Street" as a neutral, detached observer, an anthropological visitor from another culture. He was intimately involved in the market society he explores. Put more generally, like any of us and like any writer, Melville's consciousness was deeply affected by the dominant-class hegemony he exposes. The remarkable variety and intensity of response not only within Melville's work but also within that of his predecessors, contemporaries, and successors will occupy us in the succeeding chapters.

16. Michael Paul Rogin, *Subversive Genealogy: The Politics and Art of Herman Melville* (New York: Knopf, 1983), pp. 15–41.

17. John Stark, "Melville, Lemuel Shaw, and 'Bartleby,'" in *Bartleby the Inscrutable: A Collection of Commentary on Herman Melville's Tale "Bartleby, the Scrivener,"* ed. M. Thomas Inge (Hamden, Conn.: Archon Books, 1979), pp. 166–73, establishes that Shaw was an influential representative of a generally pro-industry, pro-development outlook centered around a dominant-class view of "prudence." Although like any complex mind Shaw is not mechanically consistent, his basic allegiances emerge in a series of precedent-setting decisions. Dan Schiller, *Objectivity and the News: The Public and the Rise of Commercial Journalism* (Philadelphia: University of Pennsylvania Press, 1981), pp. 20-24, analyzes the role Chief Justice Shaw and others played as they transformed American law so that "it reinforced market inequality with crucial support from the state sector" (p. 20). Michael Rogin does a revealing analysis of Shaw's role in Melville's life in *Subversive Genealogy* (see p. 353, index entry under "Shaw").

two

FATHERS, BROTHERS, AND "THE DISEASED"
The Family and Alienation in *Huckleberry Finn*

Four decades before Twain had Huck talk about lighting out for the territory, in *Typee* Melville had shown that the young American takes his own and his country's divided consciousness with him. The experience of the Typee's cohesive society as a joyful, loving family was crucial for Melville. It gave him an indispensable vantage point on the fragmenting market society he probes in "Bartleby, the Scrivener" and in different ways in *Moby-Dick*, *The Confidence-Man*, and *Billy Budd*. We need Tocqueville's analysis of nineteenth-century America to deepen our understanding of why the contrasting culture of the Typees was so important to Melville and why, to round out our emphasis on community and fragmentation in America, the Afro-American conjure world and the family idyll on the river were central for Chesnutt in *The Conjure Woman* and for Twain at the height of his powers in *Adventures of Huckleberry Finn*.

Early in the nineteenth century, Tocqueville diagnosed the restlessness of Americans who, he observed, are chronically striving and dissatisfied in the midst of their prosperity. Tocqueville's American, freed from traditional restraints and ties, pushes his way through a crowd of equally striving men, equally free and equally on the move. But with everyone moving, Tocqueville recognized, each individual finds his own way blocked by others, so that, although his expectations are of limitless freedom, his actual freedom is restricted. The striving individual also encounters the limits of personal ability, which for Tocqueville are intrinsic and cannot be altered by any social system, however egalitarian. Even more important, no matter where a person is in an open society, someone else is always in a position slightly higher, looking down on and in a way devaluing his achievement. On all these counts Tocqueville defined a basic conflict between the American's expectation

28

of limitless mobility and equality and his experience of restraints and inequality.[1]

As a result, Tocqueville's Americans are never satisfied. They restlessly strive to demonstrate to themselves and others that they are the equals of men similarly striving. The process is endless and insatiable. Tocqueville perceptively realized that the American's notorious pursuit of money conceals a more basic problem, a problem of the self. For Tocqueville, what drives people in the new world is a need to establish a sense of self-worth in a competition with men similarly driven to achieve in a changing world where traditional ties, supports, and restrictions have been left behind along with their assurances about a person's self-worth and identity. Competitive people thus accumulate great wealth and are powerfully motivated to accumulate even more. They are perpetually disappointed, however, because their underlying hunger is for a sense of self-worth that material possessions cannot satisfy. For those who fail in the competitive struggle, the results are even more demoralizing. Tocqueville's insights need to be supplemented to take account of those class, wealth, and power divisions he underestimated. But on his own territory Tocqueville is revealing. Analysts of American capitalism focus on the system's privatizing, alienating power and on capitalism's dynamics of expansion. Tocqueville independently confirms their analysis.

For Tocqueville, the restless, acquisitive American withdraws from a stable, communal world and faces the final threat of isolation. Tocqueville's American individualist "severs himself from the mass of his fellows and draws apart with his family and his friends, so that after he has thus formed a little circle of his own, he willingly leaves society at large to itself" (DIA, 2:104). These family ties, however, prove to be inadequate; they cannot hold an entire society together. Tocqueville pointedly observes, "Aristocracy had made a chain of all the members of the community, from the peasant to the king; democracy breaks that chain and severs every link of it." For Tocqueville "democracy" is a shorthand word for the individualism, competitiveness, and restless mobility of an open, egalitarian, nontraditional market society. He associates democracy with the American belief that as competitive individuals we are self-made. For Tocqueville, Americans thus tend to cut their ties with their fellows, their ancestors, and their descendants. "They owe nothing to

1. *Democracy in America*, ed. Phillips Bradley, 2 vols. (New York: Vintage Books, 1945), 2:144–47. Subsequent references will be abbreviated DIA and cited by volume and page numbers in the text.

any man," and "they expect nothing from any man; they acquire the habit of always considering themselves as standing alone, and they are apt to imagine that their whole destiny is in their own hands." Under the impulses of democratic individualism, separated from ancestors, descendants, and contemporaries, the American is thus thrown "back forever upon himself alone." The threat is that in the end he will be confined "entirely within the solitude of his own heart" (DIA, 2:105).

Tocqueville does not make his exceptionally telling observations about whites and blacks in America central to his analysis of the dominant fragmenting and isolating tendencies of the Americans. Like the country he is studying, Tocqueville segregates the racial part of his account but he does include it. Tocqueville says that the Northern black, legally free and equal, was in fact systematically discriminated against, deprived of his rights as a citizen, and held in contempt as an inferior being. Based on his observations of the depth and intensity of Northern white race prejudice against blacks, he concluded that in the South, if the blacks were to gain their freedom, the situation would be even worse. In addition to the general prejudice against blacks by the English speaking people, whom Tocqueville saw as of all nations "having mixed least with the Negroes" (DIA, 1:389), the Southern white man would refuse out of "fear of being assimilated to the Negroes, their former slaves" (DIA, 1:390), so that for Tocqueville slavery compounded race prejudice. On Tocqueville's analysis, moreover, the strongest motive of Americans in general is to be equal, to be the same as everyone else. But to be black in a land where most are white is to be visibly different, another powerful barrier against assimilation in both North and South and one rooted in what for Tocqueville is a basic impulse of American democracy. In addition, Southerners would refuse to mix with blacks because of "the dread of sinking below the whites, their neighbors" (DIA, 1:390), so that for them race prejudice is further intensified by the dynamics of self-worth and personal insecurity in an open society. "If I were called upon to predict the future," Tocqueville concluded in 1835, "I should say that the abolition of slavery in the South will, in the common course of things, increase the repugnance of the white population for the blacks" (DIA, 1:390). Tocqueville comes close to showing that white racism functions to allay some of the anxieties generated by a restless, competitive market society that systematically undermines a person's sense of self-worth. On this view white people have a special need for a despised group they can look down on and feel superior to because then at least they can feel they are above someone else and to that extent feel they are worth something.

In Tocqueville's America, men cut their ties with each other and with the land (DIA, 2:166), restlessly pursue material advantages that, even when attained, fail to satisfy them, and confront the ultimate prospect of total, dehumanizing isolation. Racism is rooted in the underlying dynamics of the society. If cohesive values exist at all, they are under extreme pressure. Tocqueville is observing in their new-world setting the dynamics of what C. B. Macpherson has analyzed as the possessive market society. The tendencies Tocqueville had perceived in the 1830s, far from being diminished, became even more pervasive in post–Civil-War America. The accelerating changes of industrialization, urbanization, and immigration intensified the sense of market-society rootlessness. More and more people experienced the loneliness of urban life in a society that continued to define people on the basis of their acquisitions. At least in Tocqueville's period, people had the relative cohesion of their village communities; increasingly after the Civil War they cut their ties and moved to the new, impersonal, industrial-commercial cities. The extremes of wealth and poverty became even more apparent and disturbing. For an increasingly large number of Americans, the pressures of this new life resulted in an experience of weightlessness, "a vapid, anonymous existence—a death-in-life."[2] This sense of weightlessness was an intensified version of the strains Tocqueville had perceived. On the surface Americans were self-assured and confident. Internally, as in Tocqueville's period, they drove themselves relentlessly, made and lost fortunes, and continued to face the threat of isolation. Not accidentally, by the end of the century white racism had also intensified: the Jim Crow laws, lynching, and the racist underpinnings of American imperialism in the Caribbean and the Philippines are simply reminders.[3]

At first glance, *Adventures of Huckleberry Finn* seems remote from the new post–Civil-War world, but in his masterpiece Twain in fact engages the basic tendencies of his contemporary America. The rootlessness and striving, the unsettling impact on the self, and the racism and the other threats to community are deeply rooted in the earlier America Tocqueville had examined and in which Twain had grown up. After the Civil War these tendencies became even more pronounced. Twain's concern with cohesive values and the threats to them reflects his sensitivity to, and acute understanding of, the most important human and social problem of his period. By concentrating on his treatment of the family and

2. T. Jackson Lears, *No Place of Grace: Antimodernism and the Transformation of American Culture, 1880–1920* (New York: Pantheon Books, 1981), p. 33.

3. See C. Vann Woodward, *The Strange Career of Jim Crow* (New York: Oxford, 1955, 1966); Willard B. Gatewood, Jr., *Black Americans and the White Man's Burden, 1898–1903* (Urbana: University of Illinois Press, 1975), and Joel Williamson, *The Crucible of Race: Black-White Relations in the American South Since Emancipation* (New York: Oxford, 1984).

individualism in *Huck Finn*, we can deepen our own understanding of both his novel and the American market society it emerges from and illuminates.

At its best, the late nineteenth-century American family embodies those possibilities of community and security the larger society undermines. In *Huck Finn* the actual families—Pap's, the Grangerford's, the Phelps's, and the widow and Miss Watson's—fall revealingly short of this cohesive ideal. As Kenneth Lynn first showed, however, Huck and Jim create a family.[4] Their family embodies an ideal of community that highlights the shortcomings of the actual families and society in the novel.[5] Considering the family and the issue of community also obliges us to examine the individual. In traditional societies, particularly in Europe, the family has a history and a future that transcend any one individual. From an American point of view these traditional societies, however attractive, are restrictive and even threatening, as Melville's Tommo discovered. In America, the development of the individual takes precedence. Americans find it difficult to imagine an individuality that develops fully in the context of a community or group like the family. As Americans, we usually think of the self opposed to society, the individual versus the community, the emerging person in conflict with the family.[6] Twain's satiric treatment of the actual families and society in *Huck Finn* shows the considerable extent to which such opposition is necessary. Through the relation between Huck and Jim, however, Twain also suggests the possibility of an individualism compatible with community. On the old-world model, people gain security and identity, but at the price of their unique individuality. Twain suggests an American individualism appropriate to the new world. This individualism differs both from the restless, market-society individualism Tocqueville and Macpherson characterize and from the traditional subordina-

---

4. "Huck and Jim," *Yale Review* 47 (1958): 421–31. See also A. N. Kaul, *The American Vision: Actual and Ideal Society in Nineteenth-Century American Fiction* (New Haven: Yale University Press, 1963), p. 293.

5. James Grove, "Mark Twain and the Endangered Family," *American Literature* 59 (1985): 377–94, focuses on "the tragedies haunting Twain's own life" and "his abiding ambivalence toward the family" (p. 377). He shows that Huck "creates families for himself and then imagines them disrupted or destroyed," that his "lies reflect Huck's repeated desire to escape families which attract, confuse, and endanger him," and that Huck is "drawn to the ideal of the strong, loving family—although he usually feels restricted within the everyday realization of this ideal" (pp. 390, 391). I am placing Grove's biographically based view of family tensions in a larger social-political context.

6. Ellen Wood, *Mind and Politics: An Approach to the Meaning of Liberal and Socialist Individualism* (Berkeley: University of California Press, 1972), perceptively examines the philosophical sources of this outlook.

tion of the individual to the family or society. Inevitably, this alternative individualism is not easy to sustain.

In *Huck Finn*, the relation between Huck and Jim is basic; self-fulfillment is a necessary but not sufficient condition for achieving a real individuality. James M. Cox reoriented Twain criticism by showing the importance of satisfying a boy's need for pleasure, fun, and the expression of his own nature in opposition to the social conventions Tom Sawyer and the widow and Miss Watson represent.[7] What has not been shown, however, is that Huck thus embodies a style of individualism different from the debased romantic individualism of Tom Sawyer, the anarchic individualism of Pap, and, most especially, the acquisitive individualism of the Duke and the Dauphin. Equally important, in the great, idyllic moments on the river, Huck fully if briefly realizes his individuality in the context of a human community with Jim and a natural community with the surrounding world. Since in American thought "self" and "society" are usually opposed, it is worth stressing Twain's intuitive understanding of the possibility of an individualism inseparable from rather than opposed to or threatened by community. In practice, the dominant market-society individualism of the Duke and the Dauphin undercuts both the ideal community and the alternative individualism Huck and Jim develop.

In *Huck Finn*, the family is the focus for these concerns about differing versions of individualism and community. "Father," "child," "family," "brother," "friend"—in the novel these related words come to form a core of values centering on Huck and Jim's relation. These cohesive family values are as basic to the human world of the novel as the river is to the natural world. Genuine feelings of joy and grief, real laughter and tears, the authentic language of the heart all contribute to the value of the family Huck and Jim create. Huck and especially Jim use a verbal and nonverbal language of the heart to express their feelings for each other. These feelings and the way Huck and Jim express them are exceptionally important in a world dominated sometimes by the suppression of compassion, as with Miss Watson, and sometimes by the calculated expression of false compassion, as with the Duke and the Dauphin. The human ties and responsibilities centering on Huck and Jim's family similarly counter powerful tendencies toward a fragmented isolation.

Because of the family Huck and Jim create, and because of Jim's feelings for his wife and children, the novel, however precariously, gives substance to the idea of the larger family of man, not as an empty abstraction but as an endangered value without which modern life is

7. *Mark Twain: The Fate of Humor* (Princeton University Press, 1967).

reduced to the barrenness Tocqueville foresaw. To dramatize the danger and to highlight the value, Twain imagines a sequence of fragmented families, culminating in the Duke and the Dauphin's. These two frauds, in their vitality, inventiveness, and merciless pursuit of self-interest, provide a deeply comic, realistic counterbalance to Huck and Jim as family. The novel is organized around the tension between these two created families and their values as much as it is around the tension between the river and the shore.

At the outset of the novel Huck is part of a fragmented family. There is no father or husband at the widow and Miss Watson's, and this incompletion is symptomatic. The widow and her sister treat Huck differently, but even the kindly widow thinks she knows what is best for Huck and, without taking his needs, feelings, or nature into account, tries to fit him into the mold of respectability, to "sivilize" him.[8] For her part, Miss Watson, impatient with a boy's need to move about and implacable in her religion of prayers and guilt, represents a debased form of what Philip Greven describes as an "evangelical" parent.[9] From the seventeenth century into the nineteenth century these authoritarian fathers and mothers trained their children to love and to fear them, to hate pleasure and their bodies, and to subordinate their wills and selves to their parents. Later such children did assert themselves, only to experience guilt and to be reborn, to become again as children and to relate to God as they had to their parents, loving and fearing an all-powerful God to whom they subordinated themselves. The widow is a more attractive version of the "moderate" parents Greven analyzes, authoritative rather than authoritarian parents who strove to bend rather than break the will of their children. Moderate parents exercised careful supervision and control over their children and sought through love to bring their children to God and to a restrained, disciplined, useful life.[10]

The widow and Miss Watson reveal the decline or weaknesses of both the "evangelical" and the "moderate" parent. In the opening episodes of *Huck Finn* both types of parent, and by extension the middle-class family as an instrument of socialization, are effectively satirized. Even well-meaning adults like the widow impose a code of social respectability at odds with Huck's real needs. In the widow and Miss Watson's family, Huck's genuine individuality is stifled, not developed. Religion, more-

---

8. Samuel Clemens, *Adventures of Huckleberry Finn; A Facsimile of the First Edition*, ed. Hamlin Hill (Scranton, Pa.: Chandler Publishing Co., 1962), p. 17. Subsequent references will be abbreviated AHF and cited by page number in the text.

9. *The Protestant Temperament: Patterns of Child-Rearing, Religious Experience, and the Self in Early America* (New York: Knopf, 1977), especially pp. 21–48.

10. Ibid., pp. 151–261.

over, is not a life-giving force but is comically reduced to the level of manners and dress. It is no wonder that Huck, estranged from his adopted family and under the pressure of social and religious demands he can live with but that fail to satisfy his needs, "felt so lonesome I most wished I was dead" (AHF, p. 20). Ideally, families provide a sense of belonging, of cohesiveness, and they encourage the individual to develop his unique potentialities as part of the family and society. At best the family is also a counterforce to those feelings of loneliness and isolation Tocqueville showed to be especially American. The families in Huck's early experience, however, intensify rather than mitigate these feelings.

Conventional religion and the code of respectability, then, are not negligible: they do have real power. Like the families that transmit them, they promote a cohesion that Huck experiences as isolating and fragmenting. A central reason is that, manifested throughout the novel from the strictures of the widow and of Miss Watson to the rhetoric of piety at the campmeeting and at the Grangerford's church and culminating in Huck's fear of hell when he decides not to turn Jim in, official religion and the code of respectability are integral to the hegemonic process that legitimizes slavery and money as the cornerstones of Huck's society. These related powers unify society and separate people from each other and from their own humanity. They do so as external and especially as internalized forces. Huck reacts against the widow and Miss Watson but their training has deeply affected him, as his crisis of conscience dramatizes. In the prevalent view, sanctioned by religion and by all the forces of respectability—as well as by Pap—slaves are not people. When it comes down to it, the widow feels justified in selling Jim for eight hundred dollars. For her, as for the Judge and Pap and the Duke and the Dauphin—quite a range—money counts. As different as they are in some ways, the widow and Miss Watson agree with each other and with Pap and the Duke and the Dauphin about money, race, and slavery. Huck bears their stamp even as he intuitively resists them.[11]

In the design of *Huck Finn* the fragmented family life and the anarchic individualism Pap represents are at the opposite extreme from Huck and Jim's natural individualism and cohesive family. Pap is at one extreme of a continuum that also includes the widow and Miss Watson's declined Protestant individualism and feminine world of middle-class respectability. Ann Douglas shows that during the nineteenth century women

11. Michael Wilding, *Political Fictions* (London: Routledge, 1980), pp. 21–31, has a revealing account of the underlying similarities between Pap and the widow and Miss Watson and the "sivilization" they represent.

and ministers created a counterideology as an alternative to the masculine-dominated world of power.[12] This domestic ideology celebrated
the "feminine" values of the family, motherhood, and religion. Unfortunately, as Douglas demonstrates, these values formed a sentimental
culture integral to the genteel tradition and the emerging consumer
society. In his treatment of the widow and Miss Watson and of Em-
meline Grangerford's sentimental poetry and painting, Twain reacts
against the prevailing "feminine" sentimentality and religiosity. In imagining Huck and Jim as a family, Twain makes authentic family values an
alternative to the "feminized" families of the widow and Miss Watson
and Aunt Sally as well as to the "masculine" extremes Pap and the Duke
and the Dauphin represent.

From another point of view the contrast between Pap and the widow
and Miss Watson is not between nature and civilization, as might first
appear, but between a decayed civilization viewed from the bottom and
the more genteel version of the widow and Miss Watson. In the
swamp of Pap's life, because he feels none of the positive ties of family
and affection, he is cut off from civilization's most basic force of human
cohesion. Pap embodies a nightmare version of what can happen to the
American individualist cut off from sustaining family ties and from any
positive involvement in the larger society. Instead, Pap tries to acquire
money without working and to satisfy himself through the most self-
destructive drinking he can manage. He is vehemently racist. He is a
caricature of Tocqueville's acquisitive individualist, the isolated, self-
centered American at his worst but in Pap's degenerate version without
the prototypical restless striving and energy. His racism is systematically
related to his failure on the individualistic standards he embodies. The
broken family life with Pap is a main source of Huck's alienation and of
his conventional view of "niggers." Paradoxically, however, Pap's situation on the edges of society leaves Huck free to develop in his own way
and to develop a genuine relation with Jim.

But when Pap takes Huck away from town into the woods, instead of
freeing his son, he confines him even more than his genteel counter-
parts did. The cabin in the woods becomes a prison, and Huck, though
he likes losing the trappings of civilization, is not really free or natural.
In the throes of delirium tremens, Pap tries to murder his son. This
terrifying scene brings to life the full reality of Huck's loneliness and
danger, his separation from sources of security, and his unnatural condition of imprisonment. Through the immediacy of dramatic action,
Twain conveys the same threatening sense of isolation that Tocqueville

12. *The Feminization of American Culture* (New York: Knopf, 1977).

more abstractly shows as the ultimate danger in the American situation. Huck's relation with Pap, however, provides the impetus for him to escape; and thereafter Huck moves gradually, unintentionally, precariously toward a world of genuine freedom and life-giving ties with Jim on the journey down the river.

In the opening chapters of the novel, though, Jim is not a father either to his family or to Huck but is instead an object, a stage nigger, for Tom Sawyer to play tricks on and for Twain to exploit for his comic superstitions. When Jim first appears, Huck refuses to play along with Tom's trick of tying him up, not because he rejects the racism or respects Jim's humanity but because he is worried that Jim "might wake and make a disturbance, and then they'd find out I warn't in" (AHF, p. 23). But later, on the island, he says, "I was ever so glad to see Jim. I warn't lonesome now" (AHF, p. 67). Thereafter, the human ties between Huck and Jim deepen. Like a father initiating his son, Jim almost immediately passes along to Huck what he knows about the mysteries of nature. As Daniel Hoffman has shown, this marvelously nonscientific lore constitutes an indispensable alternative to the rationalistic outlook of the middle-class white world.[13] What has not been stressed, however, is that Jim also comically outlines his failure as a speculator, as a man involved with money, investment, and financial manipulation. Recall the way Balum's Ass conned Jim and made an ass of him for playing the investment game, an episode that comically calls to mind both the general atmosphere of financial speculation in the Gilded Age and Twain's own penchant for pouring his money into bad investments. But Jim has learned his lesson about making money through financial speculation, a basic enterprise of the market society.

Later, when the Duke and the Dauphin appear, a restless pursuit of money and property contrasts with Jim and Huck's nonacquisitive relation to each other and to the world around them. In chapter 4 Huck gives the Judge his money when Pap shows up, and, more ominously, he later hides the money in the coffin in the Wilks episode, a revealing, unconscious association of money and death. Huck thus basically agrees with Jim about money and property. But in chapters 16 and 31 Huck also feels he should turn Jim in because Jim is someone else's property. These contradictory feelings about money and property divide Huck's consciousness and give urgency to his central moral choice. In *Huck Finn*, Twain probes deeply along a major fault line of his market society: its contradictory feelings about both property values and human values.

---

13. *Form and Fable in American Fiction* (New York: Oxford University Press, 1961), pp. 322–42.

From the point of view of official society, Jim embodies this conflict. Legally he is a commodity worth eight hundred dollars on the market. In contrast to the compelling, impersonal values of money and property, however, Jim's quality as a human being emerges subtly and convincingly. Jim, for example, refuses to let Huck look at the dead man who turns out to be Pap. Jim is again more a true father than the father who is now literally dead. After Huck puts the snakeskin in Jim's bed, however, they both suffer the consequences. Huck has still not fully realized Jim's humanity and the human responsibilities their relation entails.

Twain has Jim and Huck develop these issues unpretentiously in their comic argument about Solomon. Jim wins the first round by seeing clearly that what is at stake is not a half-child but "'a whole chile,'" a whole person, alive and functioning, "'en de man dat think he kin settle a 'spute 'bout a whole chile wid a half a chile, doan know enough to come in outn de rain'" (AHF, p. 112). Jim loses the second round, however, because he can't understand why a Frenchman doesn't talk like a man. To counter Huck, Jim has piled up a series of examples to show that cats and dogs and cows aren't men, but a Frenchman is a man, "'so dad blame it, why doan' he *talk* like a man? You answer me dat!'" (AHF, p. 114). But Huck, who speaks for pluralism, reminds us that, just as cats and dogs and cows talk different from each other, "'then, why ain't it natural and right for a *Frenchman* to talk different from us? You answer me that!'" (AHF, p. 114). The joke is intensified because Jim has just argued for the importance of the whole child, the whole man, and has accused Solomon of being limited by his upbringing, but because Jim also has his provincial limitations, the joke turns against him.

The argument between Huck and Jim centers on an idea of man. Huck and Jim raise the issues of the whole child, talking "like a man," and, to use Huck's words, what is "natural and right." Huck gets the better of the argument when he speaks for an idea of man large enough to include foreigners. Twain, however, knows that actual men often fail to live up to their best insights, as he has both Huck and Jim demonstrate in this episode—Huck at the very end when he says, "'I see it warn't no use wasting words—you can't learn a nigger to argue. So I quit'" (AHF, p. 114). The final twist on the joke is that, because of his view of "a nigger," Huck contradicts the basic argument that everyone is "a man."

What is at issue in the joke as in the novel is an idea of the unalienated person as a member of the human community, as a member of the family of man. Like the novel, the joke turns on the contrast between the whole child and the fragmented half-child, on the contrast between the whole man and alienated versions of this wholeness in the form of "nigger" or "Frenchman." The joke, which Twain delighted in reading

on the lecture platform, is a preliminary exercise on the themes of divided consciousness, of the alienation of our humanity, of racism and fragmentation versus the family of man.

In the fog scene and its sequel these issues about alienation, wholeness, and what is "natural and right" are basic to the consciousness and
central choices of the characters at the heart of their dramatized relation.
Huck and Jim have been close and in the fog they are separated. In this
nightmarish, almost surreal episode Twain renders what it means to
Huck to be separated, to have lost his bearings, to be alone again, this
time in "the solid white fog," and "tangled good, now," totally confused
and disoriented. "If you think it ain't dismal and lonesome out in a fog
that way, by yourself, in the night, you try it once—you'll see" (AHF,
pp. 116, 117). The episode has the power of a disturbing dream. It brings
alive the extreme Tocquevillean, market-society condition of being absolutely alone and separated, and it is also a metaphor for the dislocation
of Huck's consciousness and moral sense after his return, a disturbance
the experience in the fog both provokes and represents.

When they are reunited Jim responds to Huck's return like a father to
a lost, loved "chile" (AHF, p. 119). But instead of telling Jim how relieved
he is, Huck thoughtlessly belittles Jim by playing a Tom Sawyer-like
trick on him. In one of the novel's most crucial passages Jim then lets
Huck know what real feelings are and what real friendship involves. Jim
speaks the language of the heart—"'my heart wuz mos' broke'" (AHF,
p. 121), he says—a language of genuine feeling and concern that expresses in tears the depth of his friendship for his "chile." "Friend,"
"father," and "child" lose their distinction in Jim's language of the heart.
Huck gradually learns its rules and its inflections and the Duke and the
Dauphin exploit it for ends that threaten the very life of that society
whose cohesive values they pretend to speak for, even as they act out its
dominant and divisive individualism. In contrast to the destructive self-
interest of the Duke and the Dauphin, Huck develops through his
choices and grows closer to Jim. After the trick with the snakeskin, Huck
feels bad but keeps quiet; after he tricks Jim in the fog scene, Huck
begins to speak Jim's language of feeling, humbles himself to this friend,
and resolves not to "do him no more mean tricks, and I wouldn't done
that one if I'd a knowed it would make him feel that way" (AHF, p. 121).

But Twain immediately puts Huck to the test. Jim keeps talking about
being "a free man" (AHF, p. 123) and thus brings into sharp focus the
novel's concern with what it means both to be free and to be a man. As
an exemplary "free man," in the full normative sense of these key
words, Jim wants to be reunited with his family. For Jim, to be a free
man is to be fully human, a condition that for him is inseparable from

the intimate, cohesive ties of the family. But his proposal to buy his wife and steal his two children shocks Huck. Huck is on the verge of turning Jim in. Although Jim's basic humanity is inseparable from his feelings for his family, Huck also sees Jim as property, as someone who "would steal his children—children that belonged to a man I didn't even know; a man that hadn't ever done me no harm. I was sorry to hear Jim say that, it was such a lowering of him" (AHF, p. 124).

Because Huck is both Jim's friend and metaphorically his child, the comic inversions illuminate basic values and go to deep contradictions in Huck's consciousness and his American society. The novel is set in the 1850s and the specific issue is Jim's status as a slave. But the implications of this conflict between human values and property values, it should be stressed, go beyond the issue of slavery in the 1850s. More significantly, they involve a fundamental division in American capitalism. Twain has contrived the novel so that Jim is a commodity as well as a human being, a salable object as well as a free man and a true friend. As a piece of property he is worth eight hundred dollars and his children belong to someone else. Jim, however, emerges as a whole man, not as a divided person who has accepted the dominant society's definition of him as a commodity. He has freed himself of his involvement in the money world, and during the central episodes of the novel he acts and sees himself as a free man. He is intimately related to the natural world, and, though he is separated from his family, he is intimately related to them, too.

Huck, not Jim, is divided because of the dominant society's views about property. Huck is torn between the human claims of friendship and the impersonal but compelling values of property and social convention. His consciousness is polarized. Huck's conflict and divided consciousness are ones most people experience, although usually in a less polarized and dramatic form. What is equally important, Twain has the genius to expose not only the social sources but also the personal, human consequences of this conflict. It is no accident, then, that Huck "just felt sick" (AHF, p. 125). The sickness he feels is the alienated consciousness that results from a split which dominates his culture. Huck has taken inside himself the central division of his market society. This division within the self, its social, economic, and racial causes, and its disturbing human results constitute, to apply the Dauphin's words in a new but related context, the most damaging illness in the world of "the diseased" (AHF, p. 213).

The imagery of disease occurs in key episodes involving alienation and the violation of humanity. Elsewhere in the novel Huck feels sick when his sense of humanity is violated by acts of cruelty, inhumanity, or injustice, acts originating from the outside, as when he sees Buck Grangerford murdered or the Duke and the Dauphin tarred and feathered. In the present episode, however, the alienation is inside Huck, or rather, his basic humanity is at odds with his internalized social values. The conflict makes Huck feel sick. Although he has lived on the margins of society, Huck nonetheless carries inside him the source of the sickness, the divisions generated by a society whose racism and commitment to property and property values conflict with the best of its own religious and humanistic values as well as the intuitively realized humanity Huck embodies. Racism, of course, is not peculiar to capitalism. But in practice the racism reinforces and is reinforced by the commitment to property.

As in "Bartleby, the Scrivener," the classic market-society form of alienation involves the person who sells his labor as a possession, whose self is then separated internally, and who engages in work dictated by external demands. Twain renders another, related form of alienation. As in "Bartleby," the self in conflict protests from the depths of its humanity against the violation of its humanity. Huck is not directly involved in the selling of his alienated self as a commodity, but indirectly he experiences the consequences, since he accepts the dominant-class view of Jim as "nigger" and as property. As a black slave Jim brings to an intense focus the contradiction between humane views of the whole self and the market-society view that part of the self can be alienated and as a commodity can be sold for what it will command as labor. The irony is that Jim is whole, Huck and the dominant society are divided.

In the world of the diseased, we cannot expect permanent cures. But the vital ties Huck establishes with Jim and the river at least temporarily heal the divisions and, for a memorable interlude, cure the sickness of alienation. However briefly, this family idyll with Jim on the raft also makes us forget the friction and the hostility that in the real world always accompany family love and affection. Far from being a deficiency, this precariously sustained interlude enhances the attractiveness of Twain's vision of freedom, cohesion, and the fusion of individuality and community. But a reader may grant that Twain has created a compelling myth of what we desire and nonetheless feel the myth is too remote from any possibility of realization to warrant our assent. Although the interlude is powerful in its claims on our imagination and in its ability to generate significant comedy in the novel, it is also vulnerable to the assaults of reality, most literally, to the assaults of the Duke and the Dauphin. Perhaps like any vision of a green world or a golden age, it is simultaneously indispensable as a reminder of human possibility and perennially beyond our grasp.

It does not discredit Twain's goals to see them as tantalizingly beyond reach. In striving toward such indispensable, perhaps unattainable goals, however, we do need to sustain a precarious tension. We need to feel that our ideals have genuine roots and at least some chance of being realized. In the concluding chapters of *Huck Finn*, Twain shifts the focus back to Tom Sawyer and away from Huck's developing sense of freedom, community, and identity. Quite aside from its explicit content, this shift in itself constitutes an indirect form of social criticism, too indirect to be fully effective but nonetheless rooted in Twain's very genuine social disillusion. For many readers the episodes with Tom and the Phelpses represent an imaginative failure, a falling off from the promising themes Twain had been exploring. One explanation is that when he came to write the last third of *Huck Finn*, Twain had finally become too aware of the fragmenting power of his society to be willing or able to keep alive his vision of freedom and community. He apparently came to feel that his most precious ideals were too far removed from their roots in a vital social world.

It is symptomatic, then, that in the Phelps episode Huck and Jim are separated. Jim is imprisoned, chained, and made to act the part of a captured slave. Jim is legally free and, as he has shown on the river, he is a whole person and in the fullest sense "a free man." Tom's make-believe in the cabin develops the imagery of acting and performances the Duke and the Dauphin have earlier perfected when they play the parts of pirates, false brothers, and Shakespearean characters. In the Phelps episode Tom Sawyer stages, directs, and stars in the play. Although he is their successor, however, Tom is much less inventive and compelling than the Duke and the Dauphin. Tom trivializes the concerns of the novel: he wants excitement and romantic adventure and Twain is content to satirize romances. Tom conceals the fact that Jim is free because he wants to invent difficulties to overcome in freeing Jim. One unfortunate result is that, except for the scene with the doctor, under Tom's influence Jim loses his eloquent humanity and emerges again as the manipulated stage figure of the opening chapters. Another unfortunate consequence is that, in taking Tom Sawyer's name, Huck loses his own identity. "It was like being born again" (AHF, p. 282), Huck says. After the scene in the fog, Huck had resolved never again to play tricks on Jim. Under Tom's influence, however, the reborn Huck plays along with such escapades as the silly, demeaning scheme of putting snakes in Jim's cabin. He has forgotten what he learned after he put the snakeskin in Jim's bed on the island. That episode had marked an important stage in Huck's growing awareness of and intimacy with Jim. When he is reborn as Tom Sawyer, Huck's developing identity changes. An individualism combined with community had been emerging in the journey down the river. That growth ends once Huck is separated from Jim and from the river.

Aside from the family Huck and Jim create on the river, if the secure good family exists anywhere in the novel, it ought to be at the Phelpses. Unlike Huck and Jim, the Phelpses are a family in the usual sense of having a mother, a father, children, nephews, aunts, and a network of family relations. This large family centers around Aunt Sally. The presence of the Phelps family in the final episode rounds out a sequence that began with another, more obviously "feminized" family, the widow and Miss Watson's. In a low-keyed way, moreover, Twain's treatment of the Phelpses at once partakes of and undercuts nostalgia about the American rural family. The Phelpses' generosity and hospitality, the abundance of food and children, Aunt Sally's concern and Uncle Silas's absent-mindedness play off against their irritability and a recognition of the intolerance and the ineptitude that exist along with their affection. For Twain, rural life includes the mob that joins the Phelpses to hunt the escaped slave. But the Phelpses also bring Jim special food, even as they imprison him.

Tom Sawyer conditions our view of the Phelps family. Tom controls events—the petty thefts of shirts, spoons, candles, and sheets; the ratholes filled and the escape hole dug. The turmoil he causes brings out Aunt Sally's irritability and repeatedly makes her and Uncle Silas look foolish. Partly because interest centers on the tricks and on taking in the adults, the relation between husband and wife consists mainly of Aunt Sally's yelling at Uncle Silas for oversights he did not really commit. Kind as they are, Aunt Sally and Uncle Silas do not provide instances of a web of affectionate relations between husband and wife. Contrary to stereotypes about the authoritarian husband, moreover, Aunt Sally is the main authority in the Phelps family. Uncle Silas is gentle and absent-minded and provides openings for jokes about preaching and religion. The children are in the background to be smacked, hugged, and well fed.

Aunt Sally is at the center of the family. Like Jim, she has real feelings. She tucks Huck in "and mothered me so good I felt mean, and like I couldn't look her in the face" (AHF, p. 353). She cries when she thinks Tom is missing and in trouble. But unlike Jim, her tears and her concern confine rather than free Huck. "'The door ain't going to be locked,'" she tells him, "'and there's the window and the rod; but you'll be good, *won't* you? And you won't go? For *my* sake'" (AHF, p. 353). Huck wants to go "but after that, I wouldn't a went, not for kingdoms" (AHF, p. 354). Aunt Sally's compassion keeps Huck in line; it locks him up without keys. Here is a perfect example of hegemony. Huck reacts against this compassionate pressure to make him good in a way society approves. As with the widow and Miss Watson, to satisfy Aunt Sally, Huck must give up his individuality. Lighting out for the territory may not be the answer, but Huck is going to try it "because Aunt Sally she's going to adopt me and sivilize me and I can't stand it. I been there before" (AHF, p. 366). The problem is that Huck carries the divisions of the dominant society within his own consciousness, quite aside from the violence and the acquisitiveness he will find in the territory.

In contrast to both the territory and Aunt Sally's family, the relationship Huck and Jim develop on the river brings to memorable if temporary life the possibility of unalienated cohesion and individuality. The Duke and the Dauphin provide the most basic contrasts to the sustaining ties Huck and Jim create. Aside from the Duke and the Dauphin and Huck and Jim, Twain's comic probing of the family ranges from Pap's at one extreme of the class ladder through the widow and Miss Watson's and the Phelpses' in the middle to the Grangerfords' at the other extreme. With the Grangerfords, though, the comedy turns on our perception that these aristocrats are not far removed in position and bad taste from the rest of their rural countrymen. The fact that Huck and Jim are outside this conventional scheme suggests both their value and their vulnerability.

In contrast to Huck and Jim's informal rituals, the Grangerfords have a formalized code of respect and of dignity. In the idyll on the Mississippi, Huck and Jim take off their clothes and are at one with each other and the river. The Grangerfords, in splendid contrast, "dressed in white linen from head to foot, . . . and wore broad Panama hats" (AHF, p. 144), and they express their regard for each other in elaborate ceremonies with the decanter and the order of seating. Women and their honor are important in this set of conventions but when Miss Sophia falls in love with a Shepherdson, her feelings and her interests are ignored. The conventional values of the clan or family honor take empty precedence over her personal feelings and best interests, so that this "aristocratic" family reenacts the same pattern that characterizes Huck in his relations with Pap, Tom, the widow and Miss Watson, and Aunt Sally. If Pap cares too little for the family, moreover, the Grangerfords care too much, and in the wrong way. Despite the Sunday values they pay lip service to, the Grangerfords separate brotherly love and positive family feeling from what they are really committed to: killing in the name of conventional honor. The split has gruesome results: the family is decimated and Huck feels "sick" (AHF, p. 154). When he feels sick about turning Jim in, Huck shares the alienation of his society. At the

Grangerfords, though, the alienation is not inside Huck but in the world of the diseased; his sick feeling is his human response to the senseless violence and divisions of the culture.

After the violence and divisiveness of the Grangerfords' conventional society, Huck and Jim are reunited, "free and safe once more" in the "home" they have made together (AHF, pp. 155, 156). The cohesive family idyll on the river comes briefly and unforgettably alive. Huck describes his harmony with Jim and with the natural world. They are at one with each other and with the universe around them. They light up their pipes, dangle their legs in the water, and talk "about all kinds of things—we was always naked, day and night, whenever the mosquitoes would let us" (AHF, p. 159). They shed the clothes that symbolize the Grangerfords' civilization: "The new clothes Buck's folks made for me was too good to be comfortable, and besides I didn't go much on clothes, nohow" (AHF, p. 159). Open to each other and to nature, including the mosquitoes, they speculate about the origins of the vital universe they inhabit. "We had the sky, up there," Huck says, "all speckled with stars, and we used to lay on our backs and look up at them, and discuss about whether they was made, or only just happened." Their explanations, their canons of reason and probability, align them not with rationalistic scientists or theologians but with the ancient mythmakers. "Jim he allowed [the stars] was made, but I allowed they happened; I judged it would have took too long to *make* so many. Jim said the moon could a *laid* them; well, that looked kind of reasonable, so I didn't say nothing against it, because I've seen a frog lay most as many, so of course it could be done" (AHF, p. 159).

The Duke and the Dauphin, however, immediately bring civilization and its dissonances into this world of natural relations. The Duke and the Dauphin are a parody of the positive family Huck and Jim create. Instead of developing ties of real affection and concern, the two con men in the end fight each other. The younger one, who trusts no one, says to his old, bald-headed partner, "'and I a trusting you all the time, like you was my own father'" (AHF, p. 264). This final, comic reminder underscores the basic differences between these two created families, differences that define structure and values in the central sequences of *Huck Finn*. What holds the Duke and the Dauphin's family together is not trust, affection, or a journey toward community, freedom, and identity but rather the prospect of profit. The Duke and King are out for themselves at the expense of victims, primarily along the shore and finally on the raft itself. But since these acquisitive motives and values are central to the American market society, the Duke and the Dauphin also comically image the society they fleece.

As representatives of the larger society, they immediately introduce rank and social differences into the harmonious relation Huck and Jim have developed. Their fake genealogies and demands for deference satirize the fascination with rank and inequality of our supposedly egalitarian society. On a raft, however, conflict over status "would have been a miserable business," and Huck speaks for the precarious, resonant countervalue of "peace in the family" (AHF, p. 166). Although the acquisitive restlessness and greed of the Duke and the King finally destroy Huck's peaceful family, they highlight rather than diminish the need for the values Huck celebrates.

They do so most interestingly through a series of roles and identities they invent. We never know the real names of the Duke and the Dauphin. We know only their style, the parts they play, and the fact that they are constantly acting, performing. They embody the energy, resourcefulness, and greed of a culture in which men are cut off from fixed social and moral ties and are free to move and to exploit. Because the market society they emerge from is fluid and unstable, it does not provide the Duke and the Dauphin with stable identities, so that they are constantly creating themselves. Instead of fixed identities, they have only their socially generated restlessness, inventiveness, and eye for the main chance. In their unlikely costumes, they come to assume mythic proportions. They bring to imaginative life essential tendencies of modern America and a familiar style of acquisitive individualism, certainly one Tocqueville would recognize. The Duke and the Dauphin look ahead to the commodified society of appearance that became increasingly important as America in the 1880s and 1890s moved toward an economy stressing advertising and the manipulation of images.

Huck and Jim, on the other hand, embody a cohesive family and an individualism compatible with community. Their individualism also leads to personal growth, not to the exploitation of other people. For insight into the contrasting world of the Duke and the Dauphin, consider the series of performances that culminates in one of the novel's funniest and most suggestive episodes, when the King plays the part of a pirate who wants to return to do good in the Indian Ocean. The King brilliantly satirizes and exploits "'them dear people in Pokeville campmeeting, natural brothers and benefactors of the race—and that dear preacher there, the truest friend a pirate ever had'" (AHF, p. 174). Huck and Jim show that natural brotherhood and true friendship are at the heart of the novel, but again and again Twain also shows that these values are easily sentimentalized and drained of their real meaning. The king "busted into tears," a collection is taken up, and this pirate puts the cohesive values of brotherhood and friendship to the uses of private gain.

Because of its insights into the audience, its counterpoint of true and exploitative brotherhood, and its awareness of self-interest masked by religious pretense, the camp-meeting scene provides an intensifying mirror for the performances that follow. The exposure of Bricksville and the loafers, the performance of Boggs and Sherburn, the acting out of the murder, the circus performance and Huck's response, and finally the Royal Nonesuch act are all played out against the backdrop of the camp-meeting. Each episode develops one or another of the themes that the King brings into comic focus.

What is particularly significant is that the organizing metaphor of acting, shows, and performances emerges from and illuminates the instability and fluidity of a society whose members are bored, rootless, and hungry for entertainment. For them improvisation is important and the difference between the real and sham is difficult to establish. They are vulnerable to the Duke and the Dauphin and to the emerging consumerism that was waiting in the wings. It is worth stressing that the traditional, old-world imagery of shows and performances—Shakespeare is only the most famous practitioner—thus gains new meaning in *Huck Finn* specifically because of the American social setting. Twain's imagery of duplicity and role-playing is also rooted in and exposes the fragmentation of his market society, particularly when the Duke and the Dauphin play the parts of Peter Wilks's loving brothers. Cumulatively, Twain's handling of the organizing imagery of acting and performances provides a major instance of the intimate relation between an important formal pattern and its social origins and implications.[14] The related imagery of sickness and decay powerfully reenters the novel in the description of the town eaten away by the river and its inhabitants wasting away in a boredom broken by spasms of cruelty.

To contrast with the degradations of "the diseased" and to prepare for the Wilks episode, his most intense exploration of true and fake families, Twain has Jim again bring alive what real family feelings are, what real grief and tears are. He is stricken, "moaning and mourning," as he thinks "about his wife and children, away up yonder, and he was low and homesick; because he hadn't ever been away from home before in his life" (AHF, p. 201). Jim's natural feelings for his family emerge even more deeply as he recalls that he once hit his daughter for not minding him. In one of the most touching examples of the language of the heart he then says, "'Oh, Huck, I bust out a-cryin' en grab her up in my arms, en say, 'Oh, de po' little thing! de Lord God Amighty forgive po' ole Jim,

14. For another view of the theme of acting and performing, see George Carrington, *The Dramatic Unity of "Huckleberry Finn"* (Columbus: Ohio State University Press, 1976), pp. 47–108.

kaze he never gwyne to fogive hisself as long's he live!' Oh, she was
plumb deef en dumb, Huck, plumb deef en dumb—en I'd ben a-treat'n
her so!'" (AHF, p. 202).

Jim is not acting. He really feels deep love for his daughter and genuine remorse for what he has done. His tears and words mean what
they say. Continuing Twain's imagery of performance, however, the
Duke and the Dauphin immediately disguise Jim "in King Lear's outfit"
(AHF, p. 203), the most inappropriate choice imaginable for a loving
father with Jim's feelings for his family. The two con men then put on
their own costumes and, in an orgy of acting, begin to play the roles of
Peter Wilks's brothers. They fake the feelings of grief and concern Jim
has shown naturally. Further underscoring the contrast with Jim, one of
them even plays the "deef and dumb" brother.

Like Jim, the Duke and King "bust out a crying" (AHF, p. 210), and in
this and other ways they systematically parody and deprave the language of the heart. The king takes in his audience and tearfully "slob-
bers out" his speech "about its being a sore trial for him and his poor
brother to lose the diseased, and to miss seeing diseased alive." The
king also exploits "this dear sympathy" he pretends to feel and gives
thanks "out of his heart and out of his brother's heart . . . till it was just
sickening" (AHF, p. 213). Throughout Huck's report of the speech, the
imagery of disease, of sickness, has the force of the imagery of corruption in *Hamlet*. In the presence of death, which calls for human honesty
and a community of the living, these false brothers violate and exploit
the claims of human sympathy and the ties of family. The family, however vulnerable and fallible in practice, is also the most basic force of
social cohesion in the world of the novel. To convey the intensity of his
reaction against this violation of family ties and the language of the
heart, Twain invents the malapropisms of "the diseased" and "the funeral orgies" (AHF, p. 217) and he has Huck emphasize "the rot and
slush." For Huck "it was just sickening," and at the end the doctor says,
"'you're going to feel sick whenever you think of this day'" (AHF, p.
219). Part of the illness is that the townspeople lack the resources to see
through the act, to detect the fake language, to tell true from false
feeling, real from sham brothers and brotherhood. More basically the
sickening disease is the abuse and rotting out of the bonds of family
feeling and finally of the brotherhood of man in the interests of personal
gain. The resulting alienation is the most basic disease of Twain's America.

During Twain's formative years, "American institutions were still oriented toward a community life where family and church, education and
press, professions and government, all largely found their meaning by

the way they fit one with another inside a town or a detached portion of a city. As men ranged farther and farther from their communities" after the Civil War, Robert Wiebe continues,

they tried desperately to understand the larger world in terms of their small, familiar environment. They tried, in other words, to impose the known upon the unknown, to master an impersonal world through the customs of a personal society. They failed, usually without recognizing why; and that failure to comprehend a society they were helping to make contained the essence of the nation's story.[15]

But in telling his and his nation's story, Twain did comprehend. The violation of family ties is crucial to Twain, is a sickening disease, because, rooted as he is in "the customs of a personal society," he is especially well situated to sense and to judge the divisive power of self-interest and the accelerating fragmentation of the market society, tendencies he knew from observation and his own painful experience. For Mark Twain, the debasing of the language of the heart and the attacks on the family, the most intimate institution of social order, threaten to leave people with no other supports or ties, to leave them with no possibility of human community.

Adventures of Huckleberry Finn is poised between this vision of "the diseased," an alienated world presided over by the Duke and the Dauphin, and the myth of Huck and Jim's cohesive family. In America we usually see the individual opposed to society, the self versus the community, the person distinct from the group. Huck and Jim, however, are able to develop as individuals within and not opposed to the community they create. Huck, though, is also subject to the divisions of his market society; he carries as well as counters the sickness. Until the Phelps episode Twain kept the contest even. Although the Duke and King are run out on a rail in chapter 33, no one, least of all the Twain of the final chapters, believes that the style of individualism and the sense of community Huck and Jim develop has triumphed, either in the novel or in the restlessly changing market society it grows from and illuminates. The triumph is that, knowing as intimately as he did the divisive power of acquisitive individualism, Twain nonetheless managed to sustain for as long as he did a life-affirming myth of cohesion and genuine individuality undercut by the dominant tendencies of that world of the diseased he both exposed and continued to live in.

15. *The Search for Order, 1877–1920* (New York: Hill and Wang, 1967), p. 12.

three

THE CONJURE WOMAN
Double Consciousness and the Genteel Tradition

In *The Conjure Woman* (1899), Charles Chesnutt gives us his telling insights into the world of the diseased and its alternative, the conjure world rooted outside the dominant American society Chesnutt, like Twain, was ambitious to succeed in. Chesnutt renders his sense of American alienation through the contrast between his two narrators. The divided consciousness of the genteel white narrator of the frame tales in *The Conjure Woman* contrasts with the consciousness of Uncle Julius, the black narrator of the stories about conjuring and slavery at the center of the work. In the frame tales, moreover, the narrator's wife, Annie, is sick. Uncle Julius diagnoses the disease and does his best to cure it.

To appreciate what is at stake, we need to recall the 1880s and 1890s, when Chesnutt was beginning to make his way by publishing *The Conjure Woman* stories in *The Atlantic*. The genteel tradition was the dominant cultural force in America. In his classic definition, "The Genteel Tradition in American Philosophy," Santayana focuses on a divided America, "a country with two mentalities, one a survival of the beliefs and standards of the fathers, the other an expression of the instinct, practice, and discoveries of the younger generations." Even as late as 1912, Santayana continues,

in all the higher things of the mind—in religion, in literature, in the moral emotions—it is the hereditary spirit that still prevails, so much so that Mr. Bernard Shaw finds that America is a hundred years behind the times. The truth is that one-half of the American mind, that not occupied intensely in practical affairs, has remained, I will not say high-and-dry, but slightly becalmed; it has floated gently in the backwater, while, alongside, in invention and industry and social organization the other half of the mind was leaping down a sort of Niagra Rapids. This division may be found symbolized in American architecture: a neat reproduction of the colonial mansion—with some modern comforts introduced surreptitiously—stands beside the sky-scraper. The American Will inhabits the sky-scraper; the American intellect inhabits the colonial mansion. The one is the sphere of the American man; the other, at least predominantly, of the American woman. The one is all aggressive enterprise; the other is all genteel tradition.[1]

Although the two mentalities he examines need to be related to the actual processes and power relations of the society, Santayana nonetheless clarifies an important polarity. By the end of his definition, it is worth noting, the beliefs of the fathers have become feminized. In effect Santayana defines the hegemony of the market society and the counter-hegemony of "feminized" intellectuals who sometimes support, sometimes oppose, the male-dominated world of power. Every American writer of the post–Civil War period responded to the tension between the two forces Santayana focuses on. In particular, they had to take the genteel tradition into account, especially those writers, like Twain and Chesnutt, who wanted to break into magazines like *The Atlantic* and to win the approval of important ministers of culture like Howells and Richard Watson Gilder.

Because women were the major consumers of literature, the literary marketplace is an especially revealing arena. Profits, acceptability on conflicting standards, the desire to maintain quality and popularity all complicate the scene. In *The Conjure Woman*, Chesnutt deals with these problems subtly and deeply. Instead of giving us abstract analysis of external forces, Chesnutt takes us inside representative consciousnesses. He creates and undercuts a white narrator whose divided consciousness is characterized not only by the aggressive will of American enterprise and but also by the religion, literary taste, and moral emotions of the genteel tradition. Chesnutt also creates a sympathetic woman, John's wife, Annie, and has her respond eagerly to the black vernacular energy of Uncle Julius's narratives.

As a talented, moderate writer, Chesnutt, a black author white enough to pass, had to deal not only with the divisions Santayana outlines but also with the realities of American racial divisions. In *The Conjure Woman* he does so inside the experience and consciousness of his characters. Some reminders of the external world are nonetheless necessary. The separation between blacks and whites was formalized in the separate-but-equal doctrine of *Plessy* vs. *Ferguson* in 1896. Supreme Court decisions have a reassuring dignity about them even when they enforce and reflect the ugly passions of a polarized but hardly equal society. It was acceptable in *The Atlantic* of Chesnutt's period for articles

---

1. *The Genteel Tradition: Nine Essays by George Santayana*, ed. Douglas L. Wilson (Cambridge: Harvard University Press, 1967), pp. 39–40.

on the status of the mulatto seriously to debate whether mulattoes were indeed black devils, an unnatural adulteration of "pure" white and black. This widely shared view of the mulatto is symptomatic of the hostility to the coming together of blacks and whites, in contrast to their separation into supposedly "pure" and "equal" realms.

At a less genteel level, Thomas Dixon, Jr., made a fortune from portraying depraved, ape-like blacks and noble whites in *The Leopard's Spots* (1902) and *The Clansman* (1905). As a symbol of assimilation, for Dixon the mulatto represents "pollution."[2] Turn-of-the-century racism has an uncensored directness, as in Dixon's portrait of "a negro of perhaps forty years, a man of charming features for a mulatto, who had evidently inherited the full physical characteristics of the Aryan race, while his dark yellowish eyes beneath his heavy brows glowed with the brightness of the African jungle" (C, p. 93). Dixon justifies total white domination by appealing to fears of the negro mob in control of the city government while "gangs of drunken negroes, its sovereign citizens, paraded the streets at night firing their muskets unchallenged and unmolested. A new mob of onion-laden breath, mixed with perspiring African odor, became the symbol of American Democracy" (C, p. 155).

At the impeachment trial of Andrew Johnson, Dixon rises to the occasion. Johnson's fatally ill antagonist, Stoneman, radical leader of Congress, has left the arms of his mulatto mistress and is carried into the Senate by "two gigantic negroes. . . . The negroes placed him in an armchair facing the semi-circle of Senators, and crouched down on their haunches beside him. Their kinky heads, black skin, thick lips, white teeth, and flat noses made for the moment a curious symbolic frame for the chalk-white passion of the old Commoner's face. No sculptor," Dixon concludes, "ever dreamed a more sinister emblem of the corruption of a race of empire builders than this group. Its black figures, wrapped in the night of four thousand years of barbarism, squatted there the 'equal' of their master, grinning at his forms of justice, the evolution of forty centuries of Aryan genius" (C, pp. 170–71). Elsewhere, Dixon has his spokesman for Aryan civilization unpolluted by Barbarism observe, "The negro . . . in his civilized way lived as his fathers lived—stole his food, worked his wife, sold his children, ate his brother, content to drink, sing, dance and sport as the ape!" (C, p. 292).

Dixon's characterization of blacks, his treatment of the power relations between whites and blacks, and his glorification of the original Ku Klux Klan remind us of the force of the underlying attitudes Chesnutt had to confront. Dixon, moreover, vividly shows that from the vantage

2. *The Clansman: An Historical Romance of the Ku Klux Klan* (New York: Doubleday, 1905), p. 291. Subsequent references will be abbreviated C and cited by page number in the text.

point of the turn-of-the-century, a writer's stand on the immediate post–Civil War period had important contemporary implications. The battles of the present were often fought on the terrain of the past, so that Chesnutt's characterization of blacks and whites and his stories about slavery had significant resonances for the generation of *Plessy* vs. *Ferguson* and *The Clansman*.

The battles were also fought in the present. The statistics on lynching during Chesnutt's writing career hardly convey the emotional impact of the white reassertion of the absolute control of slavery and the black resistance and fear.[3] In 1892, Frederick Douglass warned,

If the Southern outrages on the colored race continue, the negro will become a chemist. Other men besides Anarchists can be goaded into making and throwing bombs. This terrible thirst for the blood of men must cease in the South, or as sure as night follows day there will be an insurrection. Anarchists have not a monopoly on bombmaking and the negro will learn to handle the terrible instrument of destruction unless the wrongs against him cease.[4]

A series of armed black uprisings in the early 1890s show that blacks did not passively accept these outrages and that race war in a divided country was a possibility.[5] More common, however, was the violent suppression of blacks, as in the 1898 Wilmington "riots" that Chesnutt used at the center of *The Marrow of Tradition*. W. E. B. Dubois characterized the South of Chesnutt's period as "an armed camp for intimidating black folk."[6] Looking back on the 1910s, Richard Wright vividly describes the impact of lynching. He writes,

Nothing challenged the totality of my personality so much as this pressure of hate and threat that stemmed from the invisible whites. . . . I had already grown to feel that there existed men against whom I was powerless, men who could violate my life at will. . . . It was as though I was continuously reacting to the threat of some natural force whose hostile behavior could not be predicted. I had never in my life been abused by whites, but I had already become as conditioned to their existence as though I had been the victim of a thousand lynchings.[7]

3. For the statistics on lynching, see NAACP, *Thirty Years of Lynching in the United States, 1889–1919* (1919; Westport, Conn.: Greenwood Press, 1970). On the reassertion of white dominance, see C. Vann Woodward, *The Strange Career of Jim Crow* (1955; New York: Oxford University Press, 1966).

4. Quoted in the *New York Tribune*, 8 May 1892, p. 1.

5. See, for example, the *New York Tribune*, 8 July 1892, p. 1; 13 July 1892, p. 7; 8 August 1892, p. 1; 16 February 1893, p. 1.

6. *The Souls of Black Folk: Essays and Sketches*, ed. Saunders Redding (1903; New York: Fawcett, 1961), p. 85.

7. *Black Boy: A Record of Childhood and Youth* (New York: Perennial Classics, 1945, 1966), pp. 83–84.

As a result, Wright went through a long period of inner paralysis but he finally affirmed his integrity through the fierce rebellion he chronicles in *Black Boy, American Hunger,* and *Native Son.*

Booker T. Washington's response was to accommodate, to accept the black person's status as a hewer of wood and tiller of fields, and, in a variation on *Plessy* vs. *Ferguson,* to remain "as separate as the fingers" in the social and personal realms.[8] Another kind of separation is the focus of Dubois's brilliant analysis of the double-consciousness of American blacks. For the black person, Dubois sees, America is

a world which yields him no true self-consciousness, but only lets him see himself through the revelation of the other world. It is a peculiar sensation, this double-consciousness, this sense of always looking at one's self through the eyes of others, of measuring one's soul by the tape of a world that looks on in amused contempt and pity. One ever feels his twoness,—an American, a Negro; two souls, two thoughts, two unreconciled strivings; two warring ideals in one dark body, whose dogged strength alone keeps it from being torn asunder.

"The history of the American Negro," Dubois continues,

is the history of this strife,—this longing to attain self-conscious manhood, to merge his double self into a better and truer self. In this merging he wishes neither of the older selves to be lost. He would not Africanize America, for America has too much to teach the world and Africa. He would not bleach his Negro soul in a flood of white Americanism, for he knows that Negro blood has a message for the world. He simply wishes to make it possible for a man to be both a Negro and an American, without being cursed and spit upon by his fellows, without having the doors of opportunity closed roughly in his face.[9]

Santayana defines one set of polarities, incentives, and inhibitions Chesnutt had to contend with; Dixon another; and Dubois an even deeper alienation, the self divided and at odds as an internalization not only of class but also of racial power.

The Conjure Woman is in part a commentary on and alternative to the polarities of the genteel tradition. Chesnutt also responds to the racism Dubois pinpoints. He creates a white narrator of the frame tales and a black narrator of the stories. For white readers the narrator of the frame tales gives a reassuring credibility to the enterprise but in subtle ways he is also undermined. In one of Chesnutt's versions of double-conscious-ness, the white, genteel speech and consciousness of John and his wife,

8. *Up from Slavery* in *Three Negro Classics*, ed. John Hope Franklin (New York: Avon, 1973), p. 148.
9. *The Souls of Black Folk,* pp. 16–17.

Annie, frame and contrast with the vital world Uncle Julius brings alive in his vernacular stories about slavery. In another version, Chesnutt shows that John's consciousness, not Julius's, is divided. As in *Huck Finn*, Chesnutt's blacks are whole; it is the white people who suffer the sickness of self-division and separation from each other, their emotions, and the natural world. Dubois on double-consciousness defines Chesnutt's authorial and personal situation but not the black consciousness of *The Conjure Woman*.

In contrast to Uncle Julius's black vernacular, John narrates the frame tales in the conventional language of the cultivated middle class. His consciousness epitomizes the decency, divisions, and limitations of the white males who controlled American business and technical life. As it was in the process of asserting its dominant characteristics, Chesnutt subtly exposes and subverts the hegemony John speaks for.[10]

The decorum of John's language, its moderation, its perfectly modulated, cultivated tones, its tolerant accents of quiet superiority over the amusing antics of Uncle Julius and the sentiments and sickness of Annie—this language speaks to and for the educated white Americans who controlled the middle levels of American society both as "practical affairs" and as genteel tradition. Part of the drama of *The Conjure Woman* turns on our initial acceptance of John's control and outlook, our initial acceptance of his reasonable views and his stance of unforced superiority over the old black man and the sensitive wife. Uncle Julius's vernacular tales gradually open up a complex, passionate world much more intimately in touch with the powers of nature and the depths of human joy and suffering than John can fathom. *The Conjure Woman* finally allows the reader but not John to become aware that the conventional, socially sanctioned hierarchy is misplaced. Our own involvement in John's position intensifies this subtle drama of exposure and counter-assertion.

In the racial climate of the 1890s Chesnutt is subversive but understandably indirect as a condition of publication and even minimal acceptance. Like Melville, Poe, and Hawthorne, Chesnutt develops his own techniques of indirection as a response to the pressures of American society. As a nearly white black man, Chesnutt transforms his own

10. For insight into the developing world of professional, technological, and corporate rationality and control, see Burton Bledstein, *The Culture of Professionalism: The Middle Class and the Development of Higher Education in America* (New York: Norton, 1976); David F. Noble, *America by Design: Science, Technology, and the Rise of Corporate Capitalism* (New York: Knopf, 1977); Robert Wiebe, *The Search for Order, 1877–1920* (New York: Hill and Wang, 1967); and Alan Trachtenberg, *The Incorporation of America* (New York: Hill and Wang, 1982).

double-consciousness into the speech and values of John, Annie, and
Uncle Julius.[11] Situated as he is between blacks and whites, he gives full
play to his gift for imitating and judging speech and all it stands for. He
does both John's genteel speech and Uncle Julius's black vernacular with
extraordinary assurance. His achievement with Uncle Julius is central
but he also gets inside John. Chesnutt is so convincing with his version
of John that it is easy to miss the extent of the undercutting.

In the frame tales of *The Conjure Woman* Chesnutt focuses on the
perfectly acceptable, conventional relation between John and Annie.
The first sentence of the first story is characteristic: "Some years ago my
wife was in poor health, and our family doctor, in whose skill and
honesty I had implicit confidence, advised a change of climate."[12] Annie's sickness figures again and again, always as an unobtrusive, familiar part of the landscape. Why, we ask, is she in poor health? Why does
her poor health take the form of depression (CW, p. 133)? Her husband
cares for her, and they have money enough to move, to set up a prosperous wine-growing business in North Carolina, and for her to live a
leisurely life without children. But as her interest in Uncle Julius's stories
reveals, her life also lacks intensity, community, and the full range of
human emotions. John's rationality screens out a depth dimension of
life Annie needs and is attracted to in Uncle Julius's tales. John's scientific belief in the doctor plays off against Uncle Julius's belief in the
conjure woman and the entire Afro-American world the conjure woman
epitomizes. Particularly significant is that John separates himself and
Annie not only from emotional intensities but also from involvement
with a complex network of other people. In contrast to the community
Uncle Julius brings alive, John and Annie live a privatized middle-class
existence. On Sundays they are alone, they go to a church that does not
touch their inner lives, and John reads missionary reports, sentimental
novels, or devitalized, abstract philosophy. His intellectual and moral
life is that of the genteel tradition; the rest of his life is that of the
American market society. John embodies both of the divided tendencies
Santayana analyzes. No wonder Annie welcomes the life-giving energy,
human insight, and companionship Uncle Julius brings to them both in
his own person and in the community he evokes in his stories. Uncle

11. For an account of Chesnutt as a "middle-class riser" with moderate views on race, see
J. Noel Heermance, *Charles W. Chesnutt: America's First Great Black Novelist* (Hamden,
Conn.: Archon Books, 1974), pp. 32–56, 74–87. See also the standard biography, Helen
Maria Chesnutt, *Charles Waddell Chesnutt: Pioneer of the Color Line* (Chapel Hill: North
Carolina University Press, 1952).

12. *The Conjure Woman* (Ann Arbor: University of Michigan Press, 1899, 1969), p. 3.
Subsequent references will be abbreviated CW and cited by page number in the text.

Julius's stories implicitly diagnose Annie's sickness and John's un-acknowledged disease, a complex illness our writers show runs through post–Civil War America.

The world of the conjure woman brings together into a human, natu-ral unity the science and the religion John and his generation have separated. In the world of the conjure woman, people are related not only to the natural world but also to each other in a precariously sus-tained human community. This community is threatened by but sur-vives the arbitrary power of white owners who can at will separate lovers, parents and children, husbands and wives. As slaves they have limited power, but they assert the power they do have. In the face of the elemental forces of nature and human nature and under the pressure of white domination Uncle Julius and his black people body forth pos-sibilities of human life lacking in the dominant white society of the 1890s. The world of the conjure woman has deep roots in an agrarian, pre-modern way of life. It fuses ancient African practices and beliefs with the demands and the conditions of American slavery. In its full dignity the African conjure world expresses the human need to exercise a measure of control over the elements responsible for the growth of crops. It relates people to their ancestors, to each other, and to the natural world and gives ritual expression to the anxieties and the needs inseparable from human life. In its African version it is untouched by the science and the capitalism that dominate John's consciousness. John looks down on the conjure world. But mediated through Uncle Julius and his black vernacular speech, the American version of the conjure world finally offers Annie more possibilities of cure than she finds in John or in the doctor or in the minister or in the white owners. In *No Place of Grace*, T. Jackson Lears has shown the extent to which during Chesnutt's lifetime upper-class white intellectuals reacted against the negative results of modernism and turned for alternatives to the Orient or to the medieval past. Chesnutt performs the same service through his evocation of the Afro-American world and through his insights into the dominant white consciousness of the narrative present and the imag-ined past.

The white owners of the stories are both like and unlike John. Through them Chesnutt extends and complicates his treatment of domi-nant-class consciousness and practice. In "The Goophered Grapevine" the owner's main interest is getting as much yield as he can from his crops. He gets his pleasure from outsmarting his slaves and his neigh-bors. Mars Dugal even takes advantage of the conjure woman, Aunt Peggy, pays her a pittance, and takes real satisfaction in the way she goophers the grapevines so that the slaves stop eating the grapes. Mars

Dugal, "monstrous keerless man" (CW, p. 14) despite his lively interest in money and efficiency, manages to shoot himself in the leg with cow-peas before he turns to Aunt Peggy to protect his grapevines. He feels one up on the conjure woman and the other blacks, but Uncle Julius establishes that the owner is comically fallible and needs Aunt Peggy. John never sees the leg-pulling parallel, the deadpan way Uncle Julius puts John and the owner down and establishes their dependence on Aunt Peggy and her successor, the conjure man who calls this entire world to life. These reversals do not deny the real power John and the owner have, but they do establish that counterpowers also exist.

At the center of Chesnutt's black American version of the myth of Dionysus is Henry, a goophered slave intimately related to the rhythms of the seasons, to the growth and death of the grapes. Henry is a black American nature god. Anointed with the sap of the grapevine, Henry's bald head begins to change. As the season progresses and the young leaves begin to come out, "Henry's ha'r begun to quirl all up in little balls, des like dis yer reg'lar grapy ha'r, en by de time de grapes got ripe his head look des like a bunch er grapes" (CW, p. 22). Henry is one with the life energies of nature itself. In the summer, old Henry becomes "ez spry en libely ez any young nigger on de plantation." In the fall, though, he declines "when de sap begin ter go down in de grapevimes" (CW, p. 24). He loses his curly hair and, appropriately, he loses his interest in "de gals." His generative powers are quiet through the winter and re-turn in the spring. "W'en he rub de sap on ag'n, he got young ag'in, en so soopl en libely dat none er de young niggers on de plantation could n' jump, ner dance, ner hoe ez much cotton ez Henry" (CW, p. 24). Henry has the same traits of dancing and sporting that Dixon views as those of the ape. For Chesnutt, in contrast, Henry is a black folk figure integrated into the cycles of nature. He enjoys and produces but does not exploit nature.

His white owner, however, immediately treats this vital energy as a commodity to make money from. Anointed with the sap, Henry is part of the conjure world. The owner, however, sees him as part of the market society. Henry and his owner's exploitation of him epitomize and judge the way black people as commodities and labor were the basic source of wealth in the Southern version of the market society. Mars Dugal realizes he can make more by selling and reselling Henry than he can from his direct labor. He sells Henry to an unsuspecting buyer for fifteen hundred dollars when the sap is up, and, in a gesture to "his good fren," he buys Henry back for five hundred dollars when the sap is down and Henry is creaky and sick. He continues to trade Henry for money for several years. Like Mars Dugal and Uncle Julius we enjoy the trickery, but like Uncle Julius and not Mars Dugal we also see that in a market society people pay a price to make money. In the first round of the joke, the price is friendship and the exploitation rather than the acceptance of natural and human energies.

In the next phase of the story, Mars Dugal intensifies his market-society impulses, but this time the joke is on him. Another kind of conjuring goes on as a Yankee "bewitches" (CW, p. 29) the owner and cons him into believing he can scientifically increase the yield on the grapes. In contrast to the conjure woman, the Yankee represents the contemporary cult of efficiency, science, and profits. He comes from the world of the market society, scientific agriculture, and Frederick Taylor's *The Principles of Scientific Management*. Unlike the conjure woman, who respects and works with the forces of nature even as she tries to control them, the Yankee works against them. He prunes the vines too close to the roots and kills them with a lime and ash fertilizer that makes them luxuriant for a while before they finally wither. The Yankee has no respect for the land or for those who work it. He is deadly. He burns the life out of the vines. When they "turned yaller en died, Henry died too" (CW, p. 31). The owner loses money, but the black man loses his life and the natural world is blighted.

Uncle Julius has his revenge partly by exposing as deadly the money-efficiency values of the whites and the gullibility of the owner. He also gets back at his former master in a beautifully placed afterthought. "He say he wuz mighty glad dat wah come, en he des want ter kill a Yankee fer eve'y dollar he los' 'long er dat grape-raisin' Yankee. En I 'spect he would 'a' done it, too, ef de Yankees had n' s'picioned sump'n en killed him fus" (CW, pp. 32–33). The play of controlled aggression is exquisite: Uncle Julius uses his Yankee audience to protect him as he undercuts the white Southern owner even as Julius has been undercutting the Yankee—and the Yankee in John and the reader.

In the frame tale John reduces the entire story to a self-interested attempt on Julius's part to keep him from buying the vineyard. John's "rational" explanation and formal language reveal more about his own consciousness than about Uncle Julius. John identifies himself with "Northern capital in the development of Southern industries" (CW, p. 34). As he characteristically does, as a representative of the emerging dominant class, he sees Julius's utilitarian motives but not the deeper satire of the market society John, the owner, and the Yankee all accept. For the same reason John also fails to see the celebration of black people at one with the energies of nature and suffering the consequences of the market society in its slave-owning version. The subversive parallel with the present is also concealed from the reader who uncritically shares

John's dominant-class vision. To achieve his ends in the racial-literary world of the 1890s, for the frame tale Chesnutt uses a white narrator who can be misread as reassuringly normative and who is undercut but only covertly.[13]

In the frame tale of "Sis' Becky's Pickaninny" Annie's depression is especially acute. Not only is she separated from her former home but also in John she has someone who believes that "frequent letters from the North kept her in touch." John also thinks that reading conventional novels, listening to plantation songs, and having friends "come in sometimes and talk" will supply what is missing in their lives (CW, p. 133). John never questions the value of his privatized, controlled and controlling way of life. Chesnutt rounds out this economical sketch of a dominant-class consciousness by having John generalize to Uncle Julius that "your people will never rise in the world until they throw off these childish superstitions and learn to live by the light of reason and common sense" (CW, p. 135). The conjure world is lighted from other sources. To bring it to life requires a language, a storytelling, totally different from John's. John speaks for both the genteel tradition and the market society with its evolving link with science and the new technology. From John's representative vantage point, Julius's vernacular stories and their concerns and vision have an inferior status. From the same point of view the old black man and Annie have an inferior status.

13. My awareness of the ironic interplay between frame tales and stories is indebted to the ground-breaking essay of Richard E. Baldwin, "The Art of *The Conjure Woman*," *American Literature* 43 (November 1971): 385–98. Baldwin focuses on the way the white narrator's racism blinds him to the deeper implications of Julius's stories. Baldwin also establishes that "Chesnutt aimed to modify white minds to feel the equality of the black man, and with the conjure tales he developed a perfect vehicle for his artistic needs" (p. 386). Although race is a central concern for both John and Julius, I see it as only one significant strain in the dominant-class consciousness and its alternative in *The Conjure Woman*. As for the tradition *The Conjure Woman* belongs to, Baldwin correctly shows that "the tales which Uncle Julius tells stand in the tradition of subterfuge, indirection, and subtle manipulation of whites developed by the slaves as a strategy for surviving in the face of oppression" (p. 387).

William L. Andrews, *The Literary Career of Charles W. Chesnutt* (Baton Rouge: Louisiana State University Press, 1980), in contrast, reduces *The Conjure Woman* to Chesnutt's "expansion and occasional transcendence of the historical assumptions and traditional social purposes of plantation-dialect fiction." Andrews misses most of Chesnutt's irony: he sees Annie as normative and believes that "if Julius has a role outside that of Chesnutt's 'mouthpiece' for discussion of slave life, the role is that of the petted servant whose disingenuous devices are often allowed to succeed by a forbearing employer" (pp. 41, 60, 52).

Chesnutt perceptively establishes an alignment between Julius and Annie, between blacks and women.

Chesnutt also raises the central issue of the truth value of stories. As opposed to the novels and the letters John endorses--and elsewhere the abstract philosophy, the piano music, and the missionary reports— Chesnutt affirms the black vernacular stories of Uncle Julius. In their vitality, their imaginative depth and range, and their grasp of human complexity, Uncle Julius's stories are an alternative to and commentary on the privileged status of the dominant society both as genteel tradition and as market society. The genteel tradition combines conventional fiction, philosophy, and Christian religion—note John's reading. Uncle Julius uses black vernacular to body forth unconventional fictions whose philosophy and religion are rooted outside Christianity in African practices and American slavery.

As for the market society, the white owners in Uncle Julius's stories repeatedly get into debt, mismanage their money, lose on trades, and are forced to sell their slaves. The ups and downs of the market society combine with the frequent ineptitude of the white owners to bring hardship to the slaves. In a matter-of-fact way, in "Sis' Becky's Pickaninny," Uncle Julius shows that "co'se Becky went on some 'bout losin' her man [who has been sold to pay debts], but she couldn' he'p herself; en 'sides dat, she had her pickaninny fer ter comfo't her" (CW, p. 137-38). The refrain line in the story is "of course":

"Co'se Becky had ter wuk en did n' hab much time ter was'e wid her baby." (CW, p. 138)

"Co'se w'en [Cunnel Pen'leton] went ter de races, he tuk his hosses, en co'se he bet on 'is own hosses, en co'se he los' his money." (CW, p. 138)

"Co'se Sis' Becky cried en went on 'bout her pickaninny, but co'se it did n' do no good." (CW, p. 144)

The refrain line establishes what is "natural," inevitable. Becky at first accepts the hard work and the separation from husband and child—"of course"—but through Uncle Julius, Chesnutt registers a quiet, deadly protest. For Colonel Pendleton, "a kind-hearted man," a racehorse is more valuable than Becky. He would rather not separate mother and child, but he is dealing within a system that places black people on a level with animals and he is "forced" to. By the 1890s slavery is in the past, but the power of white people and the demeaning view of black people is still very much in the present.

To counter that negative view, Chesnutt has Uncle Julius establish the basic humanity of black people. In "Sis' Becky's Pickaninny," the humanity is the love between mother and child. Separated from his mother, little Mose sickens. When the white doctor can't cure him, his surrogate mother turns to another kind of doctor, the conjure woman, Aunt Peggy. In the face of arbitrary white power, the black people in Chesnutt's stories repeatedly turn to the conjure woman to satisfy their need to have some control over their own lives. This time, working gently with the forces of nature, Aunt Peggy turns little Mose into a hummingbird who flies back to Becky's plantation. Repeated visits to his mother cure little Mose but not Becky, who sickens from the separation. The conjure woman is again persuaded to intervene. Like most significant healers, her power is based partly on her insight into human beings. In particular, Aunt Peggy has a shrewd understanding of what makes white people tick. She works out an ingenious scheme to keep Becky ill and to use hornets to cripple the race horse, Lightnin' Bug. Nature works for her and so does the human nature the market society has produced. Faced with losing his investment in Becky, her new owner writes Colonel Pendleton. "My conscience . . . has be'n troublin' me 'bout dat ringbone hoss I sol' you . . . I is made up my min' dat, w'iles a bahg'in is a bahg'in, en you seed Lightin' Bug befo' you traded fer 'im, principle is wuth mo' d'n money er hosses er niggers. So ef you'll sen' Lightnin' Bug down heah, I'll sen' yo' nigger 'oman back, en we'll call de trade off, en beez good frien's ez we ever wuz, en no ha'd feeling's' (CW, pp. 156–57). Friendship, principle, and conscience—Chesnutt has a lively sense of the way we use and abuse these central values as we grasp for money and advantage. In particular he exposes the contradiction between "principle" and the equation of "niggers" with horses and money.

In the frame tale John sees that Annie's face "had expressed in turn sympathy, indignation, pity, and at the end lively satisfaction" (CW, p. 158). John himself, though, questions "the truth" of the story. Like a formalistic critic, John pokes fun at "the humming-bird episode, and the mocking-bird digression, to say nothing of the doings of the hornet and the sparrow" (CW, p. 158). Annie accepts the story as "true to nature" and also accepts Uncle Julius's gift of a rabbit's foot: "de fo'-foot ain' got no power. It has ter be de hin'-foot, suh,—de lef' hin'-foot er a grabeya'd rabbit, killt by a cross-eyed nigger on a da'k night in de full er de moon" (CW, p. 135). The rabbit's foot comes from a world Annie is willing to enter more fully than John, though even she withdraws from its darkest, fiercest, most "primitive" and non-Christian intensities.

The power and the truth of the rabbit's foot in its natural setting, including the context of Uncle Julius's precise knowledge and vernacular, contrast with the power and the truth of the market society and the genteel tradition. As a gift-giver and storyteller, Uncle Julius also has recognizable power and truth. Like the conjure woman, he understands and cares for the people he lives with. Uncle Julius is as willing as the next person to make a profit, but the rabbit's foot is a gift that cannot be bought for "no 'mount er money" (CW, p. 135). He offers the rabbit's foot as a way of helping Annie in her illness. He also offers his story as a way of helping her. More gently than in his other tales, in "Sis' Becky's Pickaninny," Uncle Julius responds to Annie's situation.

Annie is childless in a period that made motherhood the central female value. Annie is unusually susceptible to this and the other stories' narration of the separation of mother and child. Uncle Julius's story, moreover, stresses sickness and separation from home and the power of men and the market society to damage women and children and the power of the conjure woman to make some of it right. The story is not an ironic allegory of Annie's situation with John, but it does have suggestive resonances and it suggests a positive outcome. No wonder Annie shows lively satisfaction. Along with his sympathy, however, Uncle Julius has a complex critical power that phrases like Annie's phrase, "true to nature," distract us from. In its full implications, Uncle Julius's story asks for basic changes in an entire way of life, changes that are unlikely in Annie and John's America. Uncle Julius's concern, insight, and rabbit's foot are not enough to effect a cure, but, like the conjure woman, they help.

To further develop his diagnosis of John's dominant-class consciousness, its effects, and the powerful alternative of the conjure world, Chesnutt uses Uncle Julius's stories about conjure men and their revenge. Unlike the conjure woman stories, one of these tales offends Annie; in the concluding frame tale of the other, Chesnutt simply leaves Annie out of account. In the background is the problem of the post–Civil War author writing for a primarily feminine audience.

In the frame tale of "The Gray Wolf's Ha'nt," Annie is bored. "'I wish you would talk to me, or read to me—or something,' she exclaimed petulantly. 'It's awfully dull here today'" (CW, p. 163). The alternative of the "or something" is fleshed out in the passions of love and hate at the center of Uncle Julius's conjure man story. Instead of the "or something" of passionate involvement, John reads Annie a devitalized piece of abstract philosophy on transmutation. He takes it as a sign of feminine intellectual inferiority that Annie is totally uninterested. Chesnutt then has Uncle Julius offer his own vernacular story involving transformation as an alternative to the language, philosophy, and inhibitions of the genteel tradition.

The black lovers in the story are powerful and attractive. "Dan wuz big en strong en hearty en peaceable en good-nachu'd most er de time, but dange'ous ter aggervate" (CW, p. 168). For her part Mahaly "wuz a monst'us lackly gal,—tall en soopl', wid big eyes, en a small foot, en a lively tongue, en w'en Dan tuk ter gwine wid 'er eve'body 'lowed dey wuz wellmatch', en none er de yuther nigger men on de plantation da' ter go nigh her, fer dey wuz all feared er Dan" (CW, p. 169). In a fight over Mahaly, Dan ends up killing the son of a conjure man. For protection he goes to Aunt Peggy, who works out a charm. In a contest of powers, though, the conjure man finally prevails. The slaves think he is in touch with "de ole Debbil hisself," and he does control the dark energies of storm and flood (CW, p. 176). In his primal world he knows his son was wrong but he nonetheless demands retribution. He takes us back beyond Christianity to a sense of harsh, elemental justice he shares with the Greeks of Aeschylus and the Hebrews of an eye-for-an-eye.

In carrying out his ingeniously cruel scheme of revenge, with their own connivance the conjure man transforms Dan into a "creetur" and Mahahy into a black cat. He wants Dan as a "creetur" who "kin bite, en bite fer er kill," who will go for the throat of a black cat and whose teeth will go through the neck "at the fus bite" (CW, p. 185). At the climax, "lo en behol'! no sooner had de blood 'mence ter flow dan de black cat tu'nt back ter Mahaly, en Dan seed dat he had kilt his own wife. En w'iles her bref wuz gwine she call' out: 'O Dan! O my husban'! come en he'p me! Come en sabe me fum dis wolf w'at's killin me'" (CW, p. 186–87). The torture is exquisite and enacts the suppressed hatred that goes along with a love as intense as Dan and Mahaly's. In the final act Chesnutt returns to the conjure man's primal revenge: even on his death bed the conjure man betrays Dan and with his dying breath makes sure that his enemy will remain a wolf forever.

In the concluding frame tale, John overlooks the contrast between Uncle Julius's vital view of transformation and his own genteel philosophy of transformation and the even more basic contrast between the passions in the story and his own passionless relation with Annie. Instead, John makes an issue of Uncle Julius's utilitarian attempt to preserve for his own use a bee-tree John is going to destroy. Julius may well feel that as a former slave and long-time resident, he has certain claims on the land. In his own voice, Julius also speaks again for a philosophy of nondevelopment. Beyond the bee-tree, he believes that you pay a price for disturbing the land. "It mought cos' mo', en it mought cos' less, ez fuh ez money is consarned. I ain' denyin' you could cl'ar up dat trac' er lan' fer a hund'ed dollahs,—ef you wants ter cl'ar it up. But ef dat 'uz my trac' er lan', I wouldn' 'sturb it, no, suh, I wouldn'; sho's you bawn, I wouldn" (CW, p. 166). John is committed to technological progress and profits. Uncle Julius may have mixed motives, but he also has a genuine intellectual position at odds with John's. Instead of seriously discussing their differences, however, John patronizes Uncle Julius. Uncle Julius is in fact perceptive, complex, deep, and well-aware of the prevailing power relations and the acceptable modes of response. In view of John's patronizing control, are the themes of hatred and revenge in "The Gray Wolf's Ha'nt" a displaced version of feelings Julius expresses indirectly through the conjure man? If so, as the conjure man behind the conjure man, Chesnutt has performed another act of transformation that allows him to handle powerful, threatening feelings in an indirect way acceptable to a respectable white publisher and a primarily white audience.

In the process, in *The Conjure Woman* Chesnutt gives us his versions of double-consciousness through the divisions within John and through the contrast between the two narrative voices of the frame tales and the vernacular stories. John's official voice expresses the accents and values of the emerging dominant class, a consciousness Chesnutt shows to be as divided as it is influential, as insensitive as it is decent, as condescending to women and blacks as it is assured of the rightness of technology, efficiency, and profits. As a diagnostician of the resulting sickness, Uncle Julius is a perceptive folk doctor, a conjure man himself. His vernacular voice subtly understands, exposes, and offers as an alternative a conventionally despised residual culture he brings alive as his twentieth-century successors were to do again and again.[14] However threatening, for the dominant society that residual culture is a vital necessity. In the late twentieth-century, however, as we move further from Uncle Julius's African and agrarian sources, the material conditions of consumerism make his alternative culture seem as valuable as it is increasingly difficult to sustain.

14. Recall, for example, the central role of the black vernacular world of Janie in Zora Neale Hurston's *Their Eyes Were Watching God* (New York: Lippincott, 1937); the central position of Trueblood and Peter Wheatstraw in Ralph Ellison's *Invisible Man* (New York: Random House, 1952); the analogous role of Reverend Brown and black mud in Ishmael Reed's *Mumbo Jumbo* (New York: Doubleday, 1972); and the celebration and exposure of life in rural Georgia in Alice Walker's *The Color Purple* (New York: Harcourt, 1982).

four

BILLY BUDD
Identity, Ideology, and Power

Melville wrote *Billy Budd, Sailor* (1886–1891) in the same decade as
Chesnutt's *The Conjure Woman* (1886–1899), and he conceived it during
the same troubled years of the late 1880s that saw the Haymarket Riot
and executions, Howells's *A Hazard of New Fortunes* (1889), and Twain's
A Connecticut Yankee in King Arthur's Court (1889). In *Billy Budd*, Melville
goes even deeper than his perceptive contemporaries into the power
relations and the alienation of selves and society in the emerging bureaucratic America. *Billy Budd* is set on an English warship in a period of
revolutionary threat in 1797 and it has roots in Melville's family drama
because of his reimagining of the *Somers* case in which his cousin Guert
Gansevoort played a key role in 1842.[1] But in his final masterpiece
Melville uses the historical setting to go deep into the contemporary
realities of the early phases of bureaucracy and professionalism. Forty
years before, well in advance of his times, in "Bartleby, the Scrivener,"
he had responded to the power relations, way of seeing, and impact on
consciousness of the emerging urban market society. By the 1890s the
society of high capitalism was assuming new dimensions. At the end of
his life, in *Billy Budd*, Melville tests his old social and religious preoccupations against the new, emerging realities that lead to the modern
bureaucratic state and to the divided selves who run it even as they are
shaped by it.

The received criticism of *Billy Budd*, however, unfortunately abstracts
the story out of its American social and historical context. Critics usually
treat such concerns as "civilization," for example, as universals having
almost no connection with the specific civilization Melville knew best.
As a customhouse employee, he was intimately familiar with one of the

---

1. Harrison Hayford, ed., *The Somers Mutiny Affair* (Englewood Cliffs, N.J.: Prentice-
Hall, 1959), and Michael Paul Rogin, *Subversive Genealogy: The Politics and Art of Herman
Melville* (New York: Knopf, 1983), pp. 288–316.

66

worst of the new bureaucracies. As a New Yorker during the Gilded Age and after, Melville was in daily contact with the energies of late capitalism, a society that made urgent the question he explores in "Timoleon" and *Billy Budd*—is "Indolence . . . heaven's ally here, / And energy the child of hell"?[2]

Billy Budd is rooted in American history and society and so is the standard criticism of the story. During the big growth period of American academic criticism during the 1940s and especially during the 1950s, the social concerns of the 1930s were in disfavor. The politics of the war and even more of the Cold War made it prudent to do socially detached close reading, myth criticism, or psychoanalytic interpretation. In the history of *Billy Budd* criticism the theological and psychoanalytical emphasis of the 1940s and 1950s succeeded in abstracting the story from its American social roots.[3] The *Billy Budd* criticism of the 1950s and the 1960s provides an interesting insight into the impact of the Cold War on the academy. "Testament of Resistance" critics were still publishing.[4] But the prevailing assumptions emerge in the way Wendell Glick detaches *Billy Budd* from American history and society and gives the readers of *PMLA* a lesson in 1950s accommodation. Melville, Glick argues,

was fully aware that a regimented society abridged many private rights, but he realized also that in the absence of such a society a state of anarchy and chaos inevitably arose in which every human right was sacrificed. An ordered society at least guaranteed the preservation of *some* rights; and though this fell far short of the ideal of the preservation of *all*, it was far better than the sort of "society" which, in the idealistic attempt to guarantee all rights, degenerated into chaos and so permitted their complete and total destruction.[5]

More recently, deconstruction has the same effect of separating *Billy Budd* from American social reality and of taming the story's political impact.[6] In his valuable chapter, in focusing on *Billy Budd* and the *Somers* mutiny, Michael Rogin goes to another extreme: he provides a social

2. "Fragments of a Lost Gnostic Poem of the 12th Century," *Collected Poems of Herman Melville*, ed. Howard P. Vincent (Chicago: Hendricks House, 1947), p. 234.

3. See, for example, William Braswell, "Melville's *Billy Budd* as 'An Inside Narrative,'" *American Literature* 29 (May 1957): 133–46, and Richard Chase, *Herman Melville: A Critical Study* (New York: Macmillan, 1949), pp. 269–77.

4. See, for example, Phil Withim, "*Billy Budd*: Testament of Resistance," *MLQ* 20 (June 1959): 115–27, and Alfred Kazin, "Ishmael in His Academic Heaven," *New Yorker*, 12 February 1949, pp. 73–77.

5. "Expediency and Absolute Morality in *Billy Budd*," *PMLA* 68 (March 1953): 105–6.

6. See, for example, Barbara Johnson, *The Critical Difference: Essays in the Contemporary Rhetoric of Reading* (Baltimore: Johns Hopkins University Press, 1980), pp. 79–109.

context that is too narrow, too historical.[7] Alan Trachtenberg corrects this tendency in his illuminating treatment of *Billy Budd*.[8] For their part, radical critics of *Billy Budd* tend to overlook Melville's ambivalence and to make him more one-sided than he is.[9] Liberal critics sometimes present Melville as more moderate than he is.[10] Because he has been deeply affected by the dominant-class hegemony he criticizes, Melville sensitively registers the crosscurrents of the hegemonic process. Conservative critics respond to one strain.[11] The received criticism of *Billy Budd* is, however, more energized than ordinary academic discourse. Critics are challenged and their responses are challenging. I have been especially stimulated by Joyce Sparer Adler, Phil Withim, Kingsley Widmer, Michael Rogin, and Alan Trachtenberg.[12]

As I see *Billy Budd*, Melville illuminates the self under the pressure of the emerging centralized military state and the threat of revolutionary crisis. The police and military powers have traditionally belonged to the state. Sensitive as he is to the America of Haymarket and the emerging new bureaucracies, Melville anticipates the twentieth-century war world in which the state has increasingly centralized its control of the police and the military. The threat of outside enemies and internal subversion can always be used to justify the extraordinary measures that are always called for to protect the very existence of the state. The degree of emergency varies, but the fact of emergency remains constant. *Billy Budd* has spoken deeply to contemporary Americans partly because it subtly explores an archetypal drama. Because critics have examined the traditional biblical and classical archetypes, it is worth stressing the extent to which *Billy Budd* gives us a modern archetype of state military and police power used against its most innocent and vulnerable members.

7. *Subversive Genealogy*, pp. 286–316.

8. *The Incorporation of America: Culture and Society in the Gilded Age* (New York: Hill and Wang, 1982), pp. 202–7.

9. H. Bruce Franklin, *The Victim as Criminal and Artist: Literature from the American Prison* (New York: Oxford, 1978), pp. 67–70, and Carolyn L. Karcher, *Shadow Over the Promised Land: Slavery, Race, and Violence in Melville's America* (Baton Rouge: Louisiana State University Press, 1980), pp. 293–306.

10. Michael Gilmore, *The Middle Way: Puritanism and Ideology in American Romantic Fiction* (New Brunswick: Rutgers University Press, 1977), pp. 182–94.

11. See Hannah Arendt, *On Revolution* (New York: Viking, 1973), pp. 74–83, and Thomas J. Scorza, *In the Time Before Steamships: Billy Budd, the Limits of Politics, and Modernity* (DeKalb: Northern Illinois University Press, 1979).

12. Adler, *War in Melville's Imagination* (New York University Press, 1981), pp. 160–85; Withim, "Testament of Resistance," pp. 115–27; Widmer, *The Ways of Nihilism: A Study of Melville's Short Novels* (Los Angeles: The California State Colleges, 1970), pp. 16–58; Rogin, *Subversive Genealogy*, pp. 286-316; and Trachtenberg, *The Incorporation of America*, pp. 202–7.

The power is not only of military force. As "Bartleby, the Scrivener" reminds us, Melville knows about the more subtle power that pervades consciousness and results in the willing consent characteristic of hegemonic dominance. In place of Bartleby's rebellion or the clerks' uneasy acceptance of this dominance, in his final work Melville has Billy Budd gladly accept his position and execution. As Melville uses him, Billy Budd becomes a vehicle for criticizing and illuminating the hegemonic process he uncritically accepts. Melville, moreover, shows the way the alienating dynamics of *ressentiment* drive Claggart as he manipulates the bureaucratic hierarchy and the condition of crisis to achieve personal ends. As a displaced modern man, Claggart, too, has been deeply affected by the prevailing hegemony. But, unlike Billy, he moves to a position of police power and uses that power to gratify his darkest needs.

Exploring Vere's situation, however, is Melville's central achievement. Through Vere, Melville not only examines the use of state power to enforce order but he also and even more basically probes the subtleties of the modern hegemonic process from the point of view of a member of the dominant group. Like the lawyer and Captain Delano, Vere's consciousness is permeated with dominant-class values and categories of perception and belief. In a familiar process that is nonetheless easy to overlook, Vere identifies his version of class and nation with "the peace of the world and the true welfare of mankind."[13] He "disinterestedly" elevates his conservative class and national interests to the higher plane of the universal. Dominant classes achieve their hegemony precisely by this preempting of the high ground of the universal. They control partly because, in a way that pervades society, they have convinced themselves and others that they represent the interests not of "the privileged classes" (BB, p. 62) but of peace and mankind. Because of his ability to generalize, Vere is finally a more effective representative of his class than are those aristocrats who focus narrowly on the threats to their privileges.

Vere is committed to a narrow interpretation of the military code. In the courtroom scene he conducts a brilliant exercise in the use of polarized categories to achieve the ends he has previously decided on. Melville does full justice to Vere's either-or mode of thought and to the arguments that support his rigid sense of order. In the process, Melville dramatizes the inadequacies of an administrative outlook that is too

13. *Billy Budd, Sailor (An Inside Narrative)*, ed. Harrison Hayford and Merton M. Sealts (University of Chicago Press, 1962), p. 63. Subsequent references will be abbreviated BB and cited by page number in the text.

rigid, too committed to order, regularity, and the state, all at the expense of human values, compassion, humanity. Vere represents a habit of mind that divides things into neat, mutually exclusive categories. The result is that he dehumanizes himself and kills Billy Budd. At the moment of Billy's execution, Vere appropriately stands "rigid as a musket" (BB, p. 124). He has made himself into an impersonal instrument of the state. To further his view of order and the true welfare of mankind, Vere fragments himself internally. Acting in accord with the new professional ethos that was developing during the 1880s, Vere denies his personal feelings in favor of his conception of his duties as an official in a bureaucratic hierarchy.[14]

The political ideology he develops in the courtroom scene generalizes this fragmentation to society at large. As a professional, Vere argues that the state cannot recognize the values of compassion, sympathy, or private conscience. He also posits an absolute split between nature and the state. He argues for a conception of the law as a reified presence absolutely separated from those who administer it. Under conditions of crisis, he asks, "Would it be so much we ourselves that would condemn as it would be martial law operating through us?" Administrators, he argues, are not responsible for the rigors of the law; they simply "adhere to it and administer it" (BB, pp. 110–11). Underlying and running through this administrative outlook is an extreme form of alienation: the state is alienated from and turned against the humanity of its members. Under conditions of crisis, the protection of the state becomes an end transcending the humanity it ostensibly protects. Early in the development of professionalism, moreover, Melville shows that the impersonal administrative outlook turns against the well-being of those the professional ostensibly exists to serve. Melville is alert to the way class and bureaucratic hierarchies become ends in themselves, at the expense of the common humanity that justifies their existence.

As an intellectual, Vere's identity is inseparable from his most deeply held ideas. To challenge these ideas about the nature of man and society is to challenge Vere's identity. Especially for an intellectual, to call into question his sense of what holds the world together is to call into question the structure of his own identity. In the story, Vere's depersonalized, dichotomized outlook is put to the test. Part of what is at stake is his own identity. He acts impersonally in part to preserve his sense of personal identity by showing that man and society are in fact as he believes they are. In his last masterpiece Melville deepens his life-

14. On the development of professionalism during the 1880s, see the references in Chapter 3, note 10.

long sensitivity to the connections between identity, ideology, and power. What is remarkable is the way Melville brings his old concerns to bear on the developing new realities that culminate in the twentieth-century's centralized state and its professedly impersonal administrators.

Vere is a patrician who has made his way as much by ability as by birth. He is a prototype of those capable modern patricians who from the 1880s on have controlled the upper levels of the American state and corporate bureaucracies. Disciplined, aloof, and thoughtful, Vere is an exemplary version of the rigorous training that produced the austerities of the Protestant character structure. As Max Weber first established, the new, professionalized bureaucracies required precisely the character structure shaped by the Protestant discipline: a dedication to efficiency, regularity, and order; a willingness to subordinate personal claims to those of duty and the organization. Officials trained "under the discipline severe" of traditional Protestantism made the perfect professionals of the new bureaucratic order. Melville, however, is alert to the way this impersonal professionalism can mask personal and class interests not as conscious manipulation but as the expression of a deeply interiorized consciousness.

Vere's professionalism and political ideology are secular. Underlying them are the rigors not only of a Protestant character structure, however, but also of a Calvinistic belief system. Vere's Calvinism pervades his consciousness and colors and structures his entire way of seeing and feeling. As ideology, however, his Calvinism appears at only one key moment, immediately after Billy kills Claggart. Vere's response reverberates through the story but Melville characteristically understates its sources. For Melville silence, understatement, and indirection are devices of emphasis. They force the reader to participate actively and they call attention to the hidden, subterranean depths that for Melville underlie conscious, public surfaces.

To appreciate Vere's response, we need to recall that Melville gives Billy a world-ranging host of associations. Instead of confining Billy's significance, he has the narrator or other characters see Billy variously as a Tahitian (BB, p. 121), a young Alexander (BB, p. 144), a Hercules (BB, p. 51), an Apollo (BB, p. 48), a young Achilles (BB, p. 71), and a "cheerful sea Hyperion," (BB, p. 88) as well as "a Catholic priest striking peace in an Irish shindy" (BB, p. 47), a "young Adam before the Fall" (BB, p. 94), and the Christ-like Billy who ascends "with a soft glory as of the fleece of the Lamb" (BB, p. 124). Vere, however, characteristically narrows this range of possibilities. For him Billy is an agent in a predetermined divine drama. He is a "fated boy" (BB, p. 99). For Vere what has happened to

Claggart "is the divine judgment on Ananias." As Vere sees it through
his Calvinistic lenses, Claggart has been "struck dead by an angel of
God! Yet the Angel must hang!" (BB, pp. 100–101). Vere decides instantly on religious grounds before he later elaborates his secular justification for Billy's trial and execution. His consciousness is saturated with
the Calvinistic categories of predestination, punishment, sacrifice, and
biblical analogies. The way he imposes these categories on the situation
causes other characters to doubt his sanity and his judgment (BB, pp.
101–2). Vere is initially presented as a moderate man knowledgeable
about the way power operates in the world of practical affairs. He reads
Montaigne, one of the world's most sensible and pluralistic writers.
Vere, however, emerges not as a flexible pluralist but as a rigid exponent
of an either-or outlook rooted in the Calvinistic dichotomies of the saved
and the damned, of difficulty equated with virtue and ease with vice,
and of love and mercy separated from a punitive sense of justice. One of
Melville's achievements in *Billy Budd* is to undercut the either-or men-
tality of Calvinism, as he had earlier in *The Confidence-Man* subverted
both the orthodox Calvinist way of seeing and its liberal Christian alternative. The exposure is as much of the arbitrary way Vere structures
experience as of the content of his views.

As a professional, Vere has a principled commitment to order, regularity, and accepted usage. As the surgeon, lieutenant, and captain of
marines all agree, however, the customary procedure would be to put
Billy in irons and delay the court-martial for the admiral to preside over
(BB, p. 102). Vere, however, has already decided the outcome on religious and personal grounds. Vere does not invoke his underlying reasons but instead articulates his patrician distrust of the people who, he
believes, "have not that kind of intelligent responsiveness that might
qualify them to comprehend and discriminate" (BB, p. 112). In his view,
explanations to the crew are beneath the dignity of his position and
exceed the capacity of the people to understand. The episode shows that
Vere has the kind of inconsistency professionals who control power can
pass off as wisdom. He stresses his commitment to "our naval usage and
tradition" and argues that the people, who are familiar with these
usages, would take advantage of any violations. Accepted usage, however, is for a delay of the court-martial. Through Vere, Melville shows
the way official power and bureaucratic attitudes about order and subordinates can be used to justify and to implement a deep structure of
unacknowledged motives and values that provide much of the energy
for the supposedly disinterested public actions.

In violating accepted usage, Vere violates a basic professional commitment to order and to regularity, values that have deep roots in his

personality and ideology. But he steps outside the professional code in order to affirm it and the structure of his own identity. His Calvinism is an underlying and unacknowledged structuring principle and source of energy. His Calvinism, that is, establishes the unstated premises of Vere's inner life and generates conflicts involving his identity and principles, conflicts he acts to resolve.

Viewed from the outside, Vere's behavior thus raises questions about his sanity. "Whether Captain Vere, as the surgeon professionally and privately surmised, was really the sudden victim of any degree of aberration, every one must determine for himself by such light as this narrative may afford" (BB, p. 102). For me the light illuminates the processes of control. Vere is used to controlling himself and others. He deliberately controls the court-martial, the apparatus of official power, but he does so for reasons so deeply rooted in his consciousness that even he is unaware of them. For the narrator, because sanity imperceptibly shades off into insanity, who can tell the dividing line (BB, p. 102)? What we can tell, however, is that under tremendous pressure a rigorously disciplined personality controls himself and the official apparatus of power for acknowledged but also unacknowledged reasons. Claggart is a clear-cut case of the same process. Melville is testing versions of the way control functions for and within officials subjected to the rigors of Protestant discipline and operating in a bureaucratic hierarchy. Melville is unusually sensitive to the way impersonal arguments become the instruments of official, class, and personal motives, to the way the impersonal rationality of bureaucratic procedures can be used to satisfy official, class, and personal needs so that outsiders see the behavior as irrational.

In Vere's case a covert domestic drama intensifies the pressures. To the extent that he sees Billy as a son, Vere's paternal affections are tapped.[15] After Billy strikes Claggart, however, "the father in [Vere], manifested towards Billy thus far in the scene, was replaced by the military disciplinarian" (BB, p. 100). Severely trained as he is, Vere has never found it easy to show his affections. His intellect is well developed and he expresses his ideas to the discomfort of his companions. His feelings, however, are controlled, and he does not express them openly. He appreciates Billy, he wants Billy stationed under his eye in a prize position, but, intelligent and resourceful as he is, Vere is unable to express his affection for Billy. Vere finally does not take good care of Billy. He does not care for Billy like a father but rather like a military

15. Edwin H. Miller, *Melville* (New York: Persea Books, 1975), pp. 346–47, and Leonard Casper, "The Case Against Captain Vere," *Perspective* 5 (Summer 1952): 150.

disciplinarian. The socially sanctioned split between the domestic and the professional, between feeling and intellect, between the feminine and the masculine gives Vere's characterization a telling resonance because of the persistence of these divisions in American selves and society.

In choosing to deny his affection for Billy, Vere affirms the dominant tendencies of his identity and ideology. In the process, however, he dehumanizes himself. He becomes a rigid musket. The contrast between the account of his end and Billy's end emphasizes Vere's spare, unfulfilled quality. Billy's death is given in expansive detail, and he lives on in legend. Vere's death is reported through the narrative device of an afterthought. In a few dry sentences of indirect narration, we learn that Vere has been killed, "cut off too early for Nile and Trafalgar" (BB, p. 129).

Melville understands the underlying processes and human costs that can occur in a threatened power hierarchy when disciplined professionals structure experience as a set of mutually exclusive, polarized alternatives. In Vere's case the result of separating the domestic and the professional gives an ironic resonance to the Marvell quotation that helps frame the narrative:

This 'tis to have been from the first
In a domestic heaven nursed,
Under the discipline severe
Of Fairfax and the starry Vere.
                              (BB, p. 61)

Billy's trial and execution and Vere's inner fragmentation give a subversive power to the "this" of the quotation. The passage, moreover, sets up ironic contrasts between "a domestic heaven" and the *Bellipotent*, a warship embodying the severities of state power. On this view the "feminine" values of domesticity, nursing, and religion ("heaven") highlight what Vere's "discipline severe" ignores and destroys. The religious connotations of "starry" in the context of "heaven" bring Vere to another value test he falls short of. Through his handling of Vere Melville shows the way established religion reinforces but also powerfully criticizes official practices and beliefs.

The sections on Nelson similarly establish a vantage point that clarifies and criticizes Vere. Because Vere is a traditionalist, it is easy to miss the way he embodies an emerging style of disciplined professionalism. Nelson, "the greatest sailor since our world began" (BB, p. 58), represents an antithetical style, heroic and poetic, not professional.

From the perspective of "the new order" (BB, p. 57), Nelson lacks "personal prudence" and is foolhardy and vain (BB, p. 59). In contrast, the narrator associates Nelson with "each more heroic line in the great epics and dramas." The narrator celebrates "those exaltations of sentiment that a nature like Nelson, the opportunity being given, vitalizes into acts" (BB, p. 58). "Those exaltations of sentiment" are precisely what Vere, "the opportunity being given," is unable to "vitalize into acts." Nelson handles the threat of mutiny "by force of his mere presence and heroic personality" (BB, p. 59). Vere "prudently" uses the impersonal structure and procedures of official power. The Nelson sections immediately precede those on Vere. They are not really a casual digression, a "bypath" (BB, p. 56), but rather a narrative device that places Vere's impersonal professionalism in the shadow of Nelson's personal, poetic, and heroic style.

Critics give two basically opposed views of Vere. Joyce Sparer Adler locates the reason inside Vere himself. She perceptively observes:

The contradiction within Vere is his very essence; the split in him is . . . central to his meaning. . . . He is the symbolic figure—not crudely, but finely and fairly, drawn—of civilized man: learned, but not sufficiently imaginative; not devoid of the ability to love, but not allowing this capacity to develop; sensitive to the difference between the good and evil signified by Billy and Claggart, but the puppet of the god he has been trained to think must rule in this world. . . . Exceptional among the officers on the *Bellipotent*, and even among captains, in his rigidity—there are a score of references to, or images of, this quality so appalling to Melville—he is the comprehensive figure of what is dominant in modern civilization.[16]

Vere allows Melville to illuminate the divided consciousness of one of the patrician officials who control the emerging power structures of "the new order." Through Billy Budd, he views matters not from the top but from the bottom. Billy, of course, cannot be confined to a class analysis, but for all his universal implications he is a common sailor, exceptional but not an officer. He may have aristocratic parentage, but he has been raised as an ordinary seaman, illiterate and unprivileged. He gladly accepts his position on the *Rights of Man* and the *Bellipotent*. The captains of both ships understandably value him. In part Billy represents the willing consent that defines hegemony. Not only is he a cooperative leader and a first-rate sailor but also, and even more important, aboard the *Rights of Man* he is a "peacemaker" (BB, p. 47). Captain Graveling celebrates the way Billy brings peace and order to the troubled forecas-

16. *War in Melville's Imagination*, pp. 177–78.

tle. Billy instinctively tames the disruptive energies below deck. The ship is a merchantman and Billy is an exemplary version of what its ruling groups value in their subordinates.

Matters are more complicated aboard the *Bellipotent*. Billy's basic inclination is to do what is expected of him. But this tendency is powerfully reinforced by the flogging he witnesses on his first full day aboard. Billy is "horrified" and "resolved that never through remissness would he make himself liable to such a visitation or do or omit aught that might merit even verbal reproof" (BB, p. 68). Although it does not take the threat of force to keep Billy in line, Melville is careful to establish the role that naked power does play. But fundamentally Billy is not coerced into being a model sailor. In the fleet at large, however, under the pressure of mismanagement and the new revolutionary ideology, the prevailing hegemony has broken down. The story turns on the fact that Billy is unaffected. He is, as the Lieutenant says, "a King's bargain"; that is, an accepting "capital investment at small outlay or none at all" (BB, p. 95). From the point of view of "capital investment," he is a splendid model of what the dominant-class values and creates in its subordinates.

Billy, however, is also "an upright barbarian," an embodiment of primitive virtues anterior to a capitalistic civilization and the state. As noble savage, as "young Adam before the fall," and as the Christ-like figure after the execution, Billy dramatizes the presence in a capitalistic civilization and the state of residual qualities the new order has gone beyond. Melville uses Billy's primitive innocence, vitality, beauty, and good spirits to highlight the value of qualities not easy to sustain in the new order. In this sense Billy functions as an implicit critic of a new order that is destructive of his admirable energy and innocence. Billy is also an Adamic and Christ-like figure killed in the crosscurrents of state demands, bureaucratic procedures, and the personal needs of Vere and Claggart. Billy's Christian associations show again that religion, a residual element in modern society, can be a powerful critic of the dominant-class hegemony it often supports.

Melville uses Billy to illuminate both tendencies. Billy's consciousness has been so deeply affected by the prevailing hegemony that at his moment of execution he expresses his consent in his famous line, "God bless Captain Vere" (BB, p. 123). Billy has interiorized conventional religion as an integral part of his own support of the established order. But as Melville uses the line, it also has a subversive power critical of a state and bureaucratic order that destroys a god-like life.

The prevailing hegemony stamps still other dimensions of Billy's characterization. "Baby" Budd is presented as child-like, innocent, and primitive. His body, beauty, and physical powers are more highly developed than his intellect. He can sing but not read. He is white but as Handsome Sailor he is aligned with the magnificent black whose description dominates the first chapter. The configuration of Billy's qualities links him with the conventional stereotypes of blacks, Indians, women, and the lower classes. In celebrating the qualities Billy shares with these groups, Melville to an extent reverses their customary denigration, but he also conceives of Billy within a framework shaped by the prevailing hegemony.

For one thing, Billy's qualities are elevated versions of those familiar class, racial, and sexual stereotypes that help keep people where the dominant groups think they belong. Billy is seen as exemplary, moreover, partly because he unprotestingly accepts his position and finally his position as victim. Melville no longer imagines rebellion as he had through Babo and Bartleby. Instead, as he had earlier, he criticizes the existing or emerging power structure not by imagining alternatives to it but by rendering the losses it causes. Those at the bottom of the social scale can take comfort from Billy's triumph in death and from the elegiac treatment of the qualities they are conventionally held to share with him. Melville is not patronizing, but he nonetheless conceives of Billy, for all his charismatic power, as an accepting victim. In his treatment of Billy, Melville thus criticizes, illuminates, and works within a hegemonic process that is uncomfortable with an overtly rebellious lower class.[17]

Although for the most part he is presented sympathetically as a victim of Claggart, Vere, and the forces they represent, Billy also contributes to his own destruction. Because he lacks "self-consciousness," a sophisticated awareness of himself, he is compared unflatteringly "to a dog of Saint Bernard's breed" (BB, p. 52). Even more than his intellectual limitations, Billy's innocence, his trusting lack of guile or "intuitive knowledge of the bad" (BB, p. 86) emerges as a simultaneously admirable and fatal cause of his death. Through both Claggart and Billy, Melville tests the way innate tendencies of human nature intertwine with the institutional settings of the new order. Billy's trusting good nature is basic to his uncritical acceptance of the new order and the officials who run it. Paradoxically, his "unconventional rectitude" is precisely what makes him susceptible to the conventional power that kills him.

Melville further illuminates the complexities of the hegemonic process through his contrast between the *Rights of Man* and the *Bellipotent*. The

17. Adler, ibid., pp. 171–73, sees the crew's response to Billy's death as a promise of growth and change. Her treatment is subtle and valuable, but she also minimizes the extent to which Melville's consciousness has been affected by the hegemony he struggles against. In the case of the crew even more than with Billy, Melville is extremely cautious and indirect in the way he handles the possibility of working-class rebellion.

Rights of Man is a merchant ship whose sensible captain is a model of "humane intelligence," "prudence," and "much conscientiousness" (BB, p. 45). After Billy brings harmony to the troubled ship, it is characterized by "love" and "peace." "It's the happy family here," Captain Graveling tells the Lieutenant (BB, p. 47). The *Rights of Man* was named after Paine's book defending the French Revolution. The narrator also mentions Voltaire and Diderot, so that the *Rights of Man* is connected not with the violence of the revolution but with the Enlightenment attack on royal and aristocratic privilege. Paine's *Rights of Man* is an eloquent example of this attack. A middle-class Scotch merchant on the rise would understandably name his ship after Paine's book. As opposed to established privilege, "Every man is a proprietor in society," Paine argues, "and draws on the capital as a matter of right."[18] Under Billy's influence, the *Rights of Man* suggests an idealized version of a merchant capitalist's civil society. The French Revolution is presented as a basic threat to this society under the aegis of "the enemy's red meteor of unbridled and unbounded revolt" (BB, p. 54). Although the state basically supports the merchant capitalist, Melville realizes that the interests of the merchantman and the state are not identical. Billy is impressed into the King's service to the disadvantage of Captain Graveling and his peaceful society.

As a natural man, Billy is at home on the *Rights of Man*. "Natural rights," Paine affirms, "are those which *always* [italics mine] appertain to man in right of his being a member of society. Every civil right has for its foundation some natural right pre-existing in the individual, but to which his individual power is not, in all cases, sufficiently competent" (ROM, p. 88). Paine concludes, "The power produced by the aggregate of natural rights, imperfect in the individual, cannot be applied to invade the natural rights which are retained in the individual, and in which the power to execute is as perfect as the right itself" (ROM, p. 89).

Aboard the *Bellipotent*, however, power and ideology combine to deny Paine's views. Billy embodies the basic natural humanity Paine assumes. Billy, though, never considers invoking Paine to justify rebellion against Vere in order to reclaim his "rights of man." Instead, Billy accepts the new order and its destruction of the natural rights and humanity he compellingly represents. Paine helped bring about "the new order." Beyond Billy, Melville is testing the extent to which this "new order" ends by destroying Paine's basic values. Can "the rights of man"

18. *The Rights of Man*, in *Thomas Paine: Representative Selections*, ed. Harry Hayden Clark (New York: American Book Company, 1944), p. 89. Subsequent references will be abbreviated ROM and cited by page number in the text.

and Paine's entire humanistic view of man exist in the new military, bureaucratic state?

As a character Billy is generally unprotesting, but he does, of course, lash out at Claggart. Billy's speech defect symbolizes his imperfect ability to express himself in language. It is part of the same pattern that has him able to sing but not able to read. Under pressure, Billy asserts his sense of right not through reasoned discourse but through an instinctive act of violence. On this view, his elemental self includes not his intellect but rather his body and instincts. There are also undertones of a virtuous but inarticulate and powerful lower class striking out not in principled rebellion but in self-defensive outrage.

At the other extreme from Billy, Claggart's innate depravity, a depravity according to nature, is central to his characterization. Melville reveals the inner dynamics of Claggart's pent-up energy and shows how "the mania of an evil nature" (BB, p. 76) intertwines with the state military and police hierarchy. Controversial as it was in an era of science and sentimental religion, Melville is not content simply with establishing Claggart's innate depravity. He opens up its inner workings and also shows how Claggart puts the institutional structure of the new order to his own uses. Claggart gravitates to a position of power in command of the police aboard the *Bellipotent*. He distinguishes himself because of his superior capacity, sobriety, ferreting genius, and ingratiating deference to those above him (BB, p. 67). He knows how to work a system that rewards skillful performance and the arts of deference, that rewards ability on the job and sensitivity to the demands of the hierarchy. As a subordinate, Claggart knows how to behave properly toward his superiors even as he manipulates those beneath him. He conceals his real nature and extends his power through his network of minor functionaries. He combines skill at his job, skill at concealment, and skill at manipulating his underground web of influence. Before the centralized power of the police had become a matter of general concern, Melville shows that this supposedly impersonal authority can be perversely controlled. Claggart casts a dark shadow on the police hierarchy, a cornerstone of the new military, bureaucratic order. Claggart illuminates the underground realities of power in the new order. Captain Vere is suspicious of Claggart but Vere's courtroom defense of state power is not supple enough to take into account the realities Claggart represents. Vere's dichotomies never touch the actualities of power Claggart and his control of the police drive home to us. Separated from these realities, Vere's ideology becomes an exercise in alienated abstraction.

Melville also uses Claggart to show the affinity between the police and their antagonists, those "lame ducks of morality" (BB, p. 65) who fill the prisons. In the eyes of the crew Claggart is a fallen patrician, a man of high quality who has perhaps fled to sea because he was involved in some mysterious swindle (BB, p. 65). Previously a morally suspect failure, on this view, Claggart becomes a success within the institutional setting of the bureaucratic hierarchy. Part of the resentful energy that animates his success as a ferreting police official perhaps comes from his loss of status, his need to truckle, and his corresponding need to dominate.

In this perverse way, Claggart shows the impact of the hegemonic process. Aboard ship he does not overtly rebel against the prevailing values and authority structures, but unlike Billy Budd he does not willingly accept them, either. Instead, he uses these structures and the revolutionary crisis to satisfy his own dark needs. As a talented, perversely alienated, socially displaced, and sexually thwarted modern man, Claggart anticipates a significant modern personality type. The perverse energy and ability of such people make them skillful manipulators of bureaucratic power. Like Claggart, they can adopt an austere patriotism and can use the threat of revolutionary apocalypse to justify themselves.

Melville thus illuminates the insanity of rationality. In part he shows that "madmen" (BB, p. 76) like Claggart conceal their real aims, but, significantly, their "method and the outward proceeding are always perfectly rational" (BB, p. 76). Melville is even more perceptive in showing that the people like Captain Vere who run bureaucracies are especially vulnerable to this manipulation. Their ordinary expectations of rationality make it hard for them to see through the facade of rationality. In this sense the basic outlook of the new order is shown to be a dangerous kind of madness. Bureaucratic power controlled by a perverse energy like Claggart compounds the danger. Melville suggests the related possibility that Vere himself, rational and controlled like Claggart, is not simply the victim of a momentary disorder but also the central embodiment of the insanity of bureaucratic rationality. On this view Vere acts from motives hidden even from his own awareness, and, like Claggart, he uses the structure of official power for complex reasons that call the rationality of official power into question.[19]

To shift to a related issue, as a mainstay of the new order the official report of the events aboard the *Bellipotent* celebrates Claggart as "patriotic," "responsible," and "respectable and discreet" (BB, p. 130). Melville's consciousness has been deeply affected by the prevailing

19. On the underlying affinity between Vere and Claggart, see Leonard Casper, "The Case Against Captain Vere," pp. 150–52, and Franklin, *The Victim as Criminal and Artist*, pp. 68–70.

hegemony, but he also reacts against it. In particular, he exposes its reliance on "patriotism" and "respectability." These values are central to the hegemonic process of which the report itself is an integral part. The contrast between the official version and the artist's "inside narrative" subversively exposes the process and content of official control. The report falsifies not for propagandistic reasons but for reasons that go deep into the process of bureaucratic control. As a result, Melville undermines confidence in official reports in general. He knows they view characters and events from a vantage point that inevitably promotes official interests.

In the "authorized" (BB, p. 130) version, Claggart is thus the valued protagonist in a drama of treasonous insurrection. As a minor official, he is affirmed because on men of his rank "the efficiency of His Majesty's navy so largely depends" (BB, p. 130). Melville understands the way officials "rationally" support those on whom the efficiency of their organizations depend. He also knows that officials control the historical record: the "authorized . . . publication" (BB, p. 130) "is all that has hitherto stood in human record" (BB, p. 131). Elsewhere Melville has the narrator say that "Billy in the Darbies" has been printed as well as passed along by word of mouth. In either version Melville recognizes that official control is pervasive but never absolute. At precisely the moment of anti-alien hysteria in the America of Haymarket and its aftermath, it is also worth stressing that Melville has the official record present Billy as "one of those aliens" involved "in some sort of plot" (BB, p. 130).[20]

Playing off against and to the disadvantage of the official story are two other narratives, "the inside narrative" of Billy Budd, sailor, and the concluding narrative of "Billy in the Darbies." The official report is one-dimensional. As an artist, Melville agrees with the narrator that "truth uncompromisingly told will always have its ragged edges" (BB, p. 128). Unlike the authorized version, the artist's "inside narrative" is ambiguous, conveys a sense of multiple possibility, and invites the reader to make up his own mind. To further this end, Melville juxtaposes the official report and the ballad, the view from the top and the view from the bottom. In contrast to the report's bureaucratic language and outlook, the simple form and simple vernacular language of the ballad bring alive an ordinary sailor, Billy Budd, who has the last word.

20. Based on their examination of the *Billy Budd* manuscript, Hayford and Sealts conclude that "the substance of the present chapter" was written in the period 1886–1888 (pp. 200, 2). This is the period of Haymarket and the outpouring of antinativist sentiment and the fears of anarchy associated with Haymarket.

In addition to his contrast with the treacherous William Budd of the official report, this Billy is less exalted and more human than the narrator's. But he, too, generally accepts his punishment: he welcomes the chaplain and jokes that "all, all is up: and I must up, too." But elsewhere this folk version is more critical than the Billy of "the inside narrative." He mentions the piping to halyards, the "forms, measured forms" (BB, p. 128) central to Vere's outlook, and then comments provocatively, "But aren't it all sham?" As opposed to the unifying sham of official ceremony and particularly the sham of his execution, this Billy invokes a sense of the community of ordinary sailors and their everyday concerns—for Bristol Mary, for a bite to eat, for the messmate who "will reach me the last parting cup," for the friends who will shake his hand "ere I sink. / But—no! It is dead then I'll be when I sink" (BB, p. 132). This Billy is not surrounded by the aura of the Resurrection: he talks to the chaplain, but his own consciousness has not been affected by conventional religion. He lives on, not in Heaven but in the consciousness of his fellows, ordinary sailors like Billy himself. In "Billy in the Darbies," Billy's language, concerns, and consciousness contrast with the narrator's, but, more important, they are an alternative to the bureaucratic world Claggart has mastered. The ballad, it is worth stressing, comes from below decks, from the strata of society at the bottom. It embodies a seaman's residual culture not easy to sustain in Claggart and Vere's bureaucratic order.

The new bureaucracies, Robert Wiebe shows, functioned to unify, to hold together a nation in "search for order." In particular, the police bureaucracy could always be called on when ordinary hegemonic consent failed, as it threatened to do when the red flag of anarchist revolt waved through the America of Haymarket, labor-management strife, and large-scale immigration during the period when Melville was writing *Billy Budd*. As the head of the police network, Claggart has a society that reflects negatively on the new bureaucracies and the kind of order they create. In contrast to the old-fashioned, free and easy companionship of Billy Budd in the society of the foretopmen or the community of the ballad, Claggart is closed in, officially secluded from sunlight (BB, p. 64). He works covertly and underground; he has "understrappers" rather than companions. Claggart is trapped not only by his nature but also by his position in the bureaucracy. His subordinates do not tell him the truth, but, like others sensitive to the demands of bureaucratic power, they tell him what he wants to hear. Lacking as it is in fellowship, trust, or honesty; based as it is on coercion, hierarchy, and subterranean power, Claggart's version of the emerging bureaucratic society is exposed as both inauthentic and dangerous. Part of Melville's legacy to the new century is the realization that bureaucratic order can have its own grim price and its own forms of madness and chaos. Vere in his controlled and controlling way also participates in these tendencies, which call into question the dominant twentieth-century response to the fragmentation characteristic of post–Civil War America.

The Impact of
Social Change

INTRODUCTION TO THE IMPACT
OF SOCIAL CHANGE

To help gauge the impact of social change, it is revealing to move from the emerging bureaucratic world of late capitalism to the pre-modern world the seventeenth-century English brought with them when they came to America. As Vere's "discipline severe" shows, the Puritanism of the early settlers makes for continuity, as does the market society of seventeenth-century England. But the seventeenth-century world was also significantly different from ours. Peter Laslett describes a baker's family in London in 1619, a household of thirteen persons headed by the father.[1] The mother was important but subordinate to him, as were the three children, the four paid journeymen, the two maid servants, and the two apprentices, all of whom worked, ate, and slept in the household. This family made bread together and their economic and domestic relations were not separated. The scale of life was human and intimate, so that affection and hatred, support and exploitation, warmth and injustice all had a personal setting. Family ties thus gave their emotional coloring to the most basic economic and political relations. The inevitable hardship, hatred, exploitation, and tyranny were inseparable from particular, intimately known members of the family. Because of the intimacy, tensions inevitably built up and could not be released "except in crisis."[2] However they were violated, expectations and relations within the family were nonetheless governed by tradition and law and had been for time out of mind.

With variations, Laslett argues, extended families like the baker's had also been the basic social unit throughout the English and European countryside for as long as anyone could remember. In this world, material hardship, plague, and disease could be very real, and, because the death of the father disrupted the family, which did not have an ongoing life like a corporation, insecurity was also a fact of existence. But the insecurity was different from ours. Because they were rooted in a family and a place, people did know who they were. The modern tensions of

1. *The World We Have Lost*, 2d edition (New York: Scribner's, 1971), pp. 1–22.
2. Ibid., p. 5.

identity were not significant. In this traditional world, moreover, change was gradual, customary ways of work persisted through generations, and people tended to remain close to where they were born.

The Englishmen who settled seventeenth-century America brought this traditional world with them in their minds, but the new settlers had displaced themselves, and the old patterns were never fully realized in America. The absence of a feudal past and the disruption of the baker's family world account for some of the most basic differences between Europe and America, since, although that family world has disappeared in Europe, too, it is not even a national memory in America. The fragmented families in *Huck Finn*; the covert and frustrated family relations in *Billy Budd*; the privatized white family, the slave community, and the broken families of the *Conjure Woman* all dramatize the impact of the change from the pre-modern, family-centered world to the emerging world of nineteenth-century industrialism and capitalism. The market society, of course, was already well developed in the seventeenth-century England of Laslett's baker. The combination of industrialism and capitalism is crucial in separating the baker's world from ours.

The baker's traditional world itself was experiencing social and economic upheaval during his lifetime, which coincides with the first English settlement of America. Enclosure of land formerly held in common displaced people in the countryside. Serious inflation and changes in the wool trade are among the other symptoms and causes of what contemporaries experienced as a disturbing disruption of social order.[3] These changes had a particularly strong impact on tradesmen and artisans like Laslett's baker or Benjamin Franklin's English ancestors, who were smiths and dyers in the silk and wool trade. Tradesmen and artisans like the baker or Franklin's ancestors were precisely the group that formed the center of the Puritan movement. More adequately than what they experienced as the old, worn-out priestly religion, more adequately than what was for them a too moderate Anglicanism, Puritanism answered to the extremity of the tradesman's felt situation.

Puritanism, Christopher Hill helps us see, appealed to two sides of the tradesman and artisan's needs and experiences.[4] It appealed, on the one hand, to his sense of being caught up in economic and social forces beyond his control—recall that powerful, all-knowing God who controlled totally and in relation to whom man was but as dust. But at the

---

3. Christopher Hill, *The Century of Revolution, 1603–1714* (New York: Norton, 1961), pp. 11–35, and *The World Turned Upside Down: Radical Ideas During the English Revolution* (New York: Penguin, 1975).

4. "Protestantism and the Rise of Capitalism," in David S. Landes, ed., *The Rise of Capitalism* (New York: Macmillan, 1966), pp. 41–52.

same time the baker also needed to feel he made a difference, that his personality and efforts counted, that in a rapidly changing world he had some control. The experience of salvation, whatever the uncertainties, gave assurance; the spiritual incentive to intense worldly effort was satisfying and functional; and the mix of confidence and uncertainty responded to both the dislocating experience of social and economic change and the need for a certain sense of individual control. The intensity of this combination may have made Puritanism a more authentic answer to the tradesman and artisan's deepest inner needs than either a relatively moderate Anglicanism or a Catholicism that emphasized ritual and the role of the priest rather than the individual. In the New World, Covenant Theology sustained the tension. Federal Theology gave a measure of contractual security to those elect individuals whose efforts were simultaneously ineffectual, necessary, and legitimized. In both the Old and New Worlds, logically but not psychologically at odds with this individualism, the experience of a community of believers, of a select minority banded together, gave a sense of assurance in a world where things seemed increasingly out of control.

Like their contemporaries in the traditional world, respectable Puritans were committed to hierarchy and order. Like almost everyone in the Old World, they knew that "God had appointed, that in every society one person should bee above or under another; not making all equall, as though the bodie should bee all head and nothing else; but even in degree and order, hee hath set a distinction, that one should be above another."[5] Rogues, beggars, and vagabonds, however, the most visible embodiments of contemporary economic dislocation, were threateningly outside the acceptable structure or body of society. "It is a foule disorder in any common-wealth," Perkins argued, "that there should bee suffered rogues, beggars, vagabonds; for such kind of persons commonly are of no civill societie or corporation, nor of any particular Church; and are as rotten legges, and armes that drop from the body" (TOV, p. 51). Perkins valued an earlier, more stable order when, at the other end of the social scale, the rich did not, as now, "spend a great part of their increase upon hawks, buls, beares, dogs, or riotously mispend the same in some sporting or gaming; and disable themselves to doe that good they should unto the Church of God." Perkins similarly invokes old stabilities when he criticizes "the meaner sort," the ordinary people who "nowadaies spend that they get in fine apparell, and good

5. William Perkins, "A Treatise of the Vocations or Callings of Men," in Edmund S. Morgan, ed., *Puritan Political Ideas, 1558–1794* (Indianapolis: Bobbs-Merrill, 1965), p. 51. Subsequent references will be abbreviated TOV and cited by page number in the text.

cheere; and by this meanes the house of God is lesse regarded; for every common man nowadaies must be a gentlemen, and it is very hard sometimes for a stranger to discerne the master from the servant" (TOV, p. 47).

Ironically, however, Puritans were among the energetic causes of the very changes they reacted against. Those who left England to establish a model, stable commonwealth in Massachusetts Bay exemplify this impulse perfectly. In the midst of the economic and social dislocations of the 1620s they uprooted themselves to found a stable, ideal order they felt England had forsaken. Once they had undergone an immense journey to an untamed land, their own energies and that of their successors transformed the land and the ideal way of life beyond recognition. They were committed to the community and fellowship of believers, knit through the love of Christ "into one body again in Christ, whereby a man is become again a living soul." "Among the members of the same body," John Winthrop continued, "love and affection are reciprocal, in a most equal and sweet kind of commerce."[6] But as Winthrop feared, their practice of worldly commerce gradually undermined their sense of loving community. Theologically, the individualism of the Saint's unmediated relation to his God was also in tension with his feelings of Christian fellowship.

The Puritans stressed traditionally established fair prices and the obligation to work "for the common good," not for individual advantage. "He abuseth his calling," Puritans from Perkins to Cotton Mather emphasized, "whosoever he be that against the end thereof, imployes it for himselfe, seeking wholly his own, and not the common good" (TOV, p. 39). And Puritans were told that they were not free to do as they wished. They were to stay in the place and the calling God had chosen for them.

Hence come treacheries, treasons, and seditions, when men, not content with their own estate and honors, seeke higher places: and being disappointed, grow to discontentments, and so forward to all mischiefe. Therefore in a word, the good estate of the church and common-wealth, is when every person keepes himself to his owne calling. And this wil undoubtedly come to passe, if we consider what be our callings; and that we are placed in them of God; and therefore judge them to be the best callings of all for us. (TOV, p. 55)

The commitment to fair prices, keeping your place, and accepting your calling without constant change, however, conflicted with the irresistible need to prosper as presumptive evidence of salvation.[7]

6. John Winthrop, "A Model of Christian Charity," in *The Norton Anthology of American Literature*, ed. Ronald Gottesman, et al., 2 vols., (New York: Norton, 1979), 1:19, 21.

7. Max Weber, *The Protestant Ethic and the Spirit of Capitalism*, trans. Talcott Parsons (New York: Scribner's, 1958), pp. 112–19, esp. p. 115.

The Puritans' commitment to hierarchy and order was also in tension with their own upward mobility and the equality of the elect regardless of traditional rank. This spiritual equality and sense of superiority over the non-elect must have appealed to rising tradesmen and artisans who gained status in God's eyes as well as in their own eyes regardless of the traditional class system they supported even as they undermined it. The move to America intensified this undermining. The guilt inseparable from such conflicts was answered to by their sense of innate depravity and their sense of insignificance before an all-powerful God. In its heyday, Puritanism thus satisfied a complex of contradictory needs. But over time in America, the pressures of internal contradictions and external changes took their toll. The earlier synthesis gradually ceased to speak to deeply felt needs.

Increasingly during the eighteenth century in the New World, the combination of religious and economic individualism came to prevail over the sense of community. The scarcity of labor and the availability of land for those with enough capital undermined traditional patterns of deference and stability. Authoritarian tendencies nonetheless persisted. In the eighteenth century, instead of compromising disagreements or living together in spite of them, when disagreements became acute, entire townships split and the dissenting group formed a separate entity, absolutist in its turn.[8] During the eighteenth century and into the nineteenth century, the myth of equality, the invidious distinctions of the work ethic, and a concealed class structure gradually replaced the earlier theology and the hierarchical, family-based traditional society. The work ethic in particular functioned to drive and to legitimize the efforts of "an immensely influential minority," "the Northern, Protestant, propertied classes," as distinct from patricians, working-class people, Irish and other immigrants, and those who lived on the frontier and in the South.[9] The Protestant ethic is integral to an early, capital-accumulating phase of a market society whose dominant members were in charge of the legitimizing educational and religious institutions as well as the new factories, banks, law offices, railroads, and stores. The work ethic thus plays an important role in the process of cultural hegemony in America.

As is well know, science, technology, and increasing material prosperity helped undermine the precarious early seventeenth-century Pu-

8. Michael Zuckerman, *Peaceable Kingdoms: New England Towns in the Eighteenth Century* (New York: Knopf, 1970).

9. Daniel T. Rodgers, "Nose to the Grindstone," *New York Times*, 16 April 1980, Op-Ed page. This essay summarizes Rodgers's *The Work Ethic in Industrial America, 1850–1920* (University of Chicago Press, 1978).

ritan synthesis. And again Puritans and their descendants contributed significantly to all these developments. Puritans were influential in the founding of the Royal Society; they helped shape the consciousness of Locke and Newton, the cornerstone theorists of the American and English eighteenth century; and, as Franklin reminds us, they contributed substantially to the increasing material prosperity.

Franklin, in fact, exemplifies all these tendencies. As much as any one person, he both epitomizes and helped create the new American world. His *Autobiography* in particular helps constitute the shared American memory, which is to say that it has played an important role in the hegemonic process of the developing nation. By considering *The Autobiography*, we can deepen our insight into this process and the impact of social change, even as these concerns can quicken our understanding of *The Autobiography*. Having established a significant point of reference, we can then go on to examine some of those who came after Franklin, a series of young protagonists who try to establish their identities in the relatively fluid, unstable American world Franklin helped create. Because their stories, too, illuminate and are illuminated by the complexities of social change, they allow us to come to know the inner, human consequences of coming of age in the changing American world.

First, however, we must examine a few preliminaries. Franklin is closely associated with the American myth of openness, mobility, and possibility, of the prospect of rising through one's own character and ability from modest circumstances to wealth and fame. Intimately tied to the work ethic as it is with Franklin, this myth of success is also basic to the process of motivating and legitimizing control in America. Winners are justified; losers must take personal responsibility for their failure. Early in the nineteenth century, Tocqueville premises his argument on American openness and equality, but unlike Franklin he analyzes the unsettling psychological consequences, that "restlessness in the midst of prosperity," that ceaseless, never-satisfied striving he acutely diagnosed.[10] Integral to his diagnosis of the dilemmas of identity in America, Tocqueville assumes throughout *Democracy in America* a general equality and mobility of conditions. In one short, brilliant section, however, he outlines the threat manufacturing poses to this equality and mobility. For Tocqueville the very dynamics of democracy in the rest of the nation intensify the pressures toward aristocracy in manufacturing, since as people become more equal they provide a growing market for the cheap goods they can afford. The manufacturer thus becomes even wealthier,

10. *Democracy in America*, ed. Phillips Bradley, 2 vols. (New York: Vintage Books, 1945), 2:144–47. Subsequent references will be abbreviated DIA and cited by volume and page numbers in the text.

and the prospects attract other men of wealth, energy, and talent to open large concerns "and by a strict division of labor to meet the fresh demands which are made on all sides" (DIA, 2:170). Their workmen, however, become increasingly "weak," "narrow-minded," and "dependent" under the conditions of the division of labor (DIA, 2:169), so that "in proportion as the mass of the nation turns to democracy, that particular class which is engaged in manufactures becomes more aristocratic" (DIA, 2:170).

Because Tocqueville sees manufacturing as only a small part of the total society, he concludes that the tendency to aristocracy is "a monstrous exception in the general aspect of society" (DIA, 2:170). As that exception becomes more and more the rule, however, his analysis becomes more and more pertinent, as does his further observation that the masters in this system have no common ties to each other or to their workers, between whom and "the masters there are frequent relations but no real associations" (DIA, 2:171).

For Tocqueville the other major exception to the prevailing equality and mobility of American life is race. His unsparing analysis exposes the depth and the persistence of white racism in America (DIA, 1:343–452). With the important qualification of his acute views on race and manufacturing, however, Tocqueville and Franklin both accept American openness and equality of opportunity as a given, a belief that has been generally accepted throughout our history. That belief, however, can no longer be accepted unqualified. Stephen Thernstrom has carefully studied patterns of mobility in a nineteenth-century New England town. His influential findings are that working-class families, after a lifetime of labor, were often able to save enough to buy a house. This stake in society sustained the belief in American possibility and drained revolutionary pressures, but it is quite different from a rags to riches story, since a working-class person on Thernstrom's findings tended to end in the same class as he began.[11] Edward Pessen makes a convincing case that income distribution in the Jacksonian period was as skewed as William Miller found it to be in the post–Civil War period, with patterns of mobility similarly limited: working-class people tended to stay that way. Fortunes were made by middle- and upper-middle-class people who had a good start.[12] Gabriel Kolko analyzes the evidence from the

11. *Poverty and Progress: Social Mobility in a Nineteenth-Century City* (New York: Atheneum, 1972).

12. Edward Pessen, "The Egalitarian Myth and the American Social Reality: Wealth, Mobility, and Equality in the 'Era of the Common Man,'" in Edward Pessen, ed., *The Many-Faceted Jacksonian Era: New Interpretations* (Westport, Conn.: Greenwood Press, 1977), pp. 7–46, and William Miller, ed., *Men in Business: Essays on the Historical Role of the Entrepeneur* (Westport, Conn.: Greenwood Press, 1962), pp. 311–28.

start of the nineteenth century and concludes that the pattern of ine-quality has been remarkably constant throughout American history.[13] The discrepancy between the belief in openness, mobility, and equal opportunity and the presence of structural patterns contradicting this belief have consequences we will examine in discussing Franklin's *Autobiography*. In the meantime it is necessary simply to establish some of the evidence for the discrepancy and to suggest through Tocqueville on American restlessness, race, and manufacturing the possibility of a darker dynamic than Franklin's.

13. *Main Currents in Modern American History* (New York: Harper & Row, 1976), p. 341.

five

THE PRACTICE AND PRICE OF MOBILITY
The Market Society
and Franklin's *Autobiography*

In *The Autobiography* at the outset of his compelling success story, Franklin traces his family history in England. At sixty-five he is writing in full consciousness of his exemplary life, an awareness that often gives resonance to the understated anecdotes of the narrative. Franklin is already famous and he has already moved from Boston to Philadelphia to England and then back to Philadelphia, where he has prospered, and then back to England, where he traveled more than once as a negotiator for the Colonies. In 1771, when he is writing the first part of *The Autobiography*, he is again doing important work for the Colonies and is living in England, as he has for many years. The contrast with the lives of his ancestors is marked, since, as he learned from a record-keeping uncle, "they had lived in the same village, Ecton in Northamptonshire, on a freehold of about thirty acres, for at least three hundred years, and how much longer he knew not."[1] Franklin characteristically leaves the inner meaning unexplored but characteristically observes the practical details we are also interested in—that since the freehold did not supply a living, his family had become smiths. They had also become Protestants and his father and uncle had become Nonconformists, so that Franklin gives us a microcosm of a family rooted in the land, practicing a craft passed on from father to son, and especially open to those changes Puritanism responded to and intensified.

The process of change includes his father's decision to go to America, persuaded by "some considerable men of his acquaintence" to leave for reasons of religious freedom (A, p. 21). In the dynamics of his father's mobility, the impulses of Protestant individualism were thus balanced

---

1. *The Autobiography and Other Writings*, ed. L. Jesse Lemisch (New York: Signet, 1961), p. 17. Subsequent citations will be abbreviated A and cited by page number in the text.

by the supports of a settled community. New World conditions, however, accelerated change. Like his brothers, Josiah Franklin had been bred a dyer, but in America the demand was insufficient to support his family, and he became a tallow chandler and a soap boiler, setting a precedent for Benjamin Franklin's even more active mobility.

These external details about the family past are revealing because they flesh out our portrait of the shift from the family-based traditional world to the emerging New World. Because relations within the family, particularly between parents and children, are important indexes of the impact of social change, we must now take a close look at Franklin's characterization of his father and mother.

His portrait of his father is of a piece with the rest of *The Autobiography*. Franklin first efficiently sketches Josiah Franklin's external appearance—he had an excellent constitution, was strong, and was of middle height. In lively detail Franklin then lists his father's skills—his pleasing musical ability and his knowledge of mechanics, the latter qualified. At the center of this attempt to get us "to know what kind of man" his father was, Franklin stresses that "his great excellence was a sound understanding and a solid judgment in prudential matters, both in private and public affairs" (A, p. 24). As a result, his father was often consulted about personal and public matters, although his means did not allow him to devote himself to civic affairs. The sketch concludes with several lines on his father's interest in good, improving conversation at meals, so that "he turned our attention to what was good, just, and prudent in the conduct of life," not to the quality of the food. One practical result, Franklin points out, is that in traveling he has always been satisfied, whereas more cultivated friends are unsettled.

As a young man, Franklin had read Locke's *On the Human Understanding* and his account of his father, like much of *The Autobiography*, shows how deeply Franklin accepts the Lockean separation of subject and object. The virtues are admirable: a clear, precise description of some external traits, equivalent to weight and mass, but not traits intimately revealing of either Franklin or his father. Then the attention to skills, judgment, and prudence, not at all joyless but also revealing a marked indifference to whole areas of the inner life in this sketch of the kind of man his father was. The moral at the end is not necessarily Lockean and neither is the professed indifference to food, but they are part of the practical Franklin we know about from school and from Max Weber. Elsewhere in *The Autobiography*, Franklin handles the moral more humorously and also remembers after fifty years exactly what he ate on his trip to Philadelphia.

What is missing from the sketch and from *The Autobiography* is any sense of an intimate relation, of emotional give and take, of feelings flowing back and forth, of two people deeply in touch with each other. In the other great eighteenth-century autobiography, Rousseau's *Confessions*, father and son cry together, hold each other, talk to each other, share their grief and joy together. This emotional reciprocity is absent from the portrait and from *The Autobiography*, as is the sensitivity to states of feeling. Physical contact between people is also foreign to the sketch and to the world of Franklin's *Autobiography*. One strains his memory to recall a single instance of people touching each other, embracing each other, hitting each other. Franklin is not cold toward his father or others; he simply keeps his physical and emotional distance and keeps his own feelings under control. The range of feeling is thus restricted. Franklin does not allow himself to suggest anger, love, hatred, fear, deep admiration, resentment, joy, or any other feelings sons inevitably have about their fathers or that any of us have about those we are close to. For purposes of *The Autobiography*, these feelings do not exist.

Equally important, through the selection and patterning of details, Franklin creates a world in which intimate relations do not exist. The words "my father" establish a relation, but the amplifying details and the point of view are not designed to develop it. On the contrary, the details and the point of view present an objective picture, not so much of a father, a person we are closely related to, but of a man standing outside. The emphasis is thus on "the kind of man" in all the generality of that phrase, not on "my father." Franklin views this man intelligently, dispassionately, and fairly, and he focuses on those qualities that make for success and standing in the world. The word "private" as he uses it does not suggest the inwardness of a person or a family but is linked to "affairs," so that it simply applies to a different form of worldly activity.

Franklin gives an even briefer sketch of his mother immediately after the one of his father. It is equally detached. It also stands alone in that it gives no sense of a relation between husband and wife or mother and son, as if Abiah Franklin, like the paragraph on her, is a self-contained unit. The only recognition of a relation comes in the commonplaces of their tombstone inscription and the comment that "they lie buried together" (A, p. 25). It is revealing that, for purposes of his narrative, Franklin's parents come together only in the grave.

During his own lifetime, Franklin's worldly activity carried him well beyond his father, his mother, and the family he grew up in. The inevitable pressures, tensions, doubts, and strains of that journey, however, do not enter into Franklin's account because they do not accord with his sense of his life as a model for others to emulate. Implicitly, though,

Franklin does recognize the tensions of mobility, and he contains them through emotional restraint and emotional distancing, through his ability to keep his feelings under control and to allow only certain feelings to surface. Equally important, Franklin does not form close ties with family or friends. In an upwardly mobile world the strains of separation and success are lessened if the ties are weak and the acknowledged feelings moderate and somewhat distant.

The Franklin of *The Autobiography* is playful, often at his own expense, and he uses his narrative skill and his sense of humor as another, more attractive, way of containing, transforming, and moderating the tensions of relation and mobility. The ten-year-old Franklin, for example, disliked the tallow-making trade he was being trained for "and had a strong inclination to go to sea, but my father declared against it" (A, p. 23). Instead of developing the intensities of this classic conflict, Franklin shifts to his swimming ability and then gives a very fine anecdote about how, as a youthful leader, he and his playmates had gotten into a scrape building a small dam with stones taken while the workmen were away from a house they were putting up. In his handling of point of view throughout *The Autobiography*, Franklin establishes a sure sense of the famous adult looking back on another character, the younger Franklin, whose ties to the narrator are in some ways no closer than between either the young or the adult Franklin and Josiah and Abiah Franklin. In this instance the joke is on both the younger and the older Franklin, since the latter invokes his adult success and has fun with it by giving this example of "an early projecting public spirit, tho' not then justly conducted." The boys were caught, "several of us were corrected by our fathers, and tho' I demonstrated the utility of our work, mine convinced me that that which was not honest could not be truly useful" (A, pp. 23–24).

If he had explored the dispute with his father, who kept him from going to sea, Franklin might well have suggested a relation, an encounter involving strong feelings on both sides and an unequal contest the father wins, though Franklin does not become a tallow-maker, either. Instead, Franklin displaces the conflict into this amusing anecdote. Instead of personal revelation, Franklin plays on his Poor Richard values and engagingly establishes a moral. In one sense he is the butt of the joke and his father wins again, but, in another sense, through the assured tone and telling of the story, through the implicit reminder of his success and skill, Franklin also scores a kind of victory for the small boy who is now a talented and famous man. It is all very indirect: the conflict about going to sea has been thoroughly displaced and transformed, none of the feelings connected with either episode are at all suggested, and no sense of a relation with his father emerges, either. Franklin's famous vanity is satisfied, but the expression is so unpretentious, indirect, and amusing that it hardly appears to be vanity. Score one more for Franklin's humor and narrative skill.

Or take Franklin's dealings with his brother James. In order to make his own way, Franklin breaks his apprenticeship agreement with his brother, who from Franklin's point of view has been unfair, unfraternal, and even tyrannous. It is a classic example of the sort of conflict Laslett suggests: the domestic and economic roles are intertwined, pressures build and are attached to particular members of the family. In the New World, however, Franklin is not confined psychologically or geographically, and he eventually leaves for Philadelphia. For him the New World values of freedom and mobility prevail over the Old World traditions of family and settled apprenticeship obligations. Franklin gives a lively sense of his brother's anger and abuse, characteristically says nothing about his own feelings, and implicitly justifies himself through the picture of his brother's "harsh and tyrannical treatment," "a means," Franklin generalizes, "of impressing me with that aversion to arbitrary power that has stuck to me through my whole life" (A, p. 33). This admirable aversion, though, occupies the space that for others is filled with the satisfactions and strains of traditional and family ties, even of broken ties.

Franklin does develop the language of family relation once in *The Autobiography*. Several months after leaving for Philadelphia, he returned to Boston, showed off at his brother's shop, and deeply offended his brother. "For when my mother sometimes spoke to him of a reconciliation," Franklin writes, "and of her wish to see us on good terms together, and that we might live for the future as brothers, he said I had insulted him in such a manner before his people that he could never forget or forgive it. In this, however, he was mistaken" (A, p. 44). Franklin does not go into further detail about either his own or his brother's feelings or relations, so that this passage must stand as a reminder of suggested but unexplored possibilities. Franklin does to this limited extent respond to the old cohesive family values, values that seem to have been alive for his mother but that he elsewhere systematically filters out of *The Autobiography*.

In the elaborate, deadpan episode with Governor Keith, for example, Franklin confirms his initial portrait of his father. If he can get help from his father, Franklin tells us, the governor is going to back him in a printing business in Philadelphia, but Josiah Franklin sensibly observes that his son is "too young to be trusted with the management of an undertaking so important." Although he perceptively questions Governor Keith's discretion, Josiah Franklin is properly pleased that his son has been favored with such flattering attention from important people. For good reasons he nonetheless declines to back his son in this enterprise. The adult Franklin approves his father's judgment and is silent about the feelings of the young boy. What the successful narrator communicates is that business values take unquestioned precedence over domestic ones, which never even enter the picture, and that feelings of disappointment or hostility do not exist.

Although Franklin grew up the youngest of thirteen, in *The Autobiography* he never gives a developed sense of what it was like to be part of this large family. For Peter Laslett's baker's family, domestic and business relations were fused. What *The Autobiography* tells us is that family relations are those having to do exclusively with business. It is not that in practice Americans lack a sense of domestic intimacy. To the extent that *The Autobiography* has been influential in establishing a sense of what is right and proper, however, it gives no value status at all to the domestic. In Franklin's America the domestic is to that extent vulnerable, as is any important area of life that lacks the support and the sanction of a genuinely felt ideology. To fill that void, to assert the counter-claims of the domestic in a world where real power had been separated off into Franklin's masculine economic realm, several generations of nineteenth-century women and ministers created a counter-ideology of domesticity.[2] Following Franklin's lead, however, it is not surprising that later embodiments of the upwardly mobile hero are imagined as orphans, as having no families whatsoever. Horatio Alger thus omits even that important degree of family involvement Franklin recognizes, as if for Alger the rising youth must be almost totally self-created and not burdened at all by the involvements of family. The tragic consequences resonate throughout American society: Faulkner's Sutpen and Fitzgerald's Gatsby are two of the most telling imaginative results.

To return to *The Autobiography*, it is not surprising, either, that Franklin presents his wife as a helpful shop assistant. He first introduces her into the narrative in the famous passage on his first entrance into Philadelphia, poor, shabby, tired, and hungry. Before he leaves for England they exchange promises, but in England Franklin neglects Miss Read, "an erratum" he regrets (A, p. 56). To underscore his rise in the world, Franklin rounds off the first part of *The Autobiography* with a summarizing passage on his successful union. It is not, however, the romantic consummation of a poor boy who ends by marrying his beloved. In his brief treatment of both his courtship and his marriage, Franklin passes

2. Ann Douglas, *The Feminization of American Culture* (New York: Knopf, 1977).

over any sense of the more intimate or tender emotions in favor of practical observations on his business prospects and, at the end, on his business success. As with parents and family, a certain moderation and distance from his wife make practical sense for a man as mobile as Franklin, who, as he was writing, had already left his wife far behind in his rise to social success in England, with his conquest of France still to come.

Franklin, though, had other sides of his personality besides the ones he presents in *The Autobiography*. The Franklin of *The Autobiography* is a creation like Poor Richard or any of the guises Franklin assumed. The "real" Franklin, if we can identify such a figure from among his many masks, is more varied than the figure I have been commenting on. In England, he lived for many years with Mrs. Stevenson, and his "Craven Street Journal" to her shows a pleasant interest in food and in the other small details of domestic life and a comfortable affection for her, not necessarily intimate but playful and affectionate. Because the ghosts of D. H. Lawrence and Max Weber haunt any attempts to deal with Franklin and since *The Autobiography* confirms some of their outlook, I want to stress my sense that *The Autobiography* represents only a portion, although an influential one, of the total Franklin.[3]

To return to that influential portrait, although he avoids the nuances and complexities of feeling and relation in his treatment of his courtships and liaisons, in *The Autobiography* Franklin does acknowledge sex, that "hard-to-be-governed passion of youth" (A, p. 87). Franklin is not prudish, but he is not a sensitive prober of passion, either. When his friend Ralph had left his mistress in difficulty, Franklin helped her with money, "grew fond of her company, and being at this time under no religious restraint, and presuming on my importance to her, I attempted familiarities (another erratum), which she repulsed with a proper resentment" (A, p. 58). Franklin records no embarrassment, disappointment, or guilt at trying for the woman his best friend has been living with. He does not suggest the possibility of her being attractive to him partly

3. On Franklin's masks and skill at role playing, see John William Ward, "Who Was Benjamin Franklin?" *American Scholar* 32 (1963): 544, 546–53; David Levin, "The Autobiography of Benjamin Franklin: The Puritan Experimenter in Life and Art," *Yale Review* 53 (1964): 258–75; Robert F. Sayre, *The Examined Self: Benjamin Franklin, Henry Adams, Henry James* (Princeton University Press, 1964), pp. 20–31; John Griffith, "The Rhetoric of Franklin's 'Autobiography,'" *Criticism* 13 (1971): 77–94, and "Franklin's Sanity and the Man behind the Masks," in *The Oldest Revolutionary: Essays on Benjamin Franklin*, ed. J. A. Leo Lemay (Philadelphia: University of Pennsylvania Press, 1976), pp. 123-38; and Melvin H. Buxbaum, *Benjamin Franklin and the Zealous Presbyterians* (University Park: Pennsylvania State University Press, 1975), esp. pp. 1–46.

because she is the woman his best friend has been living with. He suggests no feelings or crosscurrents of feeling at all, nor does he stage a drama in which the ties of loyalty to a friend conflict with the appeals of an attractive woman. Instead, as he often does in *The Autobiography*, he presents himself as a fallible person who now recognizes his earlier errors and offers them as a corrective example, so that again in place of inner probing a sensible, prudential moral caps a lively anecdote.

As the episode unfolds, Franklin continues this technique and habit of mind and extends it to his friendship with Ralph, so that the episode is revealing about Franklin's attitude toward both love and friendship, the important ties beyond a person's immediate family. Franklin describes his own reaction when Ralph learns what he has done:

He let me know he considered all the obligations he had been under to me as annulled—from which I concluded I was never to expect his repaying the money I had lent him or that I had advanced for him. This, however, was of little consequence, as he was totally unable; and by the loss of his friendship, I found myself relieved of a heavy burden. (A, p. 58)

Without downplaying the importance of money or Franklin's alert sensitivity to it, we can observe that his account book balances neatly, "loss of friendship" in one column, "relieved of a heavy burden" in the other. The balance is easy because the involvement in friendship is unspecified and remote in contrast to the immediate and compelling claims of money. What is omitted from Franklin's ledger is a sense of what he has lost besides a financial burden, of what the friendship meant positively, of what ties of loyalty he has broken and lost. But to develop this sense would detract from the moral that we gain when we lose improvident friends and that as a result the ties of friendship should not be close. To develop fully the sense of friendship, moreover, would detract from the implicit function of ending the account on a note favorable to the narrator, of balancing Franklin's wrong, his betrayal of his friend, against his even more strongly emphasized gain.

Franklin had earlier given a variation on the theme of improvident friends in his account of his friendship with Collins. As young men in Boston they were "intimately acquainted" (A, p. 28), which for Franklin takes the form of their reading and debating together, an admirable, intelligent, but peculiarly limited definition of intimacy. At the outset of their careers they leave Boston for New York together, but in New York Collins changes, takes to drink, borrows money he cannot repay, and eventually leaves for the Barbadoes, "promising to remit me what he owed me out of the first money he should receive, but I never heard of him after" (A, p. 47). Collins, talented and a reader, was initially as promising as Franklin. His role in *The Autobiography* is to suggest that in an open world downward mobility is a real possibility and that in this world the ties of friendship, though they may unfortunately touch the pocketbook, should never touch the feelings or emotions.

The brief character sketches of his friends throughout *The Autobiography* implicitly develop this moral. Franklin does not completely avoid the language of affection, since his friends often "loved books," and since he says of another, for example, "he was a lover of punning and of his friends" (A, p. 73). Social qualities are important. Franklin consistently and perceptively focuses either on a person's social disposition, his good nature and friendliness, or on the intellectual qualities important to social life, on the "wit and humor" of one or the generosity and wit of another. In his account of the Junta, the organization he founded to promote intellectual, business, and political exchange, he deliberately gives two contrasting examples: the positive one of an able, good-natured man "of sensible conversation," the negative one of a brilliant, self-taught mathematician who, however, "was forever denying or distinguishing upon trifles to the disturbance of all conversation. He soon left us" (A, p. 72). Franklin typically and acutely notes a person's intelligence, intellectual interests, skills, and accomplishments, and also his social disposition. A good mind, however, does not compensate for an offensive manner, and a person whose drinking is too sociable does not come off well, either.

As he casts up his accounts of his friends, and the sketches are usually balanced like an account book, Franklin also attends to qualities of character important to success and failure in the world of affairs, to a person's honesty or laziness, for example; or he notes traits that fuse mind and character, as in "a solid, sensible man." A cool head, a good heart, exact morals, and a distinguished career are the traits that mark William Coleman, a friend of forty years and outstanding in each of the noted categories, which define Franklin's model (A, p. 73). In none of his character sketches, however, does Franklin ever respond to traits in such a way as to say, "The most remarkable thing about him was his sensitiveness, and his affectionate, loving nature. In his large blue eyes there was such a mixture of sweetness, tenderness, and melancholy that one had only to see him to be struck by him."[4] Cool, sensible, skillful, good-hearted, successful, witty—the virtues are admirably suited to a public and a social life that does not involve depth, intimacy, or intensity

---

4. *The Confessions of Jean-Jacques Rousseau*, trans. John M. Cohen (New York: Penguin, 1953), p. 118.

of personal relations. Because feelings of sympathy and sensitivity do not exist, because feelings of any sort are controlled and seldom if ever expressed, and because generosity and good-heartedness are balanced by a cool head, the emotional bonds are moderate and somewhat distant, so that just as they can be easily broken with a Collins or a Ralph they can be comfortably sustained with a William Coleman.

Helping to sustain those ties that do endure in a world of ambitious, upwardly mobile men is a system of mutual help, of favors given and returned. As Franklin puts it with characteristic understatement, "These friends were afterwards of great use to me, as I occasionally was to some of them. They all continued their regard for me as long as they lived" (A, p. 69).

In addition to these substantive issues, the habit of mind of the upwardly mobile tradesman and artisan also affects the composition and organization of *The Autobiography*. Franklin composed *The Autobiography* on sheets of paper divided into equal parts on the model of an account book. He composed on the right and gave himself ample provision on the left for corrections, afterthoughts, and additions.[5] Having invested in the main text, Franklin left room in his ledger to record the yield on that investment. As his revisions show, he profited handsomely. Like the accounts of a going concern, the overall organization of *The Autobiography*, especially of part one, combines order and flexibility. The book does not have a mechanical regularity, but it does have discernible patterns, often those of the account book in the local episodes of "this account of my life."[6] In the dynamics of Franklin's actual life, Paul W. Conner suggests that Franklin's experiences as a typesetter, with its emphasis on the precise placement and classification of letters and type, reinforced the business virtues of keeping and balancing accounts. Conner argues that Franklin went beyond business to invest in and reap the rewards of a career on the world stage of philosophy, science, and diplomacy. "In the latter role," Conner concludes, "he could function as a *political* entrepreneur—launching new undertakings, acting as a one-man brokerage house, and rationalizing the affairs of governance as a wise storekeeper would simplify and systemize his inventory."[7]

To return to the question of Franklin's tradesman friends, their mutu-

5. See the description of Franklin's manuscript in P. M. Zall, "A Portrait of the Autobiographer as an Old Artificer," in *The Oldest Revolutionary*, p. 54.

6. For insight into these organizing patterns, see Griffith, "The Rhetoric of Franklin's 'Autobiography,'" and Charles L. Sanford, "An American Pilgrim's Progress," *American Quarterly* 6 (1954): 297–310.

7. *Poor Richard's Politicks: Benjamin Franklin and His New American Order* (New York: Oxford, 1965), pp. 204–5.

al help, and their lifelong regard for him, in the case of the young
Franklin, this regard was also based on his very real intelligence, learning, and ability, on his good conversation and his skill as a printer, on
his diligence and promise. For both the rising and the established men
who met and liked him, Franklin was a friend worth having and helping. The important reasons of mutual benefit are only part of it. In an
upwardly mobile world, there are also intangible satisfactions in identi-
fying and helping a talented man with a future, the satisfactions of using
one's own skill and judgment to identify a promising newcomer and
then to watch and to help further his career.

Along with the liabilities and strains of mobility, there are, moreover,
the satisfactions and the excitement that still make Franklin's story compelling. In a story within his story, in the very rush, energy, and variety
of the details, Franklin communicates a sense of this exhilarating American promise and openness, of "Isaac Decow, the Surveyor-Gener-
al, . . . a shrewd, sagacious old man, who told me that he began for
himself when young by wheeling clay for the brickmakers, learned to
write after he was of age, carried the chain for surveyors, who taught
him surveying, and he had now by his industry acquired a good estate;
and says he, 'I forsee that you will soon work this man out of his
business and make a fortune in it at Philadelphia'" (A, p. 69).

An index of Franklin's involvement in the dynamics of growth and
success is his scathing satiric portrait of "the croaker," a man who tried
to discourage the young Franklin by prophesying that Philadelphia
would decline, that bankruptcies would increase, and that Franklin's
new business would fail along with the rest. Franklin points to the new
buildings going up, the general rise in rents and in prosperity over his
long lifetime, and for a change allows himself to show strong, unqualified negative feelings toward this man who represents the spirit of
defeat and gloom in a land of growth.

In Franklin's upwardly mobile world, the pattern we have noted of
emotional distancing and restraint toward others also characterizes
Franklin's relation to himself. In the most famous episode of *The Autobiography*, Franklin frames his first entry into Philadelphia by establishing his present fame and prosperity, "that you may in your mind com-
pare such unlikely beginnings with the figure I have since made there"
(A, p. 38). He then vividly sketches his working clothes and dirty outward appearance on that long ago, timeless day. Without commenting
on his emotional state he then notes, "I knew no soul, nor where to look
for lodging." He goes on immediately to establish his fatigue and hunger, that is, his physical sensations; and then, instead of suggesting his
inner feelings—depression? anticipation? fear?—he characteristically

presents his exact financial state, "a Dutch dollar and about a shilling in copper coin." He amplifies by telling of his gesture of paying for his passage though he did not have to, and, again, instead of analyzing himself, he gives a shrewd generalization applicable to any person. Although it applies to the young Franklin, too, the move is away from self-analysis or self-revelation. Franklin then gives the justly famous story of how he mistakenly bought the threepenny rolls, strolled with them under his arms up Market Street, gave two away, saw his future wife for the first time, and ended by attending a Quaker meeting and falling peacefully asleep there.

The story, with its memorable physical gestures and acts, establishes Franklin's poverty, inexperience, generosity, and his unselfconscious religious skepticism. The episode, which bodies forth an American myth, obviously speaks deeply to our fascination with poor boys rising in the world. It is significant that in Franklin's version and throughout *The Autobiography*, at every point where he might move inward to give a sense of his personal feelings or his state of mind, he gives either physical or financial descriptions or acute, impersonal universal truths. In particular he avoids acknowledging the negative feelings that often accompany displacement and mobility. To this extent his mythic portrait places a burden on those who have been compelled by it and who have experienced loneliness, anxiety, and depression, since these real but unacknowledged feelings are somehow illegitimate, somehow should not exist. Franklin, in contrast, is refreshingly open and relaxed about his religious feelings or lack of them.[8]

Franklin, moreover, views his younger self in a friendly but not intimate way. The emphasis on finances, physical sensations, physical appearance, and external actions to the exclusion of personal revelation or

8. Gladys Meyer, *Free Trade in Ideas: Aspects of American Liberalism Illustrated in Franklin's Philadelphia Career* (New York: Kings Crown Press, 1941), and Conner, *Poor Richard's Politicks*, pp. 211–18, are representative of those who believe as I do that Franklin minimizes a whole range of feelings. John Griffith challenges the idea that Franklin experienced strains and deliberately played them down. He argues that Franklin was remarkably free of conflict, and he makes the engaging case that "Franklin's sense of self can best be thought of as a species of mysticism—a kind of American work-ethic folk mysticism. It is mystical in just this one crucial point: it centers on an essential *loss of self* which derives from internal conflict" ("Franklin's Sanity and the Man behind the Masks," p. 132). If so, Franklin is a very special case. Griffith's lively essay does not speak to the issue of the results of Franklin's avoidance of a range of positive as well as negative feelings. Although he exaggerates, Buxbaum, *Benjamin Franklin and the Zealous Presbyterians*, establishes that Franklin had strong feelings, particularly about the Presbyterian religious establishment, and that he deliberately projects a moderate image of himself for both personal and national reasons.

the probing of inner feelings combines with the older narrator's handling of point of view to establish a cordial but not close relation between the older speaker and the younger self. The relation with the self, both with the younger and the contemporary version, is accordingly moderate, as if to become intimately immersed in one's personal depths might make for difficulties in the upwardly mobile world of affairs. The effect is similar throughout *The Autobiography*, since Franklin pervasively maintains a certain detachment from his younger self, whom he likes, tells jokes on, and manipulates. He has a similar friendly detachment from himself as narrator and from the people who fill the pages of his book.

The habit of mind of keeping a certain distance from one's own inwardness and the tendency to view the self with some detachment, even to the extent of creating another character, a younger version of the successful Benjamin Franklin—these related tendencies bear on an important pattern in American literature and society, a pattern of fragmentation and fragmented selves. In Franklin matters are harmonious and contained but in the nineteenth century, writers repeatedly explore the divisions and splits some of whose antecedents Franklin successfully integrates. Beyond Franklin this integration, though, proved vulnerable and unstable as the reifying pressures of the American market society intensified and the inner, human resources repeatedly proved unable to hold the self together.[9] Melville's "Bartleby, the Scrivener" and Hawthorne's "My Kinsman, Major Molineux," Twain's *Connecticut Yankee* and James's "The Jolly Corner" are thus part of a continuum that also includes Franklin's *Autobiography* and the market society it emerges from and illuminates. Some of the negative consequences of tendencies in *The Autobiography* appear in later works like "Bartleby" and "The Jolly Corner"; or, to put it differently, as the eighteenth-century Franklin synthesis breaks up, some of the negative consequences become apparent.

It is accordingly worth stressing the direct connection between Franklin's sense of the individual self and the kind of social, public world he assumes. In his character sketches, in his dramatized relations with his friends, in his treatment of himself, and in his explicitly formulated morality, Franklin responds to and slights precisely those qualities in the individual self that result in a public world where people are not tied closely together, where the contracts he carefully drew up with those he helped and invested in are very important, and where in place of sym-

---

9. On the process of reification in America, see the "Preface" of this work, and especially Carolyn Porter, *Seeing and Being: The Plight of the Participant Observer in Emerson, James, Adams, and Faulkner* (Middleton, Conn.: Wesleyan University Press, 1981), pp. 57–90.

pathy, which for Hume, Rousseau, and others gives society its cohesion, we have generosity modified by a cool judgment and the imperative to be "frugal," which according to Franklin's definition means not privation but to "make no expence but to do good to others or yourself; i.e., waste nothing" (A, p. 95).[10] As a cohesive force, contracts were important but underlying them Franklin knew that "truth, sincerity, and integrity in dealings between man and man were of the utmost importance" (A, p. 70). Because sympathy, love, and affection are absent, however, those dealings are at a certain distance and involve only a limited part of the man, which for Franklin, though, constitutes "man."

Franklin himself did "do good unto others." He was public spirited and devoted the last half of his life to public service. Gladys Meyer points out the utility of this involvement for an ambitious, rising tradesman who wanted to achieve social respectability.[11] But for Franklin a valued public world did exist. Like other Lockeans, Franklin saw the world in general as separate and distinct from the individual self. For him the public world in particular was an external forum within which men competed and performed for their own good and for the good of others. Franklin was actively, intelligently involved in that world, whose stabilities and structures he and men like him helped to erode. If we can use the word "community" to describe Franklin's public realm, then we must give the word a qualified meaning. The cohesive tendencies "community" usually suggests were supplied by the structures of eighteenth-century American society and were vulnerable to the very changes Franklin's market society necessitated. Ideologically, Franklin's view of society minimized close ties and cohesiveness. The mobility he celebrates further separates "man and man," so that Franklin contributes to a dynamic that helped destroy the balance he himself so commendably achieved.

Similarly, that Franklin could see himself with detachment and create his younger self as in some sense a separate character shows an ability that is related to his well-known capacity to play roles, to adopt guises, to wear masks, and to assume different identities. To go for a moment beyond *The Autobiography*, Franklin began his writing career at sixteen by assuming the name "Mrs. Silas Dogood," so that as a young city boy he played the role of a mature woman from the country. In the course of

10. Franklin's fortune was significantly based on his practice of setting people up in the printing business, sharing in the profits for a period of years, and then selling them the plant and equipment. As Franklin stresses in *The Autobiography*, carefully drawn contracts were the key to the success of this operation (pp. 109 and esp. 120–21).

11. "The Urban Pattern of Success," ed. Charles L. Sanford, *Benjamin Franklin and the American Character* (Boston: D.C. Heath, 1955), pp. 48–53.

his career he invented, along with the Franklin stove, bifocals, and the lightning rod, such public identities as Poor Richard and Dr. Franklin and such private identities as the author of "The Craven Street Journal" and the "Bagatelles," so that he ranges from the tradesman's sensible aphorist to respected statesman to domestic humorist to amorous flirt. Through it all he does not seem divided, fragmented, or insecure in his identity. He was an exceptionally mobile person and his skill at playing roles furthered his career. In the nineteenth and twentieth centuries, in contrast, social mobility, openness, and lack of stability often correlate with insecure and unstable personal identities. But Franklin seems always to know who he is and to speak with genuine assurance, his calculated use of "perhaps" notwithstanding. His world was open but still perhaps not all that open. He was perhaps the beneficiary of the very structures he helped erode. And he was perhaps also the beneficiary of the stabilities and rootedness of that family upbringing he chooses not to detail in *The Autobiography*. In any case, for Franklin the connection between social mobility and personal identity is qualitatively different than it is for significant nineteenth- and twentieth-century role players of an apparently similar sort.

Franklin's involvement in science and technology, moreover, helped to shape the immense changes America has experienced since his lifetime. It is not that Franklin's electrical discoveries somehow brought about Henry Adams's dynamo or that his invention of the Franklin stove and bifocals somehow caused modern technology. But Franklin's experimental habit of mind, his talent for defining solvable problems, and his desire for practical solutions all contributed to those transformations we are still experiencing. For Franklin, though, the scale was still small, as were the American cities he lived in. In his Boston and Philadelphia, the pace and tone of life were still pre-modern, were still not dominated by machine technology, and were closer to the London of Laslett's baker than they are to us. In his involvement in science and technology, too, Franklin himself thus benefited from structures his own dominant impulses helped alter beyond recognition.

Having ranged beyond *The Autobiography*, we should now return to observe that the Franklin we come to like in this book is not at all priggish or inhuman, partly because his handling of point of view allows him to tell jokes on himself. In the episode with Governor Keith, the most elaborate joke in *The Autobiography*, Franklin lets us know at the outset that the governor is unreliable, and then with perfect deadpan humor he puts the younger Franklin through his paces. He shows his younger self as talented, promising, and a little swell-headed at his recognition by a governor, the second time he has been singled out, though he is not even twenty. Along with the tongue-in-cheek satire, Franklin also establishes that his world is small and manageable enough so that a talented person, however poor, can come to the notice of those who count, particularly if he is well-read and articulate. This expectation remained part of the American myth of mobility and success long after the scale of American life had destroyed its basis in reality. As the episode unfolds, Franklin's pretensions are firmly put in their place—his father plays the role we have already noted—and the joke is on the young Franklin, who is left high and dry in London, having gone there on assurances of help that never had a real foundation. The moral, however, is not that ambitious boys should cautiously stay home, since Franklin makes the best of it in England, helps Mr. Denham by giving him the damaging letters Governor Keith has sent, and is helped by Mr. Denham in return, so that his career develops without loss of momentum. The moral is rather to remind us that bright, upwardly mobile boys, even when they are as smart and as shrewd as Franklin, are likely to be pretentious, to make mistakes of judgment, and that they need to be careful about trusting people, although Mr. Denham is there to remind us that not everyone is a Governor Keith. Human nature, that is, is fallible but not evil, so that one can safely rely on a mature sense of judgment and proportion. Franklin thus allows us to profit from his mistakes and setbacks as well as from his successes. But his success is never in doubt; the assured voice of the narrator guarantees that failure and reversals are at worst only temporary.

Throughout *The Autobiography*, Franklin is a similarly likable, persuasive figure, and his authority, prestige, and assurance are reassuring. They also intensify the problems of those readers who tried and failed, who undertook the risks of mobility and were more or less defeated, who expected openness and without realizing it encountered concealed and unacknowledged patterns of stratification or economic forces beyond their personal control. Because Franklin is so obviously intelligent, diligent, and successful, because he has so convincingly risen from modest circumstances to fame and prosperity, he helps create and validate that hegemonic myth of mobility and success that for Americans intensifies the burdens of failure.

In the explicit content of this myth, success depends on personal character, as Franklin's famous list of virtues makes clear. Industry is a notoriously important virtue. Franklin complicates, humanizes, and dramatizes matters by his personal example. "I took care not only to be in *reality* industrious and frugal," he writes, "but to avoid all *appearances* to the contrary." To make the point come alive, Franklin goes on to specifics. "I dressed plain and was seen at no places of idle diversion. I never went out a fishing or shooting; a book, indeed, sometimes debauched me from my work, but that was seldom, snug, and gave no scandal." In one of his most memorable images, he concludes by saying, "And to show that I was not above my business, I sometimes brought home the paper I purchased at the stores, thro' the streets on a wheelbarrow. Thus being esteemed an industrious, thriving, young man, and paying duly for what I bought the merchants who imported stationery solicited my custom; others proposed supplying me with books, and I went on swimmingly" (A, p. 79).

As this engaging passage makes clear, in Franklin's case, success is based not only on character traits, on frugality and industry, but also and even more importantly on his keen intelligence, dramatic sense, and sense of public relations. Anyone who tries hard enough can be frugal and industrious, and so it goes with the other moral traits success is supposedly based on: honesty, temperance, diligence, and the rest. But effort and will cannot give a person Franklin's keen mind and dramatic flair. In the ideology of success Franklin helped develop and popularize, however, the emphasis on character traits enforces the conclusion that a person is responsible for his own success or failure, that anyone who chooses to can practice the virtues that lead to success, and that success and failure are thus judgments on a person's character. To the considerable extent that intellect is also involved, the myth is misleading. The myth is similarly misleading to the extent that structural inequities also exist, that forces like economic depression or war are influential, and that mobility is in fact systematically limited. Readers of *The Autobiography* who have accepted personal responsibility for situations beyond their control are both recognizably American and recognizably vulnerable.

In the portraits throughout *The Autobiography*, Franklin balances intellectual, moral, and social traits, but in the ideology of success this balance is lacking. Similarly, in *The Autobiography* Franklin goes into detail about the political skills and connections that throughout his career led to his success or that threatened to damage his career when he was young and outspoken. Our contemporaries sometimes believe, perhaps cynically, that it is not what you know but who you know that counts. Franklin believed both were important. But, like intellect, having political skills and connections is not part of the ideology of success Franklin is associated with. These gaps between the Protestant ethic and the Franklin of *The Autobiography* suggest that Franklin has been selectively absorbed and that Poor Richard and the explicit portions of *The Autobiography* have taken precedence over more implicit ones.

To return to an important issue, in episode after episode of *The Auto-*

biography, Franklin implies that we should control our emotions and suppress our feelings, especially of hostility, disappointment, or joy. Such restraint makes sense in the kind of world Franklin creates, a market society in which people are mobile, exchange favors and use and help each other, and are subject to the uncertainties of trade. Restraint and the denial of feeling help to maintain proper relations with business associates, to break off ties with people who are liabilities, and to maintain that outer air of assurance that commands respect and credit. It is prudential to inhibit direct expressions of hostility against people one may need tomorrow, just as it is sensible not to feel too close or too pleased in case fortune changes. Forty years after the event, Franklin is still unwilling to express any of the anger he must have felt against Governor Keith, and there is no recognition of feelings of depression or worry, either. Upwardly mobile people need their energy for the next enterprise and they cannot afford to slack off. For some of them, emotional restraint and the denial of feelings can thus be a buffer against the demoralizing experience of loss or failure, although the accompanying feelings of resentment or depression can be consciously denied and still have profound effects.[12]

We thus return again to Franklin's relation to later probings of split or fragmented selves, since this denial of nonetheless real feeling is part of the context for works like "Bartleby, the Scrivener" or for Hawthorne's explorations of divided selves. The emphasis on emotional restraint and the denial of feeling have social and economic roots in the underlying processes of the market society. It is not merely an interesting or isolated psychological phenomena. Granted, Franklin himself is simply an important manifestation and transmitter of a widely shared tendency of the Protestant temperament and of the reifying processes of the market society. But Franklin's balance and success at containing and transmuting feeling provide a revealing point of reference, as do his basic commitments.

Throughout *The Autobiography*, an implicit moral is that to be as mobile and as successful as Franklin, to have as shrewd a grasp of people's minds and characters as Franklin, to be able to use people and that knowledge as efficiently and as usefully as Franklin, one had better keep his emotions separate, one had better be fair and friendly but essentially distant. The implicit threat of *The Autobiography* is that the price of success in the upwardly mobile world of affairs is a kind of emotional

12. For a full account of the psychology involved, see Philip Greven, *The Protestant Temperament: Patterns of Child-Rearing, Religious Experience, and the Self in Early America* (New York: Knopf, 1977), pp. 109–24.

deadening, an unwillingness or inability to engage deeply with oneself or with others. These involvements, the implied threat goes, are impractical because if one is to move, he cannot afford deep ties, he cannot spend his energies wastefully.

Even more immediate than the dangers of self-division and inner deadness, the threat is finally that isolation Tocqueville diagnosed, the isolation of Americans who have given up Franklin's public world, with its satisfactions and unstable ties, and have contented themselves with a circle of family and friends. But Franklin suggests how insecure this bond is, too, and Tocqueville himself pointedly observes, "Aristocracy had made a chain of all the members of the community, from the peasant to the king; democracy breaks that chain and severs every link of it." In the individualistic, restlessly competitive, nontraditional market society Tocqueville saw emerging, the final threat is that the American will be confined "entirely within the solitude of his own heart."[13]

Franklin himself was not isolated and was not emotionally dead or personally fragmented, but his *Autobiography* nonetheless poses these threats. The threats are implicit in the underlying psychology, social philosophy, and sense of relations Franklin brings to life in offering his own success and mobility as an example for his successors to emulate. Franklin had a genuine ability to live comfortably under conditions of emotional restraint, to keep a friendly distance from others, to avoid tenderness and intimacy, and to avoid as well personal depths and inwardness in himself and in others. He balances humor, intelligence, dramatic skill, political understanding, scientific common sense, and a superior writing ability to give us his remarkably vital life in *The Autobiography*. But the configuration of gifts that leads to this compelling achievement also has its latent dangers and instabilities, and they, too, are worth our attention.

13. *Democracy in America*, ed. Phillips Bradley, 2 vols. (New York: Vintage Books, 1945), 2:104–6.

six

SOCIAL CHANGE AND DIVIDED SELVES
"My Kinsman, Major Molineux"

Hawthorne's "My Kinsman, Major Molineux" (1828–1832) opens up the nighttime underside of Franklin's daylight, upwardly mobile world. Along with Dick Whittington's storybook entry into London to seek his fortune, Franklin's legendary entrance into Philadelphia helps frame and establish ironic contrasts for Robin's journey by ferry across a midnight river into a confusing provincial town and into the depths of the self and the emerging new order. That the story is set on the borderline between legend and history, dream and waking, old world and new world suggests further differences with Franklin's more one-dimensional outlook. Robin's "shrewdness" is a Yankee trait he shares with Franklin, and Robin's commonsense philosophy, equally satirized, also passes judgment on Franklin's market-society outlook. In particular, through the ironic ending of the story, Hawthorne deflates "Franklinian assurances about young men rising through self-help."[1] In Robin the pretentiousness Franklin occasionally exposed in himself becomes a dominant trait. As a character, moreover, Robin is unaware of some of his deepest unconscious tendencies. Through him Hawthorne suggests un-Franklin-like depths and complexities in the human personality and in American history. These divisions within the self and the market society involve a further, indirect link with Franklin.

Franklin is an appropriate but not exhaustive focus for a character who is presented less as an individual than as a legendary representa-

---

1. John P. McWilliams, Jr., "'Thorough-Going Democrat' and 'Modern Tory': Hawthorne and the Puritan Revolution of 1776," *Studies in Romanticism* 15 (1976): 570. Denis M. Murphy, "Poor Robin and Shrewd Ben: Hawthorne's Kinsman," *Studies in Short Fiction* 15 (1978): 185–90, stresses that Hawthorne inverts Franklin's *Autobiography* and "totally negates it" (190). But Murphy inconsistently affirms that at the end Robin is truly "shrewd" and will "rise in the world" (189). On the connection with Franklin, see also A. B. England's sensible "Robin Molineux and Young Ben Franklin: A Reconsideration," *Journal of American Studies* 6 (1972): 181–88, an essay that complicates Julian Smith, "Coming of Age in America: Young Ben Franklin and Robin Molineux," *American Quarterly* 17 (1965): 550–58.

tive of his country, young, vigorous, and seeking to make his fortune, to "rise in the world."[2] As in "Bartleby, the Scrivener," implicitly and pervasively Robin's inner divisions and dominant impulses are generated by his uneasy response to the emerging new America. In particular the basic reifying pressures of the emerging capitalism influence Robin's tendency to divide himself, to separate the conflicting sides of his personality into self-enclosed entities that have a seemingly independent life of their own unrelated to human activity. The opposing sides of Robin's self specifically embody the traditional world in conflict with the aggressive new society. That Robin is satirized as "shrewd" and philosophically limited is not surprising; that for an independent American he is remarkably demanding of deference for his upper-class family connections reveals that Hawthorne is unusually sensitive to the gentry version of the market society.

In the preface that frames the tale, Hawthorne refers with typically ironic understatement to the "temporary inflammation of the popular mind" (MK, p. 209) that characterizes the events of the story about a pre-Revolutionary uprising similar to the Boston Tea Party (1773) or the Stamp Act turmoil (1765), although Hawthorne places the events "not far from a hundred years ago," which would make it the late 1720s or early 1730s.[3] Although the dress and details of circumstantial realism are those of 1730, the handling of time suggests variously the sweep of the eighteenth century, the intersection of legend and history, and the absence of any particular, sharply defined time. Robin, then, must form his identity, make his career, and come into his maturity in this ongoing, in some sense timeless, milieu of Revolutionary confusion and upheaval. The ambience of ancient ritual, of the ceremonies of midsummer night's eve and the expulsion of the scapegoat king, furthers this sense of timelessness.[4] With Robin's identity, consciousness, and divided alle-

---

2. "My Kinsman, Major Molineux" in *The Snow-Image and Uncollected Tales*, ed. J. Donald Crowley (Columbus: Ohio State University Press, 1974), p. 231. Subsequent references will be abbreviated MK and cited by page number in the text.

3. Peter Shaw, "Fathers, Sons, and the Ambiguities of Revolution in 'My Kinsman, Major Molineux,'" *New England Quarterly* 49 (1976): 562–64, examines the affinities with the Stamp Act controversy and the Boston Tea Party, whose significance Roy Harvey Pearce first discussed in "Hawthorne and the Sense of the Past; or, The Immortality of Major Molineux," *ELH* 21 (1954), rpt. in Roy Harvey Pearce, *Historicism Once More* (Princeton University Press, 1969), pp. 137–46. Robert C. Grayson, "The New England Sources of 'My Kinsman, Major Molineux,'" *American Literature* 54 (1982): 545–59, shows that the details of dress and place are those of 1730 and probably derive from Caleb Snow's *History of Boston* (1825).

4. Daniel Hoffman, "Yankee Bumpkin and Scapegoat King," *Form and Fable in American Fiction* (New York: Oxford, 1961), pp. 113–25, and Shaw, "Fathers, Sons," particularly pp. 565–76.

giances at stake and with them as its focus, the story is structured around a conflict between old world and new world, between the old authority of the Crown and the established order of his kinsman and the emerging new power of America. In part the historical setting and events of the story generate important implications about the formation of the American national identity as America cut its ties with England, the parent country, and became America instead of the Colonies.[5] Frederick Crews, moreover, has shown how deeply Hawthorne suggests the unconscious tensions and dynamics of Oedipal conflict as a young boy rebels against authority figures and forms his own identity.[6] Roy Harvey Pearce has placed this Oedipal drama in historical context to show how Hawthorne has suggested that in forming a national identity America involved itself in the history of the race through an act of original sin, represented in the story by Robin's understandable but culpable denial of his kinsman, a majestic representative of the Crown shamefully humiliated and in need of Robin's sympathy.[7]

In addition to these significant dramas of private and national identity, the story also reveals Hawthorne's sense of the present. Hawthorne uses the pre-Revolutionary setting and conflicts to probe the inner experience of coming of age amid the possibilities and instabilities of the world he himself knew best, the changing world of the early nineteenth century.[8] That world can be experienced joyfully, as Whitman shows in poem after poem, but it can also be experienced as profoundly threatening, as a nightmare world of flux and confusion. In "My Kinsman, Major Molineux," Hawthorne responds to an "inflammation" that for him and for others was not at all "temporary."[9]

5. Q. D. Leavis, "Hawthorne as Poet," *Sewanee Review* 59 (1951): 198–205.

6. *The Sins of the Fathers: Hawthorne's Psychological Themes* (New York: Oxford, 1966), pp. 72–79.

7. "Hawthorne and the Sense of the Past," pp. 137–74, and "Robin Molineux on the Analyst's Couch: A Note on the Limits of Psychoanalytic Criticism," *Criticism* 1 (1959), rpt. in *Historicism Once More*, pp. 96–106.

8. "My Kinsman, Major Molineux" was first published in *The Token* in 1832, but Hawthorne probably wrote it in 1828 or 1829. Elizabeth L. Chandler, *A Study of the Sources of the Tales and Romances Written by Nathaniel Hawthorne Before 1853*, Smith College Studies in Modern Literature, no. 7 (1926), p. 55.

9. On the basis of the work of Q. D. Leavis and Roy Harvey Pearce, a major emphasis in the study of "My Kinsman, Major Molineux" has been to ground it historically in pre-Revolutionary America. See, e.g., James Duban, "Robins and Robinarchs in 'My Kinsman, Major Molineux,'" *Nineteenth-Century Fiction* 38 (1983): 271–88; Grayson, "The New England Sources," pp. 545–59; McWilliams, "'Thorough-Going Democrat,'" pp. 549–71; and Shaw, "Fathers, Sons," pp. 559–76. I am shifting the emphasis to a neglected historical dimension.

To intensify the sense of mystery and uncertainty, Hawthorne with-holds until well into the story the nominal reason for Robin's journey; that is, his journey to seek the help of his prosperous, well-placed rela-tive, a high official of the Crown who has indicated a willingness to give Robin a start in life. But from the outset, as Robin seeks a guide to his kinsman's dwelling, his chronic misinterpretations of the rebuffs he receives show that he is vain about his family connection and that he expects people to defer to him because of it. Robin is naive and inex-perienced but he is not "innocent." He is pretentiously full of class biases, so that the story does not really fit the formula of a journey from innocence to experience. Without knowing it, Robin has been intro-duced into a world in flux, a world that is changing and in which the old guidelines and certainties no longer count. His attempts to interpret this world in the old, customary way make him appear ridiculous, and, as his frustration mounts, so does his tendency toward that same violence the story culminates in. Early in the tale Robin is viewed more critically than sympathetically. As his confusion becomes increasingly desperate, however, the intensity of his suffering becomes a mitigating considera-tion.

In the new world people speak a language Robin cannot understand. The world is new to him because he has just entered it; it is new for us because it is opposed to the old, traditional world of the Crown and Major Molineux. The code language, the covert understandings, the sense of people in on a joke he is left out of all help to define for us the changing new world as it presents itself to some young, inexperienced newcomers. Similarly, as Robin fails to find a guide and as his own efforts prove increasingly ineffectual, the streets become increasingly labyrinthine, he gropes with increasing desperation through a dark maze, and the story takes us ever deeper into his consciousness. What is revealed, along with the powerful Freudian conflicts, is a sense of confu-sion and chaos, his inner experience of the troubled world in which he is unsuccessfully trying to find his way. Written at the uncertain outset rather than at the end of Hawthorne's own career, the story is not an American success story like Franklin's but is on the edges of a counter tradition, the American failure story. In the story Hawthorne is painfully sensitive to the inner experience of failure, and, although at the end Robin has his career ahead of him, Hawthorne has rendered those feel-ings of fear, bafflement, and hate that are connected with failure and that Franklin chooses to suppress.

As the story progresses, deep in his mind Robin can no longer distin-guish between dream and waking, between inner and outer reality. Near the depths of his disorientation, his old certainties and his very identity shaken to their foundations, Robin looks into a deserted church. Instead of finding the consolations of his inherited religion, Robin sees the Bible illuminated by "one solitary ray" of a moonbeam, and the negative side of his religious heritage predominates: was the "heavenly light the visible sanctity of the place" and did it appear only because sinful, impure men were absent? The coldness of this outlook further depresses Robin, who knows a "loneliness" deeper than any he has ever experienced (MK, p. 222). He feels cut off from a sustaining God and alone in his unprotected sinfulness. In one short, moving scene Hawthorne suggests an important strain in the history of the erosion of religious belief in New England. The original Puritan synthesis of a conviction of original sin balanced by a faith in a God who would redeem the elect is no longer effective. For Hawthorne early in the nineteenth century, what remains is a sense of sin without the belief in a redeeming God, a consequence of social and intellectual changes that deeply affect the consciousness of Robin Molineux.

In his shaken, alienated frame of mind, Robin then imagines or wishes the death of the kinsman he has been searching for, that embodiment of the securities and stabilities of the old order Robin seems both to desire and to abhor. Disturbed, he attempts to comfort himself with an idyllic vision of his own home. He imagines a cohesive religious ceremony presided over by his father and joining together his father, mother, brothers, and sisters in one community with God. Robin, however, is totally excluded. Like Tocqueville's American, he is completely alone in the world, but not only is he cut off from the supports of his family, as in Tocqueville, but also he is separated from God. His confusion intensifies and becomes almost unbearable. In contrast to Franklin and with more emotional power than Tocqueville, Hawthorne suggests the complexities and the pain of separation for the young American who cuts his ties with home and strikes out on his own.

The inner and outer discord intensifies as the mob comes closer and closer with the tarred and feathered Major Molineux, although this knowledge is hidden, separated, from Robin's conscious awareness. "The shouts, the laughter, and the tuneless bray" (MK, p. 227) embody the demonic impulses of chaos and hate, ironically at odds with the church that is the public focus of the mob that "came rolling slowly towards" it (MK, p. 227). The red glare of the torches, the "vomiting" of the "fearful wind instruments," and above all the horseman, his phallic sword raised and his face divided, part red, part black, further develop the sense of primal, demonic chaos and disorder. Quite literally and whatever their other meanings, the "rioters," the discord, and the menacing horseman represent the emerging new order of America as it presents itself to Robin's confused and divided consciousness.

Robin is a young man whose early identity and expectations were formed on the traditional model. His clergyman father and especially his kinsman, his father's cousin and, in the story, his father's substitute, embody that traditional world. Robin, however, is also attracted by the man with the parti-colored face. Robin "felt a sort of brotherhood" (MK, p. 213) with the innocent countrymen in the tavern, but unconsciously he feels powerfully related to the demonic man with the grotesque visage and horns. Robin is pulled and repelled by both the leaders of the old and new orders. He is in some sense related to both. Part of what is at stake in the story is how Robin will resolve his identity, which of these conflicting authority figures he will choose, which side of his own divided identity will predominate, which "kinsman," which relation he will affirm.

Major Molineux, for his part, is associated with rank, privilege, and established wealth, with fixed position and the constituted, established authority of the Crown and the old, aristocratic order in which family is important and in which Robin's way would be smoothed.[10] He is rooted in that traditional world Laslett and Tocqueville invoke, a world whose shortcomings Hawthorne is not concerned to suggest. For both Laslett and Tocqueville, the father is especially important, and Tocqueville in particular speaks authoritatively about the role of the father in a traditional aristocracy. He writes,

The father is the natural and necessary tie between the past and the present, the link by which the ends of these two chains are connected.In aristocracies, then, the father is not only the civil head of the family, but the organ of its traditions, the expounder of its customs, the arbiter of its manners. He is listened to with deference, he is addressed with respect, and the love that is felt for him is always tempered with fear.[11]

In responding with more fear than love, in cutting his ties with the old, traditional world, and in rejecting his father or his father surrogate, his kinsman, Major Molineux, Robin is on his way to becoming a new man. At great cost he is becoming an American aligned with the emerging new world, not with the settled old world of his kinsman. That chaos and disorder are at the center of his experience, however, says as much about his initial expectations and outlook as about the outside world. In every generation, Americans with traditional expectations have been disturbed, threatened, and attracted by the fluidity around

10. Duban, "Robins and Robinarchs," pp. 271–88, connects this society of deference and patronage specifically with "Robin" Walpole and with policies that provoked the Revolution.

11. *Democracy in America*, ed. Phillips Bradley, 2 vols. (New York: Vintage Books, 1945), 2:204.

them. Henry Adams is only the most eloquent example. In the Jacksonian period, people who viewed the flux and change of their society through the lenses of eighteenth-century expectations of stability found their America especially chaotic and disorderly. Robin Molineux's experience is a powerful metaphor for their experience.[12]

Robin is divided in his situation, allegiances, and consciousness. The facts of his external situation, a young man related to the old order but living in the new land, provide in part the matrix for his inner divisions. Robin's external situation does not account for the split, the barrier, between his conscious and unconscious motives and responses as they bear on the primal Oedipal drama he acts out. But his situation does condition his inner torment, his experience of dislocation and chaos, and his very need to choose, to form a new identity instead of developing in the traditional way and instead of rising in the world with the help of his kinsman, Major Molineux, to paraphrase the suggestive ending of the tale.

In the dream logic of the story, characters and events have an external reality even as they in some sense emerge from and illuminate the depths of Robin's consciousness.[13] The leader of the uprising, the grotesque man with the split face and horns, is the most powerful embodiment of Robin's inner experience of his divided allegiances and divided consciousness, the most powerful embodiment of the story's preoccupation with splits and fragmentation and their inner consequences. This American patriot, the embodiment of the energies, authority, and power of the new world, is for Robin demonic, divided, and threatening. With his horns, his fierce colors, his tumult, his phallic sword, and his association with both Satan and Dionysus, "the Good Creature" (MK, p. 212), he suggests Robin's fear of and fascination with masculine sexual power. But even more significantly, he also suggests the connection of this masculine force with the energies of America itself, about which Robin is similarly ambivalent. For Robin, this power is grotesque, repulsive, and compelling. That the animating energies of the new nation also should be seen as deformed and destructive poses a serious problem both for the changing nation and for Robin. Among the complex implications of the divided face, moreover, are the suggestions of fragmentation, of splits, of that absence of cohesion and order the old

12. On the impact of eighteenth-century expectations on the Jacksonian response, see David Rothman, *The Discovery of the Asylum: Social Order and Disorder in the New Republic* (Boston: Little, Brown, 1971), pp. 69–70.

13. See Rita K. Gollin's treatment of the dreamstate in "My Kinsman, Major Molineux," in *Nathaniel Hawthorne and the Truth of Dreams* (Baton Rouge: Louisiana University Press, 1979), pp. 115–23.

world traditionally represents and that in this embodiment the new world conspicuously lacks. The hostility of this fierce man, moreover, answers to and is an intensified version of Robin's own hostility, as is his threatening manner. In the contest between old world and new world, the recourse to club or sword to settle disputes further comments on an American tendency, although Robin is unaware of it or of the way it relates him to the grotesque stranger. Through the parti-colored man and the "rioters" he leads, finally, the entire process of social change is pictured as violent and cruel, as threatening and callously disruptive, as both vital and deadly. At the end, although he has rejected the old order and joined himself to the new, it is no wonder that Robin feels apprehensive about rising in such a world, on his own and without the help of his kinsman.

On the testimony of later writers, that career may be as flowing and as alive as the journey of Whitman's child "who went forth every day, and who now goes, and will always go forth every day." But it could also take the maimed, powerful form Henry James imagined in "The Jolly Corner," one of the sequels to "My Kinsman, Major Molineux." For part of Hawthorne's achievement in this story is to have explored for the first time in American literature a set of themes and insights about his country that some of the deepest of his successors were to rediscover and elaborate on their own.[14]

Hawthorne's sensitivity to the connection between sexual energy and American power, and his sense of that power as grotesque, deadly, and compelling, is one theme whose persistence until the end of the century in the works of James and Adams suggests something disturbing about American masculine energy and the dynamos and changes it drove. For Adams, the American man had his hands on the throttle of the machine and restlessly, like his predecessor in Tocqueville, wanted to go sixty, seventy, eighty miles an hour. The Virgin represents the animating power of the twelfth century. She is both fully generative and powerfully spiritual; the separation of the two realms does not exist for her. The dynamo embodies not fecund, female occult power but the mysterious force associated with the modern masculine world of science, machines, and technology. For Adams, the terrible dilemma for the American woman is to remain powerless but generative or to become modern, to join the men who have abandoned her for their work, and to gain

___

14. Roy Harvey Pearce first traced from "My Kinsman, Major Molineux" on what "we may call the Molineux theme [:] . . . that guilt and righteousness are . . . imputed to us through our history ("Hawthorne and the Sense of the Past," pp. 173–74). My thinking has been stimulated by and departs from Pearce's essay.

power by becoming as mechanical, desexualized, and restless as the American man.

Adams's insights on this count complement Melville's in "The Paradise of Bachelors and the Tartarus of Maids" (1855), in which the entire sexual economy is rigidly fragmented and twisted. The men and especially the male-like machines with their cruelly raised swords and iron plungers dominate Melville's factory world and dehumanize and desexualize the women who serve the machines. For Melville, who goes even beyond Hawthorne and Adams, the processes of industrial capitalism deform our very sexuality and thereby warp humanity at its roots.

Ann Douglas's ministers and women writers responded to their loss of power, their exclusion from the masculine realm of business, industry, and authority, and they created an ideology of domesticity. This ideology emerged from and reflected on a basic split that developed in American society during the nineteenth century, a division that excluded women and ministers from real influence on practical affairs. Reacting primarily against the underlying causes of this split but also against the ideology and the genteel culture the ministers and women authors created, a series of male writers as different, perceptive, and significant as Hawthorne, Melville, James, and Adams shaped their own deep responses.

These authors all agree that masculine sexual power coincides with American power, which they see as simultaneously deformed, warped, vital, and fatal. In their daring, they challenge the deepest taboos of their culture, with its emphasis on sexual reticence, progress, and patriotism, the first closely associated with the new ideology of domesticity. In their daring and imaginative power, moreover, they give a telling criticism of the entire process and impact of social change, which for them threatens the very source of life itself, even as they respond to the fierce energy and vitality of the parti-colored men and maimed alter egos embodying the drive and the restlessness of the emerging market society. Part of the legacy of "My Kinsman, Major Molineux" is thus the unresolved paradox of American vitality inseparable from destruction.

In "My Kinsman, Major Molineux," as in different ways in the works of Melville and James, but earlier than either of them, Hawthorne also responds to the market society's reifying tendency to fragment selves and relations and in a changing or upwardly mobile world to cut people off from each other, their families, and their own personal depths, leaving people, especially the young, divided, isolated, and on their own. The maimed alter ego and divided self in "The Jolly Corner" and the tormented, divided world of "The Paradise of Bachelors and the Tartarus of Maids" are powerful, later versions. In *The Education*, Adams also develops the related themes of inner and social fragmentation and divisive social change. He stresses the image of the railroad cutting his life and the century in two, a suggestive metaphor for the impact of social and technological change and one the remainder of *The Education* confirms. Adams structures his opening chapters around a series of symbolic divisions between Quincy and Boston, between Boston and Mount Vernon, and among the conflicting roles within him of his seventeenth, eighteenth, and nineteenth-century legacies to dramatize his sense of personal division in a rapidly changing nation in which he is excluded from the power of his ancestors, even as he diagnoses his countrymen's isolation from history and each other. In *The Education*, these insights are only intermittently though tellingly linked with Adams's sense of American sexuality.

Like his successors, Hawthorne fuses his own insights into fragmentation and isolation with his sense of American power and masculine sexual energy. He goes beyond his successors, however, by locating these basic tendencies at our national origins. Like later writers, he associates these tendencies with a violent process of social change. Hawthorne was not the first to explore the divided self in America— Charles Brockden Brown's *Wieland* is earlier—but Hawthorne was the first to develop a configuration of concerns; that is, he was the first to develop a view of masculine sexual power inseparable from American power and a deep awareness of personal and social fragmentation, all in a context of profound and often violent social change.

He shows that the consequences are deep and far-reaching for the identity and consciousness of those who cut their ties with home and family and make their way alone in such a world. This holds especially for those who come to that changing world with traditional expectations, another theme that Hawthorne pioneered and that Henry Adams developed. In a variation on this theme, which Hawthorne did not originate but handles well, the naive protagonist is viewed satirically or humorously and is the butt of jokes and ridicule, in a tradition that ranges from Franklin's *Autobiography* to the deadpan antics of Mark Twain, with stops throughout the works of the Southwest humorists. For the protagonist in versions like Hawthorne's, the joke is always painful and the "merriment" is "like a funny inscription on a tombstone" (MK, p. 230).

Tocqueville, we have seen, was in on the joke, at least to the extent of deeply sharing with Hawthorne an awareness of the American tendency to cut people off from their origins, from their contemporaries, and from the ties of a settled order and to expose them to the pressures of isolation. It is an interesting historical coincidence that between 1831 and 1832

Tocqueville was forming his impressions of America at almost the same time Hawthorne was writing "My Kinsman, Major Molineux." Because the organizing principle of a tension between aristocracy and democracy informs both *Democracy in America* and Hawthorne's story, some of the differences are worth stressing, particularly Hawthorne's deeper psychological awareness. Hawthorne is able to see the impact on the depths of the self of the changing market society he and Tocqueville both respond to. They both see its fragmenting, divisive tendencies, but Hawthorne shows the deep effects on personal identity, including the strains and torments of inner division. Unlike the more analytical Tocqueville, Hawthorne as imaginative artist is also able to break through into the forbidden territory of sexuality and American power and, in exploring it, to release insights and imaginative energy that have had few equals in our literature.

seven

COHESIVE ALTERNATIVES AND
THE FEAR OF ISOLATION
Early Whitman and Market-Society Change

Franklin contains even as he contributes to the divisive energies of an emerging American market society. Hawthorne and his successors explore the fragmenting power and the darker depths of this developing hegemony. Whitman provides an indispensable alternative, a sustained attempt to counter the divisive pressures of market-society change by penetrating to residual and oppositional sources of cohesive energy. Instead of the divided selves the market society generates, Whitman affirms an unconventional coherence that fuses what we customarily separate. In "Song of Myself" and "Crossing Brooklyn Ferry," sex is the subversively unifying power. But even when his emphasis is elsewhere, as in a deceptively simple early poem like "There Was a Child Went Forth" (1855), Whitman brings together the growing child, the world of nature, and the market-society energies and change we associate with Franklin, the "men and women crowding fast in the streets," the "goods in the windows, / Vehicles, teams, the heavy-planked wharves."[1] In a way that is worth close attention, Whitman goes beyond Franklin and connects this world of goods and movement with the life of a precisely observed universe of growing plants, fish, animals, and men and women. Whitman's synthesis of the changing American market society and American nature has latent strains—they appear clearly in "Crossing Brooklyn Ferry"—but they do not detract from the importance of his achievement. Franklin's Lockean, market-society separation of subject and object, of human beings and their world is significantly altered because of Whitman's sense of the cohesion between the growing child and his equally vital natural surroundings. Even in "There Was a Child

1. Quotations from "There Was a Child Went Forth" are from *Leaves of Grass: Facsimile Edition of the 1860 Text*, ed. Roy Harvey Pearce (Ithaca: Cornell University Press, 1961), pp. 221–23.

Went Forth," Whitman is revealingly American, however, because for him the relation between people, the character of the social world itself, lacks this assured sense of cohesion. In other respects Whitman imagines cohesive alternatives to the prevailing separations. He opposes the dominant-class hegemony of Franklin's successors. At the same time, unlike Hawthorne's Robin Molineux, for Whitman's representative child American change and impermanence are finally a challenge, not a threat. But even Whitman has to an extent interiorized market-society tendencies he both resists and sensitively registers at the center of his work.

Like Robin Molineux, the child of Whitman's poem enters an open, changing world, and under the pressure of a representative American father he experiences "the doubts of day-time and the doubts of night-time." But "the doubts of night-time" notwithstanding, it is predominantly a daylight world, and he "went forth" into it "every day." Whitman has an astonishing ability to convey the child's immediate experience, to put himself into that early phase when "the first object he looked upon . . . that object he became, / And that object became part of him." Throughout the poem these objects are alive and often suggest birth. "The sow's pink-faint litter, and the mare's foal, and the cow's calf" are no more or less vital than the growing plants or the child or the "vehicles, teams, the heavy-planked wharves." For Whitman, the vitality and movement of the American material and social world are integral with the processes of natural growth. All enter into the formation of the child's self. Like "the fish suspending themselves so curiously below there" and like the child who absorbs and goes forth every day, because the plants, animals, and "the goods in the windows" are part of a vital process, they are not objectified things or commodities. The reciprocal process Whitman brings alive is an alternative to the reifying process of commodity production and exchange through which all relations "take on the character of a thing and thus acquire a 'phantom objectivity,' an autonomy that seems so strictly rational and all-embracing as to conceal every trace of its fundamental nature: the relation between people."[2]

In contrast, as much as the structure of American English will allow, from the start of the poem Whitman uses the resources of rhythm and sense to convey an impression of reciprocity and harmonious, cyclical growth rather than of compartmentalized segments and divisive change. In the 1860 version of the poem, he underscores his un-reified, un-Lockean view by naming what are for him the basic human feelings

2. George Lukacs, *History and Class Consciousness* (Cambridge: MIT Press, 1971), p. 83.

of "wonder, pity, love, or dread." Because of his human capacity to feel sympathy and dread, the basic cohesive emotions, the child is intimately tied to the objects he perceives, that he "looked upon and received." Unlike the typical market-society self, he is at home in a world that enters into him even as he flows into the world. This world has mystery without being mystified. The objects in the child's experience come predominantly from the world of farm, countryside, and seashore. In the poem the natural world has been cultivated and domesticated, but it is not tame. Whitman responds to the American land and landscape as life-giving, not as property or possessions to be bought and sold in a process of commodity exchange.

The temporal order in the poem is accordingly not the linear regularity of a market society governed by the segmented units of clock time. Whitman responds to the natural rhythms of plant, animal, and human growth and the natural rhythms of the day, of the seasons, and of even larger natural cycles. Instead of giving us a world of linear progressions, Whitman feels free to move back and forth between larger and smaller units of time, all within an emerging process of coherence. His sense of growth and development is perfectly compatible with this move from the start of day to the larger rhythms of "the stretching cycles of years" and then back in detail to the early spring of the year, followed by the growth of late spring. The poem concludes with an enlarged sense of the ending of day and the promise of more to follow. Just as his view of the graceful heads of the water-plants minimizes the separation between plants, animals and human beings, Whitman's handling of time makes the ordinary divisions fluid. Whitman uses the temporal pattern of the poem to convey a sense of flow and relation, not of rigid, market-society divisions. He achieves a similar effect through his use of parallel structure and reliance on the word *and* as a connective, often in a position of emphasis at the start of lines and reinforced by repetition within the line. *And* establishes a relation of equality among the diverse objects the child observes and that "became part of him." Some may be larger or smaller or more or less respectable, as with the drunkard and the school-mistress, but the linking word *and*, together with Whitman's tone of acceptance, makes them all equal. The recurring parallel structure is the appropriate vehicle for his view of life, particularly since Whitman varies the structure to suggest irregularity within an overall pattern of equality.

In poems like "Song of Myself" and "Crossing Brooklyn Ferry," the animating, disruptive, and unifying energies of sex are at the center of Whitman's vision, complicating and subverting market-society complacencies. Whitman is more conventionally acceptable in "There Was a Child Went Forth," but even in the pastoral sections of this poem he quietly subverts the nominal egalitarianism the dominant society professes but does not practice. The lilacs and the "sow's pink-faint litter," the apple tree and the weed are of equal value, the ordinarily despised pig as lively on this imaginatively and linguistically enlivened view as the morning glories and the apple-blossoms. And human beings of every social rank are also equal to the lowliest weed and to each other as they enter into the experience, the vision, of the growing, sympathetic child. The juxtaposition of "the commonest weeds by the road; / And the old drunkard staggering home from the out- / house of the tavern, . . . / And the schoolmistress that passed on her way to the / school" plays on and subverts the conventional hierarchies and evaluations. The drunkard and the weed have in common their lowly status, but the drunkard, the human being, is also intimately related to the natural world; he is not alienated from it and is neither superior nor inferior to the weed or the apple tree, at least on the view of the poem and the child. Similarly, the schoolmistress and the school are of equal value with the drunkard and the outhouse of the tavern, neither higher nor lower. Since drunkards and tavern outhouses are usually thought of as ugly, the perception is not an easy exercise in nostalgia but an affirmation of human equality and natural values in the face of social custom.

This turn on the customary social evaluation raises the larger question of the relation between Whitman's sense of equality and the fact and value of equality in the surrounding American social world. The radical vision of the poem, its quiet, basic insistence on equality and relation, not on hierarchy and separation, has no precedents in European literature, partly because the hierarchical character of European culture was not a likely setting for a vision as deeply egalitarian as Whitman's. Whitman's vision both extends and requires the relative openness and equality of the American social world. Whitman could not have achieved his sense of equality and process without his experience of America, but as his upsetting of the ordinary view of the drunkard and the schoolmistress suggests, Whitman goes beyond social fact in creating his myth of an egalitarian world. He thus gives a suggestive life to a central value his market society proclaims but systematically violates. Even at this early stage in his career and in this gentle, affirmative poem, Whitman as a social critic brings his society to the test of its own professed values.

In Whitman's version of the child's developing identity, his experience of the growth and movement of nature is followed by "all the changes of city and country," his experience of the changing American social world. Only now does the child's mother appear, as a source of warmth and assurance, "at home" and nurturing, not outside and competing. Like the schoolmistress, the children, and the drunkard, she is in harmony with the natural world that has thus far gone into the making of the child. This flowing harmony prevails until the father appears. Whitman delays the appearance of the child's parents until the middle of the poem. By altering the natural chronology of impressions—the parents in fact come first in the child's experience—Whitman dramatizes through contrast the father's disruptive impact.

"The father, strong, self-sufficient, manly," embodies the energies of self-reliant American masculinity. He is not Hawthorne's parti-colored man, but he is nonetheless shown as "mean, angered, unjust, / The blow, the quick loud word," so that for the child, his father is connected with angry irritability and arbitrary discipline. The manly, self-sufficient father is also associated with more public qualities, with "the tight bargain, the crafty lure" of market-society competitiveness, as well as with "the family usages, the language, the company, the furniture," a mixture of valued and devalued qualities that intensifies the child's ambivalence and speaks to "the yearning and swelling heart, / Affection that will not be gainsaid."

The child's experience of his very American father generates the central tension of the poem, the sense of uncertainty the remainder of the poem must somehow deal with,

> The sense of what is real—the thought if, after all, it should prove unreal,
> The doubts of day-time and the doubts of night-time—the curious whether and how,
> Whether that which appears so is so, or is it all flashes and specks?
> Men and women crowding fast in the streets—if they are not flashes and specks, what are they?

At the center of the poem, the child thus responds to the threat of impermanence, to the possibility that men, women, and the entire surrounding world of natural and man-made objects may simply be transitory and illusory and that his own life may be similarly impermanent. The child's disturbed experience of his father causes disturbances in his entire view of the universe, since his primary source of security and meaning is troubled and unsettled. It is not simply an exercise in individual psychology, however, since the father is a main vehicle for transmitting a masculine, self-reliant market society to the growing child. The child of the poem is more than a passive receiver, however, and because he resists these influences he experiences a crucial sense of ontological doubt inseparable from the fluidity of his American market society and his resistance to some of that society's dominant tendencies.[3]

At the center of "There Was a Child Went Forth," Whitman thus gives sensitive testimony to some of the possible consequences of forming an identity in America. His brief sketch of the father and the child's response, moreover, provides insight into inner areas of the self that do not exist in Benjamin Franklin's world. The sketch also reveals the impact of that world on a child less accepting of it than Franklin himself, and in this sense it relates to Hawthorne's treatment of several young protagonists, including Young Goodman Brown and Robin Molineux. These characters similarly experience a troubled relation with the father-figures who embody the received values of a changing American market society.

Unlike Hawthorne's Young Goodman Brown, however, the child of Whitman's poem is not overwhelmed by his doubts. Whitman immediately invokes the solid realities of American movement and materialism,

> The streets themselves, and the facades of houses, and goods in the
> windows,
> Vehicles, teams, the heavy-planked wharves.

The structure prepares us to expect a repetition of the earlier question, "If they are not flashes and specks, what are they?" Whitman never explicitly answers this question, but he does not raise it again, either. Instead, he lets the very solidity and vitality of this urban scene suggest not the impermanence and illusion of "flashes and specks" but a reli-

---

3. For alternative views, see Edwin H. Miller, *Walt Whitman's Poetry: A Psychological Journey* (Boston: Houghton Mifflin, 1968), pp. 24–40; E. Fred Carlisle, *The Uncertain Self: Whitman's Drama of Identity* (Lansing: University of Michigan Press, 1973), pp. 98–100; and Howard J. Waskow, *Whitman's Explorations in Form* (University of Chicago Press, 1966), pp. 129–34.

These representative critics write as if form and personal identity had nothing to do with the dynamics of the American market society. Form then becomes a reified technical exercise. Similarly, in treating the self in isolation from the socially complex processes of identity formation, critics participate in the privatizing tendencies of the dominant society. Multiplied by the thousands of essays on American works similarly abstracted from the American market society, Whitman's critics define a recognizable tendency. The received criticism of American literature is not so much de-natured as it is politically sanitized. Even a scholar like Jerome Loving, who has documented the central role of politics in the foreground of Whitman's life, defines politics narrowly and filters politics in the deep sense out of his account of "There Was a Child Went Forth" and its successors. *Emerson, Whitman, and the American Muse* (Chapel Hill: University of North Carolina Press, 1982), pp. 55–85, 153-71, 183–91.

able, ongoing life. As in the opening sequences, Whitman avoids any sense of a sharp break between the human and natural worlds. He modulates between them by shifting the perspective from the close-up view of buildings, goods, and vehicles to "the village on the highland, seen from afar at sunset—the river between." By the end of the sequence the eye lifts to the purity of the heavens and the bird flying to the very horizons to give a reassuring sense of ascending, never-ending life inseparable from the rank vitality of "salt-marsh and shore-mud."

Grammatically and philosophically all of these details depend for their completion on the child, since Whitman rounds out the sequence and the poem by repeating the sense and expanding rhythms of his central affirmation:

> These became part of that child who went forth every day, and who now goes, and will always go forth every day

In place of the question about "flashes and specks," Whitman supplies the implicit answer of a vital universe and a creative self intimately related to it. The vital self absorbs the energies of the surrounding world and ventures forth affirmatively and forever as a counter to the earlier doubts about death, impermanence, and illusion.

To place this vision in perspective, however, we must first stress that as far as people are concerned, the sense of harmonious, never-ending relation the poem celebrates is achieved through the experience, the medium of the child. The drunkard and the schoolmistress, for example, are related because they both enter equally and are of equal value in the child's experience. But on the evidence of the poem the two have absolutely nothing to do with each other outside their relation to the child. Although the child or the poet's sympathies suggest how they might relate, what needs to be emphasized is the absence of a rendered, deeply felt social world within which the drunkard and the schoolmistress or the "men and women crowding fast in the streets" would have real connections, quite aside from the presence of the child.

In "There Was a Child Went Forth," the process and rhythm of natural growth in the animating world of plants, birds, animals, and ocean, in contrast, do have a real existence before they enter into the child's developing self. They suggest a world of natural relations and natural patterns, moreover, not a world of fragmented, isolated parts. The child is especially close to this world. The absence of a genuine, ongoing social world and the importance Whitman places on the vitality of a harmonious natural world are not idiosyncratic responses on his part. Instead, they are his response to the relative openness and fluidity of his American market society and to residual and oppositional energies still available in America.

In a reversed, mirror-image way, Whitman is nonetheless like the workers Marx and Lukacs analyze. Whitman, too, has an obscured view of "the relations between people" in his way of seeing society, or of not seeing it. In the world of commodity fetishism and commodity structure, for the worker the society of industrial capitalism has an inexorable, commodified objectivity. Like the characters in "Bartleby, the Scrivener," the worker is fragmented and experiences the society as having an impenetrable, incomprehensible power set over and against him. Whitman goes to the opposite extreme: for him society as such has no existence at all. In a representative poem like "There Was a Child Went Forth," "the relations between people" do not exist except as these relations are mediated through the unalienated child. Whitman stresses oppositional possibilities still alive in America but neglects the emerging forces, those alienating powers Melville responds to in works like "Bartleby" and "The Paradise of Bachelors and the Tartarus of Maids."

Like other Americans, Whitman finds it easier and truer to his deepest feelings to render his relations not to the social but to the natural world. For him the growing self exists, a harmonious nature exists, and an animating divine energy exists, but society does not exist. At the end of "There Was a Child Went Forth," the processes of natural rhythm and growth reinforce the process of the child's developing self. As long as the growing child goes forth into a vital world, a meaningful existence will continue, the poem affirms. This view places a large responsibility on the creative self, on the developing individual whose involvement in the world gives existence its meaning and resolves the doubts of transience and illusion.

The absence of any sense of society, of human community, however, means that if the self encounters serious difficulty, the entire structure of meaning is threatened. The mediating presence of society does not exist either to sustain or to oppress the individual, who must deal with his inner and outer world alone and not as a member of a community. This situation speaks more to a social than to an existential condition. In "There Was a Child Went Forth," the threat of Tocquevillian, market-society isolation is only implicit, but even in Whitman's marvelously vital world of natural relations and of harmony between the child and nature, the very real possibility of human isolation is built into the basic structure of perception and experience.

Through the child of the poem Whitman acknowledges and triumphantly surmounts "the doubts of day-time and the doubts of night-time." He affirms an independent American identity related to the surrounding world, but he is ambivalent about his market society's dominant masculinity and shrewdness, is more deeply committed than his fellows to the equality they profess, and is exposed to the alienation that results from the absence of a cohesive society. Later in his career, Whitman wrote, "The fear of conflicting and irreconcilable interiors, and the lack of a common skeleton, knitting all close, continually haunts me."[4] But in "There Was a Child Went Forth," this fear, however warranted by the basic structures of the poem, has not yet surfaced to trouble the identity of Whitman's independent, sympathetic American self. As he resists and imagines vital alternatives to the cultural hegemony of the market society, Whitman nonetheless shows how deeply the privatizing tendencies of the dominant society affect the consciousness even of its most perceptive critics.

Since we, too, are part of the market society, our common sense tells us that self and society, the individual and the mass of others are opposed. Our common sense tells us that, like Ishmael and Queequeg in "The Monkey-Rope," a person's separate individuality is threatened by his ties to others, even by his connections with those he loves, to say nothing of the sharks who surround him. The structure of the English language reinforces this socially and philosophically supported sense of the separateness of individuals, if not of individuals at odds with each other. The basic subject-verb-object pattern divides and classifies subjects and objects. The compartmentalizing of nouns has the same enclosing effect. Each individual noun-subject has its own separate niche in the syntax of the sentence. An American writer thus has a real problem if he wants to celebrate the individual as a "simple separate person, / Yet utter the word Democratic, the word En-Masse," to quote from the opening lines of the first "Inscription" poem in *Leaves of Grass*. Conventionally, in the world of possessive individualism, the relation between self and others is established by competition among the atomistic players of the market-society game. In theory, contracts and the legal system are the referees and constitute the social bonds tying together the atomistic competitors. The results are unstable, but in this model the privatized, antagonistic relation between self and society is easy to understand. For the person who rejects the model of possessive individualism, however, it is not easy to conceive or to sustain the connection between "the simple separate person" and the "en-masse" of an egalitarian democracy.

Beyond "There Was a Child Went Forth," in poems like "Crossing

4. "Democratic Vistas," in *The Works of Walt Whitman: The Collect and Other Prose*, ed. Floyd Stovall (New York University Press, 1964), 2:368.

Brooklyn Ferry" (1856), Whitman makes a discovery astonishing in its simplicity and boldness. He uses the basic but tabooed experience of sexual and spiritual love to convey the fusing of self and other, the merging of one's individuality into the flow of existence, such that the person is simultaneously "separate" and "En-Masse." In sublimated versions, in his views about Comrades, it emerges as abstract and unenergized, but in the 1855–1856 poems Whitman is compelling. Love is central, but what gives urgency to a poem like "Crossing Brooklyn Ferry" is also the threat of death, of the need to affirm the ongoing life of the individual as part of the fluid, growing, but coherent whole from which the individual emerges and to which he returns.

In "My Kinsman, Major Molineux," Hawthorne shows that it can be deeply unsettling to follow the imperative to rise in the world. He brings alive the inner fragmentation and dislocations of a rapidly changing market society. In Hawthorne's view, the masculine sexual energy driving the new order is fierce, vital, and destructive. Whitman is basically at odds with the dominant society, but, in "Crossing Brooklyn Ferry," for him sexuality is cohesive, not deadly. His sexuality is an affront to the respectable decorum of the dominant society. In a deeper way, the free-flowing sexuality Whitman celebrates is a counterforce to the repressed sexuality that drives the restlessly changing market society. Whitman refuses to accept the divisions, the destabilizing competition, or the official decorum and externally imposed regularity of the market society. Instead, the implied and sometimes explicit argument in his early poems is that life is not chaos but unconventional coherence, order, plan. In his inspired view the dead end of the grave is an illusion because love, growth, and equality are the living realities. The changes he celebrates are not those of an acquisitive process of commodity exchange. The love he celebrates is an erotically charged alternative to the fragmenting power of the dominant society. Sometimes Whitman is too strident in expressing his discoveries, partly to overcome his own doubts, partly to convey his joy in perceptions he feels are infinitely precious and in need of emphasis. In "Crossing Brooklyn Ferry," though, his tone is assured.

To convey the universality and significance of his vision, Whitman progressively, provocatively insinuates an ever-increasing intimacy between himself and his readers, between what he has seen and experienced and what he affirms will continue endlessly. Building on the openness to change of his American market society, Whitman goes beyond and beneath it to oppositional sources of energy and continuity. The intimacy and its erotic culmination are similarly at odds with the restraints and discipline of the dominant market society. More acceptable on conventional standards, Whitman majestically invokes the ebb and flow of the tides and the sun "half an hour high" before sunset. They are not impersonal or even natural objects but are personified as "you" and viewed "face to face," so that they are humanized and the commonsense, market-society separation between human beings and nature is done away with.[5] As the poem progresses, other separations are similarly denied in favor of the fusing and the reciprocal relations Whitman affirms. Cumulatively, the process of crossing from shore to shore, the mundane daily process of crossing Brooklyn Ferry, assumes the heightened significance of an endless, ongoing crossing between realms. The continuity between past, present, and future eliminates distinctions. The shared sights and sounds, the ordinary details Whitman sees and delights in and affirms that others, coming after, will also be refreshed, all argue for the joy and persistence of unalienated life as an alternative to the implied shadow of death as a finality. The underlying guarantees for continuity and growth are the elemental natural rhythms of the ebb and flow of the tides, of day merging into night to be followed again by sunrise, the ongoing rhythms of the seasons, and, at the center of the poem, the elemental rhythm of sexual generation "which ties me to the woman or man that looks in my face, / Which fuses me into you now, and pours my meaning into you." As the basic source of human life, the act of sexual love is a guarantee of ongoing life. The experience, in its intensity and joy, does away with commonsense distinctions, so that

> What I promised without mentioning it, have you not accepted?
> What the study could not teach—what the preaching could not accomplish is accomplished, is it not?
> What the push of reading could not start is started by me personally, is it not?

This generating experience is pivotal.[6] Whitman then recapitulates and draws together the vital details he has previously recorded, assured that their full significance is now available. These "dumb, beautiful ministers" in their variety and flow, "you furnish your parts toward eternity, / Great or small, you furnish your parts toward the Soul." The separa-

---

5. Quotations from "Crossing Brooklyn Ferry" are from *Leaves of Grass: Facsimile Edition of the 1860 Edition*, pp. 379ff.

6. See also Edwin H. Miller's treatment of "the erotic drama of the merging of the 'I' and the 'you' with 'we,'" in *Walt Whitman's Poetry*, pp. 205, 204–7; James E. Miller, *A Critical Guide to Leaves of Grass* (University of Chicago Press, 1957), pp. 80–89, and Hyatt H. Waggoner, *American Visionary Poetry* (Baton Rouge: Louisiana State University Press, 1982), pp. 51–53.

tion between body and soul no longer holds; through the ministry of the flow of natural and human details, Whitman bodies forth an alternative to the Christian minister's vision of eternal life. For Whitman a charge of animating, sometimes erotic energy runs through existence, "ties me to the woman or man that looks in my face," and constitutes "the float forever held in solution" we emerge from and return to. This is Emerson but with a distinctive sexual charge Emerson lacks. For nonbelievers Whitman is both more offensive and more credible than Emerson because his transcendental vision emerges from the basic human realities of sex and the basic natural rhythms of tidal, human, and seasonal continuity.

During the early, capital-accumulating phases of the market society, the repression of sexuality channeled energies into productive activities and contributed to the insatiable restlessness an expanding capitalism needed. The domination and exploitation of nature and of natives was legitimized and motivated by the pervasive view that white American men were set above and apart from the natural world they were entitled to subdue, just as they were entitled to dominate black slaves and white women. Whitman provides an alternative to the prevailing alienation, sexual repression, and conventional hierarchies.

His verse rhythms and syntax reinforce the unalienated continuity and equality he celebrates. He repeatedly favors "and" to link words, phrases, and clauses and to effect balance and equality. He similarly relies on parallel structure to do away with hierarchies and to enforce a sense of equality. He has also mastered the participle to convey a sense of ongoing, never-ending activity. Whitman's reciprocal rhythms underscore the ebb and flow of the tides, of men and women crossing from shore to shore, and of the motion of the sex act itself, "the pouring in of the flood-tide, the falling back to the sea of the ebb-tide." The elemental processes, sights, and sounds he celebrates are democratic in their equal accessibility to all—the ebb and flow of the river, of seasons, of sex. Everything is animated by the unifying energy of a love that is both personal and universal.

In its personal immediacy, however, this love is also disruptive. It contributes significantly to "the old knot of contrariety" Whitman brings alive through his vital, idiomatic catalog of the negative sides of the self:

I too knitted the old knot of contrariety,
Blabbed, blushed, resented, lied, stole, grudged,
Had guile, anger, lust, hot wishes I dared not speak,
Was wayward, vain, greedy, shallow, sly, cowardly, malignant,
The wolf, the snake, the hog, not wanting in me,

> The cheating look, the frivolous word, the adulterous wish, not wanting,
> Refusals, hates, postponements, meanness, laziness, none of these
>   wanting.

The rush and energy of these details enlarge the range and credibility of a self predominantly characterized by an assured enjoyment of the ongoing human and natural panorama. The disturbance of "lusts, hot wishes I dared not speak, / . . . The cheating look, the frivolous word, the adulterous wish, / . . . Refusals, hates, postponements"—the disruptive drama of sexual involvement is thus acknowledged and absorbed. For all its universal implications, Whitman's rendering of erotic and especially of homoerotic feelings also constitutes a kind of personal invitation Whitman came to draw back from. He later eliminated the line "what the push of reading could not start is started by me personally, is it not?" And he was notoriously evasive, as in his response to inquiries from English admirers.

The universality Whitman asserts in "Crossing Brooklyn Ferry" is nonetheless rooted in an unabashed acknowledgment of personal homoerotic attraction. "But I was a Manhattanese," he asserts,

> free, friendly, and proud!
> I was called by my nighest name by clear loud voices of young men as they
>   saw me approaching or passing,
> Felt their arms on my neck as I stood, or the negligent leaning of their flesh
>   against me as I sat,
> Saw many I loved in the street, or ferry-boat, or public assembly, yet never
>   told them a word,
> Lived the same life with the rest, the same old laughing, gnawing,
>   sleeping,
> Played the part that still looks back on the actor or actress,
> The same old role, the role that is what we make it, as great as we like,
> Or as small as we like, or both great and small.

In this version, the self-made American individualist's belief that "the role . . . is what we make of it," that it is up to us, and that we can go as far or as short as we choose—this widely shared view is for Whitman not part of a program of social and economic competition but part of sexual sublimation. Whitman recognizes that the withheld words of love lead to a "laughing" camaraderie but also to a "gnawing" unfulfillment, a playing of conventional roles and a separation within the self based on inhibition, such that we are actors or actresses who play a part and make of it what we will, animated by sublimated energy.

More characteristically, however, Whitman draws on his own bisexuality, his undifferentiated interest in men and women, as a basis for an open, undifferentiated acceptance of all living beings. His emphasis is on intimacy and connection, not on separation. He moves progressively closer and involves the reader, the "you" the poem directly addresses. "Closer yet I approach you," he writes. "What thought you have of me, I had as much of you." Whitman has earlier asked, "What is it, then, between us? / What is the count of the scores or hundreds of years between us?" As he moves closer to the reader, after the lust, the unexpressed hot wishes, and the panorama of young men, the answer he insinuates becomes less general. This drama of suggestion culminates in the sexual fusing and pouring we have already noted.

The human ties Whitman brings alive in "Crossing Brooklyn Ferry" are at once intimate, vital, and impersonal. Whitman opens himself to the reader, appeals to the reader's most intimate experience, and binds the "I" of the poem to the "you," the reader, with the force of the most personal sexual communion Whitman can suggest. But it is also metaphoric and impersonal, insinuated and asserted. The feelings of love are genuine, the reader's human capacity to respond is equally genuine, but the exchange is also literary and oddly remote, for all the contrary claims. In the course of the poem itself, Whitman records his expressed and unexpressed love for undifferentiated young men and to a lesser extent women but not for any particular human being, so that the rendered ties of human love are diffuse and not particular. To that extent the asserted human ties lack the credibility of specific, complex involvements. In the *Calamus* poems, when Whitman later acknowledges the results of such involvement, he also shows that the individual, the "I" of his poems, is vulnerable to pain and to a narrowing of interests. Since for Whitman the creative individual, the bard, the "I" of his poems holds society together, the cohesion of the larger society is then threatened.

In contrast to the intense personal feeling and unparticularized love relations in "Crossing Brooklyn Ferry," Whitman observes natural objects, the sea gulls, for example, both in stereoscopic detail and in relation to the unifying rhythms of nature. He catches the suggestive, ascending motion of the sea gulls and sees "how the glistening yellow lit up parts of their bodies, and left the rest in strong shadow." This reminder of light and shadow at the end of the day, of day merging into night, reinforces and is reinforced by the seasonal emphasis on the "Twelfth Month sea-gulls," on the end of the year and the suggestion of a new year to come. These rhythms are related to the "slow-wheeling circles, and the gradual edging toward the south" of the sea gulls as guarantees of the continuity of life, of the coherence, beauty, and vitality of natural cycles—of the circling birds, of the rhythm of day and night, of old year and new year. This winter scene is immediately followed by "I too saw the reflection of the summer sky in the water," to emphasize the continuity of winter and summer, of sky and water, just as the entire scene gradually moves from the end of day into night. The reflections Whitman repeatedly focuses on enforce this sense of merging and relation--of sky merging with water, of the poet at one with the reflecting river and sun. Human beings and their creations, moreover, are as integral to this scene as the sea gulls and the scallop-edged waves, who themselves have the closely observed quality and vitality of human characters in a novel. It is part of the bonus of Whitman's democratic esthetic that natural and human objects are at once recorded in their separateness and in their flowing relation to the whole they are part of, a whole, however, that does not include society.

With this important reservation, there is no separation between the human and natural worlds; the human world of ships, sailors, and foundries has the same vitality as the glistening, ascending sea gulls, the sunlit water, and the cycle of days and seasons. At the end of the sequence, Whitman focuses on

> the fires from the foundry chimneys burning high and glaringly into the
>   night,
> Casting their flicker of black, contrasted with wild yellow light, over the
>   tops of houses, and down into the clefts of streets.

It is a potentially ominous and in any case heightened scene. The natural symbolism of the end of day and the end of life, of crossing from one shore to "the neighboring shore," of flickering "black, contrasted with wild red and yellow light"—in a Hawthorne story the imagery of demonism and death would predominate. But Whitman suggests instead a wild energy and a heightened significance appropriate to the large concerns of life and death and the continuity of existence. The unifying natural rhythms and cycles are reinforced by the poet's enclosing refrain,

> I too many and many a time crossed the river, the sun half an hour high,
> I watched the Twelfth Month sea-gulls—. . .
> I saw . . .
> I saw . . .
> I too saw . . . .
> These, and all else, were to me the same as they are to you.

This appeal to shared human experience, to common feelings, sights, and acts is a further guarantee of the continuity the poet proclaims. We, of course, are less inclined than Whitman to see the foundry fires as integral to the ongoing natural cycle, as another expression of the vitality the sunlit water and the rushing current also express. We may be inclined to see industrial pollution in both the current and the fires. The changes made by industrial capitalism register with more impact on us than on Whitman. Whitman is a reminder of the lost promises of cohesion between the natural world of sea gulls and sunset and the world of a developing industrial capitalism whose basic dynamics he failed to see as at odds with the harmony and continuity he affirms. "These and all else" are not precisely "the same" for him as for us. If the changes made by industrial capitalism do not discredit Whitman, they at least compromise one of his appeals to shared, enduring experience.

Whitman separates the foundry as spectacle from the processes of industrial capitalism the foundry is an integral part of. His urban America is vital and flowing because for Whitman it is inseparable from nature, and, on the other hand, it is separated from the dynamics of the market society.[7] His ships and foundries are alive; the men and women who endlessly cross the ferry implicitly deserve his affection by virtue of their sheer, democratic existence. To counter the fragmentation, competitiveness, and inequality, the extremes of wealth and miserable poverty of the American possessive market society, however, Whitman ignores the New York of the Five Points section, whose slums in the 1850s had the greatest density of population of any urban area in the world, more than Calcutta or London. He similarly avoids the new Fifth Avenue mansions, the alienation Melville explores in "Bartleby," or the sterile, destructive factory life of "The Tartarus of Maids." By 1856 the relative equality of the New York of Whitman's childhood no longer existed. Immigration, growth, and increases in manufacturing and trade had generated wide gaps between workingmen and owners, weakened the position of skilled and unskilled labor, and created a wealthy class that promenaded and entertained in a luxury far removed from the squalid conditions of the poor or the strains of middle-class life.[8]

Whitman pays a price for ignoring the often grim results of market-society change. His aim, however, is to provide an alternative to the divisive vision and actualities of market-society America and its conven-

7. In his focus on urban pastoral, "Pastoralism and the American Urban Ideal: Hawthorne, Whitman and the Literary Pattern," *American Literature* 54 (1982): 329–53, James Machor avoids the issues of industrial capitalism. Under the guise of celebrating the imagination he also accepts a subject-object dichotomy that misrepresents Whitman's vision and the difficult problems Whitman was attempting to resolve (pp. 332–40).

8. Douglas T. Miller, *Jacksonian Aristocracy: Class and Democracy in New York, 1830–1860* (New York: Oxford, 1967), pp. 135–39.

tional religion of guilt and rank. He speaks for a new vision of human and natural coherence and continuity, of love, equality, enjoyment, and ongoing life. Thus, he writes:

> I loved well those cities,
> I loved well the stately and rapid river,
> The men and women I saw were all near to me.

All alike are "stately and rapid"—the cities, the river, the men and women all partake of each other: the distinction between mechanical artifacts, living nature, and human beings does not arise any more than does the superiority or inferiority among people, all of whom are equal in the eyes and in the love of the poet. The sense of an ongoing society does not arise, either; Whitman is not concerned with the dense network of values and relations that constitutes a society. As an alternative to the emerging society of possessive individualism, with its systematic changes, divisiveness, and supports, Whitman instead offers a cohesion effected by the animating energy that for him runs through human beings and cities as it does through the ascending sea gulls and the cycle of the days and seasons. This energy is brought to a focus in the unifying, changing and changeless person of the "I" of the poem, the representative, godlike individual who emerges from the flow of existence and who bathes everything in his universal affection and acceptance, in his approval of "the dark patches" and the sunlit waters. His representative experience—"I too saw"; "I too lived"; "I too knitted the old knot of contrariety"—brings into the open the latent meaning of the common sights and experiences whose universality amidst change he celebrates and whose significance we would miss except for him.

In contrast to the inequalities, acquisitiveness, and instability of the American market society, Whitman taps what is for him the basic reality of love, the human form of the energy that animates and unites all of existence. This love is sometimes stately and sublimated, sometimes intense and erotic, but in any case it enlivens the universe and ties together the poet, the natural and human world, and the men and women crossing the ferry now and in the future. It is an impressive alternative to the tensions, contracts, and classes that separate and hold together the restlessly changing market society. It is also vulnerable to those pressures that result in the narrowed horizons of the *Calamus* poems. These poems have the authenticity of a complex personal involvement, but they also leave the larger society to its own divisive tendencies. With the bardic individual and his free-flowing love now concentrated on the one or two who compel him, what is to hold America together? After the crisis of personal involvement he explores in the *Calamus* poems, in "A Passage to India," Whitman tried to resolve the problem of unifying the nation through an imaginatively unenlivened reliance on conventional religion, hardly a substitute for either the cohesive self of his early poems or the sense of living community Whitman, like many other Americans, left out of account.[9]

In "Crossing Brooklyn Ferry" the disappearance or deemphasis on the "I" has a much more positive implication than in "A Passage to India." At the turning point of "Crossing Brooklyn Ferry," after the fusing and pouring, after the push of "me personally," the individual has done his provocative, integrating best. Whitman can then recapitulate the sights and sensations he has previously celebrated. Now, however, he no longer needs to stress "I watched," "I saw," "I loved well." Instead, he subsumes and absorbs the "I." He now emphasizes the panorama itself, the changing and changeless river and the scallop-edged waves, the masts and foundry chimneys. The "I" is present not at the center of the drama of the sentence or the scene but rather as an integral part of the process the poet again brings to life in full confidence that the changing, coherent process will continue and that now we are one with him in our acceptance and understanding. After the communion at the center of the poem, the individual "I" no longer has to call attention to his own authenticating feelings and experiences. He thus subsumes himself in the joyous, erotically charged flow of things:

> Frolic on, crested and scallop-edged waves!
> Gorgeous clouds of the sunset! drench with your splendor me, or the men
>   and women generations after me.

In its first appearance, the beautiful image of "the fine centrifugal spokes of light round the shape of my head in the sun-lit water" affirms the poet as a democratic saint, his aureola the natural light of the sun reflected in the water. In its second appearance, Whitman explicitly extends the meaning to everyone:

> Diverge, fine spokes of light, from the shape of my head, or any one's
>   head, in the sun-lit water

And at the end of the poem, "I" is replaced by "we":

9. Jerome Loving, *Emerson, Whitman, and the American Muse*, has a valuable discussion of the *Calamus* poems and "A Passage to India" in relation to Whitman's earlier commitments but not to his sense of America (pp. 145–71, 183–91).

We descend upon you and all things—we arrest you all,
. . . .
We receive you with free sense at last, and are insatiate henceforward

But despite the communal "we," Whitman has not established a community. As in "There Was a Child Went Forth," there is no relation among people except through the poet who sees, accepts, and celebrates, who proclaims a cohesion he shows in nature but not among citizens in a society. The love he imaginatively consummates with the reader, the love he feels for those who come after, and the love he feels for the men and women around him constitute the ties that by implication bind people together along with their shared immersion in the natural cycles of night and day, winter and summer, ebb tide and flood tide. Whitman, however, is not concerned with the way the men and the women around him relate (or fail to relate) to one another. Except for the powerful implication that his own feelings are universal, the ties (or absence of ties) among the people he sees and celebrates do not really exist for him. The poem is designed to liberate us, to appeal to our human feelings so that we can bring about in our own lives the joy and communion Whitman celebrates. Important as they are, however, Whitman does not show these human relations in the same detailed way he shows both the rhythms and objects of nature and the inner responses of the self, the concealed wishes and impulses he accurately, courageously articulates. The poem leaves it up to us to establish ties whose universal sources Whitman brings alive in convincing detail, even as this American poet slights the living texture of community.

eight

THE WAR MACHINE IN THE GARDEN
Capitalism, Republicanism, and Protestant Character Structure in *A Connecticut Yankee*

Reading the text of Twain's life, a purist might allege inconsistencies and contradictions, and he would of course be right. Many of the contradictions, though, simply establish that in a period of rapid social change Twain understood the emerging mass market and the needs of the new entertainment industry. Twain and Whitman were countrymen, but in ways that go deeper than geography they lived in different regions of America. In contrast to Whitman's sustained effort to imagine cohesive alternatives to the old-fashioned Jacksonian market society, during the period Alan Trachtenberg has characterized as *The Incorporation of America*, Twain was incorporating himself: as early as 1873 he registered "Mark Twain" as a trademark.[1] Unlike Whitman, who had a local career and uneven success as a journalist, a generation later, during the formative phase of consumer capitalism, Twain became a nationwide star in the emerging entertainment industry.[2] Twain aimed his work at ordinary readers and sold his books by subscription through his own publishing company. During the 1880s he controlled the production, distribution, and profits of his own enterprise. On the lecture circuit he developed a public personality deliberately designed to contrast with the prevailing seriousness. By the late 1880s "he had perfected the art of

1. Louis Budd, *Our Mark Twain: The Making of His Public Personality* (Philadelphia: University of Pennsylvania Press, 1983), p. 62. Subsequent references will be abbreviated OMT and cited by page number in the text.
2. For insight into the origins of consumer capitalism, see Stuart and Elizabeth Ewen, *Channels of Desire: Mass Images and the Shaping of American Consciousness* (New York: McGraw-Hill, 1982); Stuart Ewen, *Captains of Consciousness: Advertising and the Social Roots of the Consumer Culture* (New York: McGraw-Hill, 1976); Alan Trachtenberg, *The Incorporation of America: Culture and Society in the Gilded Age* (New York: Hill and Wang, 1982), esp. pp. 101–39; and Michael Spindler, *American Literature and Social Change: William Dean Howells to Arthur Miller* (London: Macmillan, 1983), pp. 1–32, 97–120.

144

acting 'natural,' of being 'as much yourself,' marveled Howells, 'as if you stood by my chimney corner'" (OMT, p. 81). As a stage performer, "Twain was a gifted actor, best at playing many versions of himself and eventually at simply radiating his 'star' presence" (OMT, p. 81). In the middle 1880s, to his later embarrassment, he capered on stage, and from the 1870s on he also appeared willing in interviews "to exchange confidences of the most literal nature, a sign that he would learn to convert his life into full-fledged public drama. Meanwhile," Louis Budd continues, "helped by his fraternizing with reporters, he was building the impression that a shrewd and 'unaffected' individualist, as cordial as a blood relation, stood tall behind his antics and occasional tongue-in-cheek publicity stunts" (OMT, p. 43).

Twain had an appetite for attention, an active taste for celebrity, and a widely shared desire for opulent living and big money. His humor, his license as America's court jester, and his ability to divide the self, to create and play roles, and to manage public relations all perfectly suited the needs of the emerging consumer society. Twain became increasingly adept at working the newspapers (OMT, pp. 96–119). As the public relations industry was beginning to develop, Twain realized that the celebrity himself was news, that his public personality was a commodity at least as valuable as his books. During his lifetime Twain's most profitable investment was, significantly, the patented Mark Twain Scrap Book. Featuring a dignified photograph of the famous celebrity and the trademarked signature, it came in a dozen versions, including one for newspaper clippings (OMT, pp. 63–66). In addition to the hundreds of news items on Mark Twain, this famous personality could have included in his own scrap book the advertisements he certainly did not discourage: "The tobacco premiums carrying his picture, the lithograph portrait given away by a 'white and fancy goods' merchant, the stereopticon slide of him at work that was for sale, and the 'Mark Twain Mazurka' published as sheet music and 'dedicated' to the 'Celebrated Mark Twain Cigars'" (OMT, p. 62).

These enterprises belonged to others, but during the 1880s Twain himself was energetically involved in a series of promotions, inventions, and investments. His "ventures into such things as a patent steam generator, a steam pulley, and a new method of marine telegraphy cost him only twenty-five or thirty thousand apiece."[3] Twain wrote *The Prince and the Pauper*, *Life on the Mississippi*, *Huck Finn*, and *A Connecticut Yankee in King Arthur's Court* during the 1880s, and he continued to create and

3. Samuel Charles Webster, ed., *Mark Twain, Business Man* (Boston: Little, Brown, 1946), p. 171.

promote the celebrity and entrepreneur, Mark Twain. During the 1880s Twain's two other major ventures were the C. L. Webster and Company publishing house and the Paige typesetter. The publishing company made money; "the typesetter was a worse monster than the Tennessee land. Year after year it swallowed money and demanded more. It consumed $300,000 before he was through with it."[4] These two enterprises combine capital investment, financial speculation, and technology, all centered on the emerging entertainment industry of the new consumer capitalism. Twain's enterprises were not sidelines but came increasingly to occupy the center of his attention. In *Huck Finn* he had Jim swear off the money-investment world, but Twain himself was too deeply enmeshed to follow Jim's example.

The investment in marine telegraphy comes from the same Mark Twain who also celebrates the true pilot of "Old Times on the Mississippi," an intuitive genius who can see in the dark and whose way of life marine telegraphy undermines, just as the railroad and the Civil War do. The creator of Huck and Jim formed his own publishing company to market *Huck Finn*, which he sold as a subscription book, necessitating the large-scale promotion and big money his novel subverts. The author of "The History of a Campaign that Failed" was also the successful publisher of the memoirs of Generals Grant, Sheridan, McClellan and Badeau and of Mrs. Custer's *Tenting on the Plains, or, General Custer in Kansas and Texas*.[5] Twain particularly admired Grant, personally supervised the details of publication of his *Memoirs*, and was generous in his terms to Mrs. Grant, who needed the money after her husband had been swindled by his business partner. The royalty check of two hundred thousand dollars was the largest in history to that time, and the company profited too, as did Mark Twain, one celebrity reinforcing another. As a publisher, while he was blistering the Catholic Church in *A Connecticut Yankee*, Twain was directing the successful campaign with the Pope to publish the authorized biography of Pope Leo XIII.[6] Not one to play favorites, Twain also went after Henry Ward Beecher's autobiography. "My valuation of Beecher's book goes up as much as double what it was. If he writes the book in that way, & heaves in just enough piousness, it will sell . . . : profit $350,000."[7]

As a celebrity himself, Twain published the lives of celebrities for a consumer audience as hungry then as now for religious uplift and the reminiscences of war heroes. Although the books Twain himself wrote were short on religious piety, he nonetheless worked within a

4. Ibid.
5. Ibid., pp. 228, 302–24, 349–51, 357, 360, 362, 371–72.
6. Ibid., pp. 347–49, 357, 364, 367.
7. Ibid., p. 376.

hegemonic process that he both accepted and subverted and that he knew from the inside because it was inside him. For an understanding of *A Connecticut Yankee*, Twain's involvement in the contradictions of finance capitalism and the emerging consumer capitalism lends authority to his probing of the new society of stock speculation, technology, advertising, and war. That he had contradictory feelings does not detract from his achievement in *A Connecticut Yankee* or make it a "confused" book as critics frequently charge.[8] Often because they shy away from the power of the social implications in the catastrophic ending, critics undervalue the novel. They typically set up a one-dimensional norm that they then fault Twain for violating.[9] Instead of an "either/or"

8. See, for example, Henry Nash Smith, *Mark Twain: The Development of a Writer* (New York: Atheneum, 1962, 1972), pp. 138, 146, 157, and *Mark Twain's Fable of Progress: Political and Economic Ideas in "A Connecticut Yankee"* (New Brunswick, N.J.: Rutgers University Press, 1964), pp. 62, 68; Robert Regan, *Unpromising Heroes: Mark Twain and his Characters* (Berkeley: University of California Press, 1966), p. 184; James M. Cox, *Mark Twain: The Fate of Humor* (Princeton University Press, 1967), pp. 199, 217; Maxwell Geismar, *Mark Twain: An American Prophet* (Boston: Houghton Mifflin, 1970), pp. 111–12; and Everett Emerson, *The Authentic Mark Twain: A Literary Biography of Samuel L. Clemens* (Philadelphia: University of Pennsylvania Press, 1984), p. 162.

9. For Henry Nash Smith, Twain's best modern critic, the problem centers on Hank as a failed vernacular hero, as an American Adam from "an almost entirely nonintellectual tradition of folk humor" who cannot sustain the burden of ideology he is made to carry (*Mark Twain's Fable of Progress*, pp. 68–69). But we need to set aside the vernacular norm and to attend to what Hank actually shows us. Smith is aware that something powerfully subversive is going on but, because he is too attached to Twain's explicit formulations and to a finally positive view of America, he cannot accept the pertinence of what the Hank Morgan figure reveals. James M. Cox, reacting against Smith's social and political emphasis, reoriented Twain criticism by stressing the pleasure principle as the central value. *A Connecticut Yankee*, however, is too deeply engaged with social and political concerns to make the pleasure principle a useful touchstone. In his hard-hitting, stimulating essay, Cox sets up the reified categories of "burlesque," "satire," and "the intention of the narrative." He claims burlesque and satire are incompatible, and, instead of following out what Twain actually does, he blames him for his "failure" to realize "the intention of the narrative" (*Mark Twain: The Fate of Humor*, p. 217). For Robert Regan, the norm Twain violates is that of the Unpromising Hero, for reasons that "lie in Mark Twain's biography" (*Unpromising Heroes*, pp. 166–67). Jeffrey L. Duncan, "The Empirical and the Ideal in Mark Twain," *PMLA* 95 (1980), is concerned with two orders of language, the empirical language of realism and the romance language of fantasy. For him the norm Twain fails to realize is that of Gass, Borges, or Barth: "He destroys a superb idea for a fiction, an idea that anticipates such works as *Henri IV*, 'Pierre Menard,' and *Chimera*" (pp. 202, 209). Everett Emerson uses romance and skeptical realism as his normative categories and then blames Twain for confusing them and the reader. Emerson's confusion is compounded because, like many Twain critics, he misuses biography. He focuses on "the slump" Twain allegedly experienced while he was writing *A Connecticut Yankee*. Emerson then reads "the slump" back as a judgment against the novel. Emerson has a bias against intensity and in favor of good humor, and he refuses to accept the full implications of the increasing violence in the novel, hence "the slump" (*The Authentic Mark Twain*, pp. 154–62).

approach, I favor a "both/and" emphasis that allows us to follow out the strains Twain actually explores. As John Kasson reminds us, especially with *A Connecticut Yankee* we need to believe the tale, not the artist.[10] I doubt if we can locate the artist, the "real" Mark Twain, from among all the roles and voices this extraordinarily gifted actor projects, each time genuinely and convincingly. The question of Twain's own attitude toward Hank Morgan is not a crucial issue. What is important is that deeply immersed himself in the contradictions of American culture and possessed of a vital comic imagination, Twain created a figure whose character structure and divided values illuminate the culture and the hegemonic process they are rooted in. I stress the comic imagination because it is so prone to turn unpredictably on its possessor and to expose the absurdities or worse of that which consciously the writer holds dear.[11]

Twain, however, makes it easy for readers then and now to minimize the force of his contemporary revelations. Despite Beard's illustrations, which sometimes substitute capitalists like Jay Gould for the feudal characters in the novel, Twain has Hank Morgan focus explicitly on the middle ages or the pre–Civil War South. Twain does not jeopardize his standing with contemporary American readers by overtly engaging with the present. During the 1880s, particularly through his losing investment in the Paige typesetting machine, as Twain became more deeply involved personally in the money-technology-promotion world of his period, he nonetheless generated increasingly darker insights into the underlying realities of the emerging America of the 1880s and 1890s. In the deep structure of character and action in *A Connecticut Yankee*, he exposes the destructive even more than the benign sides of late-nineteenth-century technology, capitalism, and republican and Protestant values, all of which form the character structure of Hank Morgan.

Drawing on his own experience and showing his grasp of the realities of the new age, in the Hank Morgan figure, Twain combines two ordinarily separated tendencies, the purely instrumental, technological,

10. *Civilizing the Machine: Technology and Republican Values in America, 1776–1900* (New York: Penguin, 1977), p. 215.

11. Aside from Henry Nash Smith, Everett Carter, "The Meaning of *A Connecticut Yankee*," *American Literature* 50 (1978): 418–40, makes the most convincing case I have seen for Twain's conscious intentions. Carter, though, underestimates the subversive complexity of Twain's comic imagination and, as Lorne Fienberg points out, "Carter's analysis falters precisely in his efforts to reconcile Twain's sympathy for Hank and the nineteenth-century creed of material progress with the premeditated slaughter and colossal destruction that this creed precipitates." "Twain's Connecticut Yankee: The Entrepreneur as a Daimonic Hero," *Modern Fiction Studies* 28 (1982): 156.

commonsense ones and those of the showman-entrepreneur. Put more generally, Hank combines features of the older, factory-based industrial capitalism and even more the new finance capitalism of stock manipulation and selling short and the emerging consumer capitalism of display, promotion, and advertising. Beyond Twain himself, the strains in Hank's character and values parallel those in the public image of another entrepreneur of the practical, Thomas Alva Edison, the "Wizard of Menlo Park."[12] P. T. Barnum, whose Bridgeport home is alluded to in chapter 1 of *A Connecticut Yankee*, is also relevant.[13] More important than particular sources or parallels, though, are the representative tendencies Hank embodies and acts out.[14]

Based on his own divided feelings and drawing on his insights into his country and his countrymen, in Hank Morgan Twain has also created a figure who moves into a backward land with his war technology and capitalism. "A one-man imperial expedition," John Kasson writes, "the Yankee regards Arthur's subjects much as nineteenth-century English and Americans viewed underdeveloped nations of black Africans and Indians of their own time. On different occasions he calls them 'white Indians,' 'modified savages,' 'pigmies,' 'great simple-hearted creatures,' 'big children,' 'sheep.' They are pictured as credulous, superstitious, gleeful, innocent, cruel, irrational, dirty, vulgar—all the 'native' virtues and vices."[15] Like the Indians or other beneficiaries of missionary

12. For a suggestive analysis of the conflicting strains in Edison's public image, see David E. Nye, *The Invented Self: An Anti-Biography, from the Documents of Thomas A. Edison* (Odense, Denmark: Odense University Press, 1983).

13. Hamlin Hill, "Barnum, Bridgeport, and *The Connecticut Yankee*," *American Quarterly* 16 (1964): 615–16.

14. Henry Nash Smith, *A Connecticut Yankee in King Arthur's Court*, ed. Bernard L. Stein, introduction by Henry Nash Smith (Berkeley: Iowa Center for Textual Studies, University of California Press, 1979), argues that "Hank Morgan is at bottom Clemens himself" and that Hank "is in some sense also Grant, a man whom Clemens admired without reservation" (p. 4). Subsequent references will be abbreviated CY and cited by page number in the text. In *Mark Twain: The Development of a Writer*, Smith also stresses that "the identification of author with narrator destroys the kind of fictional integrity Mark Twain had been able to confer on Huck Finn" (p. 144) and that Twain's increasing identification leads to "the violence of the catastrophic ending of *A Connecticut Yankee*, a violence so disturbing that one is tempted to seek a psychological explanation for it" (p. 168). Smith's influential argument distracts us from Twain's perceptive revelations, from what Twain in fact shows. Smith is unwilling to see the America Twain illuminates. He does not give Twain's imagination enough credit and does not weight sufficiently Twain's capacity to distance himself from Hank. See Roger B. Salomon, *Twain and the Image of History* (New Haven: Yale University Press, 1961), although Salomon does not follow through on his view that Twain emphasizes "the distance between himself and his hero and the particular point of view of the latter" (p. 116).

15. *Civilizing the Machine*, pp. 206–7.

zeal and Manifest Destiny, Hank wants to improve them, as Twain later observed, "down to [our] level."[16] In *A Connecticut Yankee*, the process of exposure is complicated by Twain's divided attitudes toward Hank and all he stands for and against. Rooted in this ambivalence, in Hank Morgan Twain has seized on a character structure and a set of values that combine Hank's capitalistic, republican, Manifest Destiny, and technological commitments. Together they culminate in a display of war technology that brings "the dream of a republic" to a nightmarish close (CY, p. 343). The destructive violence is not an aberration but is integral to the contradictory strains in the Yankee's representative character and ideology.

At the outset Twain has Hank define himself with engaging directness as a magician of the practical, as a man "nearly barren of sentiment" who has "learned to make everything": "boilers, engines, all sorts of labor-saving machinery." But above all, this head superintendent at the Colt works, "the great arms-factory," has learned to make "guns, revolvers, cannon" (CY, p. 50). Although he is not aware of it, from the outset his involvement in war technology is at odds with his commitment to the technology of peace and human improvement. From the beginning, Twain presents Hank as unaware of his own inner divisions of personality and ideology. Although in the course of composition Twain deepens and darkens his initial conception, the results reinforce his basic intuitions about the character. Twain needed to write *A Connecticut Yankee* in order to probe fully the meaning of what he had outlined from the beginning: the machine-gunning, the torpedoes, and the electrocutions in the culminating battle between the Yankee and the Knights were part of his original plan. In the 1886 version the war machinery is described as "plenty good enough capital to go into business . . . with."[17] In the original conception, war technology and capitalism are linked from the outset. They assume darkened meaning as the novel unfolds, as does Hank's compartmentalized consciousness.

Hank's commitment to peace and human improvement is at odds with war technology, but in Twain's perceptive version implementing the "dream of a republic" also depends on the very war technology that destroys the republic. In a more personal way, Hank comes to revel in outraged descriptions of abused women and men. This unsentimental magician of the practical has again compartmentalized himself. Not only does he have unacknowledged feelings but he also has powerful, unacknowledged hostilities. Consciously, his fascination with women and

16. "To the Person Sitting in Darkness" (1901), in *Mark Twain on the Damned Human Race*, ed. Janet Smith (New York: Hill and Wang, 1962), p. 14.

17. Smith, *A Connecticut Yankee*, p. 7 and "Appendix A," p. 502.

men under the whip establishes his republican sympathies and repugnance against the abuses of tyrants. But his descriptions of tears, screams, and bleeding wounds also suggest an unacknowledged cruelty and violence his actual behavior amply confirms. Hank, of course, puts a good face on everything he does, but he also lets us know at the start that as head superintendent at the arms factory he liked to dominate the men, that he was "full of fight—that goes without saying" (CY, p. 50)—and that in a showdown with one of his subordinates he was laid out with a crowbar (and ended up in Camelot). The contradictions that increasingly develop in the behavior and ideology of this practical magician committed to human improvement are thus foreshadowed from the beginning. They are rooted in a divided personality structure Twain knows as intimately as he knows the country the Yankee emerges from.

The concealed tensions that have plagued American republicanism from the days of Franklin and Madison reappear in the conflict between Hank's commitment to liberty and freedom and his own impulse to dominate others and become Boss, a conflict rooted in the market society and in Hank's character and related to his seriously divided feelings about the common man he is ostensibly trying to save. The early republicans sustained a delicate balance between their fear of the common man and their fear of absolute authority, between their elitist distrust of ordinary people and their recognition that a properly controlled participation was necessary. For Hank the centralized power of a united church poses the same threat of the paralysis of human thought that any strong, united faction did to the author of Federalist Paper Number Ten. Hank has the same set of liberal commitments that also evolved to support the republican hegemony—a belief in free public education and competitive examinations to assure that the meritocracy would get the most able people available; a belief in literacy and a free press to assure that the voter would be well-informed and competent to elect able people to represent him; a belief in the miracles of technology to provide a basis of material prosperity; a belief in free trade to assure that the worldwide benefits of technology would be rationally shared; and a belief in advertising, buying and selling, and stock manipulation, the forms capitalism assumes in A Connecticut Yankee. As Hank's aggressive involvement in war technology indicates, the hegemony he speaks for has a dark strain functionally related to the values and the processes that legitimize the republican system.

Equally important, the protection of human freedom, the central legitimizing value of the republican hegemonic process, functions to preserve the unequal distribution of power and property. It is a question not simply of belief but of action within a system of power, rewards, dominance, and subordination. The republican view of freedom stresses individual, privatized, competitive behavior, the alienation of the self as a commodity, and a society structured to maintain the unequal distribution of power and property, at the same time allowing outsiders sufficient entry to sustain the system and its claims to fairness. All of Hank's liberal commitments serve to justify the system and to implement the prevailing inequality. Madison, the most brilliant spokesman for the republican position, justifies the inequalities as being grounded not in social conditions that can be altered but in the inevitably unequal faculties of human nature.[18] Throughout the nineteenth century the modified Calvinism of the Founders could always break free of urbane restraints and reassert itself as a savage suspicion of that human nature the Founders themselves viewed with civilized moderation. Under the pressure of his own increasing frustration with the infernal typesetting machine he was losing everything on, Twain releases his own charge of those Calvinist attitudes he had deeply interiorized. Calvinist and republican elitism and their latent or overt hostility toward ordinary human nature, toward the common man, emerge in Hank's view of human nature as mud and scum. This tendency conflicts with his own and his republican-Enlightenment tradition's view that "a man *is* a man" (CY, p. 346). Similarly, the authoritarian tendency in Calvinism and the attraction toward it latent in the republican's ambivalence about authority surface boldly in Hank's delight in being Boss.[19] Do we really believe that all that hatred of authority doesn't someplace involve just a little love? Twain, moreover, acutely senses the destructive possibilities latent in the uneasy republican commitment to technology linked to its much less uneasy commitment to capitalism and expansionism, the latter presented under the favorable aegis of Manifest Destiny or the negative one of imperialism.[20]

18. *The Mind of the Founder: Sources of the Political Thought of James Madison*, ed. Marvin Meyers (Indianapolis: Bobbs-Merrill, 1973), esp. Federalist Paper No. 10, p. 124. From Madison's time to ours the system he helped establish has been remarkably successful at sustaining the legitimacy of the republican hegemony and at maintaining the structural inequalities. See my Introduction to Part 2, pp. 92–94 and notes 11, 12, and 13 of that section.

19. In *Civilizing the Machine*, Kasson, whose analysis is in other respects similar to mine, believes that "*despite* his professions of republicanism, the Yankee displays alarming fondness for despotic power" (p. 209; my emphasis). I see the desire for power and control as an integral but often concealed strain in the republican hegemonic system.

20. On the relation to technology, see Kasson, *Civilizing the Machine*; on the relation to capitalism, see Ellen Wood, *Mind and Politics* (Berkeley: University of California Press, 1972), pp. 154–56, and Joyce Appleby, *Capitalism and a New Social Order: The Republican Vision of the 1790s* (New York University Press, 1984); on prosperity, expansionism, and the resulting uneasiness, see Fred Somkin, *Unquiet Eagle: Memory and Desire in the Idea of American Freedom* (Ithaca: Cornell University Press, 1967).

Perhaps Hank's tendencies toward compartmentalization and division are themselves grounded in the republican system's basic tendency to preserve inequality, especially the unequal distribution of property, legitimized as the protection of freedom. On this hypothesis the republican hegemonic system itself provides strong incentives for people to develop alienated habits of thought, feeling, and behavior that encourage them to structure reality in the special ways Hank illustrates. The system's tendency to preserve inequality justified as the protection of freedom is in this view a main source of Hank's divided consciousness, and not of Hank's alone. More basically, these divisions emerge from and illuminate the reifying process inseparable from Hank's American market society. As commodity value becomes the dominant measure of worth, as money becomes the dominant means of exchange, and as the divisions and scale of factory labor make work take on a mystified inevitability the worker feels he has no control over, a commodified or reified consciousness results. The products of the worker's labor assume a commodified objectivity and seem to have a life of their own unrelated to human activity. In this system of commodity exchange people also alienate parts of themselves and sell their labor as a commodity. Hank's compartmentalized consciousness shows the impact of this pervasive reification process.

Hank has worked his way up from an ordinary workman to superintendent at the Colt arms factory, a model of the division of labor, of interchangeable parts, and of late-nineteenth-century technology. But despite his artisan origins and his factory experience, Hank shows no traces of the sort of working-class culture Herbert Gutman examines.[21] Instead, Hank has completely assimilated the prevailing dominant-class outlook: his divided consciousness epitomizes the emerging dominant-class cultural hegemony of his period. To shift from the character to his creator, when Twain first became familiar with it, the Paige typesetting machine was being made at the Colt arms factory.[22] Twain first gleefully fired the Gatling gun at the same factory.[23] The two inventions neatly symbolize two of the divided strains in Hank's representative ideology. To concentrate not on the war machine but on the Paige typesetter, it is a model of the "labor-saving machinery" Hank says he learned to make "at the great Colt arms-factory" (CY, p. 50). Twain's increasing involvement with the Paige typesetting machine may have made him unusually sensitive to the dynamics of reification. Twain, after all, had already

21. *Work, Culture and Society in Industrializing America: Essays in American Working-Class and Social History* (New York: Knopf, 1976).

22. From a Mark Twain memorandum, quoted by Albert Bigelow Paine, *Mark Twain: A Biography*, 2 vols. (New York: Harper and Brothers, 1912), 2:903.

23. Smith, *Mark Twain's Fable of Progress*, p. 43 and n. 8, pp. 110–11.

registered "Mark Twain" as a trademark and had a keen eye for the commodified value of the roles he invented. His experience with the typesetter further stresses money as a central value and has all the signs of a machine process beyond human control.

Twain was compelled by the typesetter partly because it promised unimaginable wealth, partly because in another version of the reification process the human power of thought was transferred to the machine and the machine "was automatic; the machine fed itself from a galley of dead matter and without human help or suggestion, for it began its work of its own accord when the type channels needed filling, and stopped of its own accord when they were full enough."[24] Beyond the machine itself Twain, a precise speller, consistently misspelled "Paige" as "Page."[25] "In his enthusiasm and frustration, he even developed an irrational sense of linkage between A Connecticut Yankee and the typesetter and wished to complete both projects on the same day, as if he too were a word-machine."[26] In A Connecticut Yankee, Twain fuses his involvement in the reification process with his interest in Grant's Civil War Memoirs, his fascination with the Gatling gun and other techniques of late-nineteenth-century warfare, and his own underlying hostilities toward the infernal machine he hoped would make him immensely wealthy.[27] In his novel Twain grasps key divisions in American capitalism, consciousness, and character structure. At the end, based on these realities, the result is a startling projection beyond the nineteenth century into the carnage of the twentieth.

As a capitalist, Hank uses a racy language full of the slang of stock-trading, profit-making, and get-up-and-go. "He conceives of himself as a new 'stockholder in a corporation,'" Lorne Fienberg observes. Fienberg then cites several other examples. Hank says of his predicted eclipse: "'in a business way it would be the making of me' and he is willing to charge a tactical blunder up 'to profit and loss.' Hank views the tournaments as a 'business man' would, with an eye to improving their efficiency, and knight-errantry is little more than a risky speculation." To confirm this insight, Fienberg concludes with a telling quotation from the novel:

24. Twain memoranda quoted by Paine, Mark Twain, 2:904.
25. Webster, Mark Twain, Business Man, p. 171, n. 1.
26. Kasson, Civilizing the Machine, p. 205.
27. On Grant, see the references in note 5 above and Smith, A Connecticut Yankee, p. 4; on Grant, the Gatling gun, and late-nineteenth-century warfare, particularly as it was unleashed against the Indians and the Zulus, see Kasson, Civilizing the Machine, p. 212 and n. 76, p. 262; on Twain's underlying hostilities toward the Paige typesetting machine, see Smith, Mark Twain: The Development of a Writer, p. 168, and Cox, Mark Twain: The Fate of Humor, pp. 208–10.

No sound and legitimate business can be established on a basis of speculation. A successful whirl in the knight-errantry line—now what is it, when you blow away the nonsense and come down to the cold facts? It's just a corner in pork, that's all, and you can't make anything else out of it. You're rich—yes, suddenly rich—for about a day, maybe a week: then somebody corners the market on *you* and down goes your bucket-shop. . . . [28]

The pun in "bucket-shop" refers both to the metal helmets of the knights and to "an establishment ostensibly accepting orders to buy and sell stocks, bonds, and commodities, but actually engaged in gambling on the rise and fall of their prices, or in betting secretly against its customers, speculating with funds entrusted to it, etc." (*Webster's New World Dictionary*). Hank's irreverence and comically incongruous language of bucket-shops and pork undercuts knight-errantry and Malory's elaborate syntax and archaisms. But for someone who criticizes speculation as unsound, Hank knows a lot about it. He often establishes his own business "on a basis of speculation," so that Hank, too, is deflated. His way of seeing, his penchant for ignoring his own contradictions, and his unquestioning sense of the superiority of his values make Hank a frequent object of satire.

In one of the most effective two-edged jokes in the novel, Hank harnesses a hermit to a sewing machine: "I . . . got five years' good service out of him; in which time he turned out upward of eighteen thousand first-rate tow-linen shirts. . . . These shirts cost me nothing but just the mere trifle for the materials . . . and they sold like smoke to pilgrims at a dollar and a half apiece" (CY, p. 260). The passage simultaneously exposes "the heartless capitalist and the machine-bound worker," as Allan Guttmann observes,[29] and also the commercial exploitation of religion and the ascetic monastic ideal. At the end of the episode Hank disposes of his commodified worker-machine: "I noticed that the motive power had taken to standing on one leg, and I found that there was something the matter with the other one; so I stocked the business and unloaded, taking Sir Bors de Ganis into camp financially along with certain of his friends; for the works stopped within a year, and the good saint got him to his rest" (CY, p. 260). By the end of the novel Hank has taught everyone how to trick and joke his way. Launcelot learns to practice Hank's style of capitalism, which brings on the final catastrophe.

Early in his career Hank misses the conveniences he is used to, including the insurance chromos and the "God-Bless-Our-Home" over the door, as well as tea and coffee, books, and glass windows (CY, pp. 98–

28. Fienberg, "Twain's Connecticut Yankee," p. 161.

29. "Mark Twain's *Connecticut Yankee*: Affirmation of the Vernacular Tradition?" *New England Quarterly* 33 (1960): 233.

100). Hank makes no distinctions: in his eyes his taste and values are superior, and he is going to impose them. Outside the novel the Third World is littered with the results. "I saw," Hank says, "that I was just another Robinson Crusoe cast away on an uninhabited island, with no society but some more or less tame animals, and if I wanted to make life bearable I must do as he did—invent, contrive, create; reorganize things, set brain and hand to work, and keep them busy" (CY, p. 100). The joke is partly on Hank: he brags about his own superior intelligence, but because he sees exclusively through the lenses of his market society's hegemonic assumptions he is unable to see the cohesive traditional society his own market society would privatize, to say nothing of the way he views human beings as "tame animals."

In *A Connecticut Yankee*, comedy frequently results from the strain between opposed but functionally related tendencies within the hegemonic process Hank speaks for, in this case between the republican view of "man as man" and the pervasive view that "backward" and other "inferior" people are animals. Most American readers to some extent share Hank's hegemonic assumptions and contradictions. The novel functions to expose and illuminate them, often through a comic or satiric incongruity that also catches the reader in the act. Hank later ridicules Sandy for seeing princesses instead of pigs, for viewing the world through the lenses of cultural assumptions he knows falsify reality. But Hank never deeply questions the extent to which, because of his market society's outlook, he himself sees animals instead of people and accepts pork as a normal way of doing business. In a more basic way, because Hank's entire consciousness is reified, for him "the social relations between individuals . . . are disguised under the shape of social relations between the products of labor," a process as primary for him as Sandy's view of the pigs is for her.[30]

As part of the same hegemonic process, as a capitalist, Hank never questions his right to "keep them busy" or to contrive for his own convenience and theirs. The "them" refers first to his "brain and hand" but extends to the "tame animals" Hank is going to retrain. He takes it for granted that he should control, reorganize, and change. In his own eyes his control is benign and it is important for him to believe that his title of Boss is bestowed on him by the nation. Hank becomes Boss, though, because his power is based not primarily on consent but on his

30. Karl Marx, *Capital: A Critique of Political Economy*, trans. Samuel Moore and Edward Aveling, ed. Fredrick Engels, 3 vols. (New York: International Publishers, 1967), 1:77. Interestingly enough, in this section on "The Fetishism of Commodities," Marx has been using Robinson Crusoe to contrast a capitalistic outlook with that of the Middle Ages.

mastery of war technology and showmanship and on his unquestioning belief in the rightness of his civilization of insurance chromos and meritocracy.

Hank speaks for the hegemony of the market society as opposed to that of a traditional feudal society. As part of his own legitimizing outlook, he celebrates the kind of freedom he is used to and criticizes the slavery of the feudal regime. The slavery should be opposed. The tragedy comes from the fact that Hank does not have a worthy replacement. For Hank freedom means that people are out for themselves, that they can move up and down the class-prestige ladder on the basis of ability, and that positions are won competitively, not inherited. He cannot accept the kind of "loyalty toward their King and Church and nobility" the people show (CY, p. 110). These cohesive ties are antithetical to his belief in a market-society freedom that features privatization, mobility, and individual control and individual self-interest. Public and personal ties are so unimportant to Hank that in his initial self-definition he mentions his work, his rise in position, but not the fact that he is engaged.

In their perceptive analysis of the political implications of this self-definition, Catherine and Michael Zuckert argue persuasively that Hank's privatization and his emphasis on comfort and convenience embody "the essence of bourgeois psychology," a position most clearly defined in Locke's *Essay Concerning the Human Understanding*.[31] The Zuckerts contrast this bourgeois emphasis on comfort-seeking with the King's fearless behavior in the smallpox hut. "The Yankee builds his life on the ground of comfort seeking, and thus fundamentally on the fear of death. The Yankee admires Arthur because Arthur is free from that burden that rules the Yankee's life. Manliness requires the overcoming of the fear of death" (p. 84). Stressing as it does control, privatization, competitive freedom, comfort-seeking, and an underlying fear of death, Hank's hegemonic outlook is widely shared. No wonder so many American readers from his time to ours have taken him as normative.

Hank is not normative, but, with Twain's full approval, he does effectively lay into the aristocratic class structure. His criticism is still telling because he touches the central nerve of his market society, the issues of self-interest and the freedom to control one's person and not to be subjected to the control of others. Most of us still respond strongly with Hank and Twain to the indictment of people who exist solely "to grovel before king and Church and noble; to slave for them, sweat blood for

31. "'And in Its Wake We Followed': The Political Wisdom of Mark Twain," *Interpretation* 3 (1972): 69, n. 23 and 67–69. Subsequent references will be cited by page number in the text.

them, starve that they might be fed, work that they might play, drink misery to the dregs that they might be happy, go naked that they might wear silks and jewels, pay taxes that they might be spared from paying them, be familiar all their lives with the degrading language and postures of adulation that they might walk in pride and think themselves the Gods of this world" (CY, p. 111). Like other spokesmen for the hegemony of the market society, Hank finds it easier to see the genuine abuses of foreign systems than of his own. Late-nineteenth-century America was also vulnerable to Hank's charges, but instead of focusing on the corrosive results of the Yankee's market-society theory and practice, Twain has Hank export the results to the middle ages or the pre–Civil War South. He simultaneously flatters his readers and acts out a widely shared tendency of the hegemonic process that the character, the author, and the reader all share. Justified by his abhorrence of tyranny and his commitment to personal control, Hank exercises his power. He becomes Boss, accepts a modest one percent of the profits, and begins to institute his own hegemonic system in place of the feudal one.

Henry Nash Smith observes that Hank "operates in complete defiance of the supposed laws of capital accumulation that obtain in a capitalistic system,"[32] but at a deeper level Hank's divided consciousness is permeated by his market society's conflicting values and processes. Hank is committed to efficiency, but he also stages shows. He is committed to "sound and legitimate business," but he consistently speculates and takes whoever he can into camp financially. More important, as a capitalist, he sees people as "motive power" or as "savages" to be improved through all the conveniences Hank misses and wants to manufacture—at a profit. The two views of people as commodified objects or as material to exploit and to uplift are related; in nineteenth-century America, one was for home use, the other for export. This way of seeing people coexists in tension with Hank's view that a "man *is* a man." Hank's man factory brings these contradictions to a focus. Hank believes he can manufacture men. He sees no incompatibility between humanity and the commodified processes of industrial capitalism. Hank embodies strains within the outlook and practices of industrial capitalism, finance capitalism, and consumer capitalism and tensions between a capitalistic outlook that sees people as impersonal instruments and a republican one that sees "man as man." As Hank shows, these strains are related as integral parts of a legitimizing hegemonic process that leads through

32. Quoted by Chadwick Hansen, "The Once and Future Boss: Mark Twain's Yankee," *Nineteenth-Century Fiction* 28 (1973): 67, n. 4.

increasing violence to the catastrophic final war.[33] Viewed not from Hank's nineteenth-century perspective but from that of the Arthurians Hank works out on, the war also dramatizes Hank's failure to impose his own foreign hegemony on people who finally do not accept the legitimacy of his values and practices. They fear but do not respect Hank. Because at the deepest level they have not interiorized Hank's outlook and way of operating, at the end he resorts to machine guns, land mines, and dynamite.

In the earlier parts of *A Connecticut Yankee*, the contests between Hank and his rivals, especially his rival magicians, dramatize these divisions in consciousness and ideology, show the human and inhuman faces of their practitioner, and throw light on the complex market society they emerge from. As Hank structures situations, he polarizes the superstitions of a monolithic church supporting and supported by an oppressive feudal hierarchy as over against his own technological skill, scientific knowledge, and desire to uplift the benighted inhabitants of "this dark land" (CY, p. 128). In part it is his version of the conflict between Old World tyranny and superstition and New World freedom, meritocracy, and enlightenment; in part it is his version of the White Man's Burden. Because Merlin is associated with the Church and the hierarchy, when Hank stages a show and uses the lightning to help him blow up his rival's tower, this more flamboyant latter-day Benjamin Franklin is in his eyes simply advancing a good republican cause and having a little innocent fun in the bargain. The explosion does not kill anyone and the stakes are high, since if Hank fails to perform, tyranny and superstition will prevail over the nineteenth-century technological-capitalistic civilization he is preparing. It is significant, then, that Hank totally ignores the beauty of this venerable old structure; as in the Benjamin Franklin and grass-roots versions of the Puritan tradition he emerges from, beauty does not figure in his view of this or any other situation. Even more important, he never responds to the monolithic Church behind Merlin's tower as a cohesive force helping to tie together its communicants and promoting a sense of community. In the American way, Hank wants to blow the tower sky high and to replace the Church with forty fragmented, Madisonian, American-style sects.

33. In *Mark Twain's Fable of Progress*, Smith points to the contrast between the satire of Hank as a capitalistic "entrepreneur in search of profit" and Hank as "a humanitarian emancipator of the downtrodden peasant. Mark Twain's failure to undertake the revisions that would have been necessary to confer a consistent motivation on the Yankee left an element of obscurity in the narrative that puzzles the modern reader" (p. 54). In my view the two strains are consistent and Twain has succeeded, not failed, in developing Hank's representative characterization.

Hank's increasing desire to show off and blow up things—and then people—is inseparable from his attractive, frank American common sense and technological competence. Hank sensibly figures out that a leak is causing the trouble with the Holy Fountain. But instead of simply repairing it, Hank stages an immense show full of terror-inspiring electrical tricks and exploding fireworks. The "infernal fires" of his "four furious volcanoes" (CY, p. 268) are a make-believe forecast of the final electrical storm in which "the serene volcano" of his technological civilization does "give . . . sign of the rising hell in its bowels" (CY, p. 128). Consciously, however, Hank is simply using the white magic of electrical technology to gain the admiration he revels in. But his imagery of infernal darkness and his comic curses, replete with concealed references to nihilism and Götterdämerung, suggest destructive intensities he does not consciously acknowledge (CY, pp. 267–68). He sees himself using his white magic to combat the dark forces of superstition and uncleanliness. But he also has dark tendencies concealed in the rising hell of his own bowels. These destructive impulses are rooted in his Calvinism and in his unacknowledged hostilities. In part these impulses also emerge from and reveal hidden strains in a republican position committed in its own eyes to peace, rationality, and Manifest Destiny.[34]

It is useful to outline the further implications of what is hidden in those bowels whose rising hell finally does volcanically come into the open. With the help of Philip Greven's *The Protestant Temperament*, we are able to consider the relation between Protestant child-rearing practices, toilet training, repression, and attitudes toward cleanliness, order, discipline, accumulation, work, and authority.[35] Greven explores the ambivalence that Protestant child-rearing practices generated on each of these related values. The resulting character structure is a familiar one intimately related to the technological and capitalistic achievements of Anglo-American culture. In *A Connecticut Yankee*, this configuration is also intimately related to the final destructive and self-destructive ending.

Like other bringers of light to the inhabitants of dark lands, Hank is especially satiric of the bathing habits of the childlike natives. He does not bat an eye at the terror he causes, but he is bothered by all that dirt. Huck Finn knows better, but Hank comically links soap, civilization,

34. For other views of the volcano, see Kenneth Lynn, *Mark Twain and Southwestern Humor* (Boston: Little, Brown, 1959), pp. 249, 252–54; Guttmann, "Mark Twain's Connecticut Yankee," p. 235; Smith, *Mark Twain: The Development of a Writer*, pp. 158–61; and Kasson, *Civilizing the Machine*, pp. 209–14.

35. *The Protestant Temperament: Patterns of Child-Rearing, Religious Experience, and the Self in Early America* (New York: Knopf, 1977).

and billboards, the cleanliness and advertising that go along with the technology and consumer capitalism he sponsors. In addition to soap, the stock exchange, and prophylactic toothbrushes, one of his other gifts to the unwashed natives is the bathing pool he reinstates and tricks the monks into using after he has repaired the Holy Fountain. Hank thus speaks for the hegemony of a clean, technologically advanced, capitalistic, Protestant culture insensitive to beauty and critical of the dirt and the superstition of Catholic Europe and all the other lands where people are living in darkness. The Benjamin Franklin synthesis still maintains some of its humor and energy, but in Hank it is also showing the strains of a further century of overuse.

On the one hand, as a humane American republican, Hank is genuinely opposed to the cruelty and oppression he finds in a culture with a rigid, overt structure of authority rather than the more fluid and covert one he is used to. He is eloquent about the existence of two Reigns of Terror, one lasting for centuries and the other for only a few short years. And he repeatedly brings alive the way the powerful nobles abuse those beneath them. On this count Hank comes off very well in contrast to Henry Adams's celebration of rose windows, the fecundity of the Virgin, and the unity of the thirteenth century and Adams's insensitivity to social injustice in either the nineteenth or the thirteenth century. What is called for is a fusion of Adams's sense of beauty and cohesion and Hank's sense of cruelty and injustice as these two writers use the Middle Ages as a lens on their own America.

The other side of Hank's republican hatred of cruel, arbitrary authority, however, emerges in his contest with Morgan LeFay, another of his rival magicians. Hank is appalled at the way this evil sorceress effortlessly knifes an innocent attendant as if this "poor child" were a meaningless object instead of a human being (CY, p. 190). Hank then tells a series of sentimental stories featuring a tortured husband and weeping wife and babe; a husband and wife arbitrarily separated and made old before their years, their affection deadened by wrongful imprisonment; and a husband who watched from his prison window the funerals of his family, only to discover they were all alive and the funerals were a cruel hoax invented by Morgan LeFay to torment him. The stories all play on the heartstrings of Hank and those readers attuned to the values of domesticity violated by evil, capricious authority. Hank thus implicitly declares for the virtue of New World, nineteenth-century, humane republican feeling as over against the arbitrary abuse of the family under Old World tyranny.

His own condescension toward Sandy, however, illustrates the real place of the idealized woman and family of late-nineteenth-century values. Hank simultaneously puts wife and child at the center of his world, condescends to his wife, and for the long periods he is involved in public affairs totally ignores his family. Even as he criticizes her, moreover, Hank admires Morgan LeFay's intelligence and style. Although as a woman aligned with tyranny she embodies Hank's unacknowledged feelings of hostility against women, at a deeper level Hank feels an affinity with Morgan LeFay. It is not accidental that Morgan LeFay and Hank Morgan share the same name. She also participates in the imagery of powerful, not "extinct volcano[es]" (CY, p. 210). She is thus aligned with the hell-like energy and power that erupt at the end. "And she was a Vesuvius," Hank observes. "As a favor, she might consent to warm a flock of sparrows for you, but then she might take that very opportunity to turn herself loose and bury a city" (CY, p. 210). Without realizing it, Hank is describing himself, or rather those contradictory tendencies whose darker side he consciously ignores or dignifies. Sentimentally kind to the wife and child he also ignores; opposed to tyranny but a Boss himself; compassionate but given to increasingly cruel jokes; valuing "man as man" but also feeling that people are human muck, Hank is an intensified Morgan LeFay who does in fact explode and bury a city. When he does, all the concealed negative tendencies—the authoritarianism, the contempt for human nature, the technological arrogance, the expansionist and acquisitive greed—all the dark tendencies working within the bowels of the capitalistic-republican-Protestant system explode and bury a city. Hank Morgan and Morgan LeFay, these two magicians, in Hank's view embodiments of opposed systems, turn out to have similarities disturbing to believers in republican virtue and rationality in an age of increasing technological and capitalistic power.

Hank's view of Morgan LeFay also brings into the open the determinist or environmentalist tendencies in the related Protestant and empiricist traditions Hank emerges from. Under the pressure of the new age of machines and capitalistic power, the pilot as magician of "Old Times on the Mississippi" is no longer available to give credibility to an animated world itself no longer available to Twain's imagination. Instead, Twain has Hank think seriously that "training is everything; training is all there is to a person" (CY, p. 208). Hank speaks for a tendency that was always available to people in the American Protestant tradition, the tendency to regard the self as nothing, a speck of dust in the face of an all-powerful God. Hank uses the current Darwinian language of evolution fused with telltale references to Adam and Sheol (Hell), the reminders that his outlook grows out of his Yankee Protestant upbringing.

The empiricist tendency to give priority to the world of objects and to regard the self as a passive receiver of external sense impressions also contributes to Hank's view that the external environment and the mechanisms of heredity dwarf what is unique in the self. Hank represents a benchmark in Twain's increasingly deterministic outlook. In contrast to the pilot of "Old Times," Hank's view is a perfectly understandable result of the increasing mechanization of American life and the increasing concentration on capitalistic accumulation. Americans, Twain knew, had always worshiped money, but in the post–Civil War period he believed they had learned how to get down in the mud and grovel after it. One result of the social changes of the post–Civil War period and his involvement in those changes is that Twain can no longer imagine the magician as the true pilot of "Old Times" or the conjure man Jim of *Huck Finn*. Instead, Twain responds to the reifying pressures of his period and also brings into the open the determinist, environmentalist tendencies of Hank's Yankee religious and philosophical heritage. Latent in the Protestant and republican traditions, the tendency to see the self as insignificant and to magnify the mechanical processes of nature or the external environment—these strains also contribute to Hank's use of technology to exterminate all that threatening human muck. Although respect for the inviolable human personality and the sanctity of the human soul are integral to American republicanism and Calvinism, both traditions also contain the counter impulses Hank articulates, abstractly in his views about training, more concretely in his actions at the end.

In tension with his sense of the insignificance of the self is Hank's simultaneous exaggeration of his own power. Psychologically it is the familiar pattern of feeling worthless and powerless and at the same time supremely confident and omnipotent. Philip Greven relates this syndrome to the Protestant practices of breaking or bending the child's will, demonstrating to the child his insignificance in the face of authoritarian or authoritative parents and later an authoritarian or authoritative God, depending on the intensity of the training and on the evangelical or moderate nature of the tradition. After more or less active rebellion, again depending on the tradition, the adult subordinates himself before God as before his parents and becomes again as a little child. But he also identifies with the authority figure of parent or God and participates in their power. The dynamics of self-contempt and self-righteousness follow the usual law of the return and revenge of the repressed. Hank's views on the impact of training and the punitive power of conscience (CY, p. 210) suggest the extremities of an evangelical upbringing in which "we have no thoughts of our own, no opinions of our own: they are transmitted to us, trained into us" (CY, p. 208).

More interesting than the psychological profile, however, are the political and social consequences and conflicts related to Hank's sense that he is nothing and at the same time capable of living "a pure and high and blameless life" (CY, p. 208), "humbly," of course, and as Boss and then as the war technician who humbly, purely, and blamelessly turns human beings into piles of rotting corpses. The Protestant emphasis on saving the individual soul, moreover, does not necessarily involve ignoring the rest of humanity, but the tendency is strongly present "to save that one microscopic atom in me that is truly *me*: the rest may land in Sheol and welcome for all I care" (CY, p. 208). Hank combines this self-centered indifference to the rest of the world with a conflicting missionary and imperialistic impulse to impose his and his culture's values on the rest of the world, and then, far from letting other people land where they may, he turns on them and brings them the Sheol lurking in the bowels of his system.

The divisions within Hank's personality, ideology, and actions are logically contradictory but socially and psychologically systematic and comprehensible. Hank's energy and humor, the benign side of his republican-Protestant value system, and his style of structuring situations to place himself in the right all disguise the sense of developing horror they also contribute to. At first, Hank rides along "lost in thinking about how to banish oppression from this land and restore to all its people their stolen rights and manhood without disobliging anybody" (CY, p. 167). At this stage, when he puffs on his pipe, the smoke spewing out from his helmet is magic enough to terrify his opponents into submission when two powerfully armed knights attack him. The good-natured comedy satisfies Hank's sense of the absurdity of feudal beliefs and the superiority of his own humanity and peaceful nineteenth-century practices. A pipe, after all, is a remarkably innocuous weapon. As in all his encounters, moreover, Hank is the underdog, not the aggressor, and in this instance he responds moderately and comically.

Later, however, the comedy becomes darker when Hank and the King are attacked because the disguised King forgets he is "scum" (CY, p. 316) and is supposed to get out of the way of a couple of armed knights. By now the pipe is long forgotten. Hank feels impelled to use a dynamite bomb against these picturesque upholders of chivalry and oppression who bear down on him, plumes flying and lances leveled. "When they were within fifteen yards, I sent that bomb with a sure aim, and it struck the ground just under the horses' noses. Yes," Hank goes on, "it was a neat thing, very neat and pretty to see. It resembled a steamboat explosion on the Mississippi; and during the next fifteen minutes we stood under a steady drizzle of microscopic fragments of knights and hardware and horseflesh" (CY, p. 317–18). The magic of Hank's war technology is becoming fiercer, although he himself sees the results as "very neat and pretty." This utilitarian aesthetic points up Hank's increasing dehumanization and the split between what he professes and practices or the split within his republican-Protestant position. People in that hegemonic tradition value human life and are repelled when an abused person is seen as "scum." At the same time, people in the republican-Protestant tradition delight in the use of war technology and see its victims not as human beings but as impersonal objects. The comedy, then, turns on our suppressed fascination with technological violence and death and the incongruity of human life treated as an object like hardware or horseflesh.

Hank, in contrast, is delighted when he discovers that "a man is at bottom a man, after all, even if it doesn't show on the outside" (CY, p. 343). The realization comes at the climax of a nightmarish lynching episode that demonstrates "the alacrity with which this oppressed community had turned their cruel hands against their own class in the interest of the common oppressor" (CY, p. 343). The subject is charged with contemporary implications for a society that was lynching blacks at an alarming rate and simultaneously exploiting the racial prejudices of poor whites in the interests of their own oppression. Twain has Hank point up the parallel with the poor whites of the pre–Civil War South but leaves the contemporary scene alone, just as he later suppressed publication of "The United States of Lyncherdom." Instead of confronting the dark strain in American republicanism, the continuing racism and oppression of blacks and poor whites that are among the most telling contradictions in the republican position, Twain avoids the "ages of abuse and oppression" close at hand and safely places the blame for it on monarchy and nobility. He also reconfirms Hank's republican faith in the capacities of the ordinary men who are able to withstand the crushing weight of monarchical oppression and still retain their manhood. Tendencies within Hank and his republican-Protestant system, however, turn out to be more serious than monarchical oppression as a threat to ordinary humanity and to the very "dream of a republic" that Hank has recommitted himself to (CY, pp. 343–46).

In what Hank bills as "a final struggle for supremacy between the two master enchanters of the age" (CY, p. 430), Hank presents himself as "the champion of hard, unsentimental, common-sense and reason." Like his successors into the late twentieth century, he sees no contradiction between these qualities, which might encourage compromise or the search for peaceful alternatives, and his either-or, children-of-light, children-of-dark habit of mind: "I was entering the lists to either destroy knight-errantry or be its victim" (CY, p. 430). Hank, moreover, structures situations in accord with the familiar American myth of violence.

As usual in this myth, because he must be the underdog, he is outnumbered and, because other people are on the side of darkness and are attacking him, he emerges as an innocent victim of aggression reluctantly defending himself. Also as usual, this way of structuring situations conveniently overlooks the power of technology, which more than makes up for the difference in numbers. Hank's revolver is an equalizer and in fact makes him the dominant force in a contest unfairly weighted to his advantage. Hank also minimizes his own role in precipitating the showdown. He conveniently forgets that he is an invader from the outside who is trying to impose his way of life on a reluctant native population. Hank also minimizes his own aggressive hostilities.

In his spectacular struggle with his rival magician and Merlin's knightly supporters, Hank's comic costume reinforces the sense of his innocence. Instead of heavy, medieval armor, he wears a gymnast's costume, "flesh-colored tights from neck to heel, with blue silk puffings about my loins, and bare-headed" (CY, p. 431). The costume emerges from Hank's circus, showman side. His agile horse and flexible lariat come from the world of the Wild West and the Buffalo Bill Show. Although they are not exactly what we would expect from "the champion of hard, unsentimental, common-sense and reason," they do present Hank as an embodiment of the New World. What could be more American and more innocent than circuses and Buffalo Bill displays of skill with lariat and revolver? In a long tradition going back to the English use of massed troops against the flexible tactics of American Indian warfare, Hank speaks for American mobility and resourcefulness opposed to the clumsy, massive weight of aristocratic European numbers and tradition. He also speaks for the deadly power of technology. The concealed weapon in the republican position was the machine and finally the war machine it could unleash to implement its Manifest Destiny and to demonstrate its superiority over all other forms of government. Because of their deep agrarian roots, republicans had always felt uneasy about technology even as they profited from it, and the uneasiness was intensified by prosperity. Hank, however, does not feel uneasy. Right down to his comic, flesh-colored tights he is an embodiment of the forces of light opposed to the forces of darkness. At first, Hank peacefully uses his lariat to immobilize his iron-clad opponents, but after Merlin steals the rope Hank is forced to use his gun. He is outnumbered and is being attacked. For him to stay against such odds would be "murther" (CY, p. 437). Provoked as when he bombed the knights, Hank thus waits until the last second and uses the magic of his revolver to shoot Sir Sagamore and eleven others. The issue of murder has been raised, but the structuring of the situation absolves Hank, at least in his own eyes.

Hank's war machine thus initiates "the march of civilization" (CY, p. 439), a civilization characterized by the life-affirming and the increasingly life-destroying values and practices we have been outlining. Hank sees it as a contest between "the magic of science" and "the magic of fol-de-rol" (CY, p. 439), but revealingly enough it is war technology and not science or technology in general that makes all the difference. At best, "slavery was dead and gone; all men were equal before the law; taxation had been equalized. The telegraph, the telephone, the phonograph, the typewriter, the sewing machine, and all the thousand willing and handy servants of steam and electricity were working their way into favor" (CY, pp. 443–44). But inseparable from these benefits, the "spreaders of civilization . . . went clothed in steel, and equipped with sword and lance and battle-axe, and if they couldn't persuade a person to try a sewing machine on the installment plan, or a melodeon, or a barbed wire fence, or a prohibition journal, or any of the other thousand and one things they canvassed for, they removed him and passed on" (CY, p. 444). The satire undercuts both the veneration of knightly aristocrats and the high-pressure salesmanship of late-nineteenth-century consumer capitalism and its civilization of prohibition journals, barbed wire, and installment plan melodeons and sewing machines. Hank's civilization is a mixed blessing.

When Hank begins to impose it, he pulverizes two knights, then shoots twelve knights, and as his ambitions enlarge he proposes to "take fifty assistants and stand up *against the massed chivalry of the whole earth and destroy it*" (CY, p. 443). He sees himself not as destroying human beings but as destroying an "it." We have thus reached the dead end of republican hatred of monarchy and aristocracy and the dead end as well of Protestant self-righteousness and self-hatred turned against the unregenerate; and the dead end also of the capitalistic, expansionist impulse to impose itself on "the whole earth and destroy it," which is, of course, never officially acknowledged.

A combination of Launcelot's stock manipulation and Arthur's conventional morality precipitates the final confrontation between Hank and the people sitting in darkness. As a main feature of civilization, Hank has introduced the stock exchange to bring the benighted feudal world up to the mark of capitalism. Hank is also committed to the superiority of Victorian sexual morality over the loose practices of Launcelot and Guenevere. Conventional sexual morality and the stock manipulation of finance capitalism, two cornerstones of the republican-Protestant system, are thus instrumental in bringing about the final holocaust.

Despite his eagerness to take on the whole massed might of chivalry

and destroy it, Hank presents himself as a victim of aggression. In his
own eyes Hank has as usual been attacked, this time by the Interdict of
the Church, and he is reluctantly fighting for his life and civilized values
against the overwhelming odds of the forces of darkness. To reinforce
this view of himself he has Sandy and their child reappear. Who could
be more innocent than Hank, bathed in the sentiments of domesticity,
full of real concern for his sick child, and now at last in a position to
unleash the rising hell in the bowels of his system? Hank thus perfectly
expresses the nineteenth-century separation between the masculine
world of power and the domestic realm of sentiment. In the midst of his
preparation to trap and electrocute twenty-five thousand knights, Hank,
without feeling any incongruity, "could imagine the baby goo-
gooing, . . . its fists in its mouth, and itself stretched across its mother's
lap on its back, and she a-laughing and admiring and worshipping, and
now and then tickling under the baby's chin to set it cackling" (CY, p.
473).

Also without applying it to himself, Hank attacks the "sentimental
slobbering" of the commoners who have deserted his cause for the
"righteous cause" he derides (CY, p. 306). His opponents—almost everyone on earth—are now "human muck" (CY, p. 473). In going to this
extreme Hank thus brings into the open the hostility toward ordinary
people always latent in the republican-Protestant system and its ambivalence about human nature. "The dream of a republic" is dead, but the
contradictions within Hank's Protestant-republicanism are destructively
alive.

With perfect deadpan seriousness, Hank exposes the dehumanizing
results of the Protestant work ethic commitment to technological and
economic efficiency carried to the extreme as reified ends in themselves
and separated from any awareness of the value of human lives. As he
describes his plan for electrocuting the knights, Hank emphasizes the
ingenious "economy" of his scheme to have human bodies provide the
fatal connection, so that "you are using no power, you are spending no
money" until—and he goes on in delighted technical detail—"the moment they touch [the wire] they form a connection with the negative
brush *through the ground*, and drop dead" (CY, p. 467). The comedy
turns on the way Hank is disturbed, not about his treatment of human
life but about overlooked technical details that will improve the efficiency and cut costs. "It isn't costing you a cent," he concludes, "til you
touch it off." Twain's original idea of war technology fused with capitalism is beginning to pay disturbing dividends.

The dividends accumulate. Hank arranges to have Gatling guns
slaughter any survivors. And he plants glass-cylinder dynamite tor-

pedoes in "the prettiest garden that was ever planted. . . . We laid them on the surface of the ground, and sprinkled a layer of sand over them. It's an innocent looking garden, but you let a man start in to hoe it once, and you'll see" (CY, p. 468). The war machine in the garden exposes fatal oppositions between tendencies that had coexisted since the beginning of republican ideology. Republicans were committed to peace, they valued "man as man," and they worried about a standing army. But to implement the republic, as they expanded over the continent, they also used war technology, first against the native inhabitants of the virgin land and later against other recipients of Manifest Destiny. The Civil War brought to a focus the contradiction between the peaceful aims of the republic and the war technology necessary to implement them. The new armories and the use or threatened use of armed force against recalcitrant workers were less catastrophic than the Civil War, but they did symbolize the alignment between capitalism and republicanism, an alignment also present in Manifest Destiny and in a less vivid way in the underlying concepts of republican freedom. The republican hegemony stressed peace and peaceful competition but also increasingly depended on a war power its founders distrusted.

Like the nation, Hank begins with the peaceful virgin land, the garden of the earth, a world of "cushioned turf," and the "green light that got its tint from the sundrenched roof of leaves overhead" (CY, p. 145). As Twain's imagination penetrates to the essential contradictions, Hank's war machine converts this garden into a barren waste. The land is ravaged by exploding dynamite bombs. The trenches are filled with water and then with electrocuted human bodies. The harvest is a pile of rotting corpses that poison the air and endanger the handful of survivors. Ostensibly to keep his enemies from using his own technology against him, Hank also blows up the entire factory system he had developed. He destroys the village in order to save it. He also turns his aggressive hostilities against the machines he loves.

Surrounded by his "clean-minded" young helpers (CY, p. 472), Hank dictatorially proclaims a Republic and then blows up the "human muck" who oppose him. The earlier make-believe lightning and volcanic explosions become real. His bombs explode "with a thundercrash," and his enemies become "a whirling tempest of rags and fragments; and along the ground lay a thick wall of smoke that hid what was left of the multitude from our sight" (CY, p. 476). "As to the destruction of life," Hank observes, "it was amazing. . . . Of course we could not *count* the dead, because they did not exist as individuals, but merely as homogeneous protoplasm, with alloys of iron and buttons" (CY, p. 478). The wounded are presumably carried away "under cover of the wall of smoke; there would be sickness among the others—there always is after an episode like that" (CY, p. 478). Hank has mastered the Orwellian tactic of calling a catastrophe "an episode." He then congratulates his troops, "Champions of Human Liberty and Equality" (CY, p. 478).

The contradictions of nineteenth-century republicanism are now looking ahead to the twentieth century, to the worldwide use of the slogans of liberty and equality to justify the unthinkable. "The recent annihilating wars" (CY, p. 478), moreover, have an uncanny, prophetic quality. The trenches full of rotting corpses anticipate those of World War I. The bombing anticipates the carnage of World War II. "The dead" who "did not exist as individuals but merely as homogenous protoplasm, with alloys of iron and buttons" recall both Hiroshima and the napalming of Vietnam, as does the ruined landscape and the abortive body counts. The use of war technology against native populations and justified by the noblest of political creeds is certainly not the monopoly of Hank Morgan's republican-Protestant system. But as Hank expresses "the rising hell in its bowels," we can appreciate Twain's accurate grasp of Hank's character and the market society that formed it. Rooted in the contradictions of the republican-Protestant-capitalistic system he valued and exposed, Mark Twain as magician emerges as a prophetic sorcerer.

Styles of American Individualism

INTRODUCTION TO STYLES OF AMERICAN INDIVIDUALISM

During the nineteenth century, possessive individualism was the dominant model for American individualism. The contradictions within Hank Morgan and his system dramatize that this individualism was varied and changing. Early in the century, small farmers, small businessmen, and small manufacturers actively engaged in the processes of buying and selling, producing and consuming, expanding and failing. Contrary to the received mythology of the self-sufficient independent farmer, from early in the nineteenth century, even American farmers were entrepreneurs producing for a competitive world market.[1] Except as commodities and slave labor, for the most part blacks did not count. Although women and children worked in the factories in Lowell and later in the century in the sweatshops of New York, "entrepreneurs [barred] women from most areas of manufacturing."[2] Farm women continued to do hard, useful labor—weaving, milking, raising children— but on the farms and in the new offices they worked under patriarchal dominance. The competitive system of owners and workers produced and was produced by those restless white male Americans Tocqueville analyzed.

The individual in this system exaggerated his own powers, took personal responsibility for success and failure, and was free to sell his labor and its products for what they would command. The government played an important role as a builder of roads and canals, as a source of land for railroads and land speculators, and as a military power to eliminate native Americans. Because of their communal land ownership and respect for the earth as a nurturing deity, American Indians posed a

1. William Appleman Williams, *The Contours of American History* (Chicago: Quadrangle Books, 1961). For a view that stresses the relation between city merchants and the immediately surrounding countryside, see Paul E. Johnson, *A Shopkeepers Millennium: Society and Revivals in Rochester, New York 1815–1837* (New York: Hill and Wang, 1978), pp. 1–36. But the wheat Rochester milled and exported went to those markets Williams foregrounds.

2. Carroll Smith-Rosenberg, *Disorderly Conduct: Visions of Gender in Victorian America* (New York: Oxford, 1985), pp. 12–13.

basic challenge to the system of possessive individualism, which stressed private ownership, private rights, competing individuals, and alienated labor.[3]

Those below or on the margins, the groups Herbert Gutman has studied, animate the rhythms and vision of Whitman's "Song of Myself."[4] This sustained alternative to the official work ethic individualism also reveals how deeply the dominant society affects even its most powerful critics. Put more abstractly, the mix of hegemonic and counterhegemonic forces varies from writer to writer and can change within a work or within a writer's career, as in the shift from Whitman's "Song of Myself" to *Democratic Vistas*. Because of William Dean Howells's role as a minister of culture, a middle man in the art-exchange market, Howells is especially revealing of the conflicts that in differing degrees all our writers experienced. At the height of the American Renaissance, in their lives and works, Hawthorne, Melville, and Poe exemplify the strain between the individualism of the romantic artist and the possessive individualism of the American marketplace. These conflicts are not external but internalized within selves and works. These works also remind us that, however valuable non-canonical literature is, mainstream art by mainstream writers provides crucial insights into the strains the market society generates.

A central tension is that America is both a democracy and a market society. Melville probes this conflict to its heights and depths through Ahab's titanic individualism, Fleece's sermon to the sharks, and Ishmael's subversive reflections on "Fast-Fish and Loose-Fish." Early in the twentieth century, Dreiser engages with a vastly changed America that nonetheless poses dilemmas similar to those Melville explored. From the vantage point of the new century, in *The Financier* (1912), Dreiser looks back on the formative period of American finance capitalism during and immediately after the Civil War. In *The Financier*, he focuses on one of the powerful organizers of the new system. Through Frank Cowperwood he probes the political psychology of the emerging capitalism, implicates the reader, and generates insights into the new individual constituting and constituted by a web of relations and possessions. The danger for even an individualist like Cowperwood is that he is dependent on the possessions he believes he controls.

In *Sister Carrie* (1900), Dreiser had earlier explored another phase of

3. Michael Rogin, *Fathers and Children: Andrew Jackson and American Indian Policy* (New York: Knopf, 1977), pp. 1–15.

4. *Work, Culture and Society in Industrializing America: Essays in Working-Class and Social History* (New York: Knopf, 1976).

the new capitalism, the dynamics of desire generated by the emerging consumerism. For Carrie, individual commodities and their setting, the mysterious city and its glamorous department stores and restaurants, have a power that makes her seem insignificant. Carrie's passivity, receptiveness, and theatricality are far removed from Cowperwood's imperious will, if not from Hurstwood's ability to reflect and to orchestrate the self-esteem of his prosperous clients. Through Cowperwood in *The Financier* and the rise and fall of Carrie and Hurstwood in *Sister Carrie*, Dreiser carries into the new territory of consumer and finance capitalism the dilemmas of individualism the dominant system produces along with goods, poverty, and desire.

In *The House of Mirth* (1905), Edith Wharton engages with similar issues at the highest reaches of American society. The art-commodity split that runs through the works of Hawthorne, Melville, and Poe reemerges in Lily Bart's role as a beautiful art object to be bought and sold on the marriage market. Lily is at once an individualistic entrepreneur, a commodity to be collected and displayed, and a reminder that the divisive power of American capitalism bears heavily even on the most privileged women in the society. Through Lily, Wharton shows that it is not only her male predecessors who experience America as a prison.

nine

THE ARTIST IN THE SLAMMER
Hawthorne, Melville, Poe, and the Prison of Their Times

In the generation before Twain, as romantic artists, Melville, Hawthorne, and Poe were all in crucial ways at odds with their American
market society. Two styles of individualism were in conflict, that of
American capitalism and that of the symbolically oriented romantic artist. Because the dominant society left its stamp on each of these writers,
it is not surprising that they explore this experience in their creative
work. Before considering the results, we need to recall not so much the
well-recognized affinity between the artist and the criminal as the less
frequently examined connection between the American romantic artist
and the prisoner. Prisoners live in enclosed places. They want to get out,
but if they are in for a long time, they work out ways of surviving. They
also work out ways of defying the authorities, and, if they cannot escape, at least they work out ways of communicating so as to escape
detection. In these respects they share common ground with Hawthorne, Melville, and Poe. Each of these great mid-nineteenth-century
American writers had special as well as shared reasons for simultaneously communicating and concealing in the manner both of the symbolic
artist and of the prisoner.

The symbolic mode, of course, was part of their artistic heritage. But a
heritage is never simply passively absorbed. If it is to flourish it must
satisfy the needs of a new generation. We must explain why Hawthorne, Melville, and Poe seized on the symbolic possibilities their culture made available to them. One explanation is that these writers were
attracted to the possibilities of symbolism partly because of their experience as artists in an acquisitive American society each of them came to
see as a prison. Because of the frequent conflict between their deepest
insights and the demands of the marketplace, as an integral part of their
careers as professional writers, Hawthorne, Melville, and Poe were
motivated to exploit the mode of symbolic indirection that was theirs for
the taking. In their version of the style of the inmate, the techniques of

176

symbolic indirection and symbolic intensification allowed them to communicate and conceal, to satisfy the demands of their vision and commitments and also to disguise them from unsympathetic readers. These techniques allowed Hawthorne, Melville, and Poe to defy their audience and at the same time attempt to succeed in the marketplace. In ways that differ for each of them, moreover, each of these authors came to experience his society not only as a positive resource for material and themes, of language and values, and not only as an antagonistic force hostile to their deepest needs as writers and therefore both stimulating them to express their own vision and making that enterprise difficult, but also more particularly as a prison.

Melville's "Benito Cereno" is a preliminary example. Consider the dimension of "Benito Cereno" that is the symbolic allegory of a sensitive, Dimmesdale-like artist, Cereno, trying to communicate the truth of his situation to an audience, Delano. Delano is a close relative of those commonsense representatives of official society—Peter Hovenden in "The Artist of the Beautiful" or Baglioni in "Rappaccini's Daughter"—characters who repeatedly in Hawthorne's tragedies of the creator cause problems for his artist figures. The truth Cereno wants to convey through the indirect means forced on him by his situation is that he is a prisoner and that the surfaces of the ship are deadly and totally misleading. Delano, who is a prisoner without knowing it, is an insensitive and imperceptive audience, with nearly fatal results. For his part, Cereno has been forced to do what inmates have always had to do: to find indirect ways of communicating in order to escape the detection of their keepers. Concentration camp inmates developed ways of conveying, and their friends on the outside of communicating, the truth about the camps. They did it through a code in obituary notices, an effective, macabre device all our writers would have understood. Penitentiary inmates have their devices. As usual with Melville, matters are complicated because Delano is in a sense one of the keepers and Babo is a rebellious slave and artist even more inventive than Cereno, so that even on this limited theme meanings proliferate in ways guaranteed to baffle and to antagonize the Delanoes of society.

Through both Cereno and Babo, Melville transforms his own experience as a creator. It is instructive that based on his experience as a writer in America Melville should parallel the experience of the inmate, imagine situations of confinement—the *San Dominick*, Bartleby's enclosed Wall Street office and prison—and develop the devices of symbolic indirection. The confined setting is explicitly that of the American author in the autobiographical Pierre's freezing, prison-like room where he writes his first book, after his introduction to the city in a surreal scene at a police station. Melville developed the techniques of the inmate in response to the conflicts between the demands of his vision and the demands of his public. In *Moby-Dick*, he created an exuberant, expansive version of this style. After the brutally negative reception of *Pierre*, he went underground. The techniques of the inmate were not evident in his first novel, *Typee*, although it is the narrative of a prisoner's term and escape from a valley now seen as Paradise, now as Hell. In chapter 17 of *Typee*, the indictment of the new penitentiaries is not a casual digression but a reflection of a major concern with the prison-house of the modern market society in conflict with what turns out to be the threatening freedom and confinement of the traditional world.

Before his mature development as an artist, Melville was already compelled by the prisoner's situation. It posed for him the issues of dominance and rebellion, authority and freedom, issues he was to return to again and again in his career. In the course of his development, Melville also found he needed to develop a style of symbolic indirection and symbolic intensification. As his vision darkened and deepened, as his concerns became more profound and far-ranging, Melville needed to satisfy the imperatives of his own outlook. In the marketplace where "dollars damn me," however, readers demanded official optimism and were suspicious of metaphysical probing. Melville first experimented with a symbolic style in *Mardi*, avoided it for the most part in *Redburn* and *White-Jacket*, returned to it deeply in *Moby-Dick*, and, after the reception of *Pierre*, he worked hard on an inversion of the expansive style of *Moby-Dick*. He developed an inward-turning, symbolic technique that created surfaces that would satisfy his magazine audience and depths that a few might understand. Especially in his short fiction of the 1850s and in *The Confidence-Man*, he worked out the techniques of the inmate.

In chapter 33 of *The Confidence-Man*, Melville uses the figure of harlequin to express his commitment to this intense art of symbolic indirection. In opposition to the literal realism and conventional morality called for to achieve success in the marketplace, Melville affirms a stylized but unrestrained imaginative release, a symbolic acting-out of the usually concealed realities of characters and situations. Melville's harlequin looks ahead to the suffering clowns of the twentieth-century artist. He also looks back to Poe's "Hop-Frog" (1849), one of the most disturbing enactments of the American artist's feelings of hatred against his imprisoned servitude to the public.

In this symbolic allegory, Hop-Frog, jester to the King, is a captive entertainer at the court of a gross, imperceptive monarch. Hop-Frog's situation is similar to Babo's in "Benito Cereno." Both are slaves, both feel abused and looked down on, both violently rebel, and both are

inventive dramatists who stage performances that have terrifying consequences. It is sobering that Melville and Poe, both using the techniques
of the inmate, should express such powerfully hostile feelings about the
American artist and his public. Emerging from their experience as writers in America, Melville and Poe focus on frustrated hatred, a sense of
imprisonment, and a desire to murder and to obliterate. Writing near
the end of their careers as professional authors—and for Poe in the year
of his death—in these stories Melville and Poe convey the intensity of
their response to their situation as American authors.

In Hop-Frog's case, his initial powerless subservience to his public is
combined with thwarted creative power, represented partly by his powerful teeth, arms, and chest above his crippled legs. To compound his
sense of the artist's degradation and self-contempt, Poe presents Hop-
Frog as a crippled dwarf. His employer constantly demands "invention," "characters," "something novel—out of the way."[1] The story is
dominated by the symbols of Hop-Frog's intense reaction against his
caged imprisonment to this public and its demands. The image of the
parrot's beak grating against its cage, the harsh noise dominating the
entire chamber, is one major symbol of the hatred, frustration, and
threatening, aggressive contempt the caged artist turns against himself
and even more against those who have degraded him into a parrot, no
nightingale or raven. The cruel noise dominates the final scene of awful
revenge and turns out to be the grating of Hop-Frog's fang-like teeth.

"Inspired" by the wine he is forced to drink, Hop-Frog stages a play. It
resembles the one whose violent first acts Babo directs and whose final
scenes and scenario Babo conceives and also directs, down to the costumes, props, and casting of roles. In his version, Hop-Frog tricks his
employers and with their own consent tars and feathers King and court,
chains them, and dresses them as apes. In thus reversing the conventional power relations, he makes a captive monkey of his public as he
feels they have made a caged parrot of him. The artist who has turned
his contempt against himself in the image of the crippled dwarf and
unwilling toady—hop, frog—at the end turns his hatred even more
forcefully outward against the public he feels has maimed, abused, and
imprisoned him. In another of Poe's Gothically darkened, prison-like
chambers of the mind, Hop-Frog, "with the rapidity of thought" (HF, p.
226), then illuminates the mind's destructive powers in his terrifying
final action. Hop-Frog painfully illustrates a paradox of the modern

---

1. "Hop-Frog," in *The Complete Works of Edgar Allan Poe*, ed. James A. Harrison (New
York: Thomas Y. Crowell, 1902), 5:219. Subsequent references will be abbreviated HF and
cited by page number in the text.

creative imagination under the pressures of the market society. Instead of the mind as an unequivocally free and creative alternative to the market society, Poe shows the mind as asserting its creative freedom as a punitive, destructive, self-enclosed prison. Hop-Frog's thwarted creative energies now express themselves in an act of horrible destruction. At the climax, the chamber's one source of light, the lamp, traditional symbol of imaginative creativity, becomes an implement of vicious torture, and the abused, caged victim has been goaded into inhuman, all-too-human victimizer and executioner. For those who cannot separate the story from their knowledge of Poe's life and death, perhaps the most painful turn is the sense that, whatever the origins in Poe's drinking, imaginative blocking, and difficulty in writing, whatever the actual tangle of rights and wrongs, one of our most gifted writers was impelled at the end of his life to image his career in just this way. He stresses imprisonment, primarily his own and, in reaction, that of the public he imagines in his control, chained and burned to death.

Both as an artist contemptuously at odds with a public he nonetheless depends on for support and as a man charged with powerful, unacceptable feelings, Poe was motivated to develop techniques of symbolic indirection. In "Hop-Frog" and in his detective fiction, in his stories of revenge and in his studies of the buried underside of the self, as Melville and Hawthorne do in their ways, Poe combines the techniques of the inmate with his own personally and socially revealing themes and imagery of imprisonment and punishment.

Written at almost the same time as "Hop-Frog," the first paragraph of *The Scarlet Letter* is dominated by the image of a nineteenth-century prison, not a seventeenth-century jail, which was like an ordinary house.[2] Hawthorne's prison resembles one of the new penal institutions Americans had pioneered along with everything else. Unlike the domestic architecture of the seventeenth-century jail, the prison in *The Scarlet Letter* has a massive oak door, iron spikes, and it is aligned with the "bearded men" who rule the society and who also appear in the first sentence of the novel. These iron-like, bearded men, their prison, and the scaffold define and unify the society of *The Scarlet Letter*. Characterized in this way, the society tells us much more about Hawthorne's sense of his nineteenth-century America than about the seventeenth century. Hawthorne needed the disguise of the past to free his imagina-

2. David Rothman, *The Discovery of the Asylum: Social Order and Disorder in the New Republic* (Boston: Little, Brown, 1971), analyzes the changing architecture of American jails and prisons and establishes the pioneering role of the Jacksonian reformers in developing the new prisons, reform schools, and mental institutions.

tion so that he could create what is basically a contemporary drama. It is not simply that he needed to escape the detection of the keepers but also that the keepers were part of his own identity. In "Benito Cereno" and "Hop-Frog," Melville and Poe seem fully conscious. To release his energy, however, Hawthorne had to disguise matters from a part of himself, as Poe does in stories like "Murders in the Rue Morgue." Like Melville's Babo and Poe's Hop-Frog, Hawthorne creates a costumes drama. In his version, the protagonists wear seventeenth-century dress, but the structures they live in and embody emerge from Hawthorne's sense of the present. The "Custom-House" is set in the nineteenth-century present and moves into the seventeenth-century past and into the depths of the imaginations of both Surveyor Pue and the narrator. In the deep structure of *The Scarlet Letter* proper, Hawthorne is even more profoundly concerned with the present and the depths of the imagination than he is in "The Custom-House."

As he shows in chapter 21 of *The Scarlet Letter*, Hawthorne knows that the first settlers were basically Elizabethan in their outlook, that they liked ornate clothing and the ceremonial pomp of traditional English society. But he chooses instead to emphasize a joyless, punitive society. As Winthrop tells us in his famous "A Modell of Christian Charitie," for him and his first generation contemporaries, what holds society together is the loving brotherhood of believers under God. When love fails, as it did when Winthrop was rejected as governor, he invokes the power of God. Through the medium of the people, Winthrop argues in his "Speech to the General Court," God chooses the rulers the people are bound to obey by virtue of custom and divine authority. Even under the changes of the new world, for the founding generation, the unifying force was the traditional outlook of the old world, an outlook based on ancient patterns of authority and deference sanctioned by a deep commitment to God.

For Hawthorne in *The Scarlet Letter*, however, what holds society together is not religious belief, shared traditions, and a common way of life but rather the prison and the scaffold. As ceremonial centers, they answer to Hawthorne's sense of a society lacking the traditional unifying sentiments and forced to rely primarily on punishment and repressive power. He is not giving a historically accurate portrayal of the seventeenth century or a literal description of his nineteenth-century America, but instead he is creating an image that emerges from the depths of his contemporary experience. Hawthorne's resonant image or myth comments suggestively on the grim end results of social tendencies that started in the seventeenth century. Americans who had inaugurated their society and their characters on the basis of the Protestant temperament and possessive individualism had ended with what are for Hawthorne the unifying realities of the prison and the scaffold.

The iron-like men who run the society and give it its temper are capable but insensitive, heartless. The prison and scaffold are wood, but the society and its leaders are *iron*, a word that recurs again and again in Hawthorne's descriptions of the "iron arm," the "iron links," and the "iron framework" of official beliefs, character, and society. The prevailing punitive rigidity and heartlessness define the dominant qualities of the official work-ethic society and its representative men, the keepers in what Hawthorne repeatedly presents as the prison-house of orthodox society. His gallery of the representative men who dominate this society and give it identity began with the parti-colored man in "My Kinsman, Major Molineux" and runs through such characters as Endicott in "The Maypole of Merrymount," Peter Hovenden in "The Artist of the Beautiful," and Baglioni in "Rappacini's Daughter." It includes the forefathers and all they come to stand for in "The Custom-House." Judge Pyncheon of *The House of the Seven Gables* is cut from the same iron pattern. Throughout, the historical and geographical settings are the occasion for what is primarily a contemporary American portrait. In "My Kinsman, Major Molineux," Hawthorne had explored the impact of a rapidly changing market society whose stable institutions and authority figures were being undermined. In *The Scarlet Letter*, he shifts the focus away from social change and creates an image of the rigid, repressive power that for him continued to exist. From some points of view Jacksonian America was a society in flux; from other points of view official society continued to bear down on those who were at odds with the prevailing values.

In *The Scarlet Letter*, Hester is the main alternative to the masculine-dominated official society. In contrast to the imagery and attitudes associated with society, Hester is characterized as rich and voluptuous; she has a passionate temperament that expresses itself in the oriental luxuriance of the letter and Pearl's clothing. Before it is repressed, her dark hair flows. Fluidity and passion, a depth of creative, sexual energy characterizes Hester, especially when she is freed from the deadening effects of the letter, from the rigid official punishment it in part represents. In contrast to the drab rigidities of the prison world, Hester speculates freely and dangerously and expresses herself in color and in the sexuality that animates her art—her elaboration of the letter and her other creations—and that precipitates the crisis the novel turns on. In view of his deep reservations about her, it is significant that even before Hester conforms, Hawthorne allows her mystic, passionately charged scarlet letter to become an organizing center and communal point of reference, an alternative one to the official symbols of the scaffold and prison. The scarlet letter embodies both the rebellious energies of the artist and the official attitudes of the society the artist both accepts and subverts.

As a free, sexualized, independent woman, speculative intelligence, and artistic creator, Hester embodies a compelling individualism at odds with the socially conventional version. Hester's individualism is close to Hawthorne's deepest feelings about his own creativity and identity. That he should treat Hester ambivalently reveals the most intimate strains that animate Hawthorne's imagination. He does not make matters easy for himself: he does not soften his view of the dominant, orthodox society as a way of blurring the oppositions and making his reservations about Hester more palatable. The society's accommodations to Hester do not alter the basic character of the society or Hawthorne's generally critical view of it or his ambivalent treatment of Hester's romantic individualism.

For Hawthorne, both the official society and the individualism of his characters lead to a prison-like isolation. In *The Scarlet Letter*, under the pressure of the isolating, repressive force of society and the inner energies that answer to and react against that force, characters are separated from each other. They are isolated even when, as with Chillingworth and Dimmesdale, they live under the same roof. But as with Chillingworth and Dimmesdale, they are also related by unconsummated ties of hate and love. Hawthorne only rarely allows an unequivocal expression of love to bring his protagonists together and do away with their isolation in the merging of love, and then only with equivocal results. For all their isolation, the main characters in the novel must nonetheless be seen in relation. These relations are not static or geometric; they are vital, shifting, and unstable. This dynamic quality is partly the result of the energies Hawthorne endows his characters with, partly the result of his own restless inability to find a stable, normative resting place for his divided feelings about the issues they raise for him. Hawthorne has thus contrived it so that while he may focus on Hester or the interior of Dimmesdale's heart, the energized network of thwarted relations is always present. This novel, so artfully composed and decorous on the surface, contains an inner charge of energy that requires all of Hawthorne's artful patterning to express and to contain it.

In counterpoint with the ceremonial public scenes, Hawthorne thus organizes his novel around a series of semipublic and private meetings. Under the pressure of urgent personal feelings and under the immediate influence of one they love and hate, characters suddenly come to moments of intense realization. Energy is released. Instead of a slow, logical process, the character's insight deepens instantly and consciousness is illuminated. An example is Hester's sudden awareness of how intensely she hates Chillingworth.[3] Hawthorne allows the realization to emerge from the depths of Hester's nature and the density of her relation to Chillingworth. It is an achievement because particularly for a woman the direct expression of strong hostile feelings goes so directly against the Protestant Etiquette and the nineteenth-century domestic ideal, which made these feelings unacceptable.[4] For Hester, these emotions are also inseparable from the passionate energies that relate her to Dimmesdale and animate her being.

The role of the narrator, however, is to modulate these feelings, to drain some of the force from Hester's passionate nature, and to weaken or to qualify the impact of her realization. He does so by intervening with a moral vocabulary and a moral outlook that detract from the full impact of what the novelist has allowed to emerge. The moral generalization, "Let men tremble to win the hand of woman, unless they win along with it the utmost passion of her heart" (SL, p. 176), succeeds in dampening interest and shifting attention from the particular dynamics of the "utmost passion of [Hester's] heart." The novelist illuminates those dynamics but the narrator does not. In the balanced act now of siding with Hester, now of criticizing her, the narrator uses a safe moral generalization to chastely obscure the complexity of those passions and their connection with Hester's sexuality and creativity. He then criticizes her for continuing to harbor resentment, a reminder that even after seven years of punishment she is still unrepentant. The moral-religious outlook further distracts attention from the force, depth, and dynamics of the energy Hester has expressed; or rather it is an indirect tribute to the power that requires such a moral-religious apparatus to subdue it. For the narrator, this charged moment throws a "dark light on Hester's state of mind" (SL, p. 177). It also establishes not necessarily his wisdom

3. *The Scarlet Letter*, ed. William Charvat (Columbus: Ohio State University Press, 1962), pp. 175–76. Subsequent references will be abbreviated SL and cited by page number in the text.

4. For background on the developing ideology of domesticity during Hawthorne's period, see Barbara Welter, "The Cult of True Womanhood: 1820–1860," *American Quarterly* 18 (1966): 151–74; Kathryn Kish Sklar, *Catherine Beecher. A Study in American Domesticity* (New Haven: Yale University Press, 1973); Nancy Cott, *The Bonds of Womanhood: "Woman's Sphere" in New England, 1780–1835* (New Haven: Yale University Press, 1977); and Ann Douglas, *The Feminization of American Culture* (New York: Knopf, 1978). John Murray Cuddihy, *The Ordeal of Civility* (New York: Basic Books, 1974), pp. 5–10, goes beyond Weber and characterizes what he calls the Protestant Etiquette. This comprehensive discipline of the personality was developed over a period of three hundred years and includes an ethic, aesthetics, and etiquette, all based on a deep training in moderation, restraint, and the repression of the instincts.

but his moderation, his conventionality, and, as one of the keepers, his need to put down and to assert the control of official values over the passionate energy Hester embodies. Would the structure of civilization really topple if Hester had been allowed an unchastised expression of justifiable feeling? Perhaps so for a novelist who senses the connections his narrator avoids, who is himself pulled and repelled by the values of domesticity, and who furthermore has dark doubts about the very energies his created character and his creative life depend on.

In *The Scarlet Letter*, the narrator, intelligent, perceptive, moderate, represents the more public side of Hawthorne's identity. Much of the interest in the novel is the result of the intricate play of his responses to the charged, disturbing material the novelist imagines and allows his characters and imagery to express. The narrator is an important character in this novel, as significant as the human protagonists, the forest, and the scaffold, the other major personages Hawthorne creates. Hawthorne has created the totality of the novel. The narrator has privileged insights and must be taken seriously but not normatively. He does not speak for the total Hawthorne any more than Hester or Chillingworth do. His association with the intellect, a moderate morality, and the publicly acceptable makes him attractive to a certain kind of reader. It may be, however, that characters like Hester take us closer to the "inmost Me" Hawthorne was so careful to conceal behind his veil (SL, p. 4).

Take the way the narrator reflects on a concern as vital in our period as in Hawthorne's, the situation of "the whole race of womanhood" (SL, p. 165). Unable to express her love for Dimmesdale, unable to renew herself at her sources through the direct expression of her passionate nature, Hester has been deeply thwarted by the socially imposed stigma of the letter. No wonder she questions about women, "Was existence worth accepting, even to the happiest among them?" (SL, p. 165). She has decided negatively "for her own individual existence." Then, as if entering Hester's consciousness, a consciousness darkened by the scarlet letter, the narrator develops a view appropriate to Hester's thwarted situation and to Hawthorne's skepticism about reform. The narrator never presents the radical feminist response of the Hester of the forest scene, where Hester is fully herself and in touch with her animating energies. The revitalized Hester who urges Dimmesdale to "begin all anew" would presumably accept parts of the narrator's analysis but not his hopelessness.

The narrator is properly sensitive to the immense obstacles women have to overcome. "As a first step," he begins, "the whole system of society is to be torn down, and built up anew. Then, the very nature of the opposite sex, or its long hereditary habit, which has become like nature, is to be essentially modified, before woman can be allowed to assume what seems a fair and suitable position. Finally, all other difficulties being obviated, woman cannot take advantage of these preliminary reforms, until she herself shall have undergone a still mightier change; in which, perhaps, the ethereal essence, wherein she has her truest life, will be found to have evaporated" (SL, pp. 165–66). The "ethereal essence" comes from the world of the nineteenth-century cult of domesticity. It is related to that tendency of Hawthorne's imagination connected with the spiritualizing of the "heart and sensibilities" (SL, p. 36). It is also related to Hawthorne and his culture's distrust of sexuality and the creativity it animates, since the narrator places the "essence" at some safe remove from all that Hester's passion represents.

In *The Scarlet Letter*, this fragmented, desexualized woman reaches her apotheosis in the spotless image of Divine Maternity (SL, p. 56). To compound the problem and as an unintentional reminder of the difficulties women have to overcome, the narrator not only separates women from their sexuality but also divides the head and heart. In his variation on a common nineteenth-century theme, "a women never overcomes these problems by any exercise of thought" (SL, p. 166). His customary moderation is not in evidence as the narrator boldly refuses to take refuge in question-begging qualifications. For him it is "never," not even "usually," and, in his widely shared view, "any exercise of thought" is bound to be ineffectual for a woman. Thus deprived of reliance on her intellect and separated from her sexuality, the woman is confined to a narrow, superficial sphere. The narrator dignifies it as the realm of the heart, a noble region, but then he imposes restrictions. These problems, he says, "are not to be solved, or only in one way. If her heart chance to come uppermost, they vanish." The difficulty is that if "her" heart chances to be Hester's, then the passionate energy and the defiant will associated with the heart cause problems. At best, Hester's heart beats freely and passionately, which for the narrator means that her "heart had lost its regular and healthy throb." The regular throb of domesticity is at odds with the intense beat of Hester's heart. Even the heart is thus not a secure refuge. For Hester, and perhaps not for her alone, the intensities of the heart impel a journey into "the dark labyrinth of mind," where Hester wanders "without a clew," which is to say that the intensities of her nature have pushed her beyond conventional limits and standards. Unlike Emerson or the Hudson River School painters, instead of finding a deep source of truth in the recesses of the mind and in the depths of nature, the narrator presents a terrifying landscape of the mind. Hester was "now turned aside by an insurmountable precipice; now starting back from a deep chasm. There was wild and ghastly scenery all around her, and a home and comfort nowhere" (SL, p. 166). The unrestrained openness, the total self-reliance, and the unmediated exposure to primal sexual energies are deeply threatening to the narrator. For him the alternative is sometimes "home and comfort," sometimes the iron framework of society.

For the creator of the forest scene, however, more vital possibilities are also imaginable. To the extent that the narrator is accurate about Hester, he renders her alienated state through images of wild, ghastly scenery. This alienated condition, however, may result not from her separation from home and conventional restraints but from the thwarting of a reciprocal, life-affirming, passionate love. In the shadow of the letter, nature and Hester's own nature then become terrifying, in contrast to her experience at the heart of the forest scene. For all their differences, moreover, Melville in *Moby-Dick* and Whitman in "Song of Myself" also endow the journey into the depths of nature and the depths of the mind with an affirmative energy, a commitment to the process in marked contrast to the narrator's terror. To be without a home can be exhilarating as well as disturbing. But in the nineteenth-century American tradition, it is especially disturbing for a woman.

For the narrator, Hester's nature is repeatedly "a moral wilderness," a "desert place" (SL, p. 199). He thus qualifies with negative associations of barrenness his recognition of her "free" journey into the forest, Indian regions of the self and existence. Although Hawthorne himself has hardly been uncritical of "the clerical band, the judicial robe, the pillory and gallows," if not of "the fireside, or the church," he has his narrator condemn Hester's estranged criticism of American institutions, a criticism he recognizes emerges from the "free," "wild," "Indian" depths of her being. Her entry into these regions and their energizing entry into her consciousness have deepened and elevated her, have taken her "into regions where other women dared not tread" (SL, p. 199). For the narrator, her tragedy is that, in acting from the depths of her passionate nature under the pressure of her alienating experiences, she has been both elevated and warped. As he puts it in his sober way, "They had made her strong, but taught her much amiss" (SL, p. 200).

What the narrator neglects to comment on, but Hawthorne has shown, is that Hester has been prevented from fulfilling herself through love and thus from animating her criticism from the resources of her fulfilled self. The barren estrangement has first been from Dimmesdale. Flowing like her unconfined hair, the radical criticism that may have emerged from Hester's fulfilled self could have been powerful indeed. Her tragedy may center on the waste of her human and intellectual possibilities under the pressure of distorting official constraint. In the course of the novel, Hawthorne exposes the limits of his narrator's view even as the narrator has established his own perspective on the limits of Hester's view.

Having invoked as a positive ideal the fragmented image of woman we have examined, Hawthorne's narrator explicitly presents Hester as unbalanced, as out of harmony with the "truest life" of woman (SL, p. 166). Hester is disoriented by the restrictions of society and by the urgencies of her own passionate nature; or rather, by the incompatibility between her energies and the socially approved limits and outlets. Through his narrator, Hawthorne dramatizes the value predicament of middle-class women in his period. He gives them the choice of a fragmented, etherealized "true" life separated from the intellect, from intense sexuality, and from anything more interesting than a "regular and healthy throb." In contrast is the specter of abyss and precipice, of disoriented passion, homelessness, and barren intellectual speculation. Even more than for the man, for the woman endowed with energy and mental power, the alternatives are not encouraging, and they were not intended to be.

After her formal release from prison, as she becomes vulnerable to the standards of domesticity, common sense, and the Protestant Etiquette, Hester's nature is thus truncated. She cannot directly express her passionate energy in acts of love with Dimmesdale or in intellectual and imaginative creations growing out of personal fulfillment. Her creative passions are instead repressed and express themselves overtly only in the art of her needlework. The richly elaborated, mystic letter and Pearl's dress are especially subversive of the official, commonsense, work-ethic standards. Hester is like a prisoner forced to express herself in a symbolic code to escape the censorship of the authorities. She keeps the surface barely within tolerable limits and charges her message with implications she is partly aware of, partly unaware of. This combination also applies to Hawthorne, who has his own complex reasons for expressing himself indirectly through the techniques of the inmate.

In *The Discovery of the Asylum*, David Rothman analyzes the total institutions the Jacksonian reformers created to discipline and to reform deviants. The reformers developed the strategies of solitary confinement and strict control of every detail of the inmate's environment. Because it was felt to threaten respectable middle-class social order, the sexuality of adolescents and the foreign-born was especially controlled. Like the inmates in the new prisons, reform schools, and mental institutions, Hester is compelled to repress her sexuality even more fully than her creativity, which at least has the outlet of the subsistence and charity work she is allowed. After she dons the scarlet letter, "the light and graceful foliage of her character had been withered up by this red-hot brand," and her form, though still "majestic," no longer inspires "Passion" (SL, p. 163). Explicitly, the missing quality is "tenderness," but the imagery of brands and fire suggests sexuality as well. In its official social dimension, the scarlet letter represents the pressure of the society's rigid hostility to the warm passion and defiant individualism Hester embodies. She is truncated by this hostility, is affected in the most intimate recesses of her being, but in a modified, indirect way she continues to express the defiant energy of what in "The Custom-House" Hawthorne calls "the inmost Me" (SL, p. 4). The narrator reminds us that a "magic touch" may still revive the "woman" in Hester (SL, p. 164). In the forest scene the novelist shows that Hester is still passionately alive and responsive. What revives her, however, is not a magic touch, since Dimmesdale is much too passive, but Hester's ability to love and to express her love, not safely but in a dangerous, vital way.

Before Hester momentarily comes to renewed life, Pearl reinvokes the connection between the letter and the sexualized, demonic energies that make it "glow like a red flame when thou meetest [the Black Man] at midnight" (SL, p. 185). Pearl also forces Hester to confess that she wears the scarlet letter because "once in my life I met the Black Man! . . . This scarlet letter is his mark" (SL, p. 185). Dimmesdale—whom she did meet and of whom Pearl provocatively asks, "Is it the Black Man?" (SL, p. 187)—is unfortunately not sufficiently black. The Black Man, the demon Hester has met, is the intensity of unsanctioned sexuality, the forceful, independent expression of her passion. Hawthorne always has the protection of the adultery to disguise matters, but the implication throughout is that the black, primeval quality is intense sexuality and creative energy itself. The ceremony of marriage would not alter that antagonist. Aligned as it is with the red glow of both creativity and evil, Hester's passion poses a real threat.[5]

In the forest scene, from one point of view, Hester is Hawthorne's version of Eve tempting a devitalized Adam in the uncultivated garden of the forest. In another sense, her energy and the "magnetic power" of "her deep eyes" (SL, p. 197) are characteristic of Hawthorne's powerful, masculine creators, from the painter of "Prophetic Portraits" through Matthew Maule of *The House of the Seven Gables*. Just as Hawthorne has shifted the conventional sexual roles in having Hester precede her hus-

5. For an interpretation that programmatically denies the central role of sexuality in *The Scarlet Letter*, see Michael Ragussis, "Family Discourse and Fiction in *The Scarlet Letter*," *ELH* 49 (1982): 863–88.

band to the new world, he even more fully reverses them in her relation with Dimmesdale. Hester is dark and statuesque; Dimmesdale is pale and frail. Although Hester is fully a woman, by the conventional nineteenth-century standards she is more masculine than Dimmesdale, more forceful, more aggressive, more fully in touch with her sexuality and more willing to give free rein to her sexuality and all it animates. Her unusual fusion of "masculine" and "feminine" traits is a source of her power and value, a reminder of the importance of this merging, not an easy one to effect in the American society Hester emerges from. Her fusion of the "masculine" and "feminine" also makes her unique among Hawthorne's creators, since elsewhere he divides these traits, with the resulting damage his lifelong treatment of the artist dramatizes.[6]

Revived by her meeting with the man she loves, Hester makes a forceful plea to go deeper into the Indian-filled wilderness, to leave behind the prison world of "iron men . . . and their opinions," which, Hester argues, "have kept thy better part in bondage too long already!" (SL, p. 197). Throughout the episode Hester's speech and actions are charged with undertones disturbing to respectable nineteenth-century Americans. But the surface is quintessentially American. Hawthorne allows Hester to speak forcefully and persuasively for the possibility of making a new life, of not being imprisoned by the past. "'Begin all anew!'" she urges in the nineteenth-century accents almost every American still responds to positively. "'Hast thou exhausted possibility in the failure of this one trial? . . . There is happiness to be enjoyed! There is good to be done!'" (SL, p. 198). The appeals to possibility, to happiness, to doing good touch a deep strain in the nineteenth-century American value system. In aligning Hester with these values as well as with the threatening, energizing power of the forest and of sexuality, Hawthorne has created a highly charged combination. It is the context for Hester's declaration that she will leave with Dimmesdale, that she will compound her original act of passionate love. She is still in love and from the depths of her passionate individualism she chooses again to act in defiance of convention.

Hester's sexualized creativity is both necessary and disturbing to Dimmesdale. Through Dimmesdale, Hawthorne explores another version of the romantic creator, a gifted artist whose inner dynamics necessitate the obverse of Hester's individualism. When Dimmesdale and Hester meet in the forest, Dimmesdale is in an unenergized state of

---

6. On the animating and finally debilitating strains in Hawthorne's career as a creator, see Rudolph Von Abele, *The Death of the Artist: A Study of Hawthorne's Disintegration* (The Hague: Nijoff, 1955), and Robert Shulman, "Hawthorne's Quiet Conflict," *Philological Quarterly* 47 (1968): 216–38.

despair, "listless" (SL, p. 188) and "powerless" (p. 197). For him, "death was too definite an object to be wished for, or avoided" (SL, p. 188). His condition is almost identical with the death-in-life Hawthorne attributes to himself in "The Custom-House." In the version Hawthorne imagines for his created character, Dimmesdale, too, is alienated from his sources, in his case the vitality of the sexuality Hester embodies. At the same time he is threatened by the very intensities he fears, loves, and needs. He has a capacity for passion, but only within limits. The original experience with Hester has upset the delicate balance of his inner economy. Since then he has been leading a double life. He conceals his involvement with Hester and all that suggests about his own sexual passions and "profounder self" (SL, p. 217). His saintly surface is at odds with his inner reality, which he can only express indirectly, in veiled confessions no one applies to him. Providing as they do the only genuine expression of his inner reality, his sermons become increasingly moving, partly because of his insight into the darker reaches of humanity, partly because they draw energy from his own sublimated sexuality. Hawthorne's portrait of sublimation and creativity at the expense of the artist's life is one of the most brilliant of his tragedies of the creator and one of his pioneering achievements of psychological probing. In this transformation of his own experience, instead of derogating his "soapbubble" art as he did in "The Custom-House," he celebrates the quality of Dimmesdale's psychologically perceptive symbolic allegories so much like the best of his own. He also recognizes that Dimmesdale's attenuated contact with his depths and with his lover is as fatal to his vitality as the later breakthroughs of the energy of his "profounder self." Part of Dimmesdale's tragedy is that the balance he requires is almost impossible to maintain.

Hawthorne thus makes Dimmesdale a classic conservative. To support and confine him, he requires the "iron framework" of that orthodoxy Hawthorne has severely exposed. In his perceptive, sympathetic, but not flattering, portrait, Hawthorne has dealt as searchingly and as critically with Hester's partner and polar opposite as he did with her individualism. For better or worse, to maintain his identity Dimmesdale requires the restraints, supports, and repressions of society as much as Hester needs to rebel against them to affirm her genuine self. Much of the power of *The Scarlet Letter* comes from Hawthorne's willingness to give full, complex expression to his ambivalent feelings about these divided segments of his nature.

In the forest scene, Hester offers Dimmesdale not only "human affection and sympathy" but also a passionate charge of sexualized energy to animate and complicate his glimpse of "a new life, and a true one, in exchange for the heavy doom which he was now expiating" (SL, p. 200).

The narrator then announces "the stern sad truth" that is at the heart of Hawthorne's dilemma. This truth, which puts the final damper on all that Hester's individualism embodies, is "that the breach which guilt has once made into the human soul is never, in this mortal state, repaired" (SL, pp. 200–201). Dimmesdale's peculiar makeup is the particular case that inspires the generalization, but it is supported by Hawthorne's work from "Roger Malvin's Burial" and "Young Goodman Brown" on. As in these stories, the imagery clarifies the exact nature of this "guilt," which makes a "breach" that can never on earth be repaired. It is the breach of sexuality itself. "It may be watched and guarded; so that the enemy shall not force his way again into the citadel, and might even, in his subsequent assaults, select some other avenue. . . . But there is still the ruined wall, and, near it, the stealthy tread of the foe that would win over again his unfortunate triumph" (SL, p. 201).

The military image of the "enemy" forcing his way into the "citadel," of the "stealthy tread" of the antagonist (is he an Indian?) emerging again to violate his unfortunate adversary: this masculine imagery of sexual violation is at the center of that irreparable "breach" which for Hawthorne constitutes not only Dimmesdale's but also mankind's guilt. For Hawthorne, the problem is not really with illicit sexuality but with intense sexuality, particularly masculine sexuality, that in its essence is for him illicit. This taint, inseparable from the humanity of his characters, again and again, as with Dimmesdale, constitutes an irreparable original sin that repeatedly warps the lives of his characters, beginning with the protagonists of his early *Provincial Tales*. Dimmesdale thus needs to be "hemmed in" (SL, p. 200) by the confining framework of conventional structures to protect him from being flooded by sexual impulses, by a sexual energy that Hawthorne presents as evil, destructive of Dimmesdale's tense equilibrium, and, as the source of life, also necessary for Dimmesdale's continued life. That for all his ambivalence Hawthorne can imagine and positively as well as negatively respond to Hester is an index of his achievement.

As for Dimmesdale, his personal dynamics are an extreme response to and commentary on the complex of official American values Hawthorne and his created character and narrator emerge from. The blighting threat of intense sexuality is rooted partly in the family drama of Hawthorne's upbringing, but the larger American context is what intensifies and directs this sensitivity.[7] It requires a social context strongly influenced by the discipline of the Protestant temperament and the imperatives of

7. On Hawthorne's family drama and its results, see Frederick C. Crews, *The Sins of the Fathers: Hawthorne's Psychological Themes* (New York: Oxford, 1966), and Philip Young, *Hawthorne's Secret* (Boston: Godine, 1984).

possessive individualism in order to produce the style of tragedy Hawthorne imagines for Dimmesdale and Hester and experiences in a less dramatic way himself.

To concentrate on Hester, under the influence of the official stigma of the letter and all it represents, Hester is changed and her relation to others and to society is changed. Under the influence of the letter Hester is isolated but also tied, related, to society. Hawthorne's language is significant. "The chain that bound her," he has his narrator say in chapter 5, "was of iron links, and galling to her inmost soul, but never could be broken" (SL, p. 80). The "chain" is reminiscent of "the instinct," "not love," that in "The Custom-House" Hawthorne says binds him to Salem (SL, p. 11). It is also reminiscent of the "strong traits of their nature which," Hawthorne also says in "The Custom-House," "have intertwined themselves with mine," the traits of his iron-like forefathers (SL, p. 10). When the letter in its official punitive role is foremost, when Hawthorne is answering to the iron-like, orthodox demands intertwined in his nature, and especially when for Hester the possibility of genuine love has been blighted by the "iron arm" of the official code, Hawthorne characterizes Hester's relations in the imagery of "iron links."

In the forest scene, however, Hawthorne imagines an alternative to the "iron links" the scarlet letter and the "iron arm" of society have forged within and between Hester and others. He allows Hester's passionate sexuality to show in the revived flow of her dark hair. Her smile has the requisite "tenderness" to modulate the full power of her passion, but the "gushing" and "glowing" and the revival of "her sex, her youth, and the whole richness of her beauty" establish her uncensored depths and energy (SL, p. 202). The instinct, love, establishes a vital relation that brings Hester to life again, reinvigorates Dimmesdale, and temporarily releases him from "the dungeon of his own heart" (SL, p. 201). This act of love and the relations it establishes cannot be characterized in the mechanical imagery of a prisoner's chain with iron links because it is alive, passionate, and changing. For a magic instant Hawthorne imagines a vital union animated from the depths and promising fulfillment on this earth. Given the society he knew, this vital union is necessarily in opposition to it and perhaps to some extent to all constituted societies. But it suggests the living center social relations might flow from. At the center of the forest scene, Hester is, significantly, not isolated and she is not selfish. She acts from her depths for herself and for Dimmesdale. It is revealing that the only alternative to her unifying, passionate love that Hawthorne can imagine is the iron arm and the iron links of repression, punishment, and guilt, of the iron framework of society as a supporting but isolating prison.

Even Hawthorne, the most skeptical of our great mid-nineteenth-century America writers, has an intense intuition of the individualistic sources from which a new kind of social union might develop. The heart of the forest scene is Hawthorne's equivalent of the sexually vitalized "love is a kelson of the creation" of section 5 of "Song of Myself." It is his equivalent of the erotically charged realization in "The Grand Armada" in *Moby-Dick* that "deep down and deep inland, there I bathe me in eternal mildness of joy." But for Hawthorne, as for Whitman, the insight, for all its threat to the conventional social order, is more alive than Melville's to the possibility of a new kind of society energized from the personal depths of love. It thus seems especially American that, like his great contemporaries, Hawthorne is unable to imagine the living, nonrepressive community this individualism might animate and develop in. In view of his fears about her energies, no wonder Hawthorne feels impelled to reincarcerate Hester for her full term.

Except for the marvelous interlude in the forest and with the exception of her troubled relation to Pearl, throughout the novel, Hester is accordingly isolated from her intimates as well as from society. Because her passion is threatening, Hawthorne makes Hester pay for it, but the isolation itself is not so much a punishment Hawthorne imposes on her as an acknowledgment of the isolated position in American society of a person like Hester. Her isolation from society is an intensified version of the isolation Hawthorne had experienced, in a modified form continued to experience, and had repeatedly imagined as characteristic of his fictional creators. But this isolation also has more general sources and implications.

As the recipient of the punitive ostracism of her society, Hester reveals that American tendency Tocqueville had recently analyzed. Tocqueville saw the majority as so powerful in America and the impulse toward equality, toward uniformity, as so basic that views conflicting with the majority's were, he believed, suppressed before they were born; and, if they were not suppressed early, they were punished through an informal but effective system of social ostracism.[8] Granted that the system was imperfect and that sects, splits, and fragmentation were dominant characteristics of Hawthorne's period. The tendency Tocqueville noted is nonetheless significant. It is suggestive that Tocqueville began his American investigations as a student of the new penal institutions. For him, as for Hawthorne, America is in significant ways a prison, on the one hand enforcing uniformity and punishing deviants, on the other hand driving people into the solitary confinement of their hearts.

8. *Democracy in America*, ed. Phillips Bradley, 2 vols. (New York: Vintage, 1945), 1:264–80.

In *The Scarlet Letter*, Hester's situation is also similar to that of a prisoner in one of the institutions designed to reform the deviant through isolation. Once she is released from prison, Hester has the freedom of the grounds, but "she was banished, and as much alone as if she inhabited another sphere." While it punishes and seeks to reform her by chronic public exhortation and social pressure, society may also be seeking to protect itself from contagion. The official hope, however, was not that of the seventeenth-century Puritan but of his nineteenth-century successor, the Jacksonian reformer. The official theory was that in isolation, removed from the possibility of corrupting and corruption, the prisoner would turn inward and the basic good of human nature would manifest itself in a reformed citizen. Hawthorne, however, realizes that the rich, dark depths of Hester's nature are more troublesomely complicated than the reformers assumed. His own view is divided. He or his narrator repeatedly warn us against the refractory energy in Hester that refuses to be repentant, that continually belies her surface acquiescence and repeatedly makes a mockery of the moral-spiritual reform Hawthorne simultaneously believes in and needs to deny. Finally the threat of Hester's defiant passion was too strong. Hawthorne shows the effects on Hester of her imprisonment, shows the values that are blighted—her beauty, her creative vitality, her sexuality—and returns her to the prison of his society.

Based on his complex experience and finally on his experience as an artist in America, in *The Scarlet Letter*, Hawthorne, too, came to see America as a prison. To allow Hester that release he imagines would have left unsatisfied Hawthorne's need for a balance between forest freedom and the iron framework of a supporting, imprisoning society. It would also have falsified his basic experience as an artist in America. In his own life, Hawthorne's first term of incarceration was one he chose himself, that ten-year period of relatively solitary confinement in his mother's house in Salem. This experience colored his outlook thereafter and made him sensitive to a dimension of his society that Tocqueville, himself a student of penal institutions, also found ways of characterizing. Hawthorne had special reasons for simultaneously communicating and concealing in the manner both of the symbolic artist and of the prisoner. In dealing with the threatening sexual themes and the moral and social doubts of his early stories, Hawthorne had discovered what was good for him at the very beginning of his career and after twenty years of experience in the marketplace, and, with his forefathers behind and within him and with his wife and his high-minded friends at the Old Manse, he had additional reasons for perfecting the skills of symbolic indirection.

In *The Scarlet Letter*, he brought the themes and techniques of the inmate to fulfillment. But in chastening and reincarcerating Hester, Hawthorne also acknowledged his own fears of the rebellious creative powers she embodies. In the concluding processional, he has Dimmesdale ignore Hester, side with the powerful keepers who rule society, and die. Prefigured in his treatment of Hester and Dimmesdale is Hawthorne's diminished will to explore his deepest preoccupations. With declining energy he nonetheless continued to deal with the situation of the imprisoned artist, from Clifford in *The House of the Seven Gables* through the abortive, undeveloped figures in the confined rooms and dungeons of the late romances. He came to prefer the novels of Trollope to his own books, although he knew he himself was unable to write realistic fiction. The techniques of the inmate had allowed him to survive, to satisfy his contradictory impulses, and to conceal and reveal, subvert and accept simultaneously. At the end of his career, at a banquet of the Saturday Club, surrounded by the literary friends of a lifetime, Hawthorne, Henry James, Sr., observed, "had the look all the time . . . of a rogue in a company of detectives."[9] At the end, when the techniques of the inmate had become a liability, under the surveillance of his inner and outer detectives, this rogue finally escaped into immortality.

9. Quoted in F. O. Matthiessen, *The James Family: A Group Biography* (New York: Knopf, 1948), p. 479.

ten

CAPITALISM, DEMOCRACY, AND TYRANNY
The Politics of Individualism in *Moby-Dick*

In Fleece's inverted Sermon on the Mount, in one of the most powerful, concentrated sections of social criticism in our literature, Melville satirizes the dominant style of American economic individualism. He uses black dialect, as if he is saying things that are "so terrifically true, that it were all but madness for any good man, in his own proper character, to utter, or even hint of them."[1] Fleece's sermon turns on a simple, brilliant identification of the audience of sharks with the audience of readers. One key idea is that the voraciousness of us sharks, our innate "wicked natur," can be governed. To the extent that "you gobern the shark in you, why den you be angel; for all angel is not'in more dan de shark well goberned." It cuts two ways for a black cook to insist to his "bred'ren," to his "fellow-critters," that we are all sharks, that we are all related, and that we must be "cibil," that key value, as we help ourselves from the whale. On this view Melville's predatory society is based on innate human tendencies, but the results are not inevitable since we can govern our sharkishness. Melville's unsparing metaphor for the possessive individualism of his society, however, is the spectacle of sharks, some with mouths bigger than others, competitively filling their own bottomless bellies, instead of using their strength "to bite off de blubber for de small fry ob sharks, dat can't get into de scrounge to help demselves."

As an antidote, Melville has Fleece reiterate the necessity of civility

---

1. "Hawthorne and His Mosses," rept. in *Moby-Dick*, ed. Harrison Hayford and Hershel Parker (New York: Norton, 1967), pp. 541–42. My quotations from *Moby-Dick* are from the Hayford-Parker edition. Subsequent references will be abbreviated MD and cited by page number in the text. Like all the other characters and language in *Moby-Dick*, Fleece is technically Ishmael's creation. Although the dividing line between Melville and Ishmael is not always firm, Ishmael is Melville's creation. To pretend that Melville has nothing to do with *Moby-Dick* seems ridiculous to me. Without becoming obsessive about it, I grant Ishmael his autonomy and nonetheless refer to Melville as a matter of convenience and common sense.

and brotherhood: "Don't be tearin' de blubber out your neighbour's mouth, I say." "Civil," "neighbour," "brethern," with their echo of the Sermon on the Mount and the ethics of the *civis*—these words stand for the central cohesive values, religious and secular, of Melville's culture. They also play off against the reality of sharks viciously getting as much as they can for themselves regardless of others or their own actual needs. In a subversive turn on the property values of the dominant society, for Fleece the rights of property are no justification, since "dat whale belong to some one else," presumably to God. The sharks, however, are impervious to argument, and Melville has Fleece pass a final judgment on them and the competitive, acquisitive society they represent. "Cussed fellow-critters," he has Fleece conclude, "kick up de damndest row as ever you can; fill you dam' bellies till dey bust—and den die" (MD, pp. 251, 252).[2]

This intense vision of evil at odds with the basic cohesive values of brotherhood—this outlook is rooted in Melville's sense of his individualistic American society. Melville is uncompromising about the evil of the system of possessive individualism and its total incompatibility with the Christian value of love. His torment and achievement are that he refuses to accept the compromises most people resort to in order to live with the contradictions between two of the systems basic to American culture.

Inseparable from Melville's sense of his individualistic American society is his awareness of metaphysical evil. He also brings this vision alive through the destructive energy of the sharks, who "viciously snapped, not only at each other's disembowelments, but like flexible bows, bent round, and bit their own; till those entrails seemed swallowed over and over again by the same mouth, to be oppositely voided by the gaping wound." Even the corpses of these sharks had "a sort of Pantheistic vitality," a murderous, destructive power that impels Queequeg to say, "Queequeg no care what god make him shark, . . . wedder Fejee god or Nantucket god; but de god wat made shark must be one dam Ingin" (MD, p. 257). A god who is "one dam Ingin" is a depraved god. Through the sharks, Melville has brought to life a sense of social and metaphysical evil so intense that it undermines conventional belief. The extremity of this vision challenges the underlying religious and

---

2. Robert Zoellner, *The Salt-Sea Mastodon: A Reading of Moby-Dick* (Berkeley: University of California Press, 1973), sees the treatment of Fleece as an example of Melville's racism rather than as an example of Melville's sensitivity to highly charged issues. Zoellner bases his opinion on the racist premise that it is unlikely for a black cook to be learned (pp. 220–21). More basically, Zoellner's account is weakened because he misses the indictment of sharkish capitalism (pp. 220–25).

social premises of Melville's liberal, individualistic America. Melville is passing judgment on the world of Franklin and Madison, of his father and father-in-law, of his closest friends and relatives. Although he places it at almost the exact center of his novel, no wonder he disguises his view through the outsiders' dialect of Fleece and Queequeg.

Melville is continuing into *Moby-Dick* his sense of the modern market society and its impact on religious belief, a major feature of the Launcelott-Hey and Booble-Alley sections of *Redburn*. Melville's dilemma is acute. He simultaneously takes to heart the Christian value of love, and, under the pressure of an intense vision of social and metaphysical evil, he radically questions the God who has traditionally been the sustaining source of that belief. In the absence of a supportive community, the self becomes the generating source of values, and as Ishmael and Ahab remind us, the individual is then placed under tremendous strain. At the center of the novel, in Fleece's sermon and "The Shark Massacre," Melville thus goes deeper than he had at the outset through his satire of Bildad and Peleg or, in a more positive way, of his creation of Father Mapple. Fleece's sermon is the unorthodox counterpart of Father Mapple's sermon.[3] In writing his way into *Moby-Dick*, Melville typically releases the full force of attitudes he had held in check earlier in his book.

Less intensely than in Fleece's sermon, the entire enterprise of whale hunting allows Melville to explore a range of attitudes toward possessive individualism. At the outset he is perfectly capable of celebrating the dignity and grandeur of an occupation ordinarily seen as menial. In this mood, he has Ishmael elevate the Nantucketeers who "in all seasons and all oceans declared everlasting war with the mightiest animated mass that has survived the flood." Far from seeing the whalemen as mere workers or, conversely, as invaders and exploiters, Melville has Ishmael present them as conquerors who divide the waters of the globe as England and America do the land. Ownership now becomes imperial, not exploitative, and the accumulating rhythms and allusions establish the warlike grandeur and final peace of the whaleman (MD, pp. 62, 63). But even in the early stages of *Moby-Dick*, Melville uses Bildad to expose whaling as an exploitative, blood-spilling invasion at odds with the religion of peace (MD, p. 72). Melville nonetheless values not the business practices of a sharkish capitalism but the skill and daring inseparable from the business of whaling. He takes a nationalistic pride in the American superiority to the Germans, as both pursue a blinded whale,

3. For a sensitive treatment of the orthodox position, see Robert Sherrill, *The Prophetic Melville: Experience, Transcendence, and Tragedy* (Athens: University of Georgia Press, 1979). For Sherrill, however, the "experience" of his subtitle never involves Melville's dislocating experience with the market society.

and at the same time he exposes the painful results (MD, pp. 295–302). He also delights in Stubb's Yankee trickery of the inexperienced French, who do not realize that precious ambergris is buried in the decaying whale Stubb helpfully takes off their hands (MD, pp. 336–42).

More generally, though, Melville celebrates not the business practices of whaling but the manual skills and the tools of the trade of this ordinarily despised occupation. He grounds his narrative in the solidly specified crafts and procedures of every phase of whaling.[4] As Melville has Ishmael present it, the labor is hard, demanding, but unalienated, and the men have mastered what to the landsman is an astonishing range of skills. As Melville has Ishmael present the whaling world through the texture of his voice and style, Ishmael fuses the physical and the metaphysical. Ishmael's speculative flights are integral with his precise accounts of ropes, mast-heads, and the anatomy of the tail and forehead of the whale. Through the rhythm of his narrative within chapters, Ishmael typically moves from the mundane to the furthest reaches of the universe without losing touch with cutting spades and harpoons. The result is a denial of alienation. In tension both with Ahab's political coercion of the crew and with Ishmael's comprehensive question, "Who ain't a slave?" Ishmael thinks like Marx's free man. Within his style, he brings together manual skills and free-ranging speculation as an alternative to and criticism of the separations and money-orientation of the dominant market society. This fusion is stylistic, which is Melville's way of acknowledging and resisting the power of alienated reality. He has Ishmael increasingly become a voice instead of a fully embodied character because Ishmael's unalienated style is almost impossible to embody in the social and philosophical world Melville inhabits. Melville thus takes account of the limiting pressures of those personal, philosophical, and social powers that constrain and animate both Ishmael and his American creator. The vitality, wildness, and energy of Ishmael's style and self are pervasively opposed to the moderation and orderliness of the commonsense world of market-society individualism. Drawing on the resources of the baroque tradition, Melville expresses the energies of other strata of American selves and society than those dominating the official, respectable world. He needs all the resilience available, since the pressures he must sustain are immense.

In *Redburn*, Melville began to explore the impact of his father's bankruptcy and death and his own displacement in the open world of market-society individualism. In *Moby-Dick*, he renders the full conse-

---

4. In *Hawthorne, Melville, and the Novel* (University of Chicago Press, 1976), Richard Brodhead is eloquent on this achievement (pp. 142–46).

quences of this situation. In *Redburn*, Melville radically questioned the laissez-faire world of Adam Smith and the religious certainties he associated with his dead and failed father. In *Moby-Dick*, he goes on to reject the Cartesian, Lockean world view, just as he rejects the individualistic society Locke, Adam Smith, and their successors helped to create and to justify. For Melville the Cartesian, Lockean separation between subject and object is unacceptable, but Melville is unable consistently to bridge the gap or to conceive consistently of alternatives to the received categories. Through the power of symbolic language, he achieves resolutions that temporarily do away with the conventional dualisms, but he nonetheless continues to search for a real world behind the world of appearances revealed to the senses, at the same time fearing the destructive abyss he might find. He has Ishmael probe and probe, achieve momentary fulfillments, and somehow manage to live with the uncertainties, contradictions, and inconclusiveness without demanding the final assurances he nonetheless longs for. Through Ahab, Melville powerfully imagines the alternative.

When Melville has Ishmael view whaling separated from the vitality, skill, and courage of the men, when Melville has Ishmael go to the fundamentals of the market society, he repeatedly exposes the basic premises of capitalism. After *Moby-Dick*, as his vision became even more extreme and his felt need to protect himself from hostile attack increased, Melville developed an inward-turning, understated, almost impenetrable irony quite different from the expansive, synthesizing hyperbole and symbolic energy of *Moby-Dick*. But even in *Moby-Dick*, Melville is one of the "masters of the great Art of Telling the Truth—even if it be covertly, and by snatches" (MD, p. 542). He also has a sure sense of what is central to his property-owning, Victorian society. In his account of fast-fish and loose-fish, the basic laws of ownership in a whaling world, he thus uses an outrageous phallic joke to show possession of private property as a perversion supported by an arbitrary legal system. Fleece's sermon focuses on sharks. Harpooning becomes the crucial issue as Melville defines a fast-fish as one that "belongs to the party fast to it. A Loose-Fish is fair game for anybody who can soonest catch it" (MD, p. 331).

The final implications of this general law turn out to be ominous, but the specific case is initially low-keyed and urbane. It involves a whale harpooned but then abandoned. The whalers managed to save their lives but lost the harpoons, lines, and boat attached to the fish. They sued to recover the whale and their property from the defendants who finally made the catch. In a witty, covertly insulting analogy, the defense attorney connects the abandoned whale and its harpoons with an adulterous wife, a loose-fish divorced and thus abandoned on the seas of life, "and therefore when a subsequent gentleman re-harpooned her, the lady then became that subsequent gentleman's property, along with whatever harpoon might have been found sticking in her." A modern reader even slightly touched by feminism will find it offensive to talk this way about a woman as property. For a nineteenth-century reader, the insulting sexual innuendo would have been even more disturbing, since it touches the cornerstone of Victorian propriety. Melville thus compounds the exposure of property ownership, the most basic institution of American society, by connecting property ownership with illicit sex. He intensifies the attack by using the harpoon in an outrageous phallic sense. Melville engages with two of the most sacred tenets of nineteenth-century American ideology, property and sexual propriety. In a parody of the Lockean premises underlying American property relations, Melville goes on to have the judge award the whale, harpoons, and line to the defendants: "the whale, because it was a Loose-Fish at the time of the final capture," and, especially telling, "the harpoons and line because when the fish made off with them, it (the fish) acquired a property in those articles; and hence anybody who afterwards took the fish had a right to them" (MD, p. 333). For Melville, the twin laws of Fast-Fish and Loose-Fish as interpreted by the judge constitute "the fundamentals of all human jurisprudence; for notwithstanding its complicated tracery of sculpture, the Temple of the Law, like the Temple of the Philistines, has but two props to stand on." Chief Justice Shaw would know exactly how to take this direct attack on the ideological supports and fundamental structure of capitalism.

Viewed in one way, America is a liberal democracy; viewed in another, it is a possessive market society. Liberalism prefers to stress its basic procedural fairness, respect for personal liberties, and abhorrence of tyranny. In "Fast-Fish and Loose-Fish," Melville, in contrast, has Ishmael focus on possession and argue that, "regardless of how the thing came into possession," possession is not only half of the law but is also often "the whole of the law" (MD, p. 333). His examples embarrass liberalism by exposing its tyranny and violation of Christian principles, by going to the central contradiction of a liberal republic, namely, slavery, and by aligning American slaves with "the sinews and souls of Russian serfs" as "Fast-Fish, whereof possession is the whole of the law." In the shadow of the Fugitive Slave Act of 1850, it was not at all neutral to show slaves as property and the possession of property as more important than freedom in the land of the free. Melville repeatedly uses essential similarities between Russian and American tyranny to undercut republican pretensions. In "Fast-Fish," his examples of rapacious landlords, usurers, parasitic archbishops, and hereditary dukes are commonplace, but Melville has Ishmael conclude with a series of imperialistic harpooners. In so doing, Melville forcefully seizes on the connection between the expansionism of liberal capitalism and the religious values justifying "that apostolic lancer, Brother Jonathan," in harpooning the Fast-Fish, Texas, just as England has harpooned "poor Ireland."

Melville goes even further through the doctrine of Loose-Fish. On this view, far from being a millennial, redemptive event or an occasion for patriotic eulogy, the discovery of America is one in a series of predatory captures, on a par with the tyranny of the Czar over Poland, England over India, and the approaching expropriation of Mexico by the United States. In a whaling world, the acquisitive sharks of Fleece's sermon devour as much as they can for their own benefit, and, beyond the individual, nations harpoon what they can regardless of right. Melville shows that, rooted in such a system, the highest sanctities—"the Rights of Man and the Liberties of the World, . . . all men's minds and opinions, . . . the principle of religious belief" itself—none of them are independent of the acquisitive world of sharks and harpoons, but all are Loose-Fish. "What is the great globe itself but a Loose-Fish?" Melville has Ishmael conclude. "And what are you, reader, but a Loose-Fish and a Fast-Fish, too?" (MD, p. 334). On this view, in the predatory world of possessive individualism, as individuals we are either harpooned or are soon about to be; everything is open to appropriation, everything is property to be possessed, from the great globe itself through the sanctities of human rights, liberties, and even, holiest of holies, the basic principle of religious belief.

Melville thus turns against liberalism its central claim as a protector of freedom and religious ideals. Liberalism asserts a positive connection between individual liberty and the competitive system of individual property ownership. For most mid-nineteenth-century Americans, their system also supported and was sanctioned by Christian beliefs. Far from promoting Christian certainties or "the Rights of Man and the Liberties of the World," however, for Melville, the system of possessive individualism makes everything into an unstable object of prey. His tone is good-natured, but the world of "Bartleby" and *The Confidence-Man* is in the offing.

Melville not only considered America an acquisitive, individualistic society but also responded to America as a democracy. In the nineteenth century, at the center of the controversy about liberal democracy were disagreements about the virtues and defects of the common man as distinct from an aristocracy. Other key issues involved freedom and tyranny, the individual and the mass, equality and its consequences, and the merits of a wide dissemination of culture, perhaps at the expense of excellence and a coercive demand for superficial, popular art. Early in *Moby-Dick*, Melville goes to the heart of these matters by having Ishmael celebrate the democratic dignity that, regardless of rank or externals, "shines in the arm that wields a pick or drives a spike; that democratic dignity which, on all hands, radiates without end from God; Himself! The great God absolute! The centre and circumference of all democracy! His omnipresence, our divine equality!" (MD, p. 104).

Melville's democratic faith is also grounded in his direct experience of his own depths, in what Ishmael describes as "that immaculate manliness we feel within ourselves, so far with us, that it remains intact though all the outer character seem gone." This experience is crucial. It allows Melville to have Ishmael distinguish between "man, in the ideal," and the actual individual men, "detestable as joint stock-companies and nations," who constitute the "knaves, fools, and murderers" of his confidence-man society. The existential experience of "that immaculate manliness" within turns out to be a surer basis for Melville's democratic belief than God as "the centre and circumference of all democracy." Later in *Moby-Dick*, the accumulating pressures undermine Melville's belief in a sustaining God but not in the generating power of the self. After *Moby-Dick*, when that belief, too, is affected, Melville's social vision darkens acutely.

In *Moby-Dick*, the experience of a deep, inviolable manliness guarantees democratic equality on the assumption that everyone regardless of character or external circumstance contains within the self a wellspring of infinitely precious common humanity. Ordinary people can also be seen in a positive "ethereal light" as "workmen" who "wield a pick or drive a spike." They then partake of the democratic valuation of those who do the common, productive labor of the society. But viewed as a capitalistic society of "joint-stock-companies," the same common people emerge as "mean and meagre," as "knaves, fools, and murderers." Short of a revolution that would totally transform conditions and generate a new set of challenges and problems, the dilemma is irresolvable. It has not been resolved to this day. In *Moby-Dick*, Melville lives with the contradictions. He shows the common sailors as both vital and limited, and he also exposes the acquisitive foundations of the market society. It would be simpler for him if he could show the unequivocal virtue of ordinary workmen and criticize the "detestable" venality of their exploiters, but he is too aware of human diversity and the pervasive impact of a joint stock-company society, which affects the men as well as the owners.

Melville has Ishmael deify the "just Spirit of Equality" and celebrate the "kingly commons," the source of the ordinary men who, like Bunyan and Andrew Jackson, are the champions of democratic promise. He is sufficiently at one with the ideology of his period so that he makes this celebration the heart of the powerful official invocation to his American epic. Later in *Moby-Dick*, however, he has Ahab express the dark, unofficial motto: "Ego non baptizo te in nomine patris, sed in nomine diaboli!" (MD, p. 404). For the author of *Redburn* and the creator of the tyrant, Jackson, who insists on his relation to General Jackson, Andrew Jackson also has a demonic underside. Before considering the authoritarian possibilities Melville connects with Jackson and brings alive in *Moby-Dick* through Ahab's manipulation of the crew, we must first concentrate on the divided allegiances implicit in the idea of "the kingly commons." Melville is pulled by royal and aristocratic values that both provide an alternative to the sharkish practices of capitalism and dignify ordinary life. Melville thus sustains a tension between his criticism of acquisitiveness, his democratic commitment to equality, and his patrician fascination with kings, emperors, and knights, with an elitism at odds with equality.

Although Ahab's dictatorship represents a profound threat to democracy, he also validates the democratic belief in the commons as a source of greatness. Ahab has the dignity of a Shakespearean king or a Roman emperor, and yet he is an ordinary American whaling captain in all his mundane shagginess. He is a splendid embodiment of the paradox of "the kingly commons," both a rebuttal to and a stunning confirmation of fears about the capacity and the consequences of America democracy, as well as being an elitist critic of that democracy.

In multiple ways throughout *Moby-Dick*, Melville responds to the challenge of elevating to heroic stature his crew of "meanest mariners, and renegades and castaways" (MD, p. 104). Melville plays constantly on the discrepancy between ordinary social perceptions and his own heightened perception. He creates a style distinguished by a world-ranging accumulation of allusions. The *Pequod* is compared to a French grenadier who fought in Egypt and Siberia; the masts, from Japan, are "like the spires of the three old kings of Cologne." Melville's language continues to play over the continents, to range from "barbaric Ethiopian emperors" and barbaric Icelandic heroes to the aristocratic Christian sanctity of "Canterbury Cathedral where Beckett bled." It was Peleg himself who had embellished the *Pequod* with the very bones of its prey, so as to make pursuer and pursued almost indistinguishable. The aristocratic and religious allusions to heroic achievements from barbaric Ethiopia and Iceland to feudal Canterbury and Cologne also make whaling into something other than Peleg's capitalistic business, at the same time exposing the exploitative savagery of the owners. Bildad and Peleg conduct their business from a wigwam made of whalebone while Bildad preaches Christian doctrine, fleeces Ishmael, and listens to Peleg on savage, sharkish harpooners. Melville's heightened language simultaneously dignifies the commonplace, democratic subject matter and exposes and provides a heroic alternative to marketplace realities. By dealing in a similar style with every facet of whaling, Melville grounds his narrative in observed reality and avoids the danger of a merely rhetorical exercise in elevation. At the same time, he validates his own claims as a democratic successor to Shakespeare and Sir Thomas Browne in a land where "dollars damn me."

But the very depth and complexity of Melville's style and his radical challenge to all forms of orthodoxy further compound the patrician-democratic problem, since Melville knows his audience well enough to realize it is "vain to popularize profundities, and all truth is profound" (MD, p. 161). He surrounds this perception with a series of allusions to exiled royalty, but this displaced patrician is an artist as critical of his own class as of the uncomprehending masses.

Ahab thus speaks for one side of Melville himself when he contemptuously thinks that "the permanent constitutional condition of manufactured man . . . is sordidness" (MD, p. 184), not the sordidness of factory smoke and hovels but the sordidness of the love of cash. Melville knows it is not simply an American and modern phenomenon—the Crusaders, as he has Ahab recognize, needed to rob to keep them motivated on their holy quest. That "permanent constitutional condition" may also be the universal innate depravity of the common man's human nature. The language of the passage, however, makes it seem more likely that Melville is using Ahab's caustic wit both to denigrate the manufactured mass man of an acquisitive, mechanizing society and to expose the constitutional basis of this condition.

In this sense, Ahab cuts through the official view of the Constitution as a democratic charter and brings into the open what jurists like Melville's father-in-law, Chief Justice Shaw, knew but did not like to admit, certainly not in Ahab's harsh way; namely, that the Constitution was permanently committed to the protection of a system of property ownership that by the middle of the nineteenth century increasingly involved manufacture. The "sordidness" Melville has Ahab indict is the entire cash nexus, its manufactured men, and its constitutional foundation. What appears at first to be an elite-mass opposition with Ahab looking down on and manipulating the masses turns out to be more complicated, since through Ahab Melville also questions the acquisitive motives and manufactured men generated by the constitutional system. The elites who run this system—Chief Justice Shaw is an important example—come under as sharp attack as the ordinary men who share their motives if not their returns. Through Ahab, Melville thus turns against both them and their opponents the conservative, patrician distrust of the common man manufactured by a democratic society. In the background is the ambiguity of a society that from one point of view is democratic and from another point of view is capitalistic.

Ahab turns the prevailing capitalistic motives to his own uses. He manipulates the structure of authority and the customary usages of the ship as a money-making enterprise. He uses his position of command as an instrument of his will, of his need to dominate, and he shrewdly puts the cash motive to his own uses. His tyranny and the psychological and metaphysical goals it serves, however, are in their way as dangerous as the acquisitive individualism he and his creator abhor. Melville elevates and questions Ahab's high-minded, high-handed intensities and at the same time uses them to illuminate the individualistic market society Ahab emerges from.

He thus has Ahab appeal to something powerful and irrational in the crew, something that answers to his own desire to kill the whale. In the increasingly rationalistic nineteenth-century world in which communal rituals were disappearing, Ahab stages inverted rituals that solidify his hold on the crew and give a unity to the ship beyond its official, work-a-day routine as a capitalistic, money-making venture. As a result, the members of the crew lose their own individuality in the larger purpose Ahab has defined for them. "Love is a kelson of the creation" for Whitman, but Ahab's will and individuality are "the long central keel" that holds the *Pequod* together, "welds into oneness" the individual variety of the crew, and directs them all "to that fatal goal which Ahab their one lord and keel did point to" (MD, p. 455).

This society is authoritarian, not traditional and communal. Although it has some of the features of a traditional hierarchical society, it lacks the reciprocal relations and modulations of a Burkean culture that has evolved over time. Through Ahab, Melville highlights the authoritarian possibilities that exist in an individualistic society lacking traditional communal ties and restraints, a society in which the acquisitive motives and external roles and structures of authority can be coerced by a charismatic leader. In Ahab's individualistic world, there is finally room for only one individual. This prospect is the nightmare that haunts Melville's response to his liberal, individualistic American society.

Melville rejects that society's rationalism and acquisitiveness, its destruction of communal bonds and failure to provide life-giving outlets for the buried underside of human nature. The crew members of the *Pequod* come from traditional societies around the globe. They represent a culling-out of those who are *isolatoes*, so that Melville illuminates the composition of his own individualistic society of emigrants from the traditional world. Melville also knows that a powerful leader can manipulate these *isolatoes* both by playing on the cash motive and through authoritarian appeals to the real needs an individualistic, capitalistic society only imperfectly satisfies. In a positive way, Ahab speaks to the need for community and for a ritualistically sanctioned involvement in activity transcending the self; in a darker way, he taps and redirects the primitive hatreds and racial animosities of the crew.

Madisonian republicans, who feared the tyranny of factions, created a system to fragment society so that no one faction could gain dominance and challenge what was for them the inevitably unequal distribution of property. The republicans were primarily concerned about the unchecked dominance of the majority who, if they were to consolidate their numerical power, would pose a serious threat to established property relations. The acquisitive motives the republicans assumed and intensified and the social and political fragmentation they legislated were designed to lead to pluralism and to prevent exactly the sort of tyranny Melville repeatedly imagines, from the Jackson of *Redburn* through Ahab and the political sections of "The Encantadas" into *Billy Budd*. In *Moby-Dick*, Melville is especially perceptive about the authority structures that do exist along with the human needs, acquisitive motives, and social fragmentation, all of which a powerful leader can exploit and turn to ends antithetical to the liberalism that created the very conditions from which Ahab builds his tyranny.

Melville has an ambivalent view of the shipboard society Ahab dominates, just as he has an ambivalent view of Ahab. The structure of authority is controlled by white American Protestants ruling a crew of almost every race and nationality. At times Melville presents the mates as brave, capable men adequate to command their dark, savage harpooneers. But the gigantic African, Daggoo, is superior to wooden Flask, and Queequeg has a depth of intuitive knowledge of the mysteries of life lacking in the courageous, reasonable Christian, Starbuck. This complication highlights but does not basically challenge the conventional structure of command. Ishmael, however, acquiesces in but intellectually rejects the structure, and, by the time of "Benito Cereno," Melville designs the entire work to subvert the legitimacy of any structure of authority. In *Moby-Dick*, to the extent that Christianity provides a rationale for the dominance of white Protestants over the people living in darkness, Melville also radically undercuts this ideology. He does so through his intricate play on the savagery of sharkish Christians and his tongue-in-cheek satire of Queequeg's evangelical pagan piety to expose all forms of joyless, self-righteous evangelical religion, especially the Protestant, home-grown variety.

Because of Ahab, who has "the high perception" but lacks "the low enjoying power," and because of Starbuck's decency and emotional-intuitive limitations, Melville to an extent sets up a split between the tight intensities and sensual restraints of the white Protestant officers and the instinctive passions and vitality of the harpooneers and crew. Never mechanically schematic, Melville complicates the symmetry with Stubb's celebration of appetite, Rabelaisian laughter, and sperm-filled masts. But in contrast to Ahab and Starbuck, in "Midnight—Forecastle," the crew does suggestively embody the vital energies of the uncon-scious. Their songs and dialogue repeatedly bring to life the overlooked realities of sex. "There's naught so sweet on earth—heaven may not match it," the Maltese sailor says, "as those swift glances of warm, wild bosoms in the dance, when the over-arboring arms hide such ripe, bursting grapes" (MD, p. 152). And they know, too, about the dead in their graves, about "the green navies and the green-skulled crews" (MD, p. 151). In contrast to the manufactured men of an acquisitive society, on this view, the crew is a democratic repository of energy and instinctive knowledge. But they are also violent and have primitive animosities based on race and nationality. In unifying this microcosm of America, this crew of *isolatoes*, Ahab is able to direct to his own ends the energies that animate these deep hatreds.

To underscore the point, Melville contrives it so that Daggoo and the Spanish sailor, who act out the racial pride and hostilities of black and white, are interrupted in their deadly argument by the fury of the white squall and, on Pip's association, "the white whale" and, still in Pip's mind, that "anaconda of an old man [who] swore 'em in to hunt" the white whale (MD, pp. 154, 155). On this view, an American dictator is able to compel and to redirect the racism that rages below the surface of a ship in important ways reminiscent of a liberal society on its trans-formed capitalistic quest.

The carpenter is an equivocal representative of another dimension of this society, not of its racial passions or capitalistic drive but of its me-chanical, manipulative tendencies. The carpenter is a caricature of the mechanically inventive American, the jack-of-all-trades who manipu-lates gadgets and whose technical skill makes America great. Through him, Melville raises again the issue of democratic "man, in the ideal," or, as he puts it in introducing the carpenter, "high abstracted man alone" in contrast to "mankind in mass, . . . for the most part . . . a mob of unnecessary duplicates" (MD, p. 387). Here from Ishmael's point of view is Ahab's "manufactured man" with an emphasis on his mechanical, manipulative skills.

Melville has Ishmael show that the danger for such a "pure manipulator" is that everything becomes a reified object to be worked on with equal indifference. Human beings and human values lose their distinctive quality: "teeth he accounted bits of ivory; heads he deemed but top-blocks; men themselves he lightly held for capstans" (MD, p. 388). Far from having intelligence or even the intuitive knowledge of the artisan, Melville shows the carpenter as totally literal. The carpenter sees men as objects, his superiors treat him as one, and he is willing to be used. The combination poses the threat, certainly not confined to America, of technically skilled manipulators lacking critical intelligence and awareness of humanity, at the service of superiors who open and shut them like the blades and screwdrivers on a knife (MD, p. 389). These totalitarian results are not casual but emerge from a basic American strength, its universally acknowledged mechanical genius. The carpenter is a suggestive reminder that the man who works with tools and machines may well become a machine and that powerful superiors are around to use tools. Conceived in opposition to images of the free America craftsman, the carpenter anticipates an authoritarian politics and an alienated personality type that were to become increasingly significant as American industrial capitalism developed. The coercive individualism of a powerful leader combined with the absence of independence in his reified subordinates—here is a nightmare to haunt any believer in democratic individualism.

eleven

"SONG OF MYSELF"
Whitman's Individualism and Market-Society America

Whitman's "Song of Myself" is a powerful alternative both to Melville's nightmare and to basic tendencies of the market society. In the hard-driving, hard-bargaining mid-nineteenth-century world, American men restlessly pursued their own advantage. As Tocqueville points out, having severed the ties that connect men to each other in traditional societies, the American individualist relentlessly competed with men similarly competing for wealth, power, and a sense of self-worth. Especially for respectable people in the Northeast, the work ethic provided the discipline of the personality this insatiably competitive process called for. Respectable Americans internalized and measured themselves against a set of criteria stressing restraint, frugality, order, temperance, moderation, and the other virtues appropriate to a society still accumulating capital resources. Achieving financial success, as Max Weber indicates, was "the *summum bonum* of this ethic."[1] John Murray Cuddihy has generalized the work ethic into what he usefully calls the Protestant Etiquette, a comprehensive discipline of the personality that over the course of two-and-a-half centuries had come to include an ethic, an aesthetic, and an etiquette.[2] This measure of what constituted a good person in a decent society stressed moderation, restraint, and a deep training in the repression of the instincts. Philip Greven examines this training in detail.[3] More analytically than Melville, Hawthorne, Poe, and Twain, Greven also shows the often violent ways Americans expressed those emotions they were trained to repress.

1. *The Protestant Ethic and the Spirit of Capitalism*, trans. Talcott Parsons (New York: Scribner's, 1958), p. 53.
2. *The Ordeal of Civility: Freud, Marx, Levi-Strauss, and the Jewish Struggle with Modernity* (New York: Basic Books, 1974), pp. 5–10.
3. *The Protestant Temperament: Patterns of Child-Rearing, Religious Experience, and the Self in Early America* (New York: Knopf, 1977).

211

In opposition to the world of possessive individualism and the Protestant Etiquette, Whitman's "Song of Myself" is one of the most fully developed alternatives an American has ever imagined. In contrast to the intensities and tight discipline of the capitalistic work ethic, Whitman dramatizes a totally opposed style. "I lean and loafe at my ease," he says at the outset of his American epic, "observing a spear of summer grass."[4] The poet who would bring America together and to fulfillment, who would celebrate himself and make a great poem of America, thus opposes himself to the dominant values and personality styles of his culture. He sees in himself and in America possibilities of growth, energy, and pleasure more basic than, and totally at odds with, the restraint, acquisitiveness, and common sense of market-society America. In place of the concentrated intensities, the emphasis on logic, precise categories, and the order of the account book, and in opposition to the separation between subject and object, self and other of the dominant society, Whitman offers an expanding self and universe, one merging into the other. In his world, there are no tight boundaries or restrictions. Animated by the "urge and urge and urge, / Always the procreant urge of the world," the growing self flows into the world as the world flows into the self. The result is a fundamental alternative to the Protestant Etiquette and the possessive market society this Etiquette emerges from, justifies, and perpetuates.[5]

Whitman offers instead precisely what the Protestant Etiquette suppresses: pleasure, instinctual gratification, and self-assertion, the outpouring of erotic feelings and the barbaric yawp, the whole charge of deliberately rude self-satisfaction that constitutes poor taste on the standards of the official etiquette, ethic, and esthetic. The sprawling open form of "Song of Myself" has an inner order and coherence, but they are an affront to the decorum of the dominant aesthetic, just as the unabashed self and self-expression at the center of the poem are affronts to the self-effacement called for by the Protestant Etiquette. Whitman's individual contains multitudes and gradually unfolds, grows, expresses, and is absorbed into the nation and cosmos, to "effuse my flesh in

4. *Leaves of Grass: Facsimile Edition of the 1860 Text*, ed. Roy Harvey Pearce (Ithaca: Cornell University Press, 1961), p. 23. My quotations are from the 1860 edition, but for convenience I have used the section numbers of the more readily accessible 1892 edition.

5. Although my own emphasis differs from theirs, I am especially indebted to Roy Harvey Pearce, *The Continuity of American Poetry* (Princeton University Press, 1961), pp. 69–83, and "Introduction," *Leaves of Grass: Facsimile Edition of the 1860 Text*; and to Edwin H. Miller, *Walt Whitman's Poetry: A Psychological Journey* (Boston: Houghton Mifflin, 1968), pp. 85–114.

eddies, and drift it in lacy jags," to "bequeathe myself to the dirt, to grow from the grass I love." In contrast to the suspicion of the body and the emphasis on cleanliness, two cornerstones of the official code, Whitman affirms the "flesh" and "dirt." In place of self-restraint and self-effacement, the rudely affirmed "I" is both personal and universal, both uniquely individual and a blasphemously unorthodox, mythic, unifying deity and religion, an astonishing guarantee of never-ending life.

Emerging from generating episodes like section 5, love and the pleasure inseparable from it are basic to "Song of Myself." The pleasure is rooted in and flows from a sexuality as immediate as the tongue piercing through the bosom-bone to the bare-stript heart, to use the language of section 5. For Whitman, love and pleasure do away with the isolating, divisive tendencies of market-society America. Whitman is not playing with peripheral issues: he has intuitively gone to the heart of things. His love and pleasure are radical alternatives to the dominant impulses of his capitalistic society and, in their intensity and range, perhaps of any conventional society. Later in his career, in *Democratic Vistas*, Whitman celebrates the property ownership of the ordinary middle class. And even in "Song of Myself," he values the possessions and activities of small landowners and adventurers. But his central emphasis is not on the accumulation of property and profits. Whitman suggests an entirely new basis for social life, one that emerges from the generating power of sexualized love and that stresses joy, abundance, and growth as opposed to possession and accumulation. His sustaining, opposing vision is in many ways similar to that of such Europeans as Rousseau and Kant and of such contemporaries as Emerson and Thoreau, but he differs significantly from them in stressing sexuality as an animating principle.

As an alternative to the economic expansionism of liberal capitalism, moreover, Whitman offers a free-flowing self and a vital nation and universe. The self and the America of his poem grow out of the relatively open conditions of the new world transformed by Whitman's energy and commitments. The resulting new world criticizes America by taking to heart its neglected professions about equality and by substituting the animating power of sexualized love for the competitive acquisitiveness of the market society. It may appear that by thus idealizing America, Whitman also to an extent functions as a rationalizer for liberal capitalism. But the basis for his nation is fundamentally at odds with the governing imperatives of the market society.

Instead, Whitman grounds his nation in the exceptionally precise, unsublimated love scene of section 5, set not in the seclusion of "shade and shine" but in the open air of a summer morning and fully realizing the earlier, insinuated promise of "buzzed whispers, love-root, silk-thread, crotch and vine." Now it is

> I mind how once we lay, such a transparent summer morning,
> How you settled your head athwart my hips, and gently turned over upon me,
> And parted the shirt from my bosom-bone, and plunged your tongue to my bare-stript heart,
> And reached till you felt my beard, and reached till you held my feet.

The "I" and "you" are at once body and soul, self and other, Whitman and his reader, all based on a convincing relation between Whitman and a lover. It is more comprehensive and fully rendered than in "Crossing Brooklyn Ferry," so that even more forcefully than in that poem the commonsense dualisms are replaced by the fusion and the pleasure of sexual union.

In the resulting intensity and joy,

> Swiftly arose and spread around me the peace and joy and knowledge that pass all the art and argument of the earth,
> And I know that the hand of God is the promise of my own,
> And I know that the spirit of God is the brother of my own,
> And that all the men ever born are also my brothers, and the women my sisters and lovers,
> And that a kelson of the creation is love,
> And limitless are leaves stiff or drooping in the fields,
> And brown ants in the little wells beneath them,
> And mossy scabs of the worm-fence, and heaped stones, elder, mullen, and pokeweed.

The central realization is "that a kelson of the creation is love." This love, at once sexual and spiritual, unifies existence with the basic energy of generation. Internally, Whitman's individual merges body and soul. Equally significant, he is inseparable from others: from the men and women he loves, from God, and from the panorama of democratically celebrated common objects that embody the same generating energy. This energy, this love, animates existence, guarantees ongoing life, and gives the most ordinary objects their heightened significance. The phallic leaves, "stiff and drooping in the fields," embody the same "limitless," erotically charged energy as the lovers; "the mossy scabs of the worm-fence, and heaped stones, elder, mullen, and pokeweed" are as vital and deserving as the men and women. After the intensities of passionate merging, Whitman can move out of himself and attend lovingly to the ordinary objects of existence, which flow from this generating experience and source. As opposed to conventional dualisms, individual objects retain their lovingly observed particularity and at the same time are related to an emerging whole. An unsublimated love is the basic principle of cohesion. It animates everyone and everything and does away with hierarchies and inequalities. The configuration of love, energy, pleasure, equality, and ongoing life makes for a cosmic, anarchic individualism that is Whitman's alternative to the divisive world of possessive individualism.

In its nineteenth-century version, the American market society generated and was supported by the work ethic. The emphasis on discipline, restraint, and frugality, the injunctions about moderation and the cautiousness about instinctual pleasure, however, are not integral to possessive individualism, as developments after World War II indicate. Whitman, though, should not be seen as a forerunner of contemporary narcissism and hedonism. He is too deep, too intense, and too committed to a fusion of the individual and the surrounding world, to love as a principle of cohesion as well as of pleasure. Whitman, moreover, is committed to equality, not in a lip-service way but as integral to his most basic sense of existence. He has no use for a consumerism based on systematic inequality. And though he delights in the things of this earth, in "Song of Myself," he is scathing about the acquisition of possessions. Twenty-five years later, when his exuberant hopes for America had been chastened, in *Democratic Vistas*, Whitman gives middle-class property ownership an important role as a stabilizing check on the abuses of an unregulated democracy. But at the height of his powers, in "Song of Myself," he celebrates material things not as possessions but as manifestations of the same vitality that animates the leaf of grass and the grazing cow.

Stereos and sports cars, vacation homes and TV's are for us sources of gratification, which is to say that we convert pleasure into a means both of ratifying our sense of self-worth and of shutting out the disturbing public realities we feel are beyond our control. Whitman speaks for a more authentic style of self-affirmation, one open both to the deepest energies of the self and responsive to and flowing into the surrounding world. The fact that for Whitman the surrounding world does not include a society makes him recognizably American, even as his faith that love ties us together is a source of strength and vulnerability.

In sublimated versions, this love and its accompanying delight merge into the natural energies and rhythms Whitman focuses on in poems like "Crossing Brooklyn Ferry" and "There Was a Child Went Forth"—the ebb and flow of the tides, of day merging into night to be followed by the sunrise, of the cycle of the seasons and the "stretching cycles of years," all as guarantees of relation, coherence, and ongoing life. In "Song of Myself," Whitman also relies on these natural rhythms—the perennial growth of the grass, the creative power of the sun, the conjunction of night and day, sea and shore. In "Song of Myself," however, these natural energies and cycles are even more erotically charged than in "Crossing Brooklyn Ferry," which is more focused, less cluttered, but also less intense and varied than "Song of Myself." As a result of creating the 1855 poems, Whitman discovered a way of patterning his sense of things. After the intensities and the range of "Song of Myself" and "The Sleepers," he was able to write more focused poems like "Crossing Brooklyn Ferry," but at the expense of the full charge of energy and erotic power of "Song of Myself."

The love and the pleasure at the center of "Song of Myself" animate a style of individualism that does away with the commonsense dualisms of possessive individualism, with consequences for the form of the poem, the self, and the nation Whitman brings to imaginative life. Like the energies that animate it, the form of Whitman's poem is free-flowing; it is not tightly, logically, or cerebrally organized, and to the eyes of common sense the poem appears chaotic. The development is not linear but circling and expanding. Images, insights, dramatic stances are introduced in a flow, sometimes of intimate conversation, sometimes of operatic declamation. These images and stances are later recurred to, enlarged on, expanded, just as the self that at the outset concentrates on its own inner processes comes to love others and the surrounding world, which flows into the self as the self flows into the world. This process allows Whitman the psychological freedom to move deep into the usually concealed recesses of his personality. The movement of the poem is thus one not only of expansion and the reciprocal flow of self and world but also of a gradual move into the depths. The private revelations, the recognition and celebration of his conventionally suspect imagination and sexual intensities interweave with his celebration of the vitality, variety, and virtue of the nation and universe and his proclamation of the mythic self as a religion. In the process of the poem, Whitman does away with the boundaries between these categories; or rather, he makes us see the way they flow into and interpenetrate each other.

The development is thus not logical and linear but depends on charged episodes like section 5 and on freely associated, accumulating images of the self, nation, and cosmos to body forth a stance, a style of being. At the center of the poem is the self-confident individual who is animated by the generating energy of existence. He gives us confidence in ourselves, the nation, and the universe and provides an alternative to the logic and divisiveness of the acquisitive world. Through the course of the poem, Whitman achieves cumulatively deepened realizations of what he intuitively knows at the outset, so that when he returns, for example, to the central image of the grass, he can say

> now I know it is true, what I guessed at,
> What I guessed when I loafed on the grass
> (section 33)

This perception flows from a series of intense, highly charged probings of the sexualized energy of the natural world (sections 21–22) and of the poet's own creative and sexual nature (sections 24–30). These realizations generate the deepened certainty I have quoted. Whitman then goes beyond himself to the longest and most comprehensive of the catalogs that distinguish the poem. Similarly, the passionate love sequence of section 5 leads to the less intense, more impersonal sections on the grass and then the first of the panoramas of city and nation, emerging from, generated and made possible by the sexualized love sequence. In the later sections, the self has expanded more fully than in the earlier ones and has achieved more intense personal realizations, but the movement is not consistently from the personal to the mythic. Late in the poem, Whitman can record his most intimate personal longings for "lovers [who] suffocate me, / Crowding my lips, thick in the pores of my skin, / Jostling me through streets and public halls, coming naked to me at night." It is a section we might expect early in the poem but that Whitman feels free to include in section 45, juxtaposed with his rendering of the cosmic self:

> Cycles ferried my cradle, rowing and rowing like cheerful boatmen,
> For room to me stars kept aside in their own rings,
> They sent influences to look after what was to hold me.
> (section 44)

Although there is some agreement on the centers of generating energy in "Song of Myself," moreover—sections 5 and 24–25, for example—the exact sequences and patterns of organization are bound to be open to interpretation. Even more than with most romantic poems, Whitman has created a form that calls on the reader for its completion. The appeal to the experience of sexual love powerfully invokes the participation of the reader in the process of creation. Just as others are necessary for the completion of the self, others are necessary for the completion of the poem. Others complete the poem by grasping its meaning, seeing for themselves its patterns and implications, and then acting for themselves, so that finally this poem is never-ending, since for its fulfillment it asks to be incorporated into the independently active lives of its readers.

In its 1855 version, the poem on the page was untitled and unnumbered: the undifferentiated flow of free-verse lines invited each reader to make his own configurations. As a concession to common sense and a retreat from radical self-reliance, Whitman introduced 372 numbered sections in the 1860 edition and later 52 larger groupings by the 1892 edition. The poem is nonetheless still freely patterned and still appeals to the reader to form his own configurations. As opposed to tightly structured works, Whitman has done everything in his power to stimulate the reader to make up his own mind, to make up his own poem. Thus, not only does each reader experience a different poem but also for each of us on successive readings different passages assume heightened significance, come into sharper focus; each time the poem has a different configuration and to that important extent a different meaning.

Writers and readers responding to the imperatives of the nineteenth-century market society, in contrast, were encouraged to prefer externally prescribed forms; logical, linear progressions; and an avoidance of intuitive depths. As the Elizabethan commitment to the sonnet reminds us, a preference for regular meters and forms is of course not peculiar to the ethos of the work ethic and the market society. But this ethos did have an impact on the literary preferences of educated, cultivated readers and writers. For them, regularity and uniformity of interpretation were valued goals; the ideal reader was intelligent, reasonable, but subordinate to the structure of the poem. One function of nineteenth-century American popular literature was to satisfy the emotional needs ignored by the dominant market society and to assuage the strains that society created. The popular writer, however, could not be seen as going too far below the surface or as shaping a work that was disturbingly open and irregular in either content or form. The metronomic regularity and nostalgia of the most popular American poem of Whitman's lifetime, Longfellow's *Hiawatha*, is an example. Whitman, in contrast, violates all the official imperatives. In particular, instead of subordinating the reader to the structure of the poem, Whitman seeks to empower the reader. The poem is designed to engage and then to liberate the reader, to convince him of his own powers and the beauty and virtue of his nation and universe so that he can go on to act on his own.

Whitman thus differs with post-modernist theory and practice. Postmodernism emphasizes a coterie of initiated readers, avoids social and psychological content, and stresses instead the autonomy of the word and the work as its own subject. Incomprehensibility is a valued goal. Under the guise of an avant-garde opposition to the dominant society, post-modernism thus serves the interests of the market society. It removes literature as an effective critical force and safely neutralizes the energy of disaffected graduate students and professors. It gives them a morally uplifting sense of rebellion that is at the same time certifiably harmless.[6]

For Whitman, in contrast, the open form, the free verse, the appeals to intuition, pleasure, and spontaneity function as models of the freedom and the power they simultaneously encourage in the reader. The act of reading is intended to be part of a process that leads to active living, which includes passive receptivity, Whitman's alternative to restless accumulation. The diversity of response the poem stimulates, the deliberate incitement to variety instead of uniformity and regularity of interpretation, have a radical substantive implication. So does the poet's willingness to go to the extremes, to risk that loss of conscious control official society values, and to engage with states of frenzy and intense sexuality as well as with the relaxed acceptance that leads him to say,

> I think I could turn and live with animals, they are so placid and self-
> contained,
> I stand and look at them sometimes an hour at a stretch.
> They do not sweat and whine about their condition,
> They do not lie awake in the dark and weep for their sins,
> They do not make me sick discussing their duty to God,
> No one is dissatisfied—not one is demented with the mania of owning
> things,
> Not one kneels to another, nor to his kind that lived thousands of years
> ago,
> Not one is respectable or industrious over the whole earth.
>
> (section 32)

Even in his moments of relaxed acceptance, Whitman explicitly criticizes and enacts an alternative to the world of possessive individualism. He perceptively connects and exposes its work-ethic respectability, its chronic dissatisfactions and mania for ownership, its class differences and deference, and its religion of guilt.

Whitman inspires the reader to adopt a totally opposed style of individualism. "I harbor for good or bad," Whitman tells us, "I permit to speak at every hazard / Nature without check with original energy."

---

6. See Gerald Graff, *Literature Against Itself: Literary Ideas in Modern Society* (University of Chicago Press, 1979), pp. 31–101.

This fearless, immoderate expression of "nature without check with original energy" is designed to free us, to put us in touch with the natural, originating energy that for Whitman animates the poem, poet, and universe; the energy that he believes flows within each of us and relates us to each other and all of existence. For Whitman, this natural energy is much more sexualized than it is for Emerson, although it has the same divine quality. It can thus be trusted; the free life it inspires will be at odds with conventional structures, but, for Whitman, if we act from our genuine sources of energy, we are at the same time in touch with the basic energies of the universe. This guarantee of virtue means that we can avoid the distortions of the conventional "creeds and schools" of the market society and its predecessors, that overlay of custom that keeps us from our origins and substitutes false concepts and values for the freedom, pleasure, and flowing life Whitman encourages us to live.

In his expanded, mythic version, Whitman is thus both an embodiment of and a prophet for a new religion. This divinely animated way of life is an alternative to restrictive, guilt-ridden orthodoxies and a promise of never-ending life. "Lovers of me, bafflers of graves," Whitman proclaims. In his view, what applies to Whitman, however, applies to any of us: he is not special or set apart; he has simply realized more fully than others what is possible for everyone. As bard he does have a special unifying, quickening function, but his natural divinity is as freely available as the leaves of grass and sexualized love he celebrates.

If the poem works for us, we are thus inspired to go to the original sources within and for ourselves. We are also asked to do away with the teacher and to embark on our own journeys as radically independent individuals. The journey is a metaphor for an independent life in action, in process. It is inspired by reading, not, however, as a self-enclosed enterprise but as part of the process of freeing ourselves to live from our sources. Whitman's radical, anarchic individualism thus dissolves the boundaries between religion, poetry, and social theory. This individualism is underwritten by Whitman's faith in an animating wellspring of divine, sexualized energy that guarantees ongoing life and that does away with isolation by relating the self, the leaf of grass, and the furthest star in the universe.

It is significant, however, that social action and life with others in society are slighted. Even with this important reservation, Whitman's affirmative, critical alternative to market-society individualism is impressive. His omission of community, however, shows the impact on his deepest sense of existence of the very market-society individualism he predominantly refuses to accept.

Whitman's criticism of the market society extends to the basic impulses as well as to the forms of thought and value. Whitman's image for "a few idly owning, and they the wheat continually claiming" is a dead man

> with dimes on the eyes walking,
> To feed the greed of the belly, the brains liberally spooning,
> Tickets buying, taking, selling but in to the feast never once going,
> Many sweating, ploughing, thrashing, and then the chaff for payment
>   receiving
>
> (section 42)

Through the image of the dimes placed on the eyes of corpses, Whitman catches the death and the blindness of the acquisitive world of buying and selling, of a greed that keeps people from the feast of life, and a system in which the many who sweat and do the productive labor receive only chaff and the "few idly owning" receive the wheat.

At the center of "There Was a Child Went Forth," the "tight bargain, the crafty lure" combine with the arbitrary, unjust power of the father to dislocate the harmonious green world of the child's experience. In "Song of Myself," Whitman is also sharply aware of the disruptive power of the acquisitive process and the systematic inequality it generates. In "Song of Myself," however, this awareness does not have the dramatized, central role it has in "There Was a Child Went Forth." It appears explicitly in flashes of satire or indictment, as in sections 32 and 42. More pervasively, however, it appears through omission, through the systematic contrast between the America Whitman brings alive in "Song of Myself" and the practices of the dominant market society.

In a representative catalog, section 33, Whitman, "afoot with my vision," gives form to his vision of America. He begins with "the city's quadrangular houses," but, instead of settling there and developing the solidity of those square, urban dwellings, he moves rapidly to the frontier, to open territory that is vital, unsettled, and alive with possibility. The solid, settled city is only a breath away from the adventure of "log huts—camping with lumbermen." The city and the camping of the lumbermen mutually enliven and free each other. Throughout section 33 is the variety and the flow of details, developed briefly in phrases or in clauses rarely longer than a line and succeeded by others, equally lively—this rapid, rhythmic movement enforces a sense of possibility and variety and removes from any one detail the threat of endless, routine drudgery. Work in Whitman's America is thus lively and productive, not exploitative or dull. The parallel structure and reliance on participles embody a flowing, egalitarian world at odds with the built-in inequality and class structure of the market society.

Whitman's America is both like and unlike a map of the country in the 1850s. The map shows the states east of the Mississippi, the boundaries clearly marked and many of the parcels small. Then the immense expanse of the Unorganized Territory, the Oregon Country, the Great Basin, and Texas, large spaces without clearly defined boundaries. Like parts of the map, Whitman's America is open but not empty. He has long stretches of forest and wild animals interspersed with domesticated rural scenes and the trip-hammers and whirling machines of the city. His panthers, rattlesnakes, and otters exist in close proximity to his sugar and cotton growing, as they do to his onion-weeding and carrot-hoeing. The juxtapositions mean that everything is closely related, that the conventional political and sectional separations do not exist, and that the rural and urban scenes have the same natural vitality as the forests and untamed animals.

Whitman's use of participles, moreover, emphasizes the act of growing cotton or sugar or onions or carrots. The productive acts of growing or weeding know no boundaries, although the specific products are regional. In this vital world, divisive political and regional separations do not exist and neither do their market-society causes. In particular, no mortgages or markets are in sight: farming as a business does not exist. Instead, Whitman celebrates the vitality and the value of ordinary manual labor. "Weeding my onion-patch, or hoeing carrots and parsnips" are vital, self-motivated acts, not part of a market system of commodity exchange or a process of grueling field labor. Whitman similarly focuses on the manual act of "girdling the trees" rather than on the economics or social status "of a new purchase." As an alternative to the commodified market society, Whitman's America is thus alive, active, egalitarian, and productive. Whitman emphasizes ordinary, useful labor, often with a tinge of adventure, and excludes routine, mechanical work, profit-making, acquisitiveness, and the social, occupational, and economic inequalities related to it. The individualism is of small holdings, of individual farms or the manual skill of the explorer or sailor, not of the accumulation of large fortunes or the control of factories, ships, and forces. The activity is simultaneously individual and universal, so that even when Whitman uses a possessive—"my garden"—the implication is of equal accessibility to all, rather than of exclusive ownership, an effect reinforced by the representative, mythic character of the "I." Ownership is not communal, either, but the assumption of easy, equal availability does away with proprietary claims.

Elsewhere in "Song of Myself," Whitman takes account of presidents and prostitutes in order to affirm their equal value and to undercut conventional hierarchies. The contrast between his own egalitarian vision and conventional inequalities and decorum is a major source of the striking effects Whitman achieves through sudden, surprising juxtapositions. Take the unlikely sequence of the bride, the opium eater, and the prostitute; or the prostitute surrounded by the jeering crowd and supported by the poet's sympathy and the president surrounded by his advisers, a contrast not at the expense of their dignity but to enforce a sense of the equal value of the prostitute. In this early catalog (section 15), Whitman gives vital examples of the underside of the city and the vertical and regional range and variety of American life. In section 33, however, the dominant impression is of an animated, unmonotonous uniformity of condition. The prevailing occupations are rural, with a sprinkling of explorers, prospectors, and sailors.

Productive labor, however, is significantly varied by scenes of festivals and rural merrymaking. Stimulated by genre paintings and the joyous fraternity beyond the confines of respectability, Whitman ranges with a keen eye from the acceptability of "musters, beach-parties, friendly bees, huskings, house-raisings" to "the race-course" and the even less respectable "he-festivals, with blackguard gibes, ironical license, bull-dances, drinking, laughter." There is no suggestion that these lively, communal gatherings are intervals in the hard, often lonely life of the farmer or settler or that their urban manifestations, never popular with employers, were being destroyed. There is at least as much play as work in Whitman's America, and work itself is not alienated labor.

Similarly, when he leaves the wilderness and the farms and turns to the machines of the city, they are animated, not mechanical. Whitman responds to the heightened urgency of the machines,

Where trip-hammers crash—Where the press is whirling its cylinders,
Wherever the human heart beats with terrible throes

For him the crashing, whirling machines are alive with the same energy as the human heart. In this reversal of Marx, the machines come to human life rather than men becoming like the machines they work. Unlike Melville, Whitman never relates his machines to the processes of industrial capitalism.

In the geography of Whitman's America, rural regions and wilderness share predominance; the city plays a subordinate role. It hardly comes into view in section 33, although elsewhere in "Song of Myself" this Manhattan poet does justice to the blab and rush of the New York streets. Whitman's America is inhabited, not desolate, but, especially in section 33, it is peopled as much by wild and domestic animals as by human beings. The country is thus full and animated without being crowded. In the long stretches devoted to animal life, the land is characterized by the activity of black bears searching, bats flying, and heifers browsing. Except for the implied presence of the poet and, in the domestic scenes, the implication of cultivators in the background, human beings are absent in these sequences. Interspersed as they are with scenes of human activity, they provide a sense of refuge and of animating possibility, the promise of a free, natural life within easy reach. Whitman's wild animals, his alligators, panthers, bears, and buffaloes, are wild but not fierce; his domestic animals are tame but vital.

Just when we think Whitman is giving us an excessively lush, soft country, a nation of picnics, friendly bees, and house-raisings, of the innocent fecundity of beehives and the "delicious gurgle" of the mockingbird, he wakes us up with

> Where the brood cow waits in the hovel,
> Where the bull advances to his masculine work—Where the cock is
>   treading the hen

We have been trained to disapprove of "delicious gurgles," and we know that the bull and the cock should not enter polite discourse. Whitman, however, is unembarrassed by both sentimentality and barnyard vitality. He plays with the details in the fullness of his delight in the innocence and fecundity of America and his delight in his ability to accept diversity and bring to a focus his vision of natural energy. At his frequent best, as in this sequence, his timing is perfect, and he brings us and the nation suddenly to life with surprising vignettes, often at odds with conventional decorum. He has an intuitive sense of what offends the orthodox and vitalizes the poem and country he is creating as an alternative.

For him that country is a living part of the cosmos. In the middle of section 33, he thus moves from American scenes, "hurrying with the modern crowd. . . . / Solitary at midnight in my own back yard," and juxtaposes them with his intimate companionship with God on "the old hills of Judea." He then ranges ever farther, "speeding through space— speeding through heaven and the stars," now himself a cosmic, generative god "throwing fire-balls like the rest, / Carrying the crescent child that carries its own full mother in its belly." Whitman pulls section 33 together with a series of emphatic participles that render the sense of voyaging motion and power that has characterized the entire sequence:

Storming, enjoying, planning, loving, cautioning,
Backing and filling, appearing and disappearing,
I tread day and night such roads.

The "I," "appearing and disappearing," thus returns in a central role. As self, as American, and as unifying, life-giving god and bard, the "I" holds the nation and the universe together. Grammatically and philosophically, as in "There Was a Child Went Forth," everything depends on the "I."

The individualism is not the atomized, competitive individualism of the possessive market society. It is too fluid, too sensitive to mergings and relations with all of existence, too critical of "the few idly owning," and too insistent on productive acts rather than on profit-making and social and economic hierarchies. Competition, profit-making, and rank do not exist in Whitman's America; the self has a sure sense of his intrinsic worth and is not chronically busy proving himself. The movement is thus free-flowing, not the restless striving and rootless activity Tocqueville analyzed. It is worth stressing these differences, since Whitman brings alive in "Song of Myself" an America that emerges from the relatively open nation of his formative years and that may be mistaken as an apology for or celebration of the world of liberal capitalism. Whitman's America, however, is a transformed alternative to and criticism of the dominant market society.

Whitman's America, first of all, emerges from sexual depths and intensities in the self, sexual sources conventional society fears and distrusts. The resulting love is more conventionally acceptable, but it is too free-flowing, too prone to erotic outbreaks, too disruptive of linear order to be trusted in the official world. Whitman's America also emerges from and is intuitively responsive to communal folkways, to the energy and camaraderie of blackguards and roughs, to the games and festivity of urban and rural workers. Official society, intent on regularized output, was increasingly successful in destroying these manifestations of fraternity and vitality that interfered with the employer's demand for strict schedule. No more four-day weeks, with Saint Friday given over to "drinking, laughing" and Blue Monday to recovery.[7] In Whitman's America, this fraternal festivity has an integral role, contributing to his sense of cohesion and joy and minimizing the threat of isolation. Whitman may thus seem backward-looking, rooted in an earlier period being

7. For insight into this neglected America, see Herbert G. Gutman, *Work, Culture and Society in Industrializing America: Essays in American Working-Class and Social History* (New York: Knopf, 1976).

displaced by the industrial capitalism of the new age. What he has done, however, is to draw on a stratum of American life ordinarily excluded from the province of high culture. He has made of it a resource, an integral part of his vision of a nation alive with play, frolic, and camaraderie. In the home of the capitalistic work ethic, that is not an insignificant achievement.

Whitman similarly draws on, transforms, and intensifies the possibility of free movement and of land equally available to all, not exclusively possessed and exploited for profit by a few. He eliminates the dynamics of the market society and substitutes free movement, productive work, and the animating energies of love running through everyone and everything. He may have underestimated the power of the market society—he and Melville differ basically on this count—but Whitman deserves recognition for opposing to possessive individualism elemental energies and values whose loss is tragic. This also applies to his treatment of technology, to his imagining a predominantly rural and wilderness America in which machines and science, when they do appear, are celebrated. Unlike Melville, Whitman's vision of America is of what might and should be, not of the dangers lurking in what was emerging. He may have underestimated the damage we can do with a technology linked to capitalism and overestimated the virtue in our proximity to the endless bounty of the land. But his alternative vision of a technology subordinated to human values and to human and natural energies is not dated. The ecology of open land, farms, cities, and technology mutually animating each other has a value intensified, not exhausted by the closing of the frontier and the growth of cities.

Whitman's alternative vision, however, overlaps with that of official apologists, who have offered as descriptive what Whitman presents as an imaginatively vitalized ideal for us to move toward. The resource of unsettled territory alive with wildlife in close proximity to rural and urban areas is another transformation of then-existing possibilities, a purified, stylized version that deliberately omits sectional and political conflicts and emphasizes the freely available, animating energy of forests, prairies, and dry country. Whitman drew on and put to his own uses widely shared, affirmative feelings about American nature.[8] This

8. See, e.g., Henry Nash Smith, *Virgin Land: The American West as Symbol and Myth* (Cambridge: Harvard University Press, 1950); Perry Miller, "Nature and the National Ego," *Errand into the Wilderness* (Cambridge: Harvard University Press, 1956), pp. 205–16; and Leo Marx, *The Machine in the Garden: Technology and the Pastoral Ideal in America* (New York: Oxford University Press, 1964).

urban poet responded deeply to the appeal of a country filled with wildlife. He did not, of course, anticipate the destruction of the buffalo or the strip-mining of Montana. What he did do, however, was to recall us to a sense of the possibilities of an America developing from native sources relatively untouched by market capitalism and the official religions that justified it. Whitman is in this sense a spokesman for the unofficial America, the nation that exists beyond the confines of the work ethic and the dominant market society. It is an America that has its origins in actuality and its fulfillment in the imagination. Unless we want to cede total power to what prevails, that imaginative achievement has a quickening value that still has significance.

For Whitman, the inspired bard was opposed to the divisiveness of the market society. He was, moreover, to draw together the free-flowing variety of a country that was still too diverse, still too lacking in a shared history and in shared traditions to be a nation. The bard would constitute the nation by giving it the shared myths it lacked, by bringing into focus the common, unifying elements, as in section 33, and, in his songs and person, he would constitute that unity, those cohesive ties America needed to fulfill itself. As America moved from the scattered village societies of Whitman's youth into the disruptions of the Civil War and the post–Civil War growth of mass markets, cities, and the transportation, financial, and communication systems to serve them, after a period of groping, the country achieved a measure of unity based on impersonal bureaucracies and professionalism.[9] In place of the inspired bard, we have the mass media as a source of unifying myths and values. On the whole, one might prefer the bard.

For Whitman, the bard or the class of literati were special. Not everyone was a poet specially gifted so as to give expression to common tendencies. Even the bard's own unique idiosyncrasies were reminders that everyone had his own uniqueness as well as the divine energy he shared with all of existence. The unifying "I" of section 33 is thus in part the poet, in part Whitman as a representative of the divinity of the self. As god, the "I" represents the fullness of Whitman's confidence in the natural energies he buoyantly celebrates. He feels these powers so intensely that he must express them as ultimate. He thus repeatedly imagines the "I" as cosmic god, creative, energized, and energizing. This god ranges the "orchard of spheres" and throws "fire-balls like the rest." Like the demigods of the American tall tale, he is larger than life and a guarantee of never-ending life:

9. Robert Wiebe, *The Search for Order, 1877–1920* (New York: Hill and Wang, 1967).

I am an acme of things accomplished, and I an encloser of things to be.
. . . .
Immense have been the preparations for me,
Faithful and friendly the arms that have helped me.
. . . .
My embryo has never been torpid—nothing could overlay it.

For it the nebula cohered to an orb,
The long slow strata piled to rest it on,
Vast vegetables gave it sustenance,
Monstrous sauroids transported it in their mouths, and deposited it with
     care.

All forces have been steadily employed to complete and delight me,
Now I stand on this spot with my Soul.

                                                             (section 44)

Here is man at the center of his universe, confidently emerging from
an evolving world whose energies he shares with all of existence and
which he embodies so as to make himself divine. Like the triumphant
demigods of American creation myths, Whitman's portrayal of a confident god in a universe in which "all has been gentle with me—I keep no
account with lamentation" (section 44) constitutes a dramatized figure
and setting that serve to make a difficult life bearable and to embody an
ideal. One may dissent on other grounds and prefer a tragic view or one
in closer touch with inevitable pain, but it does not discredit Whitman's
vision that his own life was hardly free of lamentation.[10] For all the
imaginative vitality of this conception, for all the exuberant affront to
commonsense decorum and joyous celebration of natural, human
capacity, it is nonetheless necessary to recall that human beings are
human beings and not gods. Gods perform miracles. Perhaps it was
asking too much of the human "I," even the comprehensive "I" Whitman conceived, to ask it to unify America, to hold together the diversity
of the new land.

An argument I have recurred to is that, for all his strengths, Whitman
lacked a sense of society, of that relation between self and society that
might have offered an alternative less vulnerable than his to the pressures of personal tragedy and the dynamics of possessive individualism.

10. On the insanity and misfortune in Whitman's family experience, see Richard Chase,
Walt Whitman Reconsidered (New York: William Sloane, 1955), p. 23.

The narrowing of Whitman's horizons under the pressure of personal tragedy emerges compellingly in the *Calamus* poems. His chastened view of America in *Democratic Vistas* is partly a response to the unfettered capitalism of the Gilded Age. In response to the relatively open, unformed America of his early years, in "Song of Myself," Whitman imagined a free-flowing alternative to the conventional market society. It is not surprising, given the America he emerged from, that he does not complement his sense of the flowing relation between self, nature, and God with an equally valid sense of the individual coming into the fullness of his individuality in the context of community. If Whitman had taken this step, perhaps he would have had to rely less on the tall tale, mythic self. The alternative I have been suggesting is not a formula for a painless life, but it does give the individual important sources of human support in the face of the inevitable personal disasters and the less inevitable inroads of the market society. It also points to a more reliable source of social cohesion than the mythic "I" as god.

Just as he was a spokesman for the unofficial America, Whitman was a spokesman for the conventionally ignored or despised regions of the self. Thus, immediately next to

Through me many long dumb voices,
Voices of . . .
. . . .
   the rights of them the others are down upon,
Of the trivial, flat, foolish, despised,
Fog in the air, beetles rolling balls of dung

he places

Through me forbidden voices,
Voices of sexes and lusts—voices veiled, and I remove the veil,
Voices indecent, by me clarified and transfigured
                                                    (section 24)

He then goes to the nerve of the Protestant Etiquette. He satirizes its deepest imperatives, not only about good manners, about genteelly pressing the finger across the mouth, but more basically about the training in repression the Etiquette enforces. "I do not press my finger across my mouth," Whitman asserts,

I keep as delicate around the bowels as around the head and heart,
Copulation is no more rank to me than death is.

In one sequence, Whitman violates and transmutes three basic taboos of official culture, its lessons in repression concerning bowels, copulation, and death. In thus sounding "a gong of revolt" against the inner structures of repression, Whitman is touching an area unusually resistant to change and one usually ignored by those who "plot and conspire" (section 23) against the structures of political repression. The inner structures are even harder to affect than the political ones they support.

"Divine am I inside and out," Whitman continues,

And I make holy whatever I touch or am touched from,
The scent of these armpits, aroma finer than prayer,
This head more than churches, bibles, and all the creeds.

This is an extreme revolt against the central ideological structure of nineteenth-century American orthodoxy, against the system of organized religion, churches, and creeds. America, of course, did not have a monolithic church, but the network of mainly Protestant churches was nonetheless crucial. The diluted forms of belief and nominal church membership in our period can obscure for us the extent to which in Whitman's time allegiance to some form of church and creed was obligatory for those who wished to be respectable. The demand for some form of conventional allegiance was intensified by the erosion of the earlier faith and enforced by those devices of ostracism that Tocqueville and more recently Anthony F. C. Wallace have examined.[11] Emerson had paid a price for affirming the divinity of the self, but he had never brought matters to life in Whitman's radically physical way. It is bad enough to celebrate the divine self, but it is real heresy to dramatize body odor as superior to prayer, to say that "touch" makes "holy," and to assert "divine am I inside and out," leaving no doubt that the bowels are "inside" and the masculine sexual parts "outside." We should not underestimate how exuberantly, offensively radical Whitman is in his free celebration as divine of those central physical, sexual pleasures orthodox society systematically repressed as "dirty" and "evil."

In the same sequence, Whitman continues to give voice to and to remove the veil from the self-satisfied sexuality, the free-flowing erotic pleasure especially threatening to official, work-ethic America. With varying degrees of intensity, the official imperatives were to be self-

11. Wallace, *Rockdale: The Growth of an American Village in the Early Industrial Revolution* (New York: Knopf, 1978), pp. 243–349. On the centrality of religion in the nineteenth century, see, e.g., Sydney E. Ahlstrom, *A Religious History of the American People*, 2 vols. (Garden City, N.Y.: Doubleday, 1975), 1:471–697, and Perry Miller, *The Life of the Mind in America from the Revolution to the Civil War* (New York: Harcourt Brace & World, 1965), pp. 3–95.

abnegating, to deny or at least to suspect the body and sexual delight, to separate the body and spirit hierarchically, and to separate the desexualized self from others and the surrounding world. It is easier for us to object to this structuring because of Whitman's pioneering efforts in behalf of alternative patterns and values. He was the first American to explore and begin to cultivate territory that has since become more familiar, though hardly commonplace. Whitman was of course not the first to deal with sexuality but the first American to affirm the sexualized body as a central value and erotic pleasure as a positive force and to explore this realm in convincing detail.

In opposition to the Protestant Etiquette, Whitman thus makes his own sexualized body the subject of worship. It is sinful enough to affirm the self as divine, but Whitman worships his own body and then goes beyond unenlivened generalities to the sort of details that tell. They deserve similarly detailed attention. Whitman launches into a rhapsody whose intensifying loss of conscious control is itself an embodiment of a style alternative and threatening to the rational, ordered restraints of official society. His imagery similarly does away with the boundaries between the body and the natural world, even as he presents as lovely the sexualized body conventionally ignored or seen as repulsive. Whitman moves from the "translucent mould of me" to his "shaded ledges and rests." He celebrates his "firm masculine colter" but also immediately returns to the rich fusion of his own flowing juices and those of animated nature:

> Whatever goes to the tilth of me, it shall be you!
> You my rich blood! Your milky stream, pale strippings of my life.

By now the fusions are increasingly sexualized, "rich blood" and the "milky stream" of semen merging, as the natural stream and body do. And the erotic mergings are not only with nature:

> Breast that presses against other breasts, it shall be you!

The refrain line, "it shall be you," originally completed the clause, "if I worship any particular thing, it shall be some of the spread of my own body." By this point, however, Whitman has lost the logical, grammatical reference and gives us an unmoored, free-flowing, sexualized incantation. Nature is first delicately, then virilely erotic:

> Root of washed sweet-flag! Timorous pond-snipe! Nest of guarded
>   duplicate eggs! it shall be you!
> Mixed tussled hay of head, beard, brawn, it shall be you!
> Trickling sap of maple! Fibre of manly wheat! it shall be you!

The hay of nature and "of head, beard, brawn" merge, just as the "trickling sap" of maple and man do. The phallic "manly wheat" (or is it the beard and pubic hairs?) is both the sexualized grain and the sexualized man.

In the official world, nature was a refuge set apart from the accelerating capitalistic activity and industrial development of the country. As picturesque or sublime, unspoiled nature was instinct with divinity; away from the struggles of industrial capitalism, Americans could commune with God by contemplating the serenity and grandeur of nature or the picturesque and sublime landscapes of the Hudson River and Luminist painters.[12] Whitman is sometimes close to the official mode, although he is always liable to show the bull at his masculine work and the cock treading the hen, hardly what Durand recommends for the aspiring lover of the picturesque. Whitman, moreover, is perfectly capable of transforming nature into a temple for the sort of worship respectable Americans were taught to see at best as in bad taste and at worst as evil. This is a nature where the sweat and dews of lovemaking fuse with those of the brook, where the winds have "soft-tickling genitals" that "rub against me," where the poet celebrates

> Broad, muscular fields! Branches of live oak! Loving lounger in my
> winding paths! it shall be you!

The temple of nature and the muscular body of man become one. The "loving lounger" is both the branches of the live oak and the lover and his branches.

> Hands I have taken—face I have kissed—mortal I have ever touched! it
> shall be you.

Unspoiled nature, the refuge of a safe, inspiring divinity, is thus not only sexualized but also made the setting for a celebration of homosexual love—all that beard, brawn, and manly wheat; all those sweaty brooks and soft-tickling genitals; all those broad, muscular fields.

12. The best primary source on the American picturesque and sublime and the religious attitudes that suffuse this outlook is Asher B. Durand, *Letters on Landscape Painting* (1855). See also Thomas Cole, "Essay on American Scenery" (1835), rpt. in *American Art 1700–1960: Sources and Documents*, ed. John W. McCoubrey (Englewood Cliffs, N.J.: Prentice-Hall, 1965), pp. 98–109; Perry Miller, "Nature and the National Ego," *Errand into the Wilderness*; and especially Barbara Novak, *American Painting in the Nineteenth Century: Realism, Idealism, and the American Experience* (New York: Praeger, 1969), pp. 61–91, and *Nature and Culture: American Landscape and Painting, 1825–1875* (New York: Oxford, 1980).

And if that is not bad (or good) enough, Whitman has the outrageous effrontery to celebrate himself, the bad taste actually to say

> I dote on myself—there is that lot of me, and all so luscious,
> Each moment, and whatever happens, thrills me with joy.

Whitman does not leave it at that. For him, beyond the self, beyond the nature of streams and fields, the cosmic heavens, the very seat of conventional divinity, are libidinized. The rays of the sunrise become "libidinous prongs"; "seas of bright juice suffuse heaven." Whitman thus transforms one of the clichés of nineteenth-century American landscape painting, the sun with its rays illuminated, the phenomenon known as "the sun drawing water," as in Thomas Cole's "The Ox Bow of the Connecticut" (1836). In the conventional iconography, this phenomenon reassures us of the divinity of nature, of the pervasive presence of God, of the landscape suffused with the natural, divine rays of the sun in heaven. Whitman continues to develop a radically contrasting view. Just as earlier, in "Song of Myself," night and day, sea and shore fused in acts of cosmic lovemaking, now it is the earth and sky at the start of day:

> The earth by the sky staid with—the daily close of their junction,
> The heaved challenge from the east that moment over my head,
> The mocking taunt, See then whether you shall be master.

In a sexualized, creative universe, a creator who has cut his ties with conventional supports to rely on himself bases his self-esteem on his own creativity. The threat in the background is loss of energy, of creative power; hence Whitman's touching statement of the dilemma of the romantic creator:

> Dazzling and tremendous, how quick the sun-rise would kill me,
> If I could not now and always send sun-rise out of me.
> (section 25).

In his most intense moments, everything for Whitman is sexualized. Touch is an immediate, physical reality, a way of establishing relations. In Whitman, it is almost always suffused with the possibility of sex, as in "I make holy whatever I touch or am touched from," where the context is of "masculine colters" and "soft-tickling genitals." Touching, with its aura of closeness and intimacy, is not one of the official American values. There is more touching in "Song of Myself" than in the rest of nineteenth-century American literature combined. Whitman, though, does not make it easy for us. At the same time that we admire his celebration of closeness, we also realize that he has an active sense of diversity but not of difference, in that he continually insists on the sameness of the objects he details and is close to. He does not establish relations based on what John Friedmann argues is the indispensable "acceptance of self and other in their radical difference from each other."[13]

Lawrence was bothered by this tendency toward what he saw as a cloying indiscriminateness in Whitman and perhaps by the homosexuality sometimes connected with it, as in the suggestive passage beginning, "Is this then a touch quivering me to a new identity?" The "new identity" is defined by the sexual intensities of

> Flames and ether making a rush for my veins
> Treacherous tip of me reaching and crowding to help them.

Is the "treacherous tip" the hands or penis? The taboos are such that specific references become obscure and the verse gains a wild, surreal power:

> My flesh and blood playing out lightning to strike what is hardly different
>   from myself,
> On all sides prurient provokers stiffening my limbs,
> Straining the udder of my heart for its withheld drip,
> Depriving me of my best, as for a purpose,
> Unbuttoning my clothes, holding me by the bare waist

This seems to be the confused intensity of a probably homosexual seduction in which the lover or lovers, the "prurient provokers," are "hardly different from myself." But it may also be a masturbatory episode in which thoughts of the "prurient provokers" are dominant. In either case, Whitman expresses the guilt, the sense of treachery and betrayal, connected with taboo sexuality.

In this episode, he combines the innocent pastoral imagery of the American landscape tradition with dark feelings connected with a defense against attacks by "the red marauder," the Indian who in the uglier side of American mythology was a demonic "traitor." This public imagery renders a private drama. "The red marauder" is not only the traitorous Indian but also the treacherous sexual passions, so that Whit-

---

13. *The Good Society* (Cambridge: MIT Press, 1979), p. 103.

man expresses the American association between Indians and the depths of the unconscious, but with a turn unique to his own sensibility:

> I am given up by traitors,
> I talk wildly—I have lost my wits—I and nobody else am the greatest traitor,
> I went myself first to the headland—my own hands carried me there.

Masturbatory confession and homosexual seduction merge, so that the absence of a sharp distinction between self and other receives a powerful sexual expression. The "villain touch," at once his own and his lover's, releases "floodgates" that "are too much for me." This poet, who is responsive to the external panorama of America, is also sensitive to the impersonal inner urgencies, the blindness, conflict, pain, and joyful relief of

> Blind, loving, wrestling touch! sheathed, hooded, sharp-toothed touch!
> Did it make you ache so, leaving me?

Whitman thus goes into uncommonly precise detail antithetical to the decorum that will have nothing to do with orgasm and certainly not with orgasm presented as

> Parting, tracked by arriving—perpetual payment of perpetual loan,
> Rich showering rain, and recompense richer afterward.

In a process that is usually ignored or presented as dirty, he captures a beauty and a fertility as natural as the "rich showering rain." He also gives us a landscape rather different from that of the official tradition, one in which

> Sprouts take and accumulate—stand by the curb prolific and vital,
> Landscapes, projected, masculine, full-sized and golden.

This is a dream landscape, perhaps a universally masculine dream, perhaps a more particularly homosexual dream—but in any case it is vital and unsublimated.

Whitman thus endows with his own dissident energy the transcendentalist commonplace, "All truths wait in all things." He has this perception emerge from a context of masturbatory and homoerotic probing. In one of his basic patterns, as in section 5, this highly charged, personal, sexualized sequence yields a more relaxed, generalized stance, the affirmation that

> All truths wait in all things,
> They neither hasten their own delivery, nor resist it,
> They do not need the obstetric forceps of the surgeon

Indeed not. Universal fecundity extends even to the non-generative sexuality Whitman has sensitively explored.

In the most radical way, Whitman has made good on his claim to give voice to

> sexes and lusts—voices veiled, and I remove the veil
> Voices indecent, by me clarified and transfigured.

The release of energy allows him to go on to dramatize the poetic possibilities of his vision of universal growth and relation. He moves from masturbatory and homosexual sex to heterosexual sex and to love, sublimated but still sexually energized. The sequence is linguistically vital, too, as Whitman places disparates in surprising juxtaposition to bring alive his belief that "soggy clods shall become lovers and lamps." He thus returns to his sense of delight in the erotically charged love that relates and animates everything in existence, from the lowliest "soggy clods" to the "lovers and lamps," both of the latter with their suggestion of illuminating light playing off against and related to the moist, uninflammable earth. Before dramatizing his sense of evolution and himself as demigod and then ranging "afoot with his vision" over the continent, Whitman first continues his intricate play on relations, the "meat" of lovers left behind and sublimated in favor of the recurring symbol of the grass, now, however, reenlivened:

> I believe a leaf of grass is no less than the journey-work of the stars,
> And a pismire is equally perfect, and a grain of sand, and the egg of the
>   wren

The lowly leaf of grass is the equal of the heavenly "journey-work of the stars," but for Whitman the grass is also an earlier form of, is "no less than," the apprentice work of the stars. The linguistic and dramatic possibilities branch out with the same vitality as the love that for Whitman relates and gives life to all existence. It is a vision yielding at best juxtapositions that surprise and delight because they unexpectedly clash with the logical expectations of conventional society and often with the religious morality supporting the official society. Whitman's mergings and fusions, brought to a focus in sections of heightened sexuality, similarly violate the demands for logic and linear order and the emphasis on a strict separation between subject and object characteristic of the dominant commonsense outlook of the market society. His mythic persona who throws fireballs with the rest and whose "palms cover continents" similarly violates the decorum and self-effacement, not to say the required rationality, of the official world. When Whitman fails to tap this dissident energy over the course of an entire poem, he produces the unenlivened catalogs of poems like "A Song for Occupations." To do his best work, Whitman needs to incorporate into his affirmative vision his opposition to dominant tendencies of official society.

In "Song of Myself," he thus speaks for despised sides of the self and the outcasts of society and also for the patriotism of the nation and for its free-flowing possibilities of equality and productive, non-acquisitive abundance. The combination of implied and explicit criticism, daring, and celebration gives Whitman his distinctive edge. When he strays too far from ordinarily despised sexuality, from frenzy and ecstasy or the calm acceptance of his affinity with animals or the criminals and mutineers of society, he loses the inclusiveness and energy of his best work. His sympathetic acceptance of everything can at worst lead to unenlivened lists, but at its frequent best Whitman's sympathy leads him to precise, startling identifications with the suffering outcasts—the hunted slaves, the mutineers, and the sexually thwarted or contemned.

Since in a diagram of his society the ordinary, productive, work-a-day democracy predominates, it is worth stressing that Whitman may celebrate the middle range of the society, but he is not moderate in his social vision. Like his map of America, a diagram of Whitman's society is both like and unlike a conventional outline. His sympathy and the resulting power and precision of his poetry effect an inversion of the conventional hierarchy; the suffering outcasts at the bottom or outside ordinary society come to such vivid life and are so fully endowed with value that they have a higher status in Whitman's American than "the few idly owning." "I am the man—I suffered—I was there": Whitman repeatedly becomes one with the maimed, the rebels, and the rejected. He juxtaposes his patriotic narrative accounts of the execution of the Texas Rangers and the victory of the *Bon Homme Richard* with precise vignettes of their rebellious or mutinous opposites, so that he not only enters into the life and death of heroes but also

Not a mutineer walks hand-cuffed to the jail, but I am hand-cuffed to him
    and walk by his side,

I am less the jolly one there, and more the silent one, with sweat on my
twitching lips.

(section 37)

The exact discrimination in the last line brings the mutineer even more
alive than the heroes who share Whitman's sympathy. In the same vein,
and in one of his great lines, Whitman writes,

Agonies are one of my changes of garments,
I do not ask the wounded person how he feels, I myself become the
wounded person.

The immediacy of this identification makes demands on us, since Whitman asks us to respond with the same humanity. And if we refuse or
find we are incapable of it?

Whitman elsewhere juxtaposes two forms of slavery, the fugitive
slave who escapes and the twenty-ninth bather, the spinster, who does
not. The escaped slave, the sexually repressed woman, the butcher-boy,
and the blacksmith—as in this sequence (sections 11–12), there is the
play of association but no real segregation in Whitman's America. Blacks
appear as victims to be helped sympathetically (section 10); elsewhere
Whitman identifies deeply with "the hell and despair" of a mercilessly
captured slave (section 33). Without actually denying the reality of slavery, Whitman thus stresses the sympathetic identification that in his
world does away with social evil. The Northern Negro emerges as a
splendid, dignified figure, equal to and in his magnificent physical presence superior to the blacksmith he immediately follows. He is a marvelous specimen, associated with powerful horses and "polished and
perfect limbs" (section 13). He is an idealized version of the black man as
sexualized body. In a poem emphasizing physical and spiritual, and not
intellectual, qualities, however, he shares common ground with the
other citizens of Whitman's democracy, composed

Of every hue, rank, caste and religion,
Not merely of the New World, but of Africa, Europe, Asia—a wandering
savage,
A prisoner, fancy-man, rowdy, lawyer, physician, priest.

(section 16)

The sheer sequence and accumulation of details does away with invidious distinctions; the idiomatic vitality of "fancy-man" makes him the
equal of the lawyer, physician, priest. The black driving his dray horses
is also lovingly particularized and equal with the rest. In giving an

egalitarian view of this representative Northern Negro, however, Whitman also ignores the systematic segregation, race hatred, and bias that in fact characterized the situation of Northern blacks.

Another, less flattering image of blacks also surfaces in "Song of Myself." Whitman has "the woolly-pates hoe in the sugar-field" (section 15), and, after a shooting contest, "the darkey brings up the rear and bears the well-riddled target" (p. 41). Although Whitman later cut the line about the darkey, racist structures turn out not to be easy to banish even from an ideal American democracy imagined by one of our most accepting creators.[14]

The same two faces characterize Whitman's Indians. On the one hand, he shows Indians as equals. The trapper marries a red bride—no segregation, no overt bias, although the image of the "dumbly smoking" relatives at the wedding gives us pause. The bride herself, with her "voluptuous limbs," however, comes from a familiar association of dark-skinned people with a sexuality denied to white spinsters. In a less questionable way, "the friendly and flowing savage" (section 39) is a bringer of vitality, a repository of savage energy, and another guarantee of the endless virtue and fecundity of the new world. The darker face of Whitman's Indian, however, appears in the episode of "the red marauder." Here Whitman expresses an opposing sense of traitorous betrayal connected with the unconscious and a tormenting, not a provocative or renewing, sexuality.

At worst, though, Whitman is benign compared with the attitudes and the practices represented by Andrew Jackson against Indians and by much of the nation against blacks. The fact of American racism raises the question of the unofficial America Whitman speaks for. In addition to existing beyond the confines of market-society respectability, isn't that unofficial America also intolerant and repressive, given to lynching abolitionists, exterminating Indians, and suppressing unpopular be-

14. In "Pictures," an early, static poem whose sequences of "pictures" evolved into the free-flowing form of "Song of Myself," Whitman presents a Southern slave-gang, "clumsy, hideous, black, pouting, grinning, sly, besotted, sensual, shameless." Whitman revealingly juxtaposes this picture with a portrait of "sturdy English heros." He dedicates the poem to these explorers lost in the Northern arctic. *Leaves of Grass*, ed. Sculley Bradley and Harold W. Blodgett (New York: Norton Critical Edition, 1973), p. 646. See also Whitman's 1866 letter to his mother describing an election procession in Washington after the Civil War. The procession features "about 3000 darkeys, old & young, men & women . . . the men were all armed with clubs or pistols . . . yelling and gesticulating like madmen—it was quite comical, yet very disgusting and alarming in some respects—They were very insolent, & altogether it was a strange sight—they looked like so many wild brutes let loose." Quoted by Roger Asselineau, *The Evolution of Walt Whitman: The Creation of a Book* (Cambridge: Harvard University Press, 1962), p. 187.

liefs? To some extent, yes, but respectable Americans were at the center
of these movements. Gentlemen anxious about their declining status in
a rapidly changing society were the leaders of the anti-abolitionist
mobs.[15] Even more important, in the nineteenth century, the ideology
and the practices of white American depredations against the Indians
drew energy from the tensions of capitalism in the post-Revolutionary
generation.[16] Racism in general has a career of its own, but not a career
independent of the dominant structures of a society. In America that
means a close connection with the needs and the fears generated by
possessive individualism.

The influence of capitalism was of course extensive. The unofficial
America that Whitman drew inspiration from and intensified and transformed in "Song of Myself" was, however, relatively untouched by the
market society. The unofficial America was not a cauldron of redneck
biases and frustrations. These frustrations and their ugly consequences
existed, but so did the real-life prototypes of the more joyous, productive, non-exploitative world Whitman creates. As it turned out, the mass
media and not the bard prevailed, just as the acquisitiveness, the corporations, the unions, the military, and the other institutions of the emerging capitalism prevailed over Whitman's dream of an America energized
from original sources. Whitman's sexualized and pleasure-loving individual, relaxed, intense, divine, assured of his identity and in touch
with others and with his own depths and heights, stands as a reminder
of lost possibilities and as an alternative as suggestive in his strengths
and limitations as the country of Whitman's imagination.

Near the end of "Song of Myself," Whitman warns, "Whoever walks a
furlong without sympathy walks to his own funeral dressed in his
shroud." He goes on to add, "And I or you, pocketless of a dime, may
purchase the pick of the earth" (section 48). The cohesive power of
sympathy may not have been a sufficient condition, but it is certainly a
necessary condition for dealing with the dominant realities of that market society in which "purchase" is a primary value and "a dime" is
hardly enough.

15. Leonard L. Richards, "Gentlemen of Property and Standing": Anti-Abolition Mobs in
Jacksonian America (New York: Oxford, 1970).

16. Michael Rogin, Fathers and Children: Andrew Jackson and American Indian Policy (New
York: Knopf, 1977).

twelve

A HAZARD OF NEW FORTUNES
The Crosscurrents of Cultural Hegemony

By the end of the nineteenth century, Whitman's America had been transformed beyond recognition. In his response to the driving force that shaped the new America, the individualism disturbing Howells in *A Hazard of New Fortunes* (1890) is that of "our competitive civilization." Howells explicates his title when he characterizes the civilization as "a state of warfare and a game of chance, in which each man fights and bets against odds."[1] The spectacle of a "decently dressed man" groveling for food in the gutters of New York "made me sick, sick at heart," Howells wrote in a letter he ended up not sending to the *New York Sun.* "The conditions in which he came to such a strait seemed to me Christless, after eighteen hundred years of Christ."[2] Howells further characterized the conditions and the state of mind that produced *A Hazard of New Fortunes* when he wrote to Henry James,

After fifty years of optimistic content with "civilization" and its ability to come out right in the end, I now abhor it, and feel that it is coming out all wrong in the end, unless it bases itself anew on a real equality. Meanwhile, I wear a fur-lined overcoat, and live in all the luxury my money can buy.[3]

Most of us can sympathize with Howells's predicament. As a middle-man of culture, Howells sensitively registers the impact of a dominant-class hegemony he both opposes and accommodates. He is in a position to write a powerful novel, depending on how intensely he dramatizes his self-irony and social disillusion.

Outside his fiction, Howells's opposition emerges in his response to

1. William Dean Howells, *Selected Letters*, ed. Robert C. Leitz, III, Richard H. Ballinger, and Christoph K. Lohmann (Boston: Twayne, 1980), vol. 3, 29 (30 May 1888).
2. *Selected Letters*, vol. 3, 238 (23 November 1888).
3. *Selected Letters*, vol. 3, 231 (10 October 1888).

the trial and execution of the Haymarket anarchists. He defended them publicly and privately. Haymarket dramatized the dark side of America—exploitative industrial conditions, the foreign-born workers' intense reaction against these conditions, the even more powerful nativist hatred of foreigners, and the use or abuse of authority against those who spoke and threatened to act to change conditions. Along with Haymarket, Tolstoy's *What Is To Be Done?* had a deep impact on Howells. He never shared the militancy of the Haymarket anarchists, but Howells was strongly attracted by Tolstoy's religious commitment to Christian love as a transforming power. In *What Is To Be Done?*, Tolstoy argues that we need to change our lives and to live simply among the urban poor. Tolstoy vividly characterizes their degraded condition in the tenements of Moscow, narrates the futility of high-minded charity, and advocates a personal change as the only genuinely Christian response. Howells wrote, "Tolstoi tells us simply to live as Christ bade us, socially and politically, severally and collectively. There's no more of it, but Heaven knows that's enough, and hard enough."[4]

In *A Hazard of New Fortunes*, Howells attempts not his usual novel of manners but a novel of ideas in which a representative range of characters respond to the challenge of the new world of social conflict and inequality that Haymarket and Tolstoy had forced on his consciousness.[5] Instead of his usual limited cast of middle-class characters, a clearly defined structural focus, and an authoritative voice and point of view, Howells opens himself to the corrosive energies of an unrestrained capitalism. The form of the novel opens up, and Howells allows representative voices and points of view to clash. The momentum of this enterprise should be to disintegrate the authoritative voice and point of view that speaks for traditional certainties. But as a minister of culture, Howells also feels his responsibility is to affirm the religious and moral truths the new world of poverty, immigration, and big money was eroding. Howells cannot bring himself to dramatize or to acknowledge that incompatibility between Christianity and the new capitalism his material repeatedly forces on his attention. He also finds it difficult to move beyond abstractions to bring alive novelistically the conditions that challenge his conscience.[6]

---

4. *Selected Letters*, vol. 3, 230 (28 September 1888).

5. On the social and personal circumstances that inform *Hazard*, see Everett Carter, "Introduction," *A Hazard of New Fortunes*, ed. David J. Nordloh, Don L. Cook, et al. (Bloomington: Indiana University Press, 1976), pp. xi–xxii. My references to *Hazard* are to this edition and will be abbreviated H and cited by page number in the text.

6. On the issue of abstraction, see George N. Bennett, *The Realism of William Dean Howells* (Nashville: Vanderbilt University Press, 1973), pp. 35–44.

The Marches are the focus for these conflicts. In the ideological spectrum of the novel, they occupy a middle ground between the extremes of the radical Lindau and the Dryfooses.[7] Howells treats the Marches sympathetically but in the first part of the novel not normatively. They only gradually become, however ironically qualified, the authoritative voice and point of view Howells found he could not dispense with. As they move around New York in search of housing, the Marches are exposed to the panoramic range of the city, particularly to the lower depths their ordinary experience separates them from. They are tourists looking in from the outside and like other middle-class tourists they respond aesthetically to picturesque details of ironwork and noisy children, to the shapes, colors, and patterns of the "burly blue bulk of a policeman" and a zig-zagging drunkard (H, p. 65).[8]

The conditions in the tenements nonetheless challenge all the ideological positions Howells presents in *Hazard*. Through the Marches, Howells intermittently develops the idea that these conditions threaten Christian commitments, that we are responsible to our fellow human beings, and that we are unworthy as long as our fellow human beings live in tenement conditions (H, p. 66). With the Marches, however, his quiet irony at their expense almost never does justice to the gap between their moderate comfort and moderate concern and the incurable disease Howells knows must be cured, even as he has difficulty bringing either the cure or the disease to imaginative life.

At best, his ironic treatment of the Marches lacks intensity, but, because Howells does not consistently maintain his distance from them, even the gentle irony often disappears. A major exception is the exposure of Mrs. March's complacent, middle-class refusal to believe that "there's any *real* suffering--not real *suffering*—among those people; that is, it would be suffering from our point of view, but they've been used to it all their lives, and they don't feel their discomfort so much" (H, p. 69). But Howells is unable to sustain this exposure. Consistent satire would run the risk of making the Marches less sympathetic than Howells wants them to be.

Satire aside, Howells could explore the human urgency of the Marches' response to the new industrial-commercial city. We know Howells himself was sickened by the spectacle of a well-dressed man eating food from the gutter. But in *A Hazard of New Fortunes*, Basil March

7. For a survey of the ideological positions in *Hazard*, see Michael Spindler, *American Literature and Social Change: William Dean Howells to Arthur Miller* (London: Macmillan, 1983), pp. 77–83.

8. On Howells as a tourist, see Alan Trachtenberg, "Experiments in Another Country: Stephen Crane's City Sketches," *Southern Review* 10 (1974): 272–73.

merely says, "I must go after him" (H, p. 70). Somewhat more forcefully, March a little later asks his wife, "What part of Christendom will you live in? Such things are possible everywhere in our conditions." Mrs. March redeems herself from her earlier insensitivity when she replies, "Then we must change the conditions" (H, p. 71). Mr. March then decides to go to the theater instead, and Mrs. March decides to return to Boston. Although Howells reveals the Marches' inability to follow through on their principles, he also conceals the full force of the original episode, which poses the threat of a Christless world. What is at stake is a direct contradiction between Christianity and capitalism, a contradiction that threatens the basis of Christian belief. Howells does not allow the Marches to raise the issue. As a result, here and elsewhere Howells does not actively pursue one of the most promising strategies open to him, the exploration of the moral responses of his representatives of the principled middle class. Howells is well situated to probe their position from the inside. Unwilling consistently and intensely to satirize them, Howells also fails to open up fully this other option available to him. As a minister of culture, the price he pays for his moderation and for his sensitivity to his audience and the side of himself responsive to that audience is that he inhibits his expression of his most challenging convictions about the damaging results of the individualistic, competitive system he knew was "a state of warfare and a game of chance." In particular, for him the structure of religious belief was too insecure to withstand even that degree of questioning he registers in his correspondence.

Religion aside, at widely separated intervals, so that they have no cumulative effect, Howells does allow March to voice eloquently his sense that

we go on, pushing and pulling, climbing and crawling, thrusting aside and trampling underfoot; lying, cheating, stealing; and when we get to the end, covered with blood and dirt and sin and shame, and look back over the way we've come to a palace of our own, or the poorhouse, which is about the only possession we can claim in common with our brother-men, I don't think the retrospect can be pleasing. (H, p. 437)

More characteristically, though, he has March respond to the "reckless picturesqueness of the Bowery" (H, p. 183). Howells's imagination is nonetheless challenged by the forces the new capitalism had unleashed. He permits March one powerful if momentary vision of the Darwinian energies at work in the chaos of New York:

Accident and then exigency seemed the forces at work to this extraordinary effect; the play of energies as free and planless as those that force the forest from the soil to the sky; and then the fierce struggle for survival, with the stronger life persisting over the deformity, the mutilation, the destruction, the decay, of the weaker. The whole at moments seemed to him lawless, Godless; the absence of intelligent, comprehensive purpose in the huge disorder and the violent struggle to subordinate the result to the greater good, penetrated with its dumb appeal the consciousness of a man who had always been too self-enwrapt to perceive the chaos to which the individual selfishness must always lead. (H, p. 184)

This impressive vision of a lawless, Godless universe at first shifts the focus from a deranged society men have created to natural energies beyond anyone's control. The emphasis is not at all on the competitive world as a warfare and a game of chance, although March's observation of the social world is the source of this grim outlook. Howells, though, does not sustain the view of a Godless universe. In his version of Darwin, there is a reassuring if "violent struggle to subordinate the result to the greater good." By the end, March is put in his place as "too self-enwrapt to perceive the chaos to which the individual selfishness must always lead" (H, p. 184). "The individual selfishness" is a euphemism for capitalism. Instead of invoking the powerful system men have collectively created, Howells, in the accepted American fashion, uses a moral vocabulary and places responsibility on the individual. What begins as a bleak Darwinian vision of a Godless universe turns by the end into a comforting, moralistic view that individual selfishness leads to a chaos that is nonetheless tending toward the greater good.

The passage perfectly illustrates Howells's role as a middleman of culture. He is caught up in conflicting currents. He responds to the destructive power of the new capitalistic, urban world and to the subversive Darwinian implications appropriate to that world. But he also needs to find an affirmative meaning and to downplay the very idea of capitalism. Through March and the narrator's comments, Howells shows the moderate American intellectual in the process of cushioning himself and his audience. When he is operating by way of ideas and direct commentary, essayistically as opposed to dramatically, Howells's secularized religion can thus insulate him and his readers from the full impact of contemporary conditions. By making these conditions appear to be part of a scheme tending toward ultimate good, Howells's residual Christianity serves to support the predatory system his religious and moral convictions oppose in other contexts.

To move from religion to politics, consider the crosscurrents in Howells's treatment of Lindau. Lindau gives Howells his best chance to extend his range beyond the limits of his middle-class narrator and the Marches. Through Lindau he can test and bring alive views more extreme than theirs. He can also use Lindau to get inside the lower depths as a native, not as a tourist. Howells endows Lindau with ideas and commitments that should make him sensitive to the feel of things in the strata of society he has deliberately chosen to live in. He fulfills the Tolstoian imperative of living his commitment to the poor. Howells has Lindau recognize that "you must zee it all the dtime--zee it, hear it, smell it, dtaste it—or you forget it" (H, p. 190). What is unfortunately lacking is any sustained sense from Lindau's point of view of what he does see, hear, smell, and taste. *A Hazard of New Fortunes* falls short as a novel of ideas partly because of Howells's failure to bring novelistically alive the conditions the novel's ideas center on.

Lindau's sense of brotherhood, his unpatronizing commitment to the poor, and his acting on his beliefs are partially realized attempts to flesh out these alternatives both to the ruthless individualism of capitalism and to the Marches' well-intentioned but tepid sympathies. As for his ideas, Howells has Lindau express them sometimes in a forceful, conventional English when he is ostensibly speaking German, sometimes in a dialect that partially obscures them. Lindau represents a particularly challenging voice and point of view for a novelist seeking to break free of middle-class confinements and to embark on an open voyage of discovery. But although he wants Lindau's point of view in the novel, Howells is not really committed to rendering Lindau's language or voice. Unlike Chesnutt's respect for dialect and dialect characters, Howells uses dialect to disguise Lindau's ideas and to distance himself from these opinions he himself is attracted to.

For the purposes of disguise and distancing, even more effective than the dialect is the strategy of dramatic irony. Howells has middle-class characters like Mrs. March or the Marches' son, Tom, summarize Lindau's views in conventional English. Their disapproving or baffled responses to Lindau's provocative criticism almost always incline us toward his ideas. Although Lindau's position is secular, he comes wrapped in the mantle of religion. He has a noble head, a flowing white beard, and at the outset he is a model for both saints and Judas in religious paintings. The thieves and beggars he aligns himself with have Christ-like echoes, as does his Tolstoian dedication. At the end his "grand, patriarchal head, foreshortened to their view, lay white upon the pillow, and his broad white beard flowed out over the sheet" (H, p. 443). He has become a figure in a late-nineteenth-century sentimentalized religious painting. In the spectrum of the novel, Lindau is the radical, but Howells contrives it so that Lindau is a domesticated radical, designed to win the assent of the respectable middle class.

For all of that, Lindau is not presented in an entirely favorable light. He is made to drink a little too much, partly to account for the vehemence of his views, partly to put some distance between his ideas and the author's, partly to characterize him as a Bohemian radical. The Judas reference also suggests a minor strain of reservation. It allows some readers to believe (mistakenly, in my judgment) that at the streetcar strike Lindau somehow betrays Conrad, the novel's Christ figure, and is somehow responsible for Conrad's death. The prevailing characterization of Lindau is nonetheless sympathetic.[9]

Like most of the Haymarket anarchists, Lindau is a German. He is an idealized version of the foreign radical who aroused passionate nativist sentiment in the years following Haymarket. To combat this prejudice, Howells associates his radical with the good revolution of 1848, not with the red revolution of 1870. Lindau is also dignified as a veteran who has lost an arm fighting to end slavery in the Civil War. He is old. Unlike the Haymarket protagonists, vigorous men in their prime, by virtue of his age and crippled arm, this venerable man with his noble head and flowing, patriarchal beard is safely removed from the arena of actual combat. His bark is worse than his bite, as he says at one point (H, p. 193). Also unlike the Haymarket anarchists, his politics are those of a literary man, not a revolutionary or a working-class radical.

Howells further makes Lindau an effective social critic for an American middle-class audience by the way he handles, or rather obscures, the class issue. The Haymarket radicals forcefully argued that class conflict between workers and owners was inevitable. Even when his dialect is foreign, however, Lindau speaks for traditional American values. He exposes our falling away from our traditions of the "free and brafe." He takes seriously every man's right to "life, liperty, and de bursuit of habbiness." Like Howells, Lindau accepts and appeals to the residual individualism of small businessmen, artisans, and ordinary land-owning farmers to oppose the dog-eat-dog individualism of the emerging finance capitalism.

What is worth stressing about his exposure of the abuses of "our competitive civilization" is the absence of any real hint of class conflict. Lindau voices hostility to big money, emphasizes the abuses of the monopolies and trusts and combines, and is dedicated to the values of the Declaration of Independence and the Star-Spangled Banner. Work-

9. Edwin H. Cady, *The Realist at War: The Mature Years of William Dean Howells* (Syracuse University Press, 1958), p. 105, dismisses Lindau as a fanatic. Kermit Vanderbilt, *The Achievement of William Dean Howells: A Reinterpretation* (Princeton University Press, 1968), downplays him because of his impaired social outlook (p. 164) and because of his "'romantic' spirit of violence, revolution, and disorder" (p. 177). For an opposing and, I believe, more accurate view, see Spindler, *American Literature and Social Change*, pp. 78–79.

ers, however, appear not as a class but as individual men, as in the phrase "no man that vorks" (H, p. 318). In contrast to Madison's precise awareness of class differences and the danger of class conflict, Lindau in effect recognizes only one class, the un-American because un-republican class of "aristocracy" or "mill-serf owners" or the oligarchy of monopolists. The rest of the nation is classless; they are implicitly lumped together, so that Lindau creates a moral drama of the oligarchy taking advantage of the rest of the nation, depriving individual men of their right to life, liberty, and the pursuit of happiness, and violating the standards of traditional American values.

Because he does not recognize workers as a class, however, Lindau begs the key question of violent conflict between workers and owners. Fulkerson says, "'I don't like that dynamite talk of his'" (H, p. 320), thus aligning Lindau with the main popular symbol of the Haymarket radicals, the dynamite bomb. But "dynamite"—the role of violence—simply does not enter into Lindau's analysis. Instead, Howells shifts attention to the vehemence of Lindau's passions, his indignation, his tone. He expresses himself violently, and, by a kind of transference, he is associated with violence. Howells wants to have it all ways: to use Lindau as a vehicle for telling criticism, to make him acceptable to a middle-class audience and to Howells himself, and also to be somehow connected with violence. His compromise is to avoid the issues of violence and class conflict in Lindau's social criticism and to slip in the violence indirectly through his tone.

Lindau's social criticism is effective as far as it goes, which is to say as far as Howells goes in his letters and as far as his sense of his audience will allow him to go. An alternative, though, would have been to go further, to attempt to give imaginative credibility to a critique like that of August Spies, the leading Haymarket radical. The challenge would be to do justice to a position Howells did not personally believe in. Howells would then have had to test openly his feelings and his ideas about violent class conflict.[10]

As Howells knew from reading Spies's autobiography and speeches, Spies believed that capitalists would not peacefully give up their power, that violence against workers was a pervasive condition of capitalist rule, and that violence would be inevitable in the change to socialism. In the meantime, Spies believed workers should be able to protect them-

10. Howells was familiar with Spies's views from *August Spies' Autobiography: His Speech in Court and General Notes* (Chicago: Nina Van Zandt, 1887), and Dyer D. Lum, *A Concise History of the Great Trial of the Chicago Anarchists in 1886, Condensed from the Official Record* (Chicago: Socialist Publishing Co., 1886).

selves, that they should know how to use arms, and that to protect themselves they should know how to make bombs. In his view, the power of the workers would ultimately prevail but not without armed struggle. In the meantime, they needed to be able to defend themselves. Spies did not think the day of the revolution was at hand, however, and he refused to print a leaflet that urged workers to come armed to the Haymarket protest meeting. Although he took account of it, Spies's emphasis was not on violent revolution, but on the injustices of the wage system and the misery and inequality he used the theory of surplus value to expose.

Through Lindau, Howells flirts with Spies's intellectual ambience, the ambience of radical criticism and the threat of violence. The culmination is Lindau's appearance at the streetcar strike. He is not one of the leaders but is an onlooker, "a tall old man with a long white beard. He was calling out at the policeman. 'Ah yes! Glup the strikers—gif it to them! Why don't you co and glup the bresidents that insoalt your lawss, and gick your Boart of Arpidration out-of-toors? Glup the strikers—they cot no friendts! They cot no money to pribe you, to dreat you!'" (H, p. 421– 22). Howells arranges it so that Lindau is not inciting anyone to violence and is not seriously interfering with the police. The Haymarket meeting had been called to protest police brutality against the strikers at the McCormick works. In contrast to this meaningful protest, Howells contrives it so that Lindau makes a private, individual gesture that has no public impact. In a novel structured around social ideas and representative social positions, his final speech is devoid of intellectual content. It succeeds in keeping Lindau-as-radical acceptable to middle-class readers, but at the expense of intellectual and rhetorical vitality.

Howells has consistently avoided probing the issues of violence and class conflict. At what should be a climax of the novel, he has nothing to build on, nothing to give his radical figure intellectual edge and the significance that comes from engaging with real concerns. Howells in effect vindicates the innocence of the Haymarket anarchists by showing that Lindau is a harmless victim. Howells, though, avoids the more challenging matter of the legal innocence of the anarchists and their actual views on violence. He offers Lindau as a radical insider, someone who has committed himself to the dispossessed. But it turns out that Lindau is simply another onlooker, another tourist from the world of the middle class.

As a spectator, Lindau has no more involvement in the strike than March has. Howells does not use Lindau to take us inside the world of the workers, to help us feel what it is like to be out of work, under pressure, and fighting for survival. Nor does Howells involve Lindau in any way in the world of the radical strike organizers or defenders. A move in this direction would have allowed Howells as a novelist of ideas to test and to dramatize the complex issues the strike symbolizes. Instead, Howells gives Lindau a white beard and has him lose his other arm to show that he is a harmless victim and is morally protected by the aura of religion. Because he does not even give Lindau a vocabulary that recognizes workers, moreover, Lindau cannot deal with the strike as a conflict between workers and owners. No wonder his response has almost no intellectual content. Lindau is an emissary from a middle class responsive to the symbols of religiosity and uneasy about the realities of workers as a class forcefully opposed to owners. Significantly, the brotherhood Lindau asserts is not with workers but with "the beccars and the thiefes," a brotherhood presided over by the chirping urchins he feeds like so many happy birds (H, p. 190).

These children and the religious allusions and aura are part of the iconography of the sentimental fiction Howells opposed but could not avoid as he tried to legitimize his radical. In order to register even the moderate criticism he uses Lindau to develop, Howells apparently felt he had to protect himself and his character. For a middle-class audience in Haymarket America it was finally more acceptable to offer the "foreshortened" perspective of a religious painting than to offer the full probing of the radical ideas that the structure of his novel calls for. In the process of criticizing the oligarchy and monopolists and the buyers of legislatures and opinion-makers—the emerging dominant class of the 1880s and 1890s—Howells thus serves their interests. He shares and reinforces a sentimentalized religion that offers false solace and ineffectual opposition to their exercise of power.

Howells similarly falsifies the radical position by domesticating it. To make them acceptable, he brings "radical" ideas within the limits of middle-class categories and a middle-class vision. He narrows the arena of acceptable controversy, screens out a meaningful probing of violence and class, and has Lindau ignore the felt reality of immigrant and working-class life. He substitutes pity for imaginative understanding. As a result, he diminishes the quality of his fiction. He cuts himself off from the challenge of imagining threatening alternatives that could also give energy to the novel and completion to the intellectual structure he perfunctorily fills out.

Viewed in one way, this failure as a novelist of ideas is an index of the pressures Howells responded to. He was a conscientious middle-class man of letters as uneasy about class and violence as his audience. More particularly, the trial of the Chicago anarchists and the outpouring of vituperation against them had systematically distorted the views of anarchists and socialists. What confronted Howells was the dominant opinion that foreign agitators had planned an immediate armed revolution, that they were committed to the aggressive use of the dynamite bomb, and that they were a foreign menace to everything the American flag symbolized: lawful society, the rights of the people, freedom itself. Anti-anarchist sentiment served different needs for different classes of Americans. The fear of anarchy and the hatred of foreign agitators was especially urgent among middle-class citizens caught up in the displacements of a rapidly changing urban, industrial world. In their hatred of the foreign anarchist they were able to find an acceptable outlet for deep frustrations, including the tensions resulting from the conflict between systematic, repeated economic depressions, with their attendant failures and unemployment, and the prevailing belief in individual responsibility for success and failure.[11]

For corporate owners, the identification of anarchists and unions functioned effectively to discredit and to break the power of organized labor. Immediately after Haymarket, in Nast's full-page cover in *Harper's Weekly*, an evil-looking "agitator" with a whip rides on the back of an honest workman. "Too Heavy a Load for the Trades-Unions," the caption reads. "The Competent Worker Must Support the Incompetent."[12] "Obey Orders or You Die," the banner in an earlier cartoon reads. The foreign "agitator" promoting strikes is the tyrant, not the honest owners or working men. To this set of images Haymarket added the anarchist bomb, a threat to America's free institutions. The complexities of class conflict were transformed by wrapping them in the flag. In the official view, what was at stake was American freedom, the existence of lawful society itself. "In the commission of such crimes it is those who instill the idea in more ignorant minds, those who justify the deed, who point out the criminal means, and who inflame murderous passions to the utmost, who are morally guilty."[13] The Haymarket anarchists are the immediate object of this judgment, but, as Howells read the editorial in *Harper's Weekly*, he might be pardoned for taking it personally. He had been corresponding with the editor, George Curtis, on behalf of the anarchists.[14]

---

11. For this analysis of the middle-class response to Haymarket, see Richard Sennett, "Middle-Class Families and Urban Violence: The Experience of a Chicago Community in the Nineteenth Century," in *Nineteenth-Century Cities: Essays in the New Urban History*, eds. Stephen Thernstrom and Richard Sennett (New Haven: Yale University Press, 1969). See also John Higham, *Strangers in the Land: Patterns of American Nativism 1860–1925* (New York: Atheneum, 1973), pp. 54–56.

12. *Harper's Weekly*, 15 May 1886.

13. "The Anarchists at Chicago," *Harper's Weekly*, 1 October 1887, p. 702.

14. Clara and Rudolf Kirk, "Howells, Curtis, and the 'Haymarket Affair,'" *American Literature* 40 (1969): 494–96, and *Selected Letters*, vol. 3, 194, notes 1–2.

In any case, when Howells came to deal with the radical position in *A Hazard of New Fortunes*, he takes the official view into account. The process is subtle. In place of the anarchist as foreign demon, Howells gives us old Lindau, his ideas clothed in the America flag and his characterization clothed in American religion. Howells then simply avoids dealing with the issues of class and violence and revolutionary change at the heart of the radical position. In the face of the anti-foreign, anti-anarchist sentiment, Howells apparently felt that to keep his credibility with his middle-class audience he could not deal accurately with the radical position. Even the distancing devices of foreign dialect and dramatic irony were not sufficient protection. In his treatment of Lindau, Howells makes sure he will not be seen as a morally guilty influencer of ignorant minds.

The official response to the anarchists is an example of the workings of dominant-class hegemony. This response satisfied the needs of corporate owners and provided outlets for middle-class people vulnerable to the emerging new world of power. By focusing on the anarchists rather than on the real causes of their problems, middle-class people reinforced the structures and practices that were main sources of their discontent. In his editorials on Haymarket, the editor of *Harper's Weekly* was an instrument of dominant-class hegemony. Howells did not accept the prevailing view of the Chicago anarchists. He courageously spoke out publicly in their defense, on the grounds that they were unjustly convicted of murder when in fact they were being punished for their ideas. In his novel, Howells had the freedom to examine matters with the intellectual and imaginative fullness a fiction makes possible. Howells, however, was freer in his own voice than in his fiction. As he shows in his treatment of Lindau's ideas, Howells as novelist was susceptible to the prevailing hegemony, in this case more than he was in his own person. This pattern is revealing both of Howells's conception of himself as a novelist and of the subtleties of the hegemonic process.[15]

Ideas aside, not a minor matter in a novel of social positions, Howells was poorly equipped as a novelist to further his readers' understanding by bringing alive the taste and feel of immigrant and working-class life. This imaginative failure unintentionally serves the interests of the emerging dominant class. Like the conceptual avoidance of class, it keeps a major reality of American life unexamined and reassuringly under control. Like harmless old Lindau whose bark is worse than his

15. For other views of Howells and Haymarket, see Cady, *The Realist at War*, pp. 67–80; Kirk, "Howells, Curtis, and the 'Haymarket Affair,'" pp. 487–98; and Kenneth S. Lynn, *William Dean Howells: An American Life* (New York: Harcourt, 1971), pp. 288–92.

bite, for Howells the underside of the city is there to be pitied. It is better to pity than to hate and to fear (Howells did some of the latter), but it is even better to understand intellectually and imaginatively. Even Mrs. March momentarily thinks "we must change the conditions" (H, p. 71). To do so would involve changing power and class and money relations. These changes would threaten the evolving ruling groups in Howells's America. By substituting pity for an active probing of these issues, Howells contributes to the dominance of those who profited in position, power, and income from the very arrangements he deplored.

Through the religious figures Conrad and Mrs. Dryfoos, on the one hand, and the finance capitalist, old Dryfoos, on the other, the members of the Dryfoos family are at the opposite extremes from Lindau in the ideological spectrum of the novel. Howells uses the history and the structure of the Dryfoos family to write a perceptive allegory on his view of the moral decline of America as it moved from its agrarian origins into the capitalistic world of big cities and big money after the Civil War. On the farm near Moffitt, Indiana, before the war, the Dryfooses had a productive life close to the land, to each other, and to their community. Their farm life embodies Howells's version of the republican agrarian myth. He outlines an agrarian, pre-capitalistic Eden before the fall into post–Civil War finance capitalism. On the farm Dryfoos works the land directly and prospers. Although his holdings are substantial, he does not own more than he can handle with his own labor. His prosperity is the reward for his hard work. His material rewards are ample but not excessive; they are of a scale with the rest of his life. The farm is the center of his prosperous life, a life that is harmonious and integrated. His family flourishes. Mrs. Dryfoos is healthy. She comes from a Dunker family, for Howells an embodiment of the purity of primitive Christianity. Dryfoos himself "was awfully old-fashioned in his ideas. He hung onto the doctrines as well as the dollars of the dads" (H, p. 87). Beyond his own farm and family, Dryfoos is an intelligent, well-informed citizen. When oil is discovered, he resists selling the land and takes the lead in trying to persuade others to hold onto their farms.

In Howells's version of the republican agrarian myth, the tempting, sinful apple is a large income unearned by a person's direct labor on the land or its equivalent. Howells does not expose contradictions in the myth by having Dryfoos take the first bite of the capitalistic apple. He does not point up the acquisitiveness latent in Dryfoos's position, the difficulty a person has in both "making money on [the farm], just like he was in business somewhere" (H, p. 86) and at the same time remaining untouched by the capitalistic motives to grow and to increase profits. Instead, Howells takes the easy way out and shifts responsibility to the girls of the younger generation. In this domesticated version, the feminine and social, not the economic motive, becomes the moving force behind the immense changes of nineteenth-century America. The girls have been away at school, have picked up new ideas, and they force Dryfoos to sell for a large profit. The account is unconvincing partly because the father, whose word is the law of Sinai to his wife, suddenly turns from a patriarch to a democrat, is outvoted and agrees to change his stand on the basic principle of his life. Howells needs to account for the decision and is unwilling or unable to look carefully at the contradictions within one of the myths that sustains his inner life.

He is more successful in outlining the later stages of Dryfoos's career. Dryfoos first moves to Moffitt to live on the interest from his money. Displaced from his home and his productive life on the land, he is "'homesick and heartsick for the old place,'" although most people believe it is because he is sorry he hadn't asked more for the farm (H, p. 88). His cure for the sickness that afflicts the rest of his life is to turn the eighty acres he has kept into a real estate development. Displaced from his own home, he makes big money building houses for other displaced people. He is successful at it, continues to speculate and to invest, and cannot stop making money. As Howells presents it, the American dream of material success is turning into the American nightmare. Dryfoos further displaces himself, moves to New York, and becomes an even richer stock gambler. His career is an allegory on the America that has cut its ties with the land, has engaged in an unholy exploitation of its natural resources, and has made big money from speculation instead of productive labor. In one of the most powerful passages in the novel, "'We *can't* go back!' shouted the old man, fiercely. 'There's no farm any more to go back to. The fields is full of gas wells and oil wells and hell holes generally; the house is tore down, and the barn's goin'—'" (H, p. 234).

What they have instead of the old cohesive, productive life is money, "more of it now than I ever had," old Dryfoos says (H, p. 234). But in Howells's version, the displaced new rich do not know what to do with the money. Separated from useful labor on the land, in this view the source of genuine value, and also separated from the religious and secular faith of the fathers, they are trapped and disoriented. "I feel like I was tied hand and foot," Dryfoos says. He continues,

I don't know which way to move; I don't know what's best to do about anything. The money don't seem to buy anything but more and more care and trouble. We got a big house that we ain't at home in; and we got a lot of hired girls round under our feet that hinder and don't help. Our children don't mind us, and we got no friends or neighbors. But it had to be. I couldn't help but sell the farm, and we can't go back to it, for it ain't there. (H, p. 234)

This is an impressive, touching version of the consequences of eating the apple of finance capitalism, of moving from the farm to the city, from prosperity to wealth, from home to homelessness. In this version, the decisive, acquisitive American individualist is portrayed as inwardly confused and empty. He does not make money because he enjoys it or because of the power it gives him or because he is responding to the demands for growth and profits intrinsic to capitalism. Instead he makes money to fill a void in the self, a void created when he left his pre-capitalistic way of life on the farm. The freedom money is supposed to buy yields instead multiple forms of entrapment. As in a penitentiary, the new rich are isolated from those around them and cut off from the sustaining inner values that gave meaning to their earlier lives. The portrait works partly because it touches on the facts of isolation, the lost power of old values, and the changes people felt and feel in their relations with their children.

The portrait also works because it satisfies a widely shared middle-class need to believe that the rich are unhappy. In particular, it speaks to the middle-class envy and fear of big money. Money in moderation is desirable, but large fortunes are an attraction and a threat to middle-class self-esteem. Elsewhere in the novel, Howells has the genteel Marches put the Dryfooses in their place. They are made to look down on the Dryfooses from the vantage point of their genteel taste and genteel morality. Along with Dryfoos's self-characterization, this patronizing dismissal must have been comforting to middle-class readers caught up in changes they found it hard to understand and subject to the power of wealthy men and forces beyond their control. No wonder *A Hazard of New Fortunes* became Howells's most successful novel. He has found a perfect combination: a celebration of the republican agrarian myth, a criticism of the fall into finance capitalism, and not only a confirmation of the middle-class view that the new rich are unhappy, empty, and vulgar but also the affirmation that somehow the Marches' genteel values triumph over Dryfoos. They even end up owning the magazine.

As part of his allegory and as part of his continuing response to the situation of displaced women, Howells presents Mrs. Dryfoos as a near-invalid confined to the house, unable to make contact with the outside world, and almost totally ineffectual. She represents a later stage of the sickness Howells had earlier examined in Mrs. Lapham. Mrs. Dryfoos's primitive Christianity is out of place in the capitalistic, urban world her husband's stock speculation has brought them to. Howells is honest enough to show her as sick and ineffectual. Cut off from her agrarian roots and the cohesive life of the farm, she is disoriented and unable to give moral-spiritual guidance to her children or husband.

The divisions between Dryfoos and his wife, and even more between Dryfoos and his son, are a grim commentary on the situation of religion in the new world of post–Civil War capitalism. The gentle, Christ-like Conrad has inherited his mother's religious tendencies. He is pure and decent, but he has a weak chin and is no match for his father. Old Dryfoos has power, energy, will, and money. His son, in contrast, embodies the faith of the fathers Dryfoos has fallen away from, a faith that appropriately enough is identified with the mother. Dryfoos demands allegiance from his son, demands that his son go into business and not the ministry, because Dryfoos needs to be reassured that his own choices are right. He is implacably fierce in his demands because he is trying to put down his own underlying doubts and to have his son confirm his choices and his new identity. Because his son is a living embodiment of the best that Dryfoos has rejected, Conrad's very presence is an indictment of the old man, who has a strong motive for forcing Conrad into business and away from his true vocation. Dryfoos overpowers his son, who on the surface meekly, dutifully submits. In the empirical world of affairs, money, and power, old Dryfoos prevails. Inseparable from the question of identity, what is at issue is a conflict between Christian values and the new world of finance capitalism—of stock speculation, of large fortunes earned not through honest labor on the land but through interest and the ownership of abstract certificates of control. For Howells, this is a world of morally undirected will and energy antithetical to the Christian values of mercy and love that he approves of but that he feels are being overwhelmed.

Howells does an imaginatively successful job with old Dryfoos. In his version of the American tragedy of success, Dryfoos wins the world but loses his soul and inner self. The conflict with Conrad has enough psychological power to animate and to reinforce the moral and social allegory. But Howells has a problem with Dryfoos. In putting down Dryfoos and all he stands for, Basil March says, "Having and shining are held up . . . by civilization as the chief good of life" (H, p. 437). The treatment of Dryfoos is partly aimed at exposing the tragic hollowness of this outlook. But to the extent it in fact prevails in America, what then of the moral and spiritual values Howells is committed to affirming?

To help us understand Howells's dilemma, we need to examine the split in his theory of realism. For Howells, realism in one sense is truth to what ordinary people do and say, how they look and act in everyday situations. Howells thus opposes sensationalism and contrivances of plot and is committed to fidelity to surfaces and to what is ordinary, not prettied up. For him, the novelist should be true to the notions, the impulses, the principles that shape the lives of actual men and women.[16] In his own practice this means respectable middle- and upper-middle-class men and women. This side of Howells's theory of realism calls for an empirical test: how well does a novel plausibly render the observed facts of ordinary experience?

Howells also has a metaphysical dimension to his theory of realism. "The finest effect of the 'beautiful' will be ethical and not aesthetic merely." The reason is that for this successor of Emerson "morality penetrates all things, it is the soul of all things" (CF, p. 83). Without being heavy-handed about it, moreover, "no conscientious man can now set about painting an image of life without perpetual question of the verity of his work, and without feeling bound to distinguish so clearly that no reader of his might be misled, between what is right and what is wrong, what is noble and what is base, what is health and what is perdition, in the actions and characters he portrays" (CF, pp. 98–99). The truth in this case is to moral standards metaphysically grounded in the nature of things. But what if "the notions, the impulses, the principles that shape the lives of actual men and women" are those of an acquisitive capitalism? Logically the novelist can expose the way these actual lives fall short of the absolute morality Howells assumes, but practically Howells also assumes that by and large these actual American lives confirm and embody metaphysically based virtue. Howells's criticism and novels indicate that at the very least writers should respond to those dimensions of American life that support a metaphysical optimism, as in the success of failure at the end of *The Rise of Silas Lapham*. By the time of *A Hazard of New Fortunes*, it had become more difficult than in *Lapham* for Howells to ignore the destructive power of acquisitive individualism as a widely shared American value and practice. Although he continued to talk about right and wrong as if everyone knew and agreed about what these words meant, their basis in everyday American life was being eroded and their metaphysical foundations were also being undermined by the new science and by the scale and ferocity of American capitalism. Howells nonetheless wanted to affirm his moral-metaphysical commit-

16. *Criticism and Fiction* (New York: Harper, 1891), p. 99. Subsequent references will be abbreviated CF and cited by page number in the text.

ments in spite of the gap between them and the observed realities of American economic and social life.[17]

Old Dryfoos thus dominates his religious son, but Conrad, although he acquiesces, sustains his real life in the Episcopalian social gospel missions he devotes himself to. Conrad has a degree of inner strength that plays off against his weak chin and mild eyes. But it is the persistence of the last gasp. Howells is too honest to portray Conrad as vital and articulate. In this version of the contest between religion and acquisitive finance capitalism, the best Howells can do is sketch a well-intentioned, gentle, somewhat dreamy character whose death is intended to affirm the value of self-sacrifice. After Conrad's death, his father loses interest in life. In one sense Howells is making the distinction between right and wrong as clear as his kind of realist should. He contrives it so that in a modified way right triumphs, in that the father suffers for the wrong he has done in thwarting the deepest, noblest impulses of his son. Beyond this personal drama, however, is the national drama of the capitalist retreating from life once the embodiment of religion dies. This implication is unearned; it is a kind of pious wish.

Conrad's shortcomings as an imaginatively realized character reflect Howells's unacknowledged doubts. Howells is simply not able to flesh out a religious figure who can in depth and in detail convincingly engage with and triumph over old Dryfoos. Conrad thus plays his part as a passive sufferer, a passive Christ figure wounded on the temple by his enraged father. "Father," he says "with a kind of grieving wonder" as he reenacts this sentimentalized version of the Crucifixion. He does not say "Forgive them, for they know not what they do," since the father in this case is "they." "Conrad's mild, grieving, wondering eyes, and the blood slowly trickling from the wound in his temple" (H, p. 418) precisely define Howells's view of the state of contemporary religion in conflict with the forces of capitalistic acquisition. Conrad is associated with the sentiments and the values of a Christianity that lacks real power but that for Howells still has the ability to make the capitalistic backslider feel guilty. Conrad himself unprotestingly "grieves" and bleeds.

In the last act of his career as a passive, sacrificial Christ figure, at the scene of the streetcar strike, Conrad finds himself standing next to Lindau. Without any effort on his part, Conrad is shot through the heart. He has not acted to save Lindau but by accident receives the bullet presumably aimed at the old man. The bullet pierces his heart, the seat

17. My view of the strains in Howells's theory of realism is indebted to Henry Nash Smith, *Democracy and the Novel: Popular Resistance to Classic American Writers* (New York: Oxford, 1978), pp. 81–86.

of feeling. It does not go near his brain. In a pattern epitomized by Little Eva in *Uncle Tom's Cabin*, Conrad's main function is to die to make us feel the wrong and the pathos of such a loss. As with Little Eva, we are then to rededicate ourselves somehow to his values of mercy and self-sacrifice, values antithetical to those prevailing in the masculine world of capitalistic power.

As a male, if not a masculine, successor of Little Eva, Conrad is diffusely, asexually in love with Miss Vance, a patrician who shares his social gospel interests. Conrad is not enough of this world to recognize the nature of his feelings. His feelings are appropriately sublimated and untainted with the dross of sexuality. Howells's own uneasiness about sexuality makes him accurately portray Conrad as lacking the power of ordinary sexuality, a lack that parallels and underlies the absence of energy in Conrad's religious position. Inspired by the sentiment he feels for Miss Vance, Conrad drifts in a dreamlike state to the scene of the streetcar strike. Under Miss Vance's urging, he has a vague intention of using his influence to make the men see the futility of attacking scabs. Like Howells, Conrad sympathizes with the strikers, but he, too, dislikes violence and wants the men to go home. Unlike Dreiser, Conrad and his creator do not realize that "peaceful methods meant . . . that the companies would soon run all their cars, and those who had complained would be forgotten. There was nothing so helpful to the companies as peaceful methods."[18] The inspirational effect of Conrad's death is spoiled if we see Conrad as an unwitting company man who gives the sanction of his Christ-like, sacrificial death to the cause of a peace in the interests of the owners. The crosscurrents of overt and covert meaning reveal some of the complexities of Howells's involvement in the process of cultural hegemony. His Christian values both oppose and support dominant-class rule.

Within the novel there is a certain revealing, fuzzy inconsistency concerning the nature of Conrad's sacrificial death. The implied narrator is clear that Conrad is doing nothing more than simply standing next to Lindau (H, pp. 421-22).[19] Fulkerson and Dryfoos, however, assume that

18. *Sister Carrie*, ed. John C. Berkey, Alice M. Winters, James L. W. West, III, and Nida M. Westlake (New York: Penguin, 1981), p. 421.

19. A common view is that Conrad acts to save Lindau, who as Judas is held to be culpable because of his unacceptable views. See, for example, Cady, *The Realist at War*, p. 105, and Vanderbilt, *The Achievement of William Dean Howells*, p. 164. Even Spindler, who does not share the derogation of Lindau's views, believes that "as [Conrad] moves to the old man's rescue he is shot through the heart" (*American Literature and Social Change*, p. 82). But Conrad is not planning to move. He is merely going to speak, "to say to the policeman, 'Don't strike him! He's an old soldier! You see he has no hand!'" (H, p. 422). But he is shot before he can speak.

Conrad died to save Lindau, that he sacrificed his life to protect the old man (H, pp. 442, 449). They make up a story, an interpretation. It reveals their deep-seated need to see Conrad's death as the result of a useful, sacrificial act, a death that is meaningful and not accidental. They impose the idea of a sacrificial act on an event that in reality does not confirm the interpretation. Howells could easily have described Conrad's last moments so that his actual behavior would support the interpretation characters place on it. The fact that Howells has not done so indicates a certain division in his own outlook.

What is at stake emerges in the Marches' version. They also take for granted that Conrad sacrificed himself, but in their version the sacrifice is generalized. "In an exaltation" Mrs. March says, "He suffered for the sins of others" (H, p. 451). Mr. March generalizes this exalted position even further.

It was his business to suffer there for the sins of others. Isabel, we can't throw aside that old doctrine of the Atonement yet. The life of Christ, it wasn't only in healing the sick and going about to do good; it was suffering for the sins of others! That's as great a mystery as the mystery of death. Why should there be such a principle in the world? But it's been felt, and more or less dumbly, blindly recognized ever since Calvary. If we love mankind, pity them, we even *wish* to suffer for them. (H, p. 452)

March begs the question of whether Conrad acted to save Lindau; it is enough for March that this Christ-like figure was present somehow "to suffer there for the sins of others." Fulkerson and Dryfoos at least have Conrad attempting to do something useful. For March, "the old doctrine of the Atonement" has degenerated to a *wish* to suffer for the sins of others, to self-sacrifice separated from any results. March speaks eloquently for high values Howells endorses. March's eloquent words, however, have a shaky basis in the empirical reality of Conrad's actual death. They are words imposed from the outside. It is a symptomatically dangerous situation for one of the central mysteries of Christianity to be portrayed as so far removed from the realities that should give the doctrine the breath of human life. The two strains in Howells's theory of realism are again in conflict. Playing off against the Marches' exalted words is a quiet suggestion that the words do not fit the facts of experience, which is to say that as a novelist Howells cannot bring the doctrine to imaginative life, cannot imagine a situation to make the value of self-sacrifice humanly credible.

Although the passage is not one of those that view the Marches ironically, moreover, the words come from the same couple who have shown their inability to act on their beliefs. The "we" who "even *wish* to suffer" out of love for mankind does not include the Marches. Probably without intending to, Howells has March set up a division of spiritual labor. It is "the business" of a few like Conrad "to suffer for the sins of others," just as it is "the business" of genteel intellectuals like March to pronounce exalted words that have no basis in their own life and actions and in this case no basis in Conrad's. The genteel intellectual watches the performance and praises and blames from his superior, absolute vantage point. His words are to reassure us that finally all is well, that meaning exists, that the old doctrines still hold. Early in the novel, Howells treated March with a self-irony more promising than when he speaks for a genteel religion unintentionally slanted in the interests of the owners.

March's genteel politics have a similar effect. Lindau died in a bad cause, March agrees, because "he died in the cause of disorder; he was trying to obstruct the law" (H, p. 451). If so, it was a very minor obstruction. Howells has March convert both Conrad and Lindau into symbols of representative positions. In both cases March misses or distorts the empirical reality of the strike scene. His generalizations are necessary to a novel aimed at expressing and finally allaying its author's doubts and at winning, as it did, the favor of a large middle-class audience. But March's generalizations are oddly unrooted in the narrative facts. At key moments March's way of seeing is dehumanizing. As his mind works on experience, he generalizes, but he does so at the expense of the actual human beings and the human reality of what he is generalizing from. The tendency is fatal for a novelist. It is part of the price Howells pays for glossing over his own doubts about the adequacy of tepid religious and political ideas to meet the threat of the new world Haymarket had exposed to him.

March illuminates the role and the situation of the genteel writer-intellectual caught in the crosscurrents of the hegemonic process. His sense of fair play and his religious-moral feelings are offended by the cruel excesses of the capitalistic system that throws people arbitrarily on the streets after a lifetime of work (H, p. 437). But his religious affirmations—his views about suffering and self-sacrifice, for example—support this system. So do his political ideas. He offers honest voting as the answer when his son asks, "'What's the use of our ever fighting about anything in America? I always thought we could vote anything we wanted'" (H, p. 451). Howells may or may not be ironic at March's expense. In any case, the novel exposes the gap between the immensity of the problems and the feebleness of the proposed solution. Faith in the electoral process and in Christianity are cornerstones of the republican belief system March and his creator finally affirm, although, intentionally or not, both the character and his creator reveal deep cracks in the structure.

These acknowledged and unacknowledged strains affect the structure of *A Hazard of New Fortunes*. In a positive sense, they prompt Howells to move beyond his usual limited cast of middle-class characters to organize the novel around a range of representative positions designed to bring alive the social-economic panorama of "our competitive civilization." But the strains also inhibit Howells. Unregulated capitalism is at the center of the misery, chaos, and heartlessness the novel responds to. As an absentee landowner and finance capitalist, Dryfoos could be the structural focus. Howells, however, is unwilling or unable to show in any detail how the system actually works in Dryfoos's world of finance capitalism or to establish Dryfoos's personal responsibility for the conditions that disturb Howells's conscience. To look too closely at Dryfoos's world, to structure the novel around Dryfoos, as he had earlier around Lapham, would not only take Howells beyond his area of specialized knowledge but also require a negative exposure his positive beliefs cannot sustain.

Even within the structure he creates, at the crucial dinner party, Howells displaces matters back in time and geography, away from contemporary New York to a discussion of an earlier period in Indiana when Dryfoos broke a strike. Instead of making any real connections with the new urban, capitalistic world, Howells has Lindau call Dryfoos a traitor for his strike-breaking (H, p. 342), hardly a contribution to our understanding of the relation between finance capitalism, the absentee ownership of mines, and the misery and injustices "of our competitive civilization." The dinner party is one of the climaxes of the novel. Lindau's outburst precipitates March's central moral dilemma. The avoidance of real analysis that would connect Dryfoos with contemporary conditions reduces the scope and weakens the novel. This structural weakness is another index of Howells's mixed response to the emerging dominant class. Howells is opposed to the forces Dryfoos embodies. At the same time, Howells inhibits his imagination in response to the internalized pressures of this class and the genteel middle class it is in part allied with, in part at odds with.

Howells is especially circumspect in dealing with that part of the competitive world he knows personally and professionally. March and Fulkerson's magazine is one of the organizing centers in the novel. This cooperative experiment is initially an alternative to the prevailing cut-throat individualism. The situation is alive with opportunities for exposure and conflict. In *A Provincial Celebrity in Paris*, Balzac had savaged the tawdry, power-hungry, profit-oriented journalism of his period. In Bartley Hubbard in *A Modern Instance*, Howells had earlier started to examine the decline in journalistic standards and morality he associates with a vulgar pandering to the lowest common denominator. In *A Hazard of New Fortunes*, though, Howells pulls all of his punches. By putting the saintlike Conrad in charge of the operating finances, Howells makes it impossible to examine conflicts between a desire for profits and quality or profits and religious principles. At least Howells does not develop Conrad's situation on the magazine to suggest that such conflicts are possible. Fulkerson could be the focus for dramatizing these conflicts. For all his aura of knowing exactly how men operate in the world of trading and promotion, however, Fulkerson is never allowed to push hard for a commercial success threatening to quality. He becomes an excuse for an endless, virtuoso display of Western hyperbole unrooted in the realities of that competitive civilization Howells deplores.

March and Fulkerson maintain their moral integrity, and, without any irony at their expense, they gradually turn the original cooperative idea into a businesslike device for keeping down wages (H, p. 493). At the center of March's dilemma, instead of revealing the actual, day-to-day pressures experienced by well-intentioned, divided people involved in the world of American journalism, Howells contrives an elaborate set of displacements. He makes sure March disapproves of the radical views of old Lindau, he makes sure Lindau is not advancing his ideas in the magazine, and then he contrives a showdown in which March, to save his integrity, refuses to fire Lindau at Dryfoos's command. The focus is on pride and hurt feelings and residual personal loyalties, not on the way power and money operate at the upper levels of the publishing industry. The episode throws almost no light on "our competitive civilization [as] a state of warfare and a game of chance, in which each man fights and bets against fearful odds." Since the publishing industry is what Howells knows as an insider, his lack of interest in examining it in any detail deprives him of a major source of power in dramatizing his views.

Howells's handling of the publishing industry does nothing to jeopardize his relations with his "generous" publishers, whose "confidence" rendered his "smiling destiny . . . safe and certain" (H, p. 507), as he emphasized in the original "Autobiographical" preface to *Hazard*. In his review of *Crime and Punishment*, Howells had contrasted the widespread American freedom, equality, and prosperity with European conditions. "Whatever their deserts," he had written, "very few American novelists have been led out to be shot, or finally exiled to the rigors of a winter at

Duluth."[20] Not to mention the inner exile American writers like Melville and Poe had experienced, Howells reminds us that American writers have had to face the subtle and not-so-subtle pressures of their involvement in the American marketplace. These pressures, which are less dramatic than the firing squad or the threat of exile, nonetheless affect the writer's freedom, and not the writer's alone. Howells had an understandable interest in the fur-lined overcoat and in "a smiling destiny rendered safe and certain by the confidence of [a] generous house." These concerns are inseparable from his involvement in the processes of cultural hegemony.

To appreciate the crosscurrents of Howells's involvement in the processes of cultural hegemony, we must recall his courageous defense of the Haymarket anarchists and his treatment of the issues relating to Haymarket in *Hazard*. Not only through Lindau but also and even more immediately through March and the magazine, Howells draws on the feeling that he was vilified, as indeed he was, for his unpopular defense of the anarchists.[21] Through March's conflict, Howells gives a toned-down version of his belief that the free expression of opinions was threatened in Haymarket America and that as a journalist even he was vulnerable. But March's threatened dismissal does not turn on his views or his defense of Lindau's right to express his opinions, so that Howells has been quite indirect in dramatizing his personal stand. He has played it safer in the novel than he did in real life. In this instance, again instead of being liberated by the possibilities of fiction, Howells has been more cautious than he was in his own voice. In this respect, Basil March is less interesting than William Dean Howells, and this phase of *A Hazard of New Fortunes* has less impact than Howells's letters. In the two years between Haymarket and *Hazard*, Howells apparently had a chance to reflect on the criticism he had given and received because of Haymarket. As with Lindau, in his treatment of March and the magazine, Howells has placed himself under constraints that reveal the subtle consequences of his moderation, his fair-minded unwillingness to be doctrinaire, and his unwillingness to challenge forcefully the economic and ideological powers he prudently takes into account even as he elsewhere criticizes them.

These crosscurrents characterize the treatment not only of March but also of Beaton, who together allow Howells to examine the situation of the literary and artistic intellectual in the new urban, capitalistic world. As an intellectual, Beaton, who "'probably hasn't a moral fiber in his

20. "Editor's Study," *Harper's Monthly*, September 1886.
21. *Selected Letters*, vol. 3, 145–46, 193–215 passim.

composition'" (H, p. 149), complements March, who has moral concerns but has trouble acting on them. March also tends to view things aesthetically, a tendency contemporary conditions challenge. Through his critical treatment of Beaton and his use of March sometimes as a spokesman, sometimes as an object of self-satire, Howells develops a view of what the intellectual should be, the dangers he confronts, and his mixed allegiances as both a critic and a supporter of the emerging dominant class.

Unlike the morally committed artist Howells calls for in his criticism, Beaton talks exclusively of shapes and colors. He is self-centered and dissatisfied with his way of life. His restless unfulfillment confirms Howells's diagnosis about a life and art, the life self-centered, "selfish and mean, weak-willed, narrow-minded, and hard-hearted; and aimless" (H, p. 476), the art technically skillful, and both the life and the art separated from the moral and human sources that for Howells should animate life and art. Through Beaton, Howells exorcises the temptation posed by the younger generation of artists who had youth and novelty on their side and who could simply give themselves over to their talent regardless of the truths Howells was committed to. Although he contrasts with him, as an intellectual, Beaton is related to March, but, as a self-centered, self-interested character, he is also related to Dryfoos. As artist and stock gambler, the two are worlds apart, but both are morally unmoored and pay the price of inner emptiness and rootlessness.

Christine Dryfoos is Beaton's main temptation. He can solve his financial problems by marrying her. Her passion and her beauty attract him, but he is not in love. He toys with her, sets off her willful defiance of her father, and finally does the right thing by not proposing. Christine, who is not Christ-like, has all the passionate vitality her brother lacks. As Howells typically does with sexually passionate women characters, he presents her as narrow-minded and bad-tempered. Although Howells is too inhibited to develop her fully, as a character, Christine has great potential. Her barely repressed, smoldering sexuality presses against the limits of social convention. Beautiful, willful, passionate, and ignorant, she has inherited her father's energy and is the shadow self of her devout brother. This separation of traits between the religious brother and the sexually vital sister is itself significant and reveals Howells's intuitive understanding of a fragmentation he has difficulty handling consciously. The devastation of the sexually charged woman, her inability to find outlets for her energy, and Howells's own unwillingness to give her an intellect are all illuminating of the situation confronting sexually powerful women subject to the pressures of genteel society.

Miss Vance is Christine's genteel alternative. Together she and Alma embody the respectable possibilities Howells values in young women. He declares for his version of realism as against sentimental fiction by having both women decide against marriage. A society girl increasingly attracted to social gospel activities, Miss Vance finally acts on her beliefs. She rejects Beaton, the prospect of marriage, and her comfortable society life, and becomes an upper-class nun who devotes herself to "the poor and dying" (H, p. 452). The narrator shows his approval by having her inspire Conrad's death and preside over Lindau's last moments. "Beside his bed Margaret Vance was kneeling; her veil was thrown back, and her face was lifted; she held clasped between her hands the hand of the dying man; she moved her lips inaudibly" (H, p. 443). In the exalted posture dear to sentimental religious art, her presence ennobles Lindau's passing, heals the conflicts centering on him, and somehow promises that all will be well. The Marches associate her as well as Conrad with the "love," the "pity" of "the way of Christ" (H, p. 452), although March notes that for the world to continue women must serve in the homes as well as in the hospitals. In theory Margaret Vance is a positive model, but in the practice of Howells's art she has all the energy, inner resources, and imaginative power of an admirable stick figure. Both she and Conrad illustrate Howells's difficulty in bringing his positive values to imaginative life.

They also show the extent to which religious values had become associated with uplifting final moments of redemptive death. It is an understandable association for people unable to affect matters in the world of social and economic power. Through both Conrad and Miss Vance, Howells offers pity and "the way of Christ" as his contribution to "the poor and dying." In this phase of his art, Howells uses genteel religion to undermine strikes and meaningful workers' activities. He moreover has his characters consistently refuse to use "workers" or class as categories, preferring instead words like "the unfortunate" or "the poor and dying."

In *A Hazard of New Fortunes*, pity is the prevailing social emotion. Unlike sympathy, which is a cohesive feeling implying the ties of compassion and equality, a feeling with someone, pity allows Howells's characters to look down condescendingly from a vantage point of superiority. " 'I pity them,' " Conrad says of the strikers; " 'my whole heart is with those poor men' " (H, p. 448). Conrad is above, the "poor men" are below. Like all the main characters, Conrad also pities his father—"poor father"—and in an orgy of pity in his reverie he has Miss Vance pity his father too (H, p. 421). The Marches in their turn patronize "poor Conrad" by pitying him as they repeatedly do old Dryfoos and the poor. They elevate pity to the pinnacle of religious values and use it to put down forces like those Dryfoos represents, to patronize the new power of finance capitalism. This exercise allows them to assert their superiority and to affirm the values of the heart in the face of the impersonally heartless, urban, capitalistic world. Like Conrad and Miss Vance, the Marches also turn their pity on workers and "the unfortunate," a maneuver that reinforces the capitalistic powers the Marches oppose.

As the central social and religious value, pity has functions but also certain weaknesses. Howells's reliance on pity and his unsatiric way of presenting it help define the predicament of many genteel middle-class people. They did not want to endorse the heartless powers of finance capitalism, but they were too deeply involved to reject these powers. Their inherited religion had lost touch with its agrarian roots and with emotional and intellectual depths and energies. This situation is epitomized by the emphasis on pity and death, the lack of vitality in Conrad and Miss Vance, and the genteel absence of intensity and commitment of the Marches. In *A Hazard of New Fortunes*, pity is the cohesive alternative to the unrestrained individualism of the new urban market society. We may deplore the limitations of this response, the tepid characters who result, and the unintentional support it gives to the heartless, impersonal forces Howells criticizes. But to appreciate fully what it means for compassion to have reached the low ebb it has in *A Hazard of New Fortunes*, we must wait until Chapter 14, when we will examine Dreiser's *The Financier*, a world with pity of any sort left out.

thirteen

THE HOUSE OF MIRTH
The Political Psychology of Capitalism

In *The House of Mirth* (1905), Edith Wharton shows that the values and the practices of capitalism have as deep an impact on people in the upper-class society of Fifth Avenue as they do in Howells's middle-class or Dreiser's stock-exchange versions of the market society. Wharton shows that Fifth Avenue and Wall Street are connected by ties of money and that, however concealed, money is the basic fact in the refined upper reaches of American society. In the market society, money is the ultimate commodity. The self, divided and sold as labor, is also a commodity. All of us are familiar with the results as they affect ordinary working people and entrepreneurs. In *The House of Mirth*, however, Wharton takes us into what for most of us is unfamiliar territory. She exposes the loneliness and alienation inseparable from possessive individualism at the most elevated, as at the most ordinary, levels of the American class system. Lily Bart's divided self is an especially revealing example of the power of the market society to divide people internally and to separate them from a community.

As an American individualist, Lily Bart has a career, a business, as clearly marked out for her as for any rising businessman. Her business is to find and marry a suitably rich and socially acceptable husband. As an entrepreneur, Lily's main resources are her beauty and exquisite social skills. They are the commodities her mother has trained her to exploit, to alienate, "to hand over to others for a price," in the ruthless career of acquisition Lily is expected to pursue.[1] At the pinnacle of New York society, the rough edges of crude competitiveness have presumably been smoothed by traditions of good breeding and established money. Lily has perfected the requisite arts of acquisition, she is the flower of her society, as her name indicates, but she does not have money of her

1. C. B. Macpherson, *The Political Theory of Possessive Individualism: Hobbes to Locke* (New York: Oxford University Press, 1962), p. 48.

268

own.[2] In the marriage market, she is thus the market society self reduced to its bare essentials: she is a capitalist exploiting her own alienated self in exchange for goods sanctioned by the official custodians of society. In another sense, she is a valuable object to be acquired by others, although like other consumption objects her value fluctuates. Lily both accepts and rejects her status as a beautiful commodity. At key moments she reacts against what she has been trained to do and to be. She has a long history of failure, of not catching her man. As an acquisitive entrepreneur in the marriage market, Lily has divided aims. These divisions weaken her resolve, gradually drain her energy, and finally cause her death.[3]

For critics of capitalism, the prostitute has always been a symbol of the free-market laborer or entrepreneur. The prostitute, the proprietor of her own person, alienates herself as a commodity and enjoys (or fails to enjoy) the fruits of her labor. In the most intense scene in *The House of Mirth*, Lily is forced to realize that Gus Trenor has used his money and not hers, that she is $9,000 in debt to him, and that he wants to be paid in sexual coin. Lily has a serious breakdown. She feels that she is polluted, that she is a prostitute, "for I've taken what they take and not paid as they pay."[4] In seeing herself as a prostitute, Lily, a highly specialized product of the possessive market society, reacts against her involvement in the buying and selling of her alienated self as a commodity. But Lily has also interiorized the alienated habits of mind of the society she reacts against. Her basic tendency is to compartmentalize and to divide, to separate herself from others, to feel isolated, and to feel divided internally. In a sense that goes deeper than we think when we first encounter the idea, Lily is a victim of her society.[5]

2. Elizabeth Ammons examines the biblical sources of Lily's name and Wharton's ironic use of it as applied to a woman of Lily's social class in *Edith Wharton's Argument with America* (Athens: University of Georgia Press, 1980), pp. 29–30. See also Cynthia Griffin Wolff on the floral motif in art nouveau, *A Feast of Words: The Triumph of Edith Wharton* (New York: Oxford University Press, 1977), esp. pp. 114–15 and 118.

3. Ammons, *Edith Wharton's Argument*, has a useful account of the contemporary literature on the economics of marriage and on Lily as a "totem of patriarchal power" (pp. 28–30). But she consistently oversimplifies Lily's motives because she overlooks Lily's severely divided self and contradictory aims. See, for example, pp. 30, 35.

4. Edith Wharton, *The House of Mirth* (New York: Signet Books, 1964), p. 175. Subsequent references will be abbreviated HOM and cited by page number in the text.

5. In "Edith Wharton: *The House of Mirth*," in *The American Novel from James Fenimore Cooper to William Faulkner*, ed. Wallace Stegner (New York: Basic Books, 1965), pp. 120, 131–32, Richard Poirier observes, "The members of [Lily's] society must calculate and invest their emotions with the coldness of financial speculators." He also concludes that Wharton "is a novelist of manners in a peculiarly American way: she cannot imagine a society in which her values are brought into play at the center of dramatic conflict. Instead of being

In a possessive market society, everyone wants money. Lily wants money and all it stands for even as she feels contaminated by it and what she has to do to get it. Lily finds it impossible to live without great wealth, but at moments she also loathes herself for what she desires. In seeing herself as above the contaminating world of money and sex, Lily exquisitely reflects the alienating tendencies of the market society she looks down on. To maintain her self-respect, in part of her consciousness, Lily compartmentalizes the world of wealth as pure, harmonious, and refined. Jewels symbolize that world for her. "More completely than any other expression of wealth, they symbolized the life she longed to lead, the life of fastidious aloofness and refinement in which every detail should have the finish of a jewel, and the whole form a harmonious setting to her own jewel-like rareness" (HM, p. 95). But in practice this "life of fastidious aloofness and refinement" depends on Lily's marriage and calls on her to sell herself as a commodity. Far from being fastidious, aloof, or refined, marriage for money and for social position would tie Lily to men like Percy Gryce, phlegmatic, narrowly self-centered, and conventional, or to the dyspeptic George Dorset, whose finicky appetite is the obverse of Gus Trenor's gross appetite, or to Sim Rosedale, who inspires in Lily feelings of fear and disgust that reveal more about her own self-doubts and self-divisions than they do about Rosedale.

In another part of her consciousness, Lily thus experiences the world of money, of paying and being paid, of acquiring and being acquired, as a pollution, as a disgusting form of prostitution. A combination of her own circumstances and temperament prevents Lily from integrating these polar views into a livable resolution. Lily, moreover, almost never connects the hard, jewel-like brilliance of the life she desires with either the obscure humanity it is based on or the complex actualities of the money that supports it: money as investment, as exploitation, as "dirty," as power, as appetite, as a symbol of achievement. Similarly, she never connects the delicate, vulnerable perfection of herself as a precious "hot-house flower" (HOM, p. 159) with either the rest of humanity or with the money that makes the flower possible. The result is a polarized outlook that falsifies by separating the ideal from its roots in the complexities of money and ordinary humanity and that compounds the distortion by making the ideal excessively pure and ordinary humanity

---

an aggregate of human relationships, subject to modification in the best interests of its members, society for her becomes an expression of impersonal power, even when it is being manipulated by some of its victims." I am concerned with the connection between a coldly calculating market society and the "impersonal power" Poirier correctly analyzes, a power that not only separates people from each other but also divides them internally.

excessively simple, dark, and dirty (see, for example, HOM, p. 159). Money in its negative connotation shares in this imagery of darkness and dirt, as when Lily feels "alone in a place of darkness and pollution" after she realizes she has taken Trenor's money.

A powerful shock, Wharton knows, can "sometimes decentralize a life. Lily's nature was incapable of such renewal" (HOM, p. 159). Her meeting with Trenor is the dramatized shock that could cause Lily to renew her life, that could decentralize her so as to bring together the divided elements in her self and in her view of life. Instead, Lily responds in a way that illuminates some of the dangers that confront people highly sensitive to the demands of the possessive market society.

When Trenor makes direct sexual advances and lets Lily know that he wants what he paid for, she has what amounts to a severe nervous collapse. The symptoms are characteristic and revealing and call for explanation. Not surprisingly, Lily's breakdown takes the form of an acute sense of self-division. She "seemed a stranger to herself, or rather there were two selves in her, the one she had always known and a new abhorrent being to which it found itself chained" (HOM, p. 156). This disturbing separation between the old and the new selves is in a sense misleading, however, since Lily had often experienced the old self as divided, too. In the scene with Selden at Bellomont, which parallels and counterpoints with the scene with Trenor, "there were in her at the moment two beings, one drawing deep breaths of freedom and exhilaration, the other gasping for air in a little black prison-house of fears" (HOM, p. 69). The "little black" tomb or "prison-house of fears" is the world of conventional expectation, the practical world of exchange and the marriage market. In this world Lily must constantly be on her guard and must take advantage of all the opportunities offered, particularly the chance to catch Percy Gryce. Instead, Lily allows herself to be momentarily free. "Gradually the captive's gasps grew fainter, or the other paid less heed to them; the horizon expanded, the air grew stronger, and the free spirit quivered for flight" (HOM, p. 69). Lily's ongoing debate about her "real self," the "real" Lily, centers on the contrast between the free, open air on the heights and the imagery of the tomb and prison, of the "captive self" imprisoned in the closed rooms of convention, of the possessive market society at its most stifling. The scene with Selden at Bellomont is outside in the full light of day; the one with Trenor is in a closed room at night. Lily's inability to free herself from the confines of conventional expectations about money, luxury, and freedom culminates in her death at night in one of the small rooms that symbolize the impoverished future she dreads. At the end, Lily in effect kills herself because she is afraid that, to escape this dreary way of life, she will sell out and destroy what she sees as her better self, the "real self" Selden has made her aware of. Death is the only resolution she can conceive, since her "real self" and her "captive self" cannot coexist.

The impasse between her "real" and her "captive" selves is rooted in Lily's severely alienated experience of reality. "This real self of hers which [Selden] had the faculty of drawing out of the depths" (HOM, p. 100) has no contact with either Lily's sexuality or the world of money. Cut off from these two sources of vitality, unable to act independently either from her sexual instincts or from her own economic resources, no wonder this "real self" cannot live. As a man, Selden can move amphibiously from the world of money to the rarified heights of his elitist "republic of the spirit," just as he can have and then break off his affair with Bertha Dorset. But as a woman, Lily experiences a much more polarized situation. She accepts Selden's view that "the real Lily Bart" has no contact at all with "the trivialities of her little world" but instead participates in "that eternal harmony of which her beauty was a part" (HOM, p. 142). Her "beauty" has no sexual dimensions for Selden. When Ned Van Alstyne, a connoisseur, remarks appreciatively about Lily's sexuality, Selden sets up an absolute contrast between the contemptible "world she lived in" and the ideal "real" world her beauty invokes for him. Like his "republic of the spirit," Selden's view of beauty is part of the genteel tradition's reaction against the crude vitality of ordinary American life. In separating his genteel ideal of beauty and the spirit from ordinary material life, Selden reflects the alienating processes of the capitalistic system he snobbishly looks down on and profits from.

At her triumph as Reynolds's "Mrs. Lloyd" in the *tableau vivant* scene, Lily's beauty is explicitly that of a priceless work of art. In part of her consciousness, Lily, like Selden, sees herself not only as a jewel but also as a rare work of art in a pure, timeless realm far removed from the tainting pressures of money and sex. In a possessive market society, however, art is a commodity. As "Mrs. Lloyd," at the climax of Lily's career, all of the collectors in the novel resolve to acquire her.[6]

Throughout Lily's drama of self-respect and self-disgust, the issue of money is crucial. Through Lily, Wharton poses the question of what a person can do with wealth and still feel worthwhile. Philanthropy is exposed as superficial. Lily, for all her intelligence and social sensitivity,

---

6. See Wolff's treatment of the role of art, especially of mural, portrait, and art nouveau in *The House of Mirth* (*A Feast of Words*, pp. 111–15, 126–32). Wolff sees that Lily is an object, an art object. My account places this insight in the context of the underlying dynamics of the market society. Lily is not only an object but also a commodity.

is also deliberately cast as a character without serious artistic or intellectual concerns. Her idea of poetry and literary culture is to carry with her to a country house weekend a copy of the *Rubaiyat*. Beyond the art of decorating her person, Lily is uninterested in visual art. Because her upper-class world as a whole is similarly barren of vital intellectual and aesthetic concerns, Lily is both a representative and a victim of that world. She is sensitive enough to experience that world as a prison and an airless tomb, but her imagination is unable to conceive alternatives. As an upper-class woman, she is the product of a training she is unable to transcend. Integral to her energy-draining conflicts and alienation is the force of her training and her susceptibility to conventional values. Lily, in many ways the flower of her class and sex, "could not figure herself as anywhere but in a drawing-room, diffusing elegance as a flower sheds perfume" (HOM, p. 106). The satire exposes the conventional, anti-intellectual values of Lily's upper-class New York even more than it exposes Lily.

The Gryces represent the dead center of the established New York upper class. In view of the pervasive imagery of the airless tomb and prison, it is significant that the Gryce fortune comes from "a patent device for excluding fresh air from hotels" (HOM, p. 25). The Gryces dramatize the change from an earlier period of American history when patricians like Jefferson took an active role in founding a democracy. Old Jefferson Gryce instead achieves a kind of derivative distinction as a collector of Americana. In *The House of Mirth*, American history, the American past, is reduced to a set of possessions derivatively collected by people who have no ideas of their own and whose minds are like those of "a merchant whose warehouses are crammed with unmarketable goods" (HOM, p. 23). Phlegmatic Percy Gryce has been trained by his mother never to leave the house without his rubbers. "Every form of prudence and suspicion had been grafted on a nature originally reluctant and cautious," an education that is completed downtown by his training in "the management of the Gryce estate." Percy "was initiated with becoming reverence into every detail of the art of accumulation" (HOM, pp. 25–26). Wharton pervasively uses references to business, to work, to jobs in order to undercut expectations that the New York upper class is somehow above such crass matters. In the meanest sense possible, money and accumulation are at the center of the society the Gryces embody.

Religion, which in an earlier period at least had an intense fervor, has degenerated to the sterile forms of church-going as a social exercise and to Mrs. Gryce's gift to all the clergymen of her diocese, "a special edition of the Sarum Rule printed in rubric" and hence as illegible as the Sarum

Rule is archaic. The gift is a symbol of the irrelevance of a genteel religion whose main function is to ignore the problems of contemporary New York and to elicit letters of thanks that, pasted in a gilt album, "formed the chief ornament of [Mrs. Gryce's] drawing-room table" (HOM, p. 25).

The Gryce episode is a model of Wharton's view of the possessive market society in its upper-class version. The Gryces possess and stolidly, steadily collect and accumulate. Fortunes merge and enlarge: Percy Gryce inherits both his father's and his uncle's estates, and his marriage to Evie Van Osburgh combines two already great fortunes. For Wharton, their main power is "a force of negation which eliminated everything beyond their own range of perception" (HOM, p. 152).

Lily suffers because she both accepts and rejects the values of the system the Gryces and Van OsBurghs dominate. Like everyone in her world, and not hers alone, in accord with the basic values of possessive individualism Lily equates freedom and self-respect with the control of her own person and property. To be acquired or to be in debt is a denial of this entire psychology and value structure. As a woman trained to be acquired, Lily is thus pulled in opposing directions. For Lily and the others in her world debt is highly charged emotionally, because to be in debt puts a person in someone else's power. It symbolizes a loss of power and control, a diminishing of freedom, a carelessness or failure in the handling of money. However necessary debt is in the ordinary transactions of an acquisitive society, debt also stands for failure and dependency and finally for the deepest corruption of the character. Not surprisingly, then, the novel turns on the fact of debt. Lily's gambling debts cause Mrs. Peniston to disinherit her, to deprive Lily of her best hope for independence. Even more basically, Lily's desire to clear her debt to Trenor is one of her major motives. At the end, instead of using her inheritance to set up in a business of her own, Lily spends her inheritance to satisfy her debt to Trenor. Her death follows immediately. The women in Lily's world are far removed from the actual marketplace transactions where money is made and lost. Their separation intensifies their proprietary and in some cases their moral sensitivity to money and debt. The rich women in Lily's world all draw the line when another woman borrows money from one of their husbands.

Judy Trenor is typical. She is opposed to such borrowing partly because she resists having inroads made into her fortune, partly because she is suspicious of another woman's placing herself in the power of her husband. Mrs. Peniston has a horror of debt, an ancestral, tribal fear and abhorrence intensified by her separation from the actual workings of the marketplace. A person actively involved in the ups and downs of acquisition might be more tolerant than Mrs. Peniston. Mrs. Peniston's abhorrence of debt is part of her way of life, of her need to control, to judge, and to conserve. Lily is as deeply affected by the ancestral possessive market-society values as Mrs. Peniston or Judy Trenor. Like them, she realizes that being in debt to a man gives him a claim for repayment in sexual coin. Lily protects herself by not allowing herself to see what Trenor is doing.

In addition to the question of power, in a possessive market society people are traditionally sensitive about money and sex: both are seen as scarce resources to be conserved and protected. The counter image of the prostitute hovers in the background. Lily suffers from the accumulated pressure of wanting money and despising it, of deluding herself about the transaction with Trenor and being tainted as a result. Her cumulative sense of failure, of loss of power, of a corruption like a prostitute's contributes to her "paralyzing sense of insignificance," to the blows to her self-respect. Lily has difficulty respecting herself partly because she has difficulty acknowledging how deeply she accepts the money world she despises. She conceals the depth of her involvement by imaging the world of money as jewel-like in its fastidious aloofness, by separating this bright realm from the dark world of relative poverty and sordid concerns, and by imagining the good she can do as a philanthropic benefactor.

To the extent that Lily sees her world as separate and elevated, she participates in the basic reifying process of the market society. Wharton simultaneously shows that the entire women's upper-class social world is a mirror image of the men's financial world that provides the money to support it. In both versions, money is basic. In contrast to other models, in Wharton's upper-class version, child-rearing does not play a major role for women. Instead, the women have marriage and affairs for their careers; the men have money and power for theirs, and affairs for their amusement. The women gamble at bridge; the men gamble on the stock market. More basically, as Lily's relation to the Dorsets shows, in the women's world, the dynamics of buying and selling and alienation are exactly those of possessive individualism. Lily's sympathy, moreover, is precisely the quality that dignifies her as a human being and dooms her in the competitive, alienated world of possessive individualism. Bertha Dorset, in contrast, has exactly those qualities necessary for market-society success either on Wall Street or on Fifth Avenue.

Wharton shows that the market society makes sisterhood difficult to achieve. Because Bertha does what an active, successful participant in that society should do, Lily's sympathy for her cannot survive. The women do support each other to an extent—within limits they help Lily in the marriage market—but the ties are not deep. In emergencies the only person Lily can count on is Gerty Farish, who, significantly, has dropped out of active competition. Grace Stepney, in contrast, is out but wants to be in. She successfully, maliciously undercuts Lily with Mrs. Peniston and coolly refuses to help Lily in her time of need. Grace uses the full force of conventional attitudes about money and debt to retaliate against Lily. Her name, "Grace," ironically highlights what she lacks in both the secular and the religious senses. It is an appropriate commentary on the market society that graceless Grace receives the reward of the inheritance for her diligent undermining efforts against Lily.

Wharton further illuminates "society" and the market society through Rosedale, a prime representative of possessive individualism. As a talented, wealthy outsider moving up and in, he brings with him an aura of money, persistence, and ability. Insiders like Gus Trenor, George Dorset, and Percy Gryce all attend to "the art of accumulation," but Rosedale surpasses everyone. Rosedale carries over into his social life the qualities that made him successful as a financier. As an investor and perceptive art connoisseur, Rosedale appreciates Lily's value as a beautiful, rare object, a possession worth paying a high price for. Percy Gryce, a collector of musty books and manuscripts he never reads, has no genuine appreciation of the beautiful, living Americana he can add to his collection. Rosedale is much more subtle and appreciative, but for him Lily becomes an expensive commodity in an elevated trading venture. He openly offers to exchange his money and the power and protection that go with it in return for Lily's beauty and social grace. Rosedale will put it in Lily's power to satisfy her meanest cravings. "I want my wife to make all the other women feel small," (HOM, p. 185) Rosedale tells Lily, and she responds to the appeal.

As Rosedale's wife, she can excite envy, have affairs, and exude an aura of elegance. She can exert her power over Bertha and gratify slights to her injured pride. Instead of her chronic, paralyzing sense of failure and insignificance, as Rosedale's wife, Lily can bask in the admiration that gives her a renewed sense of her power, that makes her feel she is somebody, a self. She is understandably tempted to accept Rosedale and to become fully her captive self. Always tempting, these prospects become even more insidiously attractive after the Dorset episode, as Lily declines in value as an unsullied adornment to a man on the rise. On her own, as a woman, the power reserved to Lily is to make men love her. She is especially tempted to make Rosedale marry her for love regardless of her exchange value in the social world. This exercise of her power would confirm her badly damaged self-esteem, a sense of self-worth conditioned by her mother's training. The long-term price of such conventional victory, however, would be high.

Always in reserve after the likes of Percy Gryce and George Dorset, Rosedale is Lily's fate in her role as a successful, alienated commodity on the exchange floor at the upper levels of the market society. In marrying him, Lily would be tying herself formally to that society in the crudest form possible within the limits of respectability. Given her own mixed feelings about the side of herself Rosedale appeals to, no wonder Lily often feels disgust and self-disgust in his presence.

Rosedale shows the capacity of established society to absorb wealthy, able newcomers, even when as Jews they are vulnerable to anti-Semitism. Wharton plays a complex game with Rosedale as a Jewish outsider gaining acceptance. As Lily's fortunes decline, Rosedale's improve. Lily moves further and further from social respectability as Rosedale becomes increasingly acceptable. Conventional society is thus criticized for ignoring Lily's real virtue and grace and paying back Rosedale in the coin of respectability for the tips he gives on the market. The criticism depends partly on our seeing Rosedale as a plump, short-armed Jewish beast to Lily's long-waisted beauty. The acceptance of Rosedale as a plump, commercial Jew reflects negatively on a society that can reject the slender, virtuous Lily. Rosedale, however, is undemonstrably kind to children, and, for all his shrewd bargaining, at the end he is more genuinely concerned about Lily than her patrician friends are. Having characterized Rosedale as a nouveau-riche Jew, Wharton uses a subtle form of anti-Semitism to expose the shortcomings of an established society most of whose members are shown to be inferior even to Rosedale.

Wharton's central achievement, however, is with Lily and the political psychology of market-society acquisitiveness and alienation. In one of the most powerful passages in *The House of Mirth*, she has Lily experience "an inner destitution" more deeply impoverishing than even the material poverty she has feared.

It was the clutch of solitude at her heart, the sense of being swept like a stray uprooted growth down the heedless current of the years. That was the feeling which possessed her now, the feeling of being something rootless and ephemeral, mere spindrift of the whirling surface of existence, without anything to which the poor little tentacles of self could cling before the awful flood submerged them. And as she looked back she saw that there had never been a time when she had had any real relation to life. (HOM, p. 331)

Her rootless upbringing is a metaphor of the conventional market-society values her mother has inculcated. This upbringing has deprived Lily not only of place but also of values, of the stable center "to which her heart could revert and from which it could draw strength for itself and tenderness for others." Instead, divided, rootlessly ambitious, and weakened by her contradictory aims, Lily's individualistic self is cut off and especially vulnerable to a sense of isolated mortality. Like many Americans, Lily has lacked the protection of a cohesive culture to inter-vene between the self and the storms of existence. Wharton uses the image of the house to define this intervening culture:

In whatever form a slowly accumulated past lives in the blood—whether in the concrete image of the old house stored with visual memories or in the concep-tion of the house not built with hands but made up of inherited passions and loyalties—it has the same power of broadening and deepening the individual existence, of attaching it by mysterious links of kinship to all the mighty sum of human striving. (HOM, p. 331)

This "vision of the solidarity of life" centering on the traditional "old house" and "the house not built by hands" contrasts with the alienating practices of the house of mirth Lily has inhabited. It is a contrast be-tween the traditional world and the modern world, between an ide-alized view of Europe and an acutely critical view of America. The con-trast is also between a stable aristocratic society and the new possessive market society. From a traditional, backward-looking point of view, Lily's "vision of the solidarity of life" effectively highlights central fail-ings of the modern American market society. The force of the passage is not to suggest that Lily or her individualistic society should change but rather to register a strong criticism of that society.

Wharton suggests another, less convincing alternative to the loveless, fragmented house of mirth, an alternative she indicates can be acted on in the present. She has Lily feel that Selden's "love was her only hope. . . . love was what she needed; it would take the glow of passion to weld together the shattered fragments of her self-esteem" (HOM, p. 183). This is the view of the popular fiction Wharton had satirized in stories like "The Descent of Man" (1904). Wharton develops another phase of this sentimental outlook in her celebration of Nettie Struthers, the poor working girl who has an illegitimate child and finds a man who nonethe-less has faith in her, a faith that allows her as "a woman to become what the man she loves believes her to be" (HOM, p. 332). In the warm kitchen dear to the hearts of sentimental readers, Lily holds the baby and has "her first glimpse of the continuity of life" (HOM, p. 332). This conventionally domestic outlook emphasizes the dominant role of the man who inspires love and the child who continues life. The woman is subordinate. Like the complementary view of Selden's love as "welding together the shattered fragments of her self-esteem," this outlook is basically individualistic. Lily's "vision of the solidarity of life," in con-trast, firmly places the individual in a social setting. Even in this vision, as in her view of love and children, however, Wharton does not conceive of a social-economic world within which Lily can act from her deepest sources of vitality so that she can sustain her self and self-esteem from such action as a free member of a community.

Selden's "republic of the spirit" is equally far removed from this fusion of individuality, action, and community. Selden proposes instead an elitist meritocracy cut off from most of the sources of vitality that challenge and stimulate people in the actual world. He argues for success as negative freedom: freedom from worries, "from everything—from money, from poverty, from ease and anxiety, from all material accidents. To keep a kind of republic of the spirit—that's what I call success" (HOM, pp. 72–73). His "republic of the spirit" is similar to his view of Lily's beauty as part of an eternal order separated from sexuality and all the other impurities of this world. His germ-free republic is "a country one has to find the way to one's self" (HOM, p. 73). In practice, Selden has tepid feelings and consistently fails to help Lily when she needs him. He leaves her to find her way herself. Selden develops an individualistic theory perfectly suited to his fastidious, genteel temperament and to the needs of genteel, upper-class people who live off the money and position they have become sufficiently refined to look down on.

Lily is attracted to Selden because "everything about him accorded with the fastidious element in her taste. . . . She admired him most of all, perhaps, for being able to convey as distinct a sense of superiority as the richest man she had ever met" (HOM, p. 70). Part of Lily's misfortune is that she is conventional enough to fall in love with Selden. Instead of freeing her from the dominance of her mother's views, Selden intensifies the most devitalized and elitist sides of Lily's self. As a character, Selden fails to care for her; as an internalized psychological principle, he aggravates her self-divisions and makes it difficult for her to think, act, and feel her way out of her dilemmas. Through his theory of beauty and "the republic of the spirit," moreover, Selden intensifies Lily's inner alienation with an alienated theory of society. In his elitist theory, he separates people from each other and from the complex concerns of ordinary life. He makes Lily's loneliness more acute by setting her apart from other people without supplying any compensating personal or intellectual cohesion.

Selden collects but does not write books. Gryce, Rosedale, and Selden are all collectors. Selden is the most refined of the three, but he does not have the material means to collect Lily or the inner resources to act creatively so as to offer a genuine alternative to the collection ethos of the possessive market society.

Lily has a serious problem, since she not only sees her beauty as a pure and jewel-like work of art, but she also has been trained to see her beauty as a commodity, as her main weapon and economic asset. In the struggle for success at the upper levels of society, her mother is clear that Lily's beauty is a "weapon she had slowly fashioned for her vengeance. It was the last asset in their fortunes, the nucleus around which their life was to be rebuilt. She watched it jealously, as though it were her own property and Lily its mere custodian" (HOM, p. 37). Lily enhances the desirability of her property: she wears low-cut dresses, cares for her skin and hair, displays herself to advantage. Under her mother's guidance, Lily treats her beauty as an economic asset to be improved and capitalized on. She alienates her beauty, uses it as a weapon in the pursuit of prey, as in the Percy Gryce episode, and offers it for sale at the high price rare goods can command. Her failures in the marriage market stem from her divided aims and self. Because she accepts but also despises her mother's values, she manages to follow other impulses at the crucial moments that could lead to marriage.

The view of her beauty and real self that she accepts from Selden is totally at odds with the view she has learned from her mother. These ideals of "the real self," "beauty," and "the republic of the spirit" at first sight seem to be alternatives to the dilemmas of market-society alienation. They turn out, however, to be grounded in the same market-society processes Lily responds to, and they intensify rather than mitigate Lily's inner divisions. As internalized powers, Selden and Mrs. Bart divide Lily's consciousness and polarize her inner life. Both Selden and Mrs. Bart stress alienation and as opposed as they are in other respects, both of them encourage Lily to alienate herself from her sexuality. For her mother, Lily's beauty is a weapon and an asset. Enhancing this asset involves being seductive and attractive but has nothing to do with acting from genuine sexual impulses. In this important sense, Lily's beauty and self are as desexualized, are as separated from sexuality for her mother as they are for Selden.

The conflict between her mother and Selden's views, both of which she accepts, her deep experience of economic and sexual alienation, and her inability to act independently as a sexual and economic person all contribute to Lily's frequent feeling of self-disgust. She is "oppressed by a sudden conviction of failure" after she allows Percy Gryce to escape (HOM, p. 102; see also pp. 93, 96, 105). The strain of having to keep up a front causes her to "lapse to a deeper self-disgust" (HOM, p. 105), but the underlying reason is the irreconcilable conflict between two views of success. Lily feels insignificant, humiliated, and paralyzed; her self-respect is undermined because she fails to exert her power, to capture her prey, and to achieve the success her mother, her friends, and a part of Lily herself values.

But Lily also feels self-disgust when she acts on her mother's standards. Selden then functions as her conscience, as her superego. After he brings into the open what she has sensed and acted on even earlier—namely, that her conventional ambitions are contemptible—she tells him, "I have never recovered my self-respect" (HOM, p. 100). When she does what she needs to in order to succeed, she thus feels "humiliated" when Selden is around to see. "Under the spell of his observation, Lily felt herself powerless to exert her usual arts. The dread of Selden's suspecting that there was any need for her to propitiate such a man as Rosedale checked the trivial phrases of politeness" (HOM, p. 101). Under the pressure of Selden's disapproval, "it was as if the eager current of her being had been checked by a sudden impulse which drove it back on itself" (HOM, p. 100). Wharton has Lily recapitulate the childhood origins and punitive workings of the superego. "Like a frightened child" (HOM, p. 100), Lily then feels helpless and punished, or, rather, she punishes herself by feeling worthless. In this mood she feels a self-repugnance that she projects onto Rosedale, who, she "fancied," had detected the "conjugal familiarity" in Gus Trenor's voice (HOM, p. 100). "The idea turned her dislike of [Rosedale] to [a] repugnance" that originates in Lily's feelings as much about herself as about Rosedale.

The dynamics of this representative episode have serious and finally fatal consequences. Just as she momentarily fails to act prudently with Rosedale, under Selden's influence, Lily more significantly fails to catch Percy Gryce—or succeeds in not catching him, depending on one's point of view. As a character, Selden is weak and bloodless, but, as an internalized psychological principle, he is strong enough to be a main cause of Lily's death. In this internalized form, he intensifies her sense of self-disgust, furthers her self-division, and contributes to the draining of her energy. By showing the impasse Lily reaches, by having this flawed but valuable character die in the crosscurrents of conflicting and almost equally unsatisfactory values, Edith Wharton passes a severe judgment on both Selden's devitalized views and those of Lily's mother and the conventional world. The values and psychological dynamics do not, however, exist in a vacuum: they are socially rooted and expose both the dominant practices and the genteel alternatives Lily's mother and Selden represent.

In this drama of self-respect and self-disgust, Bertha Dorset plays the role of Lily's antagonist and shadow self. A phase of Lily's alienation and internal self-division is externalized in the person of Bertha Dorset. Bertha is what Lily could be as a conventionally successful woman. Bertha has had an affair with Selden. To repay Lily for taking Selden from her, Bertha is the agent who brings Percy Gryce together with Evie

Van Osburgh. Bertha dresses well, lives luxuriously, and amuses herself with affairs. She has the power reserved to women of her class, the power to make men fall in love, to excite envy, and to avenge slights to her pride. She is a vicious, skillful infighter. At the climax of the Mediterranean episode, she coolly sacrifices Lily to preserve her own position. She shows what Lily must become in order to function successfully in the world of affairs, in the competitive arena set apart for upper-class women. As she reveals as the Dorset situation unravels, Lily is unfit for this competition partly because of the human sympathy that is her most valuable trait. Lily's first reaction is to sympathize with Bertha as another woman. As a result, she delays protecting herself and is vulnerable to Bertha's attack. To succeed with the Dorsets, Lily first had to alienate herself by selling her social skills to amuse and distract George Dorset. Finally, to be successful with them as representatives of the established upper class, Lily must separate herself from her human compassion. Wharton contrives the novel so that as her circumstances decline Lily can recoup her fortunes by marrying George Dorset. Because she has Bertha's compromising letters to Selden, Lily has Bertha completely in her power. She simply has to exert that power to destroy Bertha and to advance her own interests, to treat Bertha as Bertha has treated her. As the new Mrs. Dorset, she can then in effect become Bertha Dorset, the conventionally successful, unprotestingly alienated side of her self.

In a further development of this pattern, Lily can also use Bertha's letters to blackmail her to regain the social respectability that will allow her to marry Rosedale. Again she can unscrupulously do to Bertha what Bertha has done to her. In the process she can become Bertha or the self-serving, alienated, Bertha side of her self. It is a scathing commentary on the conventional world that only on these terms can she then regain the social respectability that will allow her to marry, now not Dorset but Rosedale. Lily is tempted and terrified by the possibility of accepting Dorset and later Rosedale. The fear is both an index of her moral value and of her inner divisions. Dorset and especially Rosedale make a powerful appeal to Lily. When Rosedale proposes that she use Bertha's letters, "it was not, after the first moment, the horror of the idea that held her spell-bound, subdued to his will; it was rather its subtle affinity to her own inmost craving" (HOM, p. 268). In rejecting Dorset and Rosedale, Lily gains a moral victory her divided self is unable to live with. Since her "real self" is unfortunately alienated from Lily's instinctual and economic sources, this alternative to her "captive" or Bertha self intensifies rather than resolves the dilemmas of alienation. Her "real self" is separated from sources of vitality, so that Lily cannot live as her "real self." At the same time, her "real self" makes it difficult for her to accommodate to the world as it is or to imagine workable alternatives.

Lily's divided aims, her divided self, make failure unusually disturbing. For Lily, the inevitable result of failure is a deep feeling of "loneliness" and "inner isolation" (HOM, p. 65). Her conventional, social self punishes her for failing by making her feel alone and isolated from the society her mother has trained her to belong to. Her meeting with Gus Trenor is the most disturbing failure of her life. As she always does when she has failed, Lily then feels "alone," and "it was the loneliness that frightened her" (HOM, p. 156). When she fails, her mother's training repeatedly makes her feel cut off from the support of society. Now in addition she feels "alone in a place of darkness and pollution." She feels she is two selves: for money she has alienated herself and, like a prostitute, has sold her sexuality. She feels she has lost her freedom and, like a corrupt debtor, has placed herself in the power of a man. The episode with Trenor involves Lily's deepest feelings about success and failure, about money and sexuality, about her own power and powerlessness. Her responses are based on inner divisions that weaken her sense of self-esteem and on the force of the conventional socialization that makes her as a woman accept all the blame for a male assault.

Lily's situation as a dependent woman intensifies her sense that she is totally alone. She cannot turn for support to her guardian, Mrs. Peniston. Like a warder in a prison, Mrs. Peniston controls the money, arranges the drawing-room blinds to shut out the light, and loves a spotless mantlepiece more than she loves Lily. Mrs. Peniston provides Lily with a joyless "house of mirth" but not a home. Lily is in a deep sense homeless; she does not feel she has even a room of her own to return to. American men may be as rootless as Tocqueville describes them, but they at least build homes of their own. These homes are integral to the self in a possessive market society. Lily has no possessions, not even a room, but she has been deeply affected by the prevailing definitions of self-worth. At the end, in her displacement, Lily is an epitome of the rootlessness and isolation of the dominant society.

In illuminating the sources and results of Lily's recurring sense of failure and the feelings of "fearful solitude" that accompany it, Wharton goes deep into the inner consequences of possessive individualism. She reveals the general implications of the hegemonic process by showing in detail the way cultural hegemony works on and within a sensitive woman at the upper levels of the American class system.

fourteen

DREISER AND THE DYNAMICS OF AMERICAN CAPITALISM
Sister Carrie and *The Financier*

As Carrie gazes from the outside into the world of wealth she longs for, she envies beautifully dressed women like Lily Bart. Lily and Carrie are sisters—they experience the same loneliness, fear of poverty, and susceptibility to the lure of wealth—but even more important, through Carrie, Dreiser takes us into previously unexplored territory. His pioneering achievement in *Sister Carrie* is to enter deeply into the process through which Carrie becomes a connoisseur of the insatiable desires released by late capitalism. Marx and Lukacs clarify the earlier stages of this process, but Dreiser shows the way it affects people especially responsive to the demands of an emerging consumerism. By the late nineteenth-century, the commodification process in America was entering a new phase.[1] Advertising, the manipulation of images, the production of needs were becoming increasingly important.[2] To absorb the commodities produced by industrial capitalism, the production and manipulation of consumer needs were becoming integral to the new capitalism. Dreiser is a pioneer explorer of this territory.

As her central trait he has Carrie respond to the allure of the glittering goods enshrined in the new department stores and in temples of consumption like Sherry's mirror-filled restaurant. Carrie worships these fetishized commodities and their settings. They are mysterious and compelling. As if she has stepped out of an updated version of "The

1. For a summary of Marx and Lukacs on commodification, see the Preface.

2. For perceptive accounts of this process, see Alan Trachtenberg, *The Incorporation of America: Culture and Society in the Gilded Age* (New York: Hill and Wang, 1982), esp. pp. 101–39; Stuart Ewen and Elizabeth Ewen, *Channels of Desire: Mass Images and the Shaping of American Consciousness* (New York: McGraw-Hill, 1982); Stuart Ewen, *Captains of Consciousness: Advertising and the Social Roots of the Consumer Culture* (New York: McGraw-Hill, 1976); and Michael Spindler, *American Literature and Social Change: William Dean Howells to Arthur Miller* (London: Macmillan, 1983), pp. 1–32, 97–120.

Fetishism of Commodities," for Carrie goods have a life of their own separate from and superior to human beings. In a perfect example of the consumer phase of the commodification process, clothes speak to Carrie more eloquently than her lovers. With Hurstwood, instead of words, she heard "the voices of the things which he represented. How suave was the council of his appearance. How feelingly did his superior state speak for itself."[3] From the outset, Carrie's heart longs for the goods and the glamorous way of life the mysterious, mystified city embodies. Her self is inseparable from these longings, from the commodities she endlessly pursues. Things impress themselves on her and penetrate her consciousness to its core, to her heart, to the center of her being. She nonetheless experiences the seductive world of commodities as superior to her and separate from her, set off against and above her. In a touching confirmation of Marx on mystification and commodification, she has no sense that human labor, hers or anyone else's, has created the baffling, alluring array of commodities. Separated from anything she can understand or anything she has had to do with, the mystified world of commodities makes her feel envious, small, and inadequate. Carrie typically views this world from the outside, from a distance. She glimpses the life of the rich from afar, through an open gate, or she peers into glass cases or through plate-glass windows: the goods are inside; she looks longingly at them from the outside.

In her passivity, Carrie perfectly embodies the compelling power of commodities to assume a magnitude and a separateness that make the self seem insignificant, unworthy. To overcome this sense of insignificance, to be happy and to feel worthwhile, Carrie adorns herself and acquires the possessions that temporarily make her feel she is as good as those who display the goods that stimulate her envy. Dreiser goes beyond Marx in revealing the dynamics of commodification and its impact on the self as consumerism became increasingly important during late capitalism.[4]

3. Theodore Dreiser, *Sister Carrie*, ed. John C. Berkey, Alice M. Winters, James L. W. West, III, and Nida M. Westlake (New York: Penguin, 1981), p. 118. This edition is based on the University of Pennsylvania Press's restored version of Dreiser's manuscript. Subsequent references will be abbreviated SC and cited by page number in the text.

4. My thinking about *Sister Carrie* has been stimulated by unpublished University of Washington essays by Bruce Byers, "Heartless in a Havenless World: The Social Origins of the Naturalistic Novel"; James Thomas, "Spectacle and Power in *Sister Carrie* and *The Financier*"; and Caren J. Town, "The House of Mirrors: Carrie, Lily, and the Reflected Self." I have also profited from Ellen Moers, *The Two Dreisers* (New York: Viking, 1969), a book that marks a turning point in Dreiser criticism; Sandy Petrey, "The Language of Realism, the Language of False Consciousness: A Reading of *Sister Carrie*," *Novel* 10 (Winter 1977): 101–13; Lester H. Cohen, "Locating One's Self: The Problematics of Dreiser's Social World," *Modern Fiction Studies* 23 (Autumn 1977): 355–68; Walter Benn Michaels, "*Sister*

In Columbia City, Carrie can understand a stonecutter working at his quarry. But she cannot understand what Dreiser tellingly calls "the stone corporation" with its complex web of railroads, its huge machinery, its incomprehensible scale and power (SC, p. 17). This impersonal system dwarfs, baffles, and excludes her. She is treated impersonally, "as one would a package" (SC, p. 26), a commodity. When she does find a job, she is led through a confusing maze of rooms to a machine that stamps out parts but not the whole of a shoe (SC, p. 36). She is left in "a portion of a stock room which gave no idea of the general character of the floor, and Carrie could form no opinion of the nature of the work" (SC, p. 28). The commodified world produces shoes, but equally important it produces mystification about its processes and a corresponding sense of discontent and inadequacy. The threat of hunger and exclusion is never far away, even as the display of wealth intensifies Carrie's longing and feeling of insignificance. Lacking any experience of community or any understanding of the process she is involved in, Carrie longs for shoes. Even in Columbia City she has been compelled by the goods in the stores; now even more intensely she longs to consume (see, for example, the telling juxtaposition on pp. 28–29). In her world of late capitalism, production and consumption are separated and the entire process has been mystified. The relation between production and consumption has been obscured and so has the role human labor plays. Laslett's baker, producing and consuming on a comprehensible scale in the same household, has long passed from the scene.

Carrie can thus see no connection between her fragmented human labor stamping out shoe uppers and her longing for shoes, jackets, and all they represent. For her and many others, the connection has been mystified, just as the mysterious city has been mystified. One result is that instead of any sense of solidarity with her fellow workers, Carrie feels variously repelled by their grossness, pity for their poverty and poor clothes, and envy for the appearance of the pretty, well-dressed shop girls. Collective action to change conditions is thus out of the question. Instead of cooperative action and a sense of individuality emerging from a community, Carrie places at the center of her self the

Carrie's Popular Economy," *Critical Inquiry* 7 (Winter 1980): 373–90, and "Dreiser's *Financier*: The Man of Business as a Man of Letters," *American Realism: New Essays*, ed. Eric J. Sundquist (Baltimore: Johns Hopkins University Press, 1982), pp. 278–95; Philip Fisher, "Acting, Reading, Fortune's Wheel: *Sister Carrie* and the Life History of Objects," *American Realism: New Essays*, pp. 259–77; Spindler, *American Literature and Social Change*, pp. 84–88, 135–49; and Rachel Bowlby, *Just Looking: Consumer Culture in Dreiser, Gissing, and Zola* (New York: Methuen, 1985), pp. 52–65.

glittering trinkets and the alluring possibilities of the commodified city. For her "expectancy, dissatisfaction, and depression" are inseparably linked (SC, p. 50). As an actress, Carrie is able to capitalize on her depression, her melancholy. Her frown captivates the audience; her melancholy is basic to that success which ensures her continued depression. Dreiser diagnoses the political-economic etiology of her version of consumerism and individualism.

He also distinguishes it from other versions of possessive individualism. Dreiser uses the Hansons to represent the traditional, mean, work-ethic, accumulating version. For Hanson, Carrie is basically the $4.00 a week she pays for room and board. Dreiser includes the humanizing touch of Hanson's affection for his child, but primarily the family relation is impersonal and economic. Reflected in the light of Hanson's view of her as income, Carrie's lack of regret for leaving is made to seem less callous than it would otherwise. Carrie, though, as different as she is from the Hansons, is like them in having a weak sense of family ties. Dreiser thus stresses the absence of cohesive ties in both the traditional and the emerging forms of the market society. As an embodiment of the traditional style, Hanson works hard at the stockyards, lives a gray life in the present, and scrimps to invest in the two pieces of real estate for the future. He avoids the theater that for Carrie is the very embodiment of what she is eager for in life. In contrast to the Hansons, from the outset, Carrie is shown as responsive to the department stores, the new theaters of display, and later to the glamorous theater of escape she eventually stars in.

Even on the train she responds with quickened interest to the clothes, manner, and money displayed by Drouet, a "drummer," a salesman, one of the new men of the consumer-appearance society. The Hansons would be as out of place in the new department stores as they are disapproving of the theater and as Carrie knows they would be of Drouet. Carrie's status as an embodiment of the new, evolving consumer-display sensibility is defined through contrasts between her attractions and the Hansons' repulsions to the representative theaters and showmen of consumption and display. Drouet, the theater, and the stores promise a life of possibility and pleasure, of the happiness Carrie longs for, as over against the impoverished life of the Hansons. In Dreiser's beautifully paced account, shifts of scenes between Drouet and the Hansons and all they represent—grindingly hard work in the impersonal system of industrial capitalism—impel Carrie toward Drouet and make him and the new way of life he embodies seem understandably attractive. The Hansons' refusal to go with her to the theater frames a narrative sequence that culminates in Drouet's taking her to the theater and then to the new apartment he has furnished for her.[5]

When Dreiser first introduces Carrie, he lets us know that "self-interest with her was high, but not strong. It was nevertheless her guiding characteristic" (SC, p. 4). The effect is to establish the importance of self-interest, the classic market-society motive, but also to qualify it, to establish it as "her guiding characteristic," and to establish that it was not overpowering, to somehow assert and withdraw simultaneously. The effect of presenting it in this form is that we can't really hold "self-interest" against Carrie, although we now know it operates with her. When Carrie leaves the Hansons, the web of contrasts, the gray world of rejection and hard labor, Hanson's view of her as income, and the Hansons' disinterest in the theater and pleasure similarly make the move to Drouet and the new apartment and the furnishings and the clothes seem understandable and not open to the ordinary criticisms. In a way Carrie is beginning her career of moving up the class ladder from the Hansons to Drouet to Hurstwood. In a way she is selling herself as a commodity and giving play to her socially inspired longing for commodities and appearances. Perhaps because of his own ambivalence, Dreiser presents, reveals fully, and nonetheless accepts and sympathizes with his representative, flawed characters.

The theaters, the apartment and its furnishings, the stores and the new clothing—in this world, money is the ultimate commodity, the measure of exchange for all the goods in the exchange system. In the great seduction scene between Drouet and Carrie, Carrie responds to the lure of the new jacket, of the new shoes. Commodities have a seductive power. After Drouet appeals to her love of clothing and the theater, the seduction is consummated when Drouet gives Carrie the "two soft, green, handsome ten-dollar bills" (SC, p. 62), not hard money but sensuous money. The qualities of human beings are transferred to the money, which is "handsome" and eloquent, more so even than the "handsome" Drouet (SC, p. 68), whose clothes and fat purse have earlier captivated Carrie. After the exchange of money, Carrie "felt bound to him by a strange tie of affection" (SC, p. 61). Because she is human, Carrie experiences the exchange relation as creating "a tie of affection." Ordinarily Carrie does not have ties; both her isolation and the vulnerable tie she does feel are representative of the dynamics of her individualistic, commodified society.

5. Julian Markels, "Dreiser and the Plotting of Inarticulate Experience," *The Massachusetts Review* 2 (Spring 1961); rpt. in *Sister Carrie*, ed. Donald Pizer (New York: Norton, 1970), p. 532.

In this instance of exchange, Carrie, too, is a commodity. Dreiser sympathetically, comprehensively shows the results of her involvement in the system of commodity exchange. A high point, the seduction scene in the restaurant, is more sexually suggestive than the scene that presumably takes place in the apartment. Throughout *Sister Carrie*, commodities have a seductive, sexual power more fully rendered than that of the human players. Dreiser has a deeper understanding of the processes of commodification and commodity fetishism than those critics who accuse him of lower middle-class sentimentality and prudery.[6] Dreiser realizes that the basic human power of sexuality has been transferred to commodities and, in the restaurant scene, to money, the ultimate commodity.

Dreiser frames the entire narrative with a passage establishing that the lights of the city have a seductive power more compelling than that of a human seducer. The glittering commodities of the market society are fetishized, and, like the "handsome" greenbacks, they are endowed with human qualities even more potent than a lover's. When this happens, Dreiser knows that it "perverts even the simplest human perception" (SC, p. 4). Carrie's consciousness, her way of seeing, is perverted in this sense. Dreiser shows in detail the results of this representative psychology, a psychology rooted in the political economy of late capitalism. Commodities are integral to the entire process. As Carrie shows, at once set off against and superior to the self, commodities also penetrate, infiltrate, and finally become integral to the self. They even penetrate the realm of the heart, that deep region of the personality we would expect to be the most resistant to commodities. Instead, Carrie sets her heart on the show and the brilliance of the commodified city, epitomized by the display of wealth and luxury on Broadway, Broadway as the ultimate theater of consumerism (SC, pp. 324–25). In this theater, the need to validate the self through external show, exhibition, display motivates the self to accumulate the commodities that also constitute the self. For Carrie, in her way the self is inseparable from the possessions that enlarge or diminish it.

Her success is thus as empty as Hurstwood's failure is painful. Both are premised on a privatized view of the self as constituted by commodities. For all her warmth, Carrie loves commodities more than she loves people. *Sister Carrie* is not organized around the growth of Carrie's self, an aborted growth that allegedly weakens the novel.[7] Carrie becomes a more sophisticated manipulator and connoisseur of appear-

6. Leslie Fiedler, *Love and Death in the American Novel* (New York: Criterion, 1960), p. 242.
7. Markels, "Dreiser and Inarticulate Experience," pp. 537–41.

ances as the novel progresses, but she does not develop an autonomous self. Appearances precisely mark the class differences between the superior Hurstwood, with his rich clothes and soft leather shoes; Drouet, with his shiny patent leather shoes; and Sven Hanson, who after work exchanges for slippers "the solid pair of shoes he wore" (SC, p. 30). Although she is initially mistaken about Hurstwood's exact position, Carrie increasingly learns to discriminate and to continue longing for ever higher realms. Ames, who appears to be a way out, is instead deeply involved in the commodified world. His criticisms and contradictions intensify Carrie's unsatisfied longings. The pathos of her career is that at the end even more than at the beginning she is enmeshed in that world of class and appearances whose emptiness she senses but which she is unable to break free of. Her early longings contribute significantly to the power of the novel, as does Dreiser's honesty in staying true to her essential characteristics. For Carrie, self-possession is a self constituted by possessions. The early phases of this process are admittedly more compelling than the later ones. But by then Dreiser is structuring his novel around the counterpoint with Hurstwood. Dreiser plays off Carrie's early longings, her experience of painful rejection and mean jobs, and her glamorous success in counterpoint to Hurstwood's decline from prosperity to an increasingly moving poverty and failure. The powerful center of gravity in the novel is the tension and paradoxical similarities between these representative careers.

Dreiser matches his sympathetic insight into the processes that impel Carrie with an even more perceptive treatment of Hurstwood. He has Hurstwood perform in the theater of Hannah and Hogg's elegant saloon (Fitzgerald and Moy's in the 1900 edition). He performs well because, as Dreiser says, "he looked the part" (SC, p. 43). Hurstwood's assets are his rich clothes, his shrewdness, and above all his assured sense of well-being and self-importance. His sense of self-esteem is inseparable from his position and the material manifestations of his self and his success: his impeccable clothes, his soft leather shoes, his office, and his glittering rings. He is "a light reflecting in his personality the ambitions of those who greeted him," men who are themselves defined by "their stout figures, large white bosoms and shining pins" (SC, p. 180). In Hurstwood's version of the market society, the dividing line between appearance and reality is blurred, obscured. In his theater, appearances are integral to reality. Hurstwood's work is producing appearances, facilitating social exchanges among men on the make, and, under the guise of recreation, stimulating the envy and emulation basic to the society (SC, p. 47). He is an exceptionally able "poser" (SC, p. 105), a

natural, consummate actor, a master of carefully modulated gregarious-
ness, a manager skillful at greeting with the appropriate measure of
friendship or distance.

As "a manager," he does not organize large resources, but he does
manage the appearances essential for social exchange. He does not own
the saloon, and, although he has property, Dreiser contrives it so that
the property is not in his name. Dreiser thus emphasizes that Hurstwood's main capital is his personality, which in turn depends on his
position, his sense of well-being and prosperity, and his "reflection of
the ambitions of those" around him. Sturdy and energetic as he appears,
his self and self-esteem are not intrinsic but are significantly constituted
by a web of possessions, position, and desire. Given sufficient capital to
invest in a really good saloon, Hurstwood may have prospered in New
York. But without enough capital, he is vulnerable to the very powers of
envy and emulation he himself had successfully manipulated in Chicago.

New York intensifies the pressures of emulation. The scale of wealth,
the visibility of luxury magnify the insignificance of those of moderate
wealth. In Chicago Hurstwood was somebody. In New York he is no-
body. He has cut his ties with his network of friends, position, and
possessions. He is a diminished self. Lacking capital, he depends on his
main resource, his personality. In an earlier period, people trained to
practice the Protestant virtues of restraint and control were necessary to
accumulate scarce resources. In its capital-accumulating phase, the market society thus produced character. As the production of appearance
becomes increasingly important, as the production and manipulation of
images accelerates, as advertising and the production of needs comes
into prominence, instead of character, the society produces personality.
In Chicago, Hurstwood was a successful player in the appearance-emu-
lation-personality theater. But in New York, under the surface of his
prosperous appearance, Hurstwood's personality has been negatively
affected. The continued comparison with his former state and the pressure of invidious comparison with those around him generate the com-
modification-emulation disease, depression (SC, p. 339). Hurstwood's
self and self-esteem have been poisoned. His main resource, his personality, has been weakened. Hurstwood's depression gradually erodes his
will to succeed, gradually infiltrates his entire consciousness, and progressively leads to his gradual and then accelerating decline. Carrie's
depression is integral to her rise; Hurstwood's depression is integral to
his fall. Carrie and Hurstwood show that the disease of depression
permeates the consciousness of those especially responsive to the de-

mands of a capitalism moving into its appearance-oriented, consumer phase.[8]

To highlight the process, Dreiser frames Carrie's entry into Chicago and Hurstwood's entry into New York. In each case he uses the city as his focus for the commodified world of display, show, and exchange (SC, pp. 4, 304–6). Dreiser establishes for both Carrie and Hurstwood that immersion in this world perverts perception and that commodities overpower people whose selves and self-esteem are inseparable from possessions and position.

Hurstwood understandably comes to feel that something is missing in his life. In Chicago, Hurstwood has increasingly centered his life on his work, on the theater of Hannah and Hogg's, with its round of activity and pleasure, its casual friendships, and its opportunities for investment. His domestic and personal life has deteriorated, withered. After meeting Carrie, Hurstwood comes to believe he must have her, that possessing her will make him happy, will rejuvenate him. Just as commodities have penetrated Carrie's heart, the ethos of possessive individualism has done the same with Hurstwood. Possessing, owning, Carrie and her love is his individualistic solution to a malaise that includes, but goes beyond, his domestic situation. For all his friends, Hurstwood is isolated. He has no one to talk to in his period of crisis. He has no experience of community. In a society of envy and emulation, a society that systematically produces discontent, Hurstwood has reached a plateau. He is not moving. He is vaguely discontent and turns for a cure

---

8. Roland E. Martin, *American Literature and the Universe of Force* (Durham: Duke University Press, 1981), stresses and often condescends to Dreiser's philosophical and scientific ideas and even more than his predecessors ignores the complex social dynamics at the center of Dreiser's most powerful fiction. For Martin, "the theory of katastates and anastates . . . somewhat spuriously accounts for Hurstwood's decline and Carrie's rise in terms of hypothetical chemicals, poisonous or helpful, respectively, engendered in the blood by bad emotions or good ones" (p. 223). See also Charles C. Walcott, *American Literary Naturalism, a Divided Stream* (Minneapolis: University of Minnesota Press, 1956), pp. 190–91; Richard Lehan, *Theodore Dreiser: His World and His Novels* (Carbondale: Southern Illinois University Press, 1969), p. 66; and Lawrence E. Hussman, Jr., *Dreiser and His Fiction: A Twentieth Century Quest* (Philadelphia: University of Pennsylvania Press, 1983), p. 23. The theory of katastates and anastates, however, plays at best a minor reinforcing role in *Sister Carrie*. Martin's approach allows him consistently to exclude Dreiser's understanding of the emerging consumer-commodity-appearance society of late capitalism. Any critical approach places some matters in the foreground and deemphasizes others. For an understanding of Dreiser's novels, perhaps his philosophical and scientific ideas are of secondary importance and should be subordinated to what the novels say in their subtlety and complexity about the society at the center of his fiction. This issue of priorities and approach is intelligently debated by Ellen Moers and Sandy Petrey, "Critical Exchange: Dreiser's Wisdom or Stylistic Discontinuities," *Novel* 11 (Fall 1977): 63–69.

to the rejuvenating illusion of pastoral love for Carrie (SC, pp. 122–23, 203). Far from being pastoral, however, Carrie longs for all the glittering things the city embodies. Her self is constituted by these longings. She is understandably attracted to Hurstwood's rich clothes, soft leather shoes, and assured manner. In Hurstwood she sees a means of entry into the world of luxury she desires. She is, as Dreiser puts it, "deluded" (SC, p. 138).

Compounding Dreiser's comedy and tragedy of commodified perception, Hurstwood for his part misperceives Carrie as a fresh, rejuvenating pastoral innocent. An embodiment of the world, Hurstwood imagines one of the sentimental escapes the commodified world produces to relieve the strains it generates. He even stages his meetings with Carrie in Jefferson Park, a pastoral retreat sheltered from the noise and energy of the surrounding city. Shrewd and practical as he is, Hurstwood is also inextricably involved in the producing and consuming of appearances. He is especially susceptible to the palliatives a society of images produces for the consumption of its discontented members.

The popular theater is the focus for these tendencies. In the crucial theater scene, Dreiser intersperses authorial commentary throughout his narrative of the rehearsal and performance of *Under the Gaslight*. By systematically breaking the illusion of the play, he achieves a Brechtian exposure of the artifice of the performance. He illuminates the different theaters Hurstwood and Carrie act in; he explores the blurring of appearance and reality in a society of show.

As a rejected job hunter and meanly paid factory worker, Carrie has had experience as a kind of outcast. She has an underlying fear of being cast out into a world of poverty and shabby clothes, even as she longs for the luxury the play presumes to represent. Her experience in the impersonal world of industrial capitalism throws into relief the glamorized, sentimentalized version of the outcast she acts as Laura in *Under the Gaslight*, even as the sentimentality of the play throws a revealing light on her socially generated aspirations and fears. The interplay of illusion is compounded because within the play Laura is exposed as an imposter, a revelation that helps make the part one that "affected Carrie deeply. It reminded her somehow of her own state" (SC, p. 163). Far from being able to draw immediately on her own emotions, fears, and desires, however, Carrie is able to shine only after Drouet gives her an admiring audience to act for. Reflected in the mirror of his admiration, she then enters into the part of the rejected outcast and exhibits the feelings that inflame both Drouet and Hurstwood and make them decide to possess her. Later, outside the theater, Carrie similarly reflects back to Hurstwood the passion he feels for her (SC, p. 301). Drouet tells

Carrie to forget about the audience, but she needs an audience as a mirror to perform for. When she practices alone in front of a mirror, Carrie makes herself into the audience. The theater and the mirroring in the face of an audience emphasize the absence of a strong, inherent self and Carrie's ability to respond to the socially generated demands of performance and display. Carrie succeeds in the theater because her melancholy, her passivity, her weak sense of self, and her responsiveness to the demands of display and performance are well suited to a society of appearances. Instead of the complete change he needs, Hurstwood gets Carrie, an exceptionally attractive embodiment of precisely what is causing his discontent.

To bring the problem to a climax, during Carrie's performance of *Under the Gaslight*, Hurstwood completely loses his sense of the difference between the player and the person, between the theater of melodrama and his own theater of appearance. He has previously imagined a pastoral Carrie. He now sees a Carrie-Laura created by the dynamics of the theater. In the process, he takes personally the melodrama's injunction, "do not let [your married life] be discontented and unhappy" (SC, p. 191). The emphasis on happiness, on a happiness identified with claiming, protecting, not losing Carrie-Laura, appeals directly to him. And no wonder, since he has earlier seduced Carrie by telling her, "You're not happy. . . . You are not satisfied with life, are you?" (SC, p. 119). He means that Carrie can be happy, that he can give her what she needs to be "satisfied with life." Dreiser, however, establishes that "things . . . are realities," that "things" equal the big North Shore houses Carrie is learning to desire (SC, p. 119), and that in the market-society theater the pursuit of happiness is endless and insatiable. Dreiser knows that in this theater discontent is systematic: *Sister Carrie* shows that people who equate self and self-worth with "things" and who identify happiness with possessions have entered into a devil's bargain. Whatever its original humanistic promise in the Declaration of Independence, in *Sister Carrie*, "the pursuit of happiness" has become integral to the dynamics of the commodified society Hurstwood and Carrie have both accepted.

Like Hurstwood's theater of appearances, the theater of melodrama promotes the illusion of happiness based on possession--in its case, possession of a loved one. The melodrama reinforces this illusion with another illusion, that the "heart," "love," is "the treasure without money and without price," worth any sacrifice (SC, p. 192). In Hurstwood's theater, things are reality. A web of money, position, and personality is the treasure that counts. Ordinarily shrewd, Hurstwood is vulnerable to a sentimental appeal that totally falsifies the realities of the theater he performs in. Carrie's youth, beautiful appearance, and her exhibition of feeling, the appeal to happiness and his desire to protect and to possess her, the competitive rivalry with Drouet, and finally the idea that "her love is the treasure without money and without price" combine to disorient Hurstwood. He resolves to have Carrie. "He would marry her, by George. She was worth it" (SC, p. 192). As he now sees her, Carrie is a commodity whose exchange value goes beyond even money. Hurstwood is willing to pay any price for the happiness he believes she will bring him. For Hurstwood, the fusion of theaters reveals the comic and finally tragic extent to which commodities have penetrated the realm of the heart and have deeply affected his perceptions.

Because Hurstwood's consciousness is commodified from the beginning, his perceptions, like Carrie's, are perverted from the outset (SC, p. 4). Under the influence of his needs and the magnetism of the play, however, his perceptions become obviously deranged. To emphasize Hurstwood's deranged perceptions, Dreiser shows him as "crazy" (SC, p. 193). In the lobby of the theater, Hurstwood wants "affectional relief"; he wants real love (SC, p. 194). But Hurstwood, the master of sham, after an evening of sham, must sham an indifference he does not feel. In Carrie, he is also going to have a "love" that is an exhibition of feelings, a reflection of his own ardor and Carrie's desire for the higher world of commodities Hurstwood embodies for her. When Hurstwood does marry Carrie, he appropriately stages a performance as misleading as *Under the Gaslight*. On the train to Detroit—or Montreal?—or the hospital?—Hurstwood and Carrie play out a melodrama of mutual dissimulation.[9] They are not hypocritical; the consciousness of each has been deeply affected by a society of display, of exhibition, of theater. Throughout *Sister Carrie*, by juxtaposing theaters and stressing theatricality, Dreiser subverts the simple opposition between "reality" and "appearance." He subtly exposes and undercuts their mutual penetration in a society of commodified appearances.

The central theater episode illuminates the state of mind that culminates in the turning point of the novel, the theft. In the period after the performance, Hurstwood's perceptions are repeatedly at odds with his ordinary world. In a glow of pleasure he returns home and sees it in a euphoric light that makes it difficult for him to deal sensibly with his wife (SC, p. 219). On the fatal evening his drinking simply reinforces the

9. Petrey, "The Language of Realism," analyzes the parody in this episode (pp. 104–5) and subtly discusses the two styles of *Sister Carrie*. See also Daryl C. Dance, "Sentimentalism in Dreiser's Heroines Carrie and Jennie," *CLA Journal* 14 (1970): 135, and Cathy N. and Arnold E. Davidson, "Carrie's Sisters: The Popular Prototypes for Dreiser's Heroine," *Modern Fiction Studies* 23 (Autumn 1977): 395–407.

process of perception or misperception the theatrical performance has brought to a climax. Even at that, his mind is divided and he wavers, unable to decide whether or not to take the money. "Chance" has been made the main actor, but the underlying role of the melodramatic theater is crucial.[10] In this drama of commodification, moreover, the sheer physical presence of "the soft green stack," of the "ten thousand dollars in ready money," "so smooth, so compact, so portable," is instrumental in tipping the scales (SC, pp. 271, 268, 270). Unlike *Under the Gaslight*, Hurstwood performs alone on a stage that has no audience. But he brings the world of the play with him to the lonely set of Hannah and Hogg's. "The ten thousand dollars in ready money" will allow him to have "the treasure without money." The fusion or confusion of theaters is complete.

In *Sister Carrie*, the fusion of theaters is pervasive. Characters repeatedly plan to conceal their affairs in the course of discussions about going to the theater, as with Drouet and Carrie (SC, p. 62) and later with Hurstwood and Carrie (p. 138). These episodes reflect on each other. As part of a pervasive pattern, the reflections and the fusion of theaters, the multiple mirroring, intensify the sense that sham, illusion, and deception penetrate every facet of life in a society of show where the boundaries between appearance and reality blur. To the same effect, characters repeatedly enact key scenes at or outside theaters, or they use the theater as bait or experience it as a reward that itself turns out to be illusory. Crucially, the theater defines the contrast between the traditional work-ethic world of the Hansons and the evolving consumer-display society of Drouet, Carrie, and Hurstwood. Inseparable from the sense of sham and illusion is the compelling appeal of pleasure, commodities, and success connected with the theater. Carrie's growing involvement with Drouet is thus framed by the theater.

Her rising and falling involvement with Hurstwood similarly centers on *Under the Gaslight* and is underscored by the contrast between the first play Hurstwood takes her to and the impact on her of *A Gold Mine* in the declining phase of their relation. At the first play, Carrie "was really hypnotized by the environment, the trappings of the box, the elegance of her companion. Several times their eyes accidentally met and then there poured into hers such a flood of feeling as she had never before experienced" (SC, p. 110). The seductive environment of the theater and Hurstwood's appearance reflect on each other and drive "into Carrie's mind that [in relation to Drouet] here was the superior man. She

10. On the role of chance see, e.g., Walcott, *American Literary Naturalism*, p. 188, and Lehan, *Theodore Dreiser*, p. 63.

instinctively felt that he was stronger and higher and yet withal so simple" (SC, p. 110). Her instincts, however, have been conditioned by that society of sexualized commodities, class, and appearances the theater intensifies and reflects on. As Hurstwood begins his decline, *A Gold Mine* appropriately reinspires Carrie's desires for the dress and luxury Hurstwood is increasingly unable to provide. By juxtaposing them, Dreiser contrives it so that the two theaters of Broadway, the theater of emulation and the theater of escapist melodrama, mutually penetrate, elevate, and subvert each other (SC, pp. 325–27).

At the same time that characters are deeply enmeshed in the processes of emulation and appearances, they also show an array of human traits that cannot be reduced to these processes. Drouet is generous and shallow, Carrie is warm and vulnerable, the early Hurstwood is variously practical and limited. These traits also intertwine with the prevailing theaters, the processes of commodification and appearance that dominate consciousness and society in *Sister Carrie*.

In this world of pervasively fused theaters, characters typically look out of or into plate-glass windows as if they were spectators watching a performance framed by the proscenium arch of the theater. They watch a performance of commodities, prosperity, and luxury, as when Carrie looks from the outside into restaurant windows, offices, and display cases or looks out from her window at the life of the commodified city. In the restaurants, Drouet or Mr. Vance perform, and Carrie watches the spectacle, sometimes turning to look outside through the ever-present window to view the crowds or the cold reminders of poverty. For both Carrie and later Hurstwood, the spectacle of hunger is inseparable from the displays in the temples and the theaters of consumption.[11]

Reflected in the light of the popular theater, Carrie's delusion about Hurstwood, her entire way of perceiving—or misperceiving—is doubly subverted. His "dress and manner" have "deluded her as to the height and luxury of his position. She imagined that his attraction to her could only mean that entrance for her in a higher world which she craved" (SC, p. 138). This passage frames a love scene Carrie and Hurstwood enact while they talk about dissimulating when they go to the theater. In the foreground, the play ironically exposes Drouet as a cuckold, but

11. Fisher, "Acting, Reading, Fortune's Wheel," discusses the way "a window theatricalizes experience" in his analysis of "the self in anticipation" in *Sister Carrie* (pp. 261–63). Fisher is also concerned, as I am, with theaters and mirroring in *Sister Carrie*, although he uses Trilling and Rousseau to take him away from the dynamics of commodification and the production of appearance and misery. For a suggestive treatment of these issues in their formative period, see Jean-Christophe Agnew, *Worlds Apart: The Market and the Theater in Anglo-American Thought, 1550–1750* (Cambridge University Press, 1986).

more deeply the emphasis on theater highlights and subverts Carrie and Hurstwood as players in a drama scripted by a commodified society of appearance. Part of the script is Carrie's craving for the world of luxury, her susceptibility to "dress and manner." Another part is Hurstwood's infatuation for Carrie, a preoccupation that originates in the social circumstances of his life and his susceptibility to the palliatives his society produces.

Even more important is the hardship the market-society theater produces and the blindness to hardship both the market-society theater and the escapist sentimental theater produce. As they leave the play, Hurstwood, preoccupied with Carrie, fails to notice "a gaunt-faced man, . . . the picture of privation and wretchedness," who pleads for the price of a bed (SC, p. 139). Hurstwood himself later enacts his own misery in scenes juxtaposed with Carrie's rise in the theater. Beyond its obvious prefiguring of his own situation, the episode establishes a subversive connection between the sentimental theater of the play, Hurstwood's preoccupation with Carrie, his representative blindness to hardship, and the inescapable presence of misery.

On the evidence of *Sister Carrie*, the impersonal market-society theater produces a glittering array of goods, and, inseparable from great wealth and the longing for luxury, it also systematically produces poverty, hunger, hardship. Carrie is always haunted by the specter of exclusion, mean jobs, and hunger. Her grim experience of poverty in the first part of the novel counterpoints with Hurstwood's decline at the end to give *Sister Carrie* much of its power. The specter of the misery inseparable from all the glittering commodities repeatedly takes concrete form in scenes juxtaposed or fused with the popular theater, as when the gaunt-faced man abruptly throws a harsh light on the "good play," the "comedy" that Hurstwood, Carrie, and Drouet have been viewing and acting (SC, p. 139). In *A Hazard of New Fortunes*, William Dean Howells has his middle-class observers, the Marches, speculate that the starving man they see groveling for food in the gutter may be shamming. Dreiser, however, uses the juxtaposition with the theater not to discredit or to call into question the hard, cold experience of hunger and poverty but to insist on its immediacy, to establish its direct relation to the producing and consuming of commodities and illusions, and, in a society where appearance and reality merge, to stress the irreducible actuality of hunger, displacement, and misery.

Take the strike episode. Dreiser frames it with scenes of Carrie prospering in the chorus line and driving with rich admirers in the park. After Hurstwood returns, cold and defeated, Dreiser flashes to the theater and Carrie, one of "the treasures of the harem" (SC, p. 430), about to capitalize on her frown and her appeal to men who, like the early Hurstwood, want to protect her. Carrie's ability to satisfy the escapist needs generated by the society leads to the richly remunerated heights, to her suite at the Waldorf. Hurstwood's depression leads in the opposite direction. To maintain a shred of dignity, to avoid disgrace, he "feels he must do something" (SC, p. 407). He gets a temporary job as a scab during a streetcar strike. The strikers repeatedly appeal to his sense of solidarity: "we're all working men like yourself" (SC, p. 423). But Hurstwood is not a working man. He is not even an "ex-manager." As he says, "I'm not anything" (SC, p. 413). He enacts a tragedy of displacement, of being without a class. Cut off from his self-constituting web of position and possessions, Hurstwood nonetheless retains a sense of his superiority to the other needy job applicants. In multiple ways Hurstwood suffers the injuries of an individualism that isolates him, makes him feel he is "not anything," and deprives him of any experience of community with his unemployed fellows or with the striking workers. At the same time, he experiences the cold, the mean food, and the painfully hard work the system produces for its laborers.

For Hurstwood, the physical and psychological pressures are intense. Sick to his depths, he returns home through the snow and turns for relief to the newspaper. He has participated in the events he now comfortably reads about as escapist fiction. The novel's rendering of Hurstwood's experience illuminates the newspaper headlines and stories as precisely that—"stories." Under the guise of fact they provide the same distracting, distorting relief for Hurstwood that Carrie's sentimental novels do for her. Hurstwood was earlier a master of appearances, a devotee and victim of the theater. At the end, as a devotee of the sensational press, he continues his career as a consumer of those escapist fictions that Dreiser uses to highlight the hardship inseparable from a society of commodified spectacle.

As Hurstwood deteriorates, Dreiser repeatedly places him outside the restaurants and theaters that embody the compelling, illusory success he has lost. Just as Hurstwood has failed to see the starving man, Carrie, in her warm tower, looks down on the spectacle beneath her and fails to see him. It is not a personal failure of compassion but rather a reflection of the invisibility of failure in a society of appearances. Hurstwood's misery is urgent, but he has become invisible. Even in his own eyes he has become nothing, worthless. " 'I'm no good now. I was all right. I had money. I'm going to quit this,' and with death in his heart he started toward the Bowery" (SC, p. 492). The commodities and appearances that he and Carrie have set their hearts on, the "money" and all it stands for that constitute the self, finally emerge explicitly as death.

In *The Financier* (1912), the drama of self and commodities is enacted not on the stage of the saloon, the theater, or the bowery but at the highest levels of power. The focus shifts from the theaters of appearance, the management of show and emulation, and the dynamics of depression, consumerism, and displacement. Passive or moderately talented figures like Carrie and Hurstwood are replaced by the forceful, commanding personality of Frank Cowperwood. But in the face of the conventional wisdom about rugged individualists, Dreiser shows that Cowperwood, too, for all his intrinsic power, is inseparable from the commodities that enlarge or diminish his self. In *Sister Carrie* and *The Financier*, Dreiser establishes a new view of the American self as constituted by the commodities, energies, and attractions of the emerging market society. He responds to two main tendencies, consumer capitalism in *Sister Carrie* and finance capitalism in the Cowperwood novels. Through Cowperwood, Dreiser concentrates on the predatory practices and effects of finance capitalism. He turns his attention to the upper reaches of the system which organizes or disorganizes the commodified world that Carrie longs for and that Hurstwood experiences as deadly. Both in the content and in the destabilizing techniques of *The Financier*, Dreiser exposes the usually hidden implications of the emerging capitalism that has increasingly dominated twentieth-century American life.

Dreiser's revelations have a continuing pertinence, although in the Cowperwood novels he is looking back on a crucial phase of American capitalism that even as he was writing had been transformed. The heyday of finance capitalism was defined by the organizing energies of individualists like Yerkes and Morgan and by the drying up of European investment capital during the 1880s.[12] Simultaneously, the American economy generated domestic surplus capital able to dominate its own investment markets, a surplus capital controlled by a few powerful firms and men.[13] Particularly during the 1890s and the first decade of the twentieth century, these men and firms consolidated to maximize profits and to minimize what they saw as destructive competition. They incorporated their competitive individualism. In the formative period, giant individualists created giant corporations like U.S. Steel, Standard Oil, and the Union Pacific. Thereafter the impersonal corporation or the large organization functioned as ruthlessly as the individualistic found-

12. Dreiser modeled Cowperwood on the traction magnate Charles T. Yerkes. See Philip Gerber, "The Financier Himself: Dreiser and C. T. Yerkes," *PMLA* (1973): 112–21.

13. Robert Wiebe, *The Search for Order, 1877–1920* (New York: Hill and Wang, 1967), pp. 24–26.

er. The corporation, a legal person, carried on the earlier possessive individualism in a new form appropriate to the changed conditions of large-scale twentieth-century capitalism.

From the vantage point of 1912, Dreiser looks back on the formative period during and immediately after the Civil War. His revelations are rooted in but not confined to the historical period he covers in *The Financier* and *The Titan*. The motives, the practices, and the isolating, energizing impact on self and society do not seem dated and neither do the more accessible relations he shows between finance, politics, law, and journalism. For us the scene has shifted from the city council to Washington, the scale of operations has expanded to billions instead of millions and to multinational corporations instead of municipal traction companies. But in reading the Cowperwood novels we feel we are being shown clearly an earlier phase of a condition still recognizably alive and rarely shown with Dreiser's intensity, understanding, and skill.

Because Dreiser's skill has been widely questioned, we should stay alert to the full implications of his masterful handling of point of view. Technically, the point of view is that of an omniscient third-person implied narrator. In effect, however, Dreiser enters into Cowperwood's point of view and generates a destabilizing dialogue with the reader. Beyond narrative technique, point of view means an entire value structure and way of seeing. In this sense, in place of a fixed, authoritative point of view with clearly defined guidelines, Dreiser responds to the corrosive, animating energies of the market society. Unlike Howells, he fully accepts the consequences of the energies he releases and confronts. Dreiser thus creates a novel whose point of view and evaluations are not stable and authoritative but vary with the reader, systematically, not in the ordinary sense that each of us of course has a perspective. Authority does not reside in the authorial voice and point of view but resides in the shifting exchange between the reader and the character. Dreiser deliberately presents Cowperwood, "the man as I see him," and he has him "stand there, unidealized and uncursed, for you . . . to take and judge according to your own lights and blindnesses and attitudes toward life."[14] The resulting judgments are implicit and indirect and emerge from the exchange between the reader's "lights and blindnesses and attitudes toward life" and the detailed unfolding of Cowperwood's attitudes, practices, lights, and blindnesses. The shifting, unsettling effect of Dreiser's handling of point of view is intensified because of the way

14. Quoted by Robert H. Elias, *Theodore Dreiser: Apostle of Nature* (New York: Knopf, 1949), p. 160.

he involves and provokes the reader. Rooted like Cowperwood in the destabilizing dynamics of the American market society, this play of perspectives has important consequences.[15]

Before we consider these consequences, however, we must return to an even more basic matter. In a distinctively different way than in *Sister Carrie*, Dreiser understands that in the emerging market society the connection between the self and commodities is subtle and reciprocal. "We think we are individual, separate, above houses and material objects generally," Dreiser observes in *The Financier*,

but there is a subtle connection which makes them reflect us quite as much as we reflect them. They lend dignity, subtlety, force, each to the other, and what beauty, or lack of it, there is, is shot back and forth from one to the other as a shuttle in a loom, weaving, weaving. Cut the thread, separate a man from that which is rightfully his own, characteristic of him, and you have a peculiar half success, half failure, much as a spider without its web, which will never be its whole self again until all its dignities and emoluments are restored.[16]

In the emerging market society of consumerism and display, Hurstwood, cut off from his dignities and emoluments, acts out the tragedy of this new view of the self as constituted by position, commodities, and their attendant dignity. In the predatory market society of *The Financier*, even an individualist like Cowperwood is not autonomous but depends on the possessions and connections that go to make his "whole self."

Cowperwood is decisive, energetic, vital. He has extraordinary powers of mind and personality. He has no use for conventional morality; his motto is "I satisfy myself" (F, p. 121). But in order to be a "whole self," the self he satisfies must have possessions and the network of

15. See also Cohen's "Locating One's Self," a suggestive treatment of Dreiser's use of shifting perspectives, for Dreiser "a fundamental principle of reality" (360), a reality Cohen shows to be socially constituted. Dreiser carries further than they did tendencies that characterize predecessors like Twain, James, and Howells. See Janet Holmgren McKay, *Narration and Discourse in American Realistic Fiction* (Philadelphia: University of Pennsylvania Press, 1982), esp. pp. 189–200. McKay's study would be more revealing and less a classification exercise if she connected the formal issues of point of view, especially the rejection of the omniscient narrator, to the destabilizing impact of the post–Civil War market society that was increasingly undermining the certainties that supported a fixed, omniscient point of view. Conversely, an omniscient point of view could also function to reassure readers that the old religious and secular certainties still held, despite daily evidence to the contrary. In their best fiction, Twain, James, and, to a lesser extent, Howells were as unwilling as Dreiser to play the reassurance game.

16. Theodore Dreiser, *The Financier* (New York: Signet, 1967), pp. 97–98. This easily accessible edition reprints Dreiser's 1927 revision of the original 1912 text. Subsequent references will be abbreviated F and cited by page number in the text.

connections he alone understands. Cowperwood embodies a new conception of the contradictions of the market-society self. As in earlier
versions of the rugged individualist, he has great intrinsic power, he has
no sense of community, and for self-fulfillment, to be a whole self, he
needs to succeed in the market place. What is new is Dreiser's awareness that for all Cowperwood's independence and disregard for others,
Cowperwood's self is intimately tied to, is inseparable from, a web of
possessions and connections that define him as he controls, or sometimes fails to control, them. Even his basic impulse, his underlying need
to organize and to control makes him vulnerable to the men and forces
he brilliantly manipulates. Dreiser explores the process by which in
post–Civil War America not only a person's "body and his psychic
powers" but also "his clothes and his house, . . . his lands . . . and his
bank-account" come to constitute what William James calls "a man's
Me," his very self.[17]

This subtle, reciprocal relation between selves and commodities, their
ebb and flow, penetrates all the social and psychological structures in
The Financier and is basic to the organization of the novel. Dreiser centers
each phase of Cowperwood's career around the buildings and the possessions that are integral to the market-society selves who accumulate,
inhabit, possess, and dispossess these structures. In *The Financier*, moreover, the organizing rhythm of Cowperwood's ascent (chapters 1–12),
his resistance to reversals (chapters 13–43), his conviction and imprisonment (chapters 44–57), and his final reemergence (chapter 58) renders
the hero's rise to success through the processes of material and psychological accumulation, loss, and magnificent recovery. Dreiser responds
with the freshness of discovery to the American fascination with the
details and the movements of this drama. In the prison scenes, drawing
on his own experience and imagination of failure, Dreiser chronicles the
depletion, the depression, and the diminishing of self Cowperwood
experiences as he struggles to maintain his integrity. This drama is at the
center of the prison episode. It speaks deeply to the American fear of
failure and hope for the triumph of the self during and after defeat. The
dominant emotions of the prison episode play off against, and intensify
through contrast, the overall rhythm of Cowperwood's rise to the financial heights.

Dreiser is especially perceptive in working out the political psychology of this process. At the turning point in Cowperwood's career, Stener, the city treasurer, decides not to lend him any more of the city
funds that until then have given the financier immeasurable power. His

17. William James, *Psychology* (Greenwich, Conn.: Fawcett, 1892, 1963), p. 167.

access to the city treasury has multiplied Cowperwood's influence and wealth and has enlarged his "whole self" with "all its dignities and emoluments," including the secret control of the Nineteenth Street line and the large shares in several other street-railway lines. His relation to Stener is part of the web of connections that began when Cowperwood successfully did secret brokerage work for Butler. Using the Butler connection, Cowperwood later makes a million dollar bid on the loan to consolidate the city debt. He comes to the favorable attention of Relihan and the Harrisburg politicians. His ordinary business is thriving, and with the profits from the loan coup Cowperwood builds his impressive house and office. "His new house, this beautiful banking office, his growing fame, and his subtle connections with Butler and others put Stener in considerable awe of him" (F, p. 139). "Like a spider in a spangled net," Dreiser concludes, "every thread of which he knew, had laid, had tested [Cowperwood] had surrounded and entangled himself in a splendid, glittering network of connections, and he was watching all the details" (F, p. 140).

When this network of connections is damaged, Stener, who has been trained to read the signs, sees a different Cowperwood. He loses his awe of the financier. Self-interest dictates that Stener continue loaning from the treasury: a loss of $800,000 is hardly more significant than $500,000, and with the additional money Cowperwood will not fail, they will not lose their holdings, and they can deal as equals with the other financial and political powers of Philadelphia. But Stener has a weak sense of self, and, as for Cowperwood, in Stener's eyes Cowperwood has been diminished. Mollenhauer, Butler and Simpson are "the big forces in [Stener's] world." They are "older and richer" than Cowperwood (F, p. 140). Instead of being connected to and enlarged by them, Cowperwood is now cut off. His innate personal ability is not enough to persuade Stener to back him. What is at issue is the conflict between two tendencies within late-nineteenth-century capitalism. One stresses traditional economic self-interest, the other is responsive to the new, emerging view of the self as comprising its web of connections. Dreiser arranges the novel so that Stener's key choice turns on and illuminates the power of that new view of the self Cowperwood opposes even as he embodies it.

In the world of finance capitalism, impersonal connections are crucial as the self aims at a self-satisfaction that finally fails to satisfy. The whole self expands and becomes ever more powerful, and yet something is missing. This realization gradually emerges through the accumulating details of The Financier and The Titan. In The Financier, the grim forecasts of unfulfillment in the concluding chapter, "The Magic Crystal," thus have particular force. They cast a shadow back on the earlier narrative and look ahead to what Dreiser dramatizes in *The Titan*, his novel of endless seductions, both sexual and financial. In contrast to Howells, Dreiser does not moralize. Unlike Howells with Dryfoos in *A Hazard of New Fortunes*, Dreiser does not show his financier as disoriented and discontent as he becomes richer. He does not make stock gambling a sin punished by unhappiness, the just result of violating republican virtue. In the republican myth Howells affirms, personal labor on the land is necessary for a merited prosperity and for well-being. Dreiser is more subtle and more profound than Howells. In place of the violated republican myth, Dreiser sympathetically shows Cowperwood in action. For the most part using indirect discourse to present Cowperwood's point of view, Dreiser shows what Cowperwood does and lets the judgment emerge. The reader's "lights and blindnesses and attitudes toward life" are crucial in this process.

Take the issue of stock gambling. Cowperwood objects to it, too, but not on moral grounds. A broker gambling on stocks, he realizes, is an agent secondary to and dependent on those who really control organizations. For Cowperwood, "a man, a real man, must never be an agent, a tool, or a gambler—acting for himself or for others—he must employ such. A real man—a financier—was never a tool. He used tools. He created. He led" (F, p. 42). On this view, human beings are not immortal souls related to God and to each other. Or to shift to a secular perspective, human beings are not well-springs of energy and possibility, precious by virtue of their existence and related by bonds of sympathy and necessity. Instead, on Cowperwood's widely shared but usually softened view, "a real man," the normative human being, sees people as tools and is himself "real" to the extent that he can control the impersonal instruments around him. They are "tools," he is alive and creative. In Cowperwood's version of commodification, other people become not so much commodities to be bought and sold as objects, tools, to be manipulated. To the extent that a person genuinely cooperates with or fails to manipulate others, he becomes less real. His selfhood, his value as a human being, diminishes. On this view, in order to be "real," a person must dominate others and treat them as depersonalized objects. "A real man" does not have close ties to other people or deep feelings for them. He exploits political connections for personal gain; he does not live in a political or social community within which he develops his individuality as he contributes to the common welfare. Parts, but not the whole, of this outlook go back to earlier stages of American society, as Franklin reminds us. But in *The Financier* and *The Titan*, the fully developed outlook emerges from and illuminates the post–Civil War society dominated by finance capitalism.

In the Cowperwood novels, this socially rooted view of "a real man" affects the most intimate social and personal relations, the most general financial and political ones, and it affects the entire narrative strategy. In place of Howells's moral judgments and moral drama, Dreiser probes, accumulates, and lets the results speak to our "lights and blindnesses and attitudes toward life." Instead of invoking a normative, authoritative point of view, Dreiser's finally destabilizing strategy is to expose the reader to Cowperwood, to stand back, and to allow the reader to respond.

Intensifying Cowperwood's dilemma and our response to it is the fact that he has great intrinsic force. "To live richly, joyously, fully—his whole nature craved that" (F, p. 57). He loves beauty—in landscapes, in art, and especially in women. His vigor is an affront to the devitalized genteel religion of post–Civil War America. And because he has a genuine and developing appreciation for art and as a financier is himself an intuitive artist, Cowperwood cannot be condescended to as vulgar millionaires are by Howells or by David Graham Phillips. Richly endowed as he is, fulfilled in many of his aspirations, why then the sense of underlying disappointment?

Dreiser illuminates the problem by developing complex insights into the new market society and its relation to the self and sexuality. Dreiser has often been accused of being too talky. He has also been ridiculed for interspersing the financial and sexual episodes.[18] In fact, Dreiser's technique of juxtaposition allows him to reveal and to subvert without explicit commentary. The organization of *The Financier* is in some ways solid and simple: Cowperwood's rise, setback, and reemergence and a pattern of juxtaposed scenes dealing with business and sex. Despite the frequent complaints about Dreiser's technical ineptitude, his technique yields complex results and is not at all pedestrian. We conventionally separate business and sex. In unconventionally showing their relation, Dreiser goes to the roots of the possessive market society.

Scenes detailing Cowperwood's youthful rise, his early successes, the exhilarating sense that he was rich and was going to become richer counterpoint with scenes detailing his developing infatuation with Lillian, his marriage, his change of attitude toward her, and his growing involvement with Aileen. After he and Aileen reach their understanding, the development of their illicit affair counterpoints with the intri-

18. Stuart P. Sherman, "The Barbaric Naturalism of Mr. Dreiser," *The Nation* (1915), rpt. in *The Stature of Theodore Dreiser: A Critical Survey of the Man and His Work*, ed. Alfred Kazin and Charles Shapiro (Bloomington: Indiana University Press, 1965), p. 78, and, more analytically, Donald Pizer, The *Novels of Theodore Dreiser* (Minneapolis: University of Minnesota Press, 1976), p. 170.

cacies of Cowperwood's ambiguously legal use of the city treasury to finance his personal control of the Nineteenth Street and other traction lines. Cowperwood has gone beyond the conventional limits in his personal life and has simultaneously moved into new territory in his business life.

From the beginning, Cowperwood has had several involvements, beginning with Prentice Barlow. His first interest in girls is juxtaposed with his first business success, his boyhood purchase and sale at a profit of seven boxes of Castile soap. Just as he succeeds in business, he soon succeeds in satisfying his masculine, combative desire to arouse Lillian. But for Cowperwood and Dreiser, change is inevitable. The account of the early, contented years of Cowperwood's marriage is charged with intimations of change ("at this time"; "for the time being," F, p. 57). Dreiser perceptively juxtaposes his account of these years with a detailed analysis of the prevailing practices in the upper reaches of the Philadelphia financial and political world (F, p. 59). What Dreiser shows through his juxtaposition is that a rapidly changing economy and the fluid rules of the big money game undermine traditional restraints and provide the context and model for Cowperwood's later business and sexual adventuring and infidelity. "For the time being," Cowperwood is faithful, as he is trustworthy in his business affairs. But fidelity is unstable in both the expanding big money marketplace and in the realm of marriage and sex. Cowperwood's sexual energies and interests are intrinsic, but the expanding market society encourages him to express his sexuality regardless of restrictive conventions.

The conventional world compartmentalizes business and sex, but Cowperwood does not. In both areas of his life he is the same man and uses the same energy and methods. The compartmentalizing of business and sex functions to make sex hard to come by. Sublimated energy is then available for business. Cowperwood, however, uses market-society values and energy in both sex and business. He is a representative of the market society and also subversive of its traditional dichotomy, a separation based on scarcity and on the need to accumulate capital resources. Cowperwood flourishes during the period of transition from the older, small-scale capitalism to the expanding, post–Civil War finance capitalism with its emphasis on organizing large resources. His father is cautious and frugal; "from the first [Cowperwood] had the notion that liberal spending was better, and that somehow he would get along" (F, p. 21). He spends his energy freely in business and sex. He is a harbinger of a new morality appropriate to a new phase of capitalism. Although his practice has a vigor and an aggressiveness appropriate to his personality and to his origins in an early, transitional stage, his

motto of "I satisfy myself" looks ahead to the culture of narcissism and
to the dilemmas of the sexual revolution, which is to say, the dilemmas
of revolving sex.

Cowperwood is naturally attracted to the youthful, vital Aileen. "Nature"—in this case, Dreiser's "chemisms," Freud's biology of sexual impulse—is, however, intertwined with the market-society emphasis on
change, on the undermining of traditional, stable values, and on the
dynamics of the market- society self. Cowperwood renews and satisfies
himself not at his own sources, not through his participation in a community, but through financial conquest and through beautiful younger
women who function to give pleasure, to satisfy his love of beauty, and
even more to extend his self through his mastery of them as possessions. When Cowperwood declares his love for Aileen, Dreiser says,
and the order is important, "A thrilling sense of possession, mastery,
happiness and understanding, love of her and of her body, suddenly
overwhelmed him" (F, p. 122). The process of acquisition, mastery, and
aesthetic and sexual satisfaction is endless and insatiable. Through Cowperwood, Dreiser again shows that the desires released by the expanding post–Civil War market society can never be satisfied. The American
tragedy for the man who says, "I satisfy myself," is that his self can
never be fully satisfied, can never be fulfilled or whole despite long
periods of contentment.

Youth is crucial because of its vitality, because of its value in the eyes
of American men, and because it revitalizes and enlarges the market-
society self and implicitly denies death. The youth of one individual is
scarce, perishable, but youth is always available. It is unfortunate for
Aileen that, like Lillian, she will become older and that Cowperwood's
ideas about beauty will change. Even while Aileen is young, Cowperwood has countless affairs, exciting, satisfying "for the time," but
cumulatively disappointing. Individually each affair has its pleasures
but also its complications. Since Cowperwood does not develop complex, continuing emotional ties, he has only the continuity of repeatedly
beginning anew. Youth does not develop into maturity, although Cowperwood himself grows older. Cowperwood has the genuine satisfaction of affirming the deepest fact of his socially and biologically conditioned self, the fact that his feelings about women change and that he
acts from his feelings. He does not joylessly trap himself in the chains of
dead convention. But he does not develop sustaining ties, either. As he
himself grows older and approaches death, what awaits him is Bernice,
the ice princess he falls in love with when she is fifteen and he is in his
fifties.

In his treatment of Cowperwood and his affairs, Dreiser has the outlines of the American tragedy of unfulfilled desire. The focus is the sexualized market-society self. The arenas are sex and finance and the built-in satisfactions and disappointments of perishable youth, endless conquests, and an absence of emotional ties and human community. Dreiser does not develop the Cowperwood novels as tragedy, but he does suggest the tragic potential of his material.

Dreiser not only sketches but also develops the tragic possibilities of Edward Malia Butler, the most compelling of the secondary characters in *The Financier*. Butler's tragedy is rooted in the conflicting viewpoints, divided allegiances, and predatory market-society practices he brings to a focus. When they first meet about the secret brokerage work he wants Cowperwood to do, "Butler wanted him to see clearly that fidelity was the main point in this case—fidelity, tact, subtlety, and concealment" (F, p. 68). But concealment is finally at odds with fidelity. Butler himself conceals from Cowperwood the full dimensions of his plans (F, p. 68). Cowperwood tactfully, successfully does his secret work for Butler but in his turn conceals from Butler the full scope of his own operations, including his use of the city treasury, his secret control of rival traction lines, and above all his affair with Aileen. Butler counts on self-interest to keep Cowperwood faithful. He knows that "this talk of political influence and connections could only whet Cowperwood's appetite" (F, p. 68). But in a market-society world of lobsters and squids and black groupers, appetites are voracious. A fidelity based on self-interest is unstable because in a predatory world self-interest can be served in shifting ways.

Butler is at home in this new world. He has come from the traditional world but has made his way in this one. He has adapted traditional European loyalties to new world conditions. His success is based significantly on the ties he has forged with a network of fellow Irish-Americans. As a devout Catholic, moreover, Butler believes in traditional religion and morality and in the cohesive, hierarchical structure and world view the Church at its best embodies. If anyone in the novel provides an alternative to Cowperwood's individualistic abuse of cohesive ties, it is Butler. In the predatory world of affairs, though, Butler functions as a man of power. He has successfully compartmentalized his life: traditional religion and morality apply at home. Cowperwood breaks down these barriers and shows the reader, though not Butler, the extent and results of Butler's double standard. Dreiser shows what happens when religion and morality have totally lost their hold on the world of power.

Traditional religion and morality simply do not apply in Butler and Cowperwood's world of business and politics. Butler has no trouble accepting the situation. He has a humane tolerance of Cowperwood's business tactics, even of his stretching of the rules about the use of the city treasury and his secret acquisition of the Nineteenth Street line. Butler is not sanctimonious like Skelton C. Wheat and other "solemn, self-righteous souls who see life through a peculiar veil of duty, and who, undisturbed by notable animal passions of any kind, go their way of upholding the theory of the Ten Commandments over the order of things as they are" (F, p. 224). What Butler accepts is that in the market-society world "of things as they are," men prey on other men.

For the young Cowperwood, as an explanation of the universe the biblical account of Adam and Eve is unbelievable in contrast to the powerful evidence of the lobster devouring the squid. As the juxtaposition at the end of chapter 1 of *The Financier* shows, this predatory behavior applies with special force to the world Cowperwood chooses to make his way in, the market-society world of money, finance, and large organizations. Butler has helped create this new market society that effectively excludes the traditional religion and morality he adheres to. In particular, he has helped create Frank Cowperwood. He uses Cowperwood, but he also supports him and extends Cowperwood's network of connections. He is proud of the younger man, who is almost like a son.[19]

As a man from the old world successfully making his way in the new world, Butler retains even in his business life some of the human qualities Cowperwood has eliminated. The contrast between Butler and Cowperwood involves the old world evolving into the new world, the older generation in conflict with the younger generation, the viewpoint of traditional morality and religion in conflict with the fully developed amorality of the evolving marketplace. In the scenes between Butler and Cowperwood, Dreiser does a masterful job of developing the conflicting viewpoints in their full implications. "You have one view of life, Mr. Butler," Cowperwood says, "and I have another" (F, p. 340). Cowperwood has a powerful intelligence, but, to his cost, he has failed to realize the depth of this difference. For all his ability and practical knowledge of men, Butler has also failed to grasp the extent of the difference. Like the techniques that reveal them, the convergence and conflict of points of view, the clash of Butler and Cowperwood's "lights and blindnesses and attitudes toward life" are grounded in and illuminate the destabilizing power of the emerging market society.

Dreiser is open and responsive, not doctrinaire or reductive. He

---

19. John O'Neill, "The Disproportion of Sadness: Dreiser's *The Financier* and *The Titan*," *Modern Fiction Studies* 23 (Autumn 1977): 409–22, discusses the family drama in *The Financier*.

shows that Butler's opposition to Cowperwood is fueled from complex sources. Dreiser suggests an underlying conflict between Butler as patriarch and Cowperwood as son, each in his own way interested in Aileen. Butler's outrage is fed from psychological as well as moral sources, or, rather, the psychological conflicts intensify the moral abhorrence. As a traditional, patriarchal father, moreover, Butler loves Aileen partly because she is *his* daughter. He does not allow Aileen her feelings and her independent life. Butler genuinely feels that the adultery is a sin, that Aileen's soul is in jeopardy, that

"It's me duty to be hard. It's my obligation to you and the Church. Ye must quit this life. Ye must leave this man. Ye must never see him any more. I can't permit ye. He's no good. He has no intintion of marrying ye, and it would be a crime against God and man if he did. No, no! Never that! The man's a bankrupt, a scoundrel, a thafe. If ye had him, ye'd soon be the unhappiest woman in the world. He wouldn't be faithful to ye. No, he couldn't. He's not that kind." He paused, sick to the depths of his soul. (F, p. 272)

Butler cannot tolerate having *his* prize wasted on a man who is in every way faithless. In the separate worlds of business and religion, "fidelity was the main point." Although Cowperwood does marry Aileen, Butler is correct about the unhappiness in store for her. The mixture of accuracy, patriarchal rivalry, personal grief, and religious violation gives Butler's response a compelling, passionate intensity.

It is appropriate and revealing that Butler finally dies of a form of religious despair. Dreiser has successfully rendered the tragedy of the man who has been able to keep his traditional old world religion separate from his new world affairs until he encounters through Cowperwood dimensions of reality so powerful that they break down the barriers and cause his death. Butler, "hale and strong like seasoned hickory" (F, p. 69), has a powerful self, but even his identity is not invulnerable to the corrosive pressures of the new market-society realities Cowperwood embodies.

Dreiser is equally good at registering his insights into the world of possessive individualism not only directly through what he shows but also indirectly through techniques that emerge from and illuminate those unsettling market-society tendencies Cowperwood embodies. Dreiser has a vital sense of relation. His technique of juxtaposition—of finance and sex, for example—registers that sense and makes us see connections where we conventionally see only isolated units. Similarly, descriptions of buildings and people are a stylistic trait of the Cowperwood novels. They have a special importance because they are rooted in and illuminate the world of possessive individualism.

Take a representative character like Edward Tighe, one of Cowper-wood's early employers. Like his "handsome green-gray stone building at 66 South Third Street," Tighe is placed in the context of a changing history and society, "in what was then, and for a number of years afterward, the heart of the financial district" (F, p. 33). As he does with almost every character, Dreiser gives a brief account of the changes in Tighe's life: his background, accomplishments, capacities, and present position. As part of his individualizing portrait, Tighe, like the others, receives an economical, telling description: his "manner . . . was as lively and good-natured as it was combative and self-reliant. His upper lip was ornamented by a short, gray mustache" (F, p. 33).

Dreiser juxtaposes the individualizing descriptions of Tighe's building and self with the first detailed exposure of the history and practices of the city and state financial world Tighe and later Cowperwood flourish in. In the world of possessive individualism, Tighe's network of socially and historically rooted possessions and connections helps define his identity, so that Dreiser has a strong motive to see Tighe and the others as individuals in a context, not as people separate from their changing history and society. Although American economic individualism pro-duces emotional isolation, Dreiser shows that, surprisingly, this individ-ualism also produces certainly not a community but a certain kind of relatedness between the self and its possessions, history, and society. Dreiser has a gift for precisely observed detail, a capacity that is called into play by the world of possessive individualism he is dealing with. Although Cowperwood dominates the novel, other characters nonethe-less have a place. They contribute to Cowperwood's self and world and also receive their own lively, individualizing descriptions.

Dreiser's techniques of description and juxtaposition are perfectly suited to the individualistic world of the Cowperwood novels. In their context, these individualizing descriptions are in effect metaphors for the world of possessive individualism; they have a special and finally subversive meaning because of the equivocal status of the individual in the evolving possessive market society. In each of the countless individ-ualizing portraits that characterize the Cowperwood novels, Dreiser tes-tifies to his unusual sensitivity to this style of individualism. In these novels, Dreiser's delight in describing a panorama of individuals is the equivalent of his delight in describing commodities in *Sister Carrie*. For Cowperwood, the individuals he encounters, manipulates, and profits from are commodities, to be used to aggrandize that "whole self" Drei-ser knows is inseparable from a web of possessions, dignities, and emoluments. To the extent that individuals like Edward Tighe merge into the flow of commodity-selves, they are "individual" in the equivocal sense that glittering, replaceable commodities exert their "individual" appeal in *Sister Carrie*.

In describing buildings as well as people, Dreiser further renders the unsettling impact of the new market society. Sensitive as he is to the reciprocal relation between the self and possessions in the post–Civil war possessive market society, Dreiser makes particularly effective use of Cowperwood's office and home. Take a routine description of the office Cowperwood is planning to buy, a building, "which, though old, could be given a new brownstone front and made very significant" (F, p. 76). The front is important and so is the appearance of openness and prosperity in this "handsome building, fitted with an immense plate-glass window; inside, his hardwood fixtures visible." As with his secret loan manipulations, however, behind the new front Cowperwood decides what the public will and will not see. The really important matters take place in his inscrutable interior or in private rooms in the private mansions the public has no access to. Like Cowperwood himself, the dominant impression the office gives is "of reserve and taste pervading the place, and yet it was also inestimably prosperous, solid and assuring" (F, p. 95). Matters are more complicated than a simple appearance-reality dichotomy, since in Cowperwood's world, appearances help constitute reality.

The office, moreover, is "solid and assuring," and yet nothing is quite what it seems. "The interior was finished in highly-polished hardwood, stained in imitation of the gray lichens which infest trees." The wood is not quite what it seems. The door is tastefully decorated with "a money-changer's sign used in old Venice, the significance of which had long been forgotten." It is a "hand, delicately wrought, thin and artistic, holding aloft a flaming brand." To the uninitiated, is the sign in some sense misleading, not quite what it seems? The same applies to the "Cowperwood & Co. lettered on [the safe] in gold." The "company" is a fiction; there is only Cowperwood. The office safe itself "was made an ornament"; it, too, is not quite what it seems.

Similarly, the architect of Cowperwood's house "was arranging and decorating [it] in such a way as to give an effect of size and dignity not really conformable to the actual space" (F, p. 95). Like Cowperwood himself, the house is solid and good-looking but also deceptive and not easy to penetrate. It features a recessed window made by using a trick wall in the facade of the house. The window is protected by a dwarf parapet or balustrade and heavily barred French casements. The effect from the street is of a pleasant sense of greenery, but from the recessed window insiders can look out through a protective screen. "The high but pierced wall" that surrounds the house has the same effect: it is pleasantly decorative, "surmounted by a white marble coping . . . sown to grass and had a lovely, smooth, velvety appearance," but it is also a barrier that keeps outsiders away and allows insiders to see out. The office is designed to appear open; the exterior of the house is apparently the same but in fact keeps people from looking in.

People enter through one of "the deep-recessed doorways" that further the sense of privacy. On the inside, the house is there for the display of decorations, art works, and other possessions, including the triangular piano that especially impresses Aileen with Cowperwood's refined, advanced taste. The larger house belonging to Cowperwood's father is mainly for entertaining, but even Cowperwood's house is oddly public in that there is no provision for intimate family life. The dining room is for entertaining. Lillian has a boudoir, Cowperwood has a tasteful private office but no bedroom is mentioned. Dreiser is alert to a new development: like the modern selves they reflect and embody, these new structures reveal an increasingly impersonal inner life oriented toward public display.

At least in Butler's older, less tasteful home, the life of the family takes place at meals around the dining room table. Butler has an office at home, and like Cowperwood and the other powerful men in the novel he transacts important business there. Doing business at home has tragic consequences for Butler. Cowperwood's home office is in perfect taste. Butler's, however, has symptomatically "no completeness or symmetry as either an office or a living room" (F, p. 66). Successful as he is, Butler has not perfected the complete separation of business and home, or, like Cowperwood, their harmonious integration.

Buildings in Cowperwood's world are handsome, stone structures. Playing off against this reassuring sense of solidity and permanence is the fact of change, the auctions that await Cowperwood's mansions, the shifts that will eventually date and displace Tighe's "handsome, green-gray stone building" from its central position in the financial district. The buildings, moreover, are solid, but, like Cowperwood's office and home, they are also deceptive, not quite what they seem. From one point of view, they are "solid and assuring," but, from another point of view, as we learn more about the deceptions, the secret maneuvering, and the predatory energy, we also see these buildings and their handsome, confident inhabitants as reassuring in much the same way as the black grouper is. Everything is solid and yet shifting and unreliable. Cumulatively, we are put slightly off balance.

Dreiser's accurate handling of Cowperwood's sense of history is also unsettling. The Civil War as a public event involving human principles does not exist for Cowperwood. For him, "the negro isn't worth all this excitement" (F, p. 32). The sweep of history culminating in the Civil War concerns Cowperwood only "in so far as it affected his immediate interests" (F, p. 47). Dreiser juxtaposes Cowperwood's views about the negro with a revealing analysis of the concealed history of city and state finances and politics. Dreiser thus plays conventional history off against Cowperwood's insider's history. Cowperwood and the others are rooted in history but in a special way. In the Cowperwood novels, Dreiser has a special slant or way of seeing history. He plays off what he actually shows against what we conventionally expect; he throws us slightly off balance by concentrating on matters that are skew with conventional historical expectations. In a more general sense, Dreiser gives us Cowperwood's amoral outlook as perfectly normal and acceptable. Cumulatively, we come to take this outlook for granted. This prolonged exposure to Cowperwood's way of seeing also throws us slightly off balance. Most of us are accustomed either to more hypocrisy or to a commitment to a different configuration of values. Participating in Cowperwood's world from Cowperwood's point of view is for most readers a destabilizing experience. Even when Cowperwood confirms our views about the way finance capitalism operates, always a satisfying and reassuring experience, the novel is nonetheless a bit unsettling.

As with his way of presenting Cowperwood, buildings, and history, Dreiser's central techniques are rooted in the destabilizing energies they reveal, so that he provides an important example of the relation between the dynamics of possessive individualism and new modes of expression. Consider his technique of juxtaposition. Dreiser uses this old technique in a new way animated from new sources—the emerging market society itself. In *Sister Carrie*, he juxtaposes the popular theater and Carrie and Hurstwood's theater of appearance and emulation to expose the merging of appearance and reality in the new commodified society of spectacle. In *The Financier*, in juxtaposing scenes of business and sex, Dreiser reveals their unsuspected relation and destabilizing sources and implications. Responsive as he is to the relation between possessions and self in the emerging market society, Dreiser similarly endows buildings with an unsuspected meaning, just as he views history in a special way and presents Cowperwood's point of view as normal. In all these cases the merging of appearance and reality Dreiser had shown in *Sister Carrie* also characterizes the manipulations at the highest levels of organization, duplicity, and acquisition in *The Financier*.

More important, as a pioneer, Dreiser shows that even a rugged individualist like Cowperwood is inseparable from the web of commodities and connections that go to make the "whole self" he is never able to achieve. In *Sister Carrie*, Dreiser shows the same process at work in the emerging society of appearance and consumerism. Even more precisely and powerfully than William James, Dreiser's achievement in these works is to establish a new conception of the American self as constituted by commodities and desires. He explores with energy and innovative drive the impact on self and society of two of the dominant forms of late capitalism. He impressively renders the satisfactions, the power, and the fragmenting, isolating consequences of these new forms of possessive individualism in which the individual is simultaneously privatized and constituted by the emerging market society. The scale has changed from Dreiser's time to ours, but the practices and underlying values have been remarkably persistent.

Throughout, Dreiser challenges the reader's "lights and blindnesses and attitudes toward life." Instead of providing a normative, authoritative voice and point of view, Dreiser responds to the unsettling energies of the new market society that was increasingly eroding the foundations of the traditional American secular and religious belief systems, the bases for a normative, authoritative voice and point of view. Dreiser withholds explicit commentary and engages the reader in a dialogue that produces multiple, shifting points of view. Dreiser involves the reader. He provokes us to respond; he does not tell us authoritatively how to respond. Readers who want a prettier picture than Dreiser presents are unsettled because they are forced to acknowledge the accuracy of what Dreiser has shown. At the other extreme, even readers who delight in Dreiser's subversive account are somewhat unsettled. For the entire range of readers, the unresolved tension between America as a democracy and America as a market society contributes to the shifting, destabilizing impact of the novel. Dreiser brilliantly exploits the ambivalence of American readers who are themselves inextricably involved in a society torn between its democratic and capitalistic commitments.

Dreiser has a well-deserved reputation for architectonic skill, for his ability to organize the large rhythms of a narrative. He organizes *Sister Carrie* and *The Financier* around the large rhythms of rise and fall. He appeals deeply to our hopes and fears about wealth and misery and to our fascination with the processes and failure of that commodified success that continues to compel us. Dreiser has developed narrative techniques to do justice to his insights into the corrosive, energizing power and appeal of the new market society. The results are as deep, disquieting, and unsettling as we could wish for. As an explorer uniquely different from modernist writers like Eliot and Faulkner, Dreiser in his own way qualifies as one of the modern masters.

AFTERWORD

One of my central concerns has been to illuminate the political psychology of capitalism as it emerges in the works and lives of our great nineteenth-century writers. Political economy is a well-understood concept. Political psychology is less familiar. Applied to American literature, for me the concept centers on the impact capitalism had on the depths of consciousness of creators and their creations. This impact differs from writer to writer, as it often does within their careers. The market society itself, for all its continuities, changed dramatically from the early, capital-accumulating days of the first-generation Puritans and the intelligent practices and advice of Benjamin Franklin. The scale and activity intensified during the Jacksonian period, as market capitalists put technology to work to produce a revolution in communications and transportation. The Civil War accelerated these tendencies. By the end of the nineteenth century, Americans were living in a world of large-scale finance capitalism, mass markets, and rapidly developing strategies of consumerism at odds with the earlier stress on restraint and accumulation.

From the start, however, along with the growing array of goods, profits, and losses, the market society produced divisions within selves, as people came to treat their labor as a separable commodity they were free to sell on the market. By the end of the nineteenth century, moreover, America had caught up with Europe. The processes of machine production and the immense, complex distribution and exchange systems of American and European capitalism seemed to have a life of their own unrelated to the people who worked the machines, did the accounting, and sold the goods. These processes were reified or commodified. People experienced them as forces more alive and valuable than the tiny human beings, each of whom performed only a small, replaceable part in a system almost no one understood. The system seemed to have a reified life of its own independent of human beings and beyond their control. One result of the large-scale production and distribution of commodities was the production of a reified or commodified consciousness. The terms are less important than the pervasive, subtle effects of the processes themselves. For working examples of

317

this consciousness we have only to turn to Twain's Hank Morgan or Dreiser's Sister Carrie or, from an earlier period, the divisions Melville explores in "Bartleby, the Scrivener" or Hawthorne in "My Kinsman, Major Molineux."

Divided selves are of course not peculiar to nineteenth-century American capitalism, as Saint Augustine reminds us. But in the American context, the divisive impact of the market society is too widespread to be ignored. Our writers repeatedly bring alive a dominant strain in the political psychology of capitalism, the divisions within selves and society that recur again and again in the major works of nineteenth-century American literature. In these achievements of the American imagination we come to know about fragmentation in depth and life-giving detail. Far from being abstracted from the dominant currents and undercurrents of nineteenth-century American society, our writers and their works are intimately involved. From the Wall Street world of Melville's "Bartleby, the Scrivener" to the factory milieu of "The Paradise of Bachelors and the Tartarus of Maids," from Twain's *A Connecticut Yankee* to Wharton's *The House of Mirth*, from the short story masterpieces of Northern writers like Hawthorne and James to the subversive strategies of Charles Chesnutt, our writers take us deep into the inner life of the American market society. They deal perceptively with the conflicts within and between classes and within and between the representative selves who embody the practices and values of their society.

The processes of domination and subordination, of control and resistance, of acceptance and rebellion are subtle, pervasive, and varied. In *Billy Budd*, Melville probes these issues in a way that transforms his own experiences in the evolving bureaucratic world of late-nineteenth-century America. Melville illuminates the dynamics of ideological control peculiarly appropriate to the total state of the twentieth-century war world. Melville has a sure grasp of the ways dominant classes legitimize their rule less by the recourse to force than by entering deeply into the consciousness of those in subordinate classes. Melville, that is, understands the dynamics of the hegemonic process. This process of conflicting cultural and political forces is not confined to the institutional world but significantly works inside the members of a society. The divisions within the lawyer-narrator of "Bartleby" are a moving, revealing example. For his part, William Dean Howells responded to Haymarket and the new industrial-commercial city in a way that provides fascinating insights into the crosscurrents of the hegemonic process, even as these dynamics give renewed interest to Howells and his work. At the other extreme from Howells, at the heart of their work, Chesnutt and Whitman show an unusual capacity to tap into sources outside the official

America and to bring into the open possibilities of pleasure, health, and energy at odds with the dominant impulses of their society.

Whitman in particular brings to imaginative life an open form and an animating sexuality as alternatives to and subversive of market-society regularities. In a darker vein, Hawthorne, Melville, James, and Adams all agree that market-society change is driven by a masculine sexuality they find vital, compelling, and fatal. In the guise of the maimed alter egos and fierce, divided selves of their stories, these writers pose the still unresolved paradox of American power as simultaneously vital and deadly. In probing the relation between sexuality and market-society power, our writers repeatedly take us into the inner recesses of American political psychology.

Like their country and countrymen, these writers are not rock-like and monolithic. Together and as individuals they illustrate the tensions and differing degrees of acceptance and resistance that characterize our writers' involvement in the emerging market society. As Whitman's open form reminds us, this involvement inevitably affected the form as well as the content of literary works. Beyond Whitman, the official demands, assumptions, and practices stimulated our great mid-nineteenth-century authors to develop counter strategies of symbolic indirection that allowed them to go to threatening extremes and at the same time to maintain a claim on marketplace acceptability. In responding to the destabilizing energies of the market society, moreover, writers as different as Dreiser and Melville involve the reader in shifting lights and points of view that call established certainties into question. Instead of an authoritative narrative point of view, Dreiser and Melville build into the deepest structure of their creations an unsettling handling of point of view that actively involves and turns on the reader.

To shift our own focus from authors to their audience, as readers we are as involved as our writers in the processes of cultural hegemony. Our expectations, assumptions, and ways of life inevitably condition what we see and value. In a sense, we help produce the literary works we consume. To the extent that we are involved in the processes of production as consumption, my hope is that we will do it intelligently and sensitively, not passively. In my own practice I have tried to be historically informed and as responsive to nuance and implication as to overt statement. Every reader brings theoretical preconceptions to bear, including the often unexamined ones I have referred to as hegemonic. Our theories help us see and, for those with opposing views, our theories distort. Some readers, for example, are uncomfortable with the theory of reification. In a reified world, literary works exist apart from readers as well as from writers and social-historical processes. I have tried to suggest alternatives to a reified approach to American literature. One of these options deserves special emphasis. At the center of our own lives, those of us interested in the relation between literature and society can counter the pervasive fragmenting tendencies of everyday life. In our own work we can affirm our freedom as responsible producers of the works we work on.

INDEX